Communication

Eighth Edition

Larry L. Barker

Deborah Roach Gaut
James Madison University

Allyn and Bacon
Boston • London • Toronto • Sydney • Tokyo • Singapore

Vice President, Editor-in-chief: Karen Hanson
Senior Editor: Karen Bowers
Series Editorial Assistant: Jennifer Trebby
Marketing Manager: Mandee Eckersley
Production Coordinator: Mary Beth Finch
Photo Researcher: Helane Manditch-Prottas/Posh Pictures
Composition and Prepress Buyer: Linda Cox
Manufacturing Buyer: Julie McNeill
Cover Administrator: Linda Knowles
Editorial-Production Service: Shepherd, Inc.
Electronic Composition: Shepherd, Inc.

Library of Congress Cataloging-in-Publication Data
Barker, Larry Lee, 1941-
  Communication / Larry L. Barker, Deborah Roach Gaut.—8th ed.
    p. cm.
  Includes bibliographical references and index.
  ISBN 0-205-29587-8 (alk. paper)
  1. Communication. I. Gaut, Deborah A. II. Title

P90 .B296 2001
302.2—dc21

                                                        2001046376

Printed in the United States of America
10 9 8   09 08 07

Dedication:
To David
With love from Deb

Contents

Preface

The first edition of *Communication* was published in 1978. In the 23 years since the publication of that first edition, our communication world has changed dramatically. Computers and the World Wide Web have made it possible for us to chat online with people from around the world. Changes in the way that organizations do business have allowed us to have a greater voice in decision making much sooner in our careers. That means we must learn to communicate faster and smarter if we want to survive and grow in the twenty-first century workplace. On the down side, technology that was developed to help us work faster and smarter has reduced the amount of time we have to nurture important human relationships.

The eighth edition of this book was written to aid you in communicating in an increasingly complex world. It has been revised substantially with some of the most recent research available in hopes of increasing your awareness and knowledge of human communication phenomena, and your skills in communicating more effectively with people at home, school, and work.

Previous editions of *Communication* incorporated several features with universal appeal, which have been retained in this edition. These include a complete mini-text on the subject of public speaking, a major emphasis on nonverbal communication, an extensive discussion of listening and intrapersonal processes, and an integrated set of chapters focusing on interpersonal and group communication. The eighth edition features:

■ A new introductory chapter that explores the most recent advances in our understanding of human communication.

■ The merger of listening and intrapersonal processes into a single chapter that reflects the most recent thinking regarding these subjects.

■ Another new chapter developed specifically for this edition on the subject of small group and team communication.

■ Substantial revision of the organizational communication chapter, including a new discussion of approaches to organizational thought.

■ A fresh approach to the subject of mass media and the addition of a new discussion of electronic communication.

■ Updated examples and illustrations.

In addition to the features noted above, the eighth edition also includes (1) key concepts and terms at the beginning of each chapter to aid you in identifying the most important concepts, (2) new chapter openings in the form of "personal e-mail messages" that set the tone for the information to come, and (3) summaries, activities, discussion questions, and exercises at the end of each chapter.

We hope that the eighth edition of *Communication* will continue to serve the needs of teachers who have used the book in the past, and will come to serve the needs of those who have not used previous editions. We welcome letters or phone calls concerning specific items in the text that you like or dislike, as well as suggestions for improvement in future editions.

Acknowledgments

During the past 23 years, countless people have contributed to the success of previous editions as well as the present one. Any attempt to acknowledge all those contributors completely and appropriately is bound to be incomplete. We do, however, want to express our thanks and appreciation to all those at Prentice Hall and Allyn and Bacon who contributed to the development, creation, and refinement of this and previous editions.

A special debt of gratitude goes to Phil and Vickie Emmert who co-authored the introductory chapter with Deb Gaut. This chapter was a labor of love that evolved over the 18 months prior to completion of this edition. Another goes to Eileen Perrigo, a fantastic colleague and friend, who contributed the chapter on small groups and teams. Her time, dedication, energy, love, and support are appreciated more than she will ever know.

In addition, several friends and students (not mutually exclusive categories) helped with research and development of individual chapters in previous editions. Special thanks to Kittie Watson, Faye Christensen, Renee Edwards, Loretta Malandro, Janice Lumpkin, Frances Sayers, Ginger Tubbs, Debbie Smith, Cheryl Fisher, Karen Harris, Sondi Feldmaier, Bob Kibler, Wini Vallely, John Garrison, Charles Roberts, Karl Krayer, Frank E. X. Dance, Kathy Wahlers, Mary Helen Brown, Mary Etta Cook, Kale Hill, Jimmie Thorn, and Gayle Houser.

We also would like to express our appreciation for the insightful comments offered by the reviewers: Eugene Michaud, Framingham State College; Penny Eubank, Oklahoma Christian University; and Juanita Dailey, University of Rio Grande.

Finally, thanks to our students during the past 18 months, who were patient with us while we worked on this revision, and to our students over the past 35 years, who helped provide examples and illustrations for our text.

Larry Barker
Deborah Roach Gaut

chapter one

Communication

Tool for Survival

*Contributed by Philip Emmert
and Victoria Emmert with Deborah Gaut*

key concepts and terms

Biological perspectives
Cultural/social perspectives
Systems perspectives
Regulative rules
Episodes
System
Second law of
  thermodynamics
Entropy
Antientropic
Interdependence
Holism
Equifinality

Linear models
Source
Encoding
Message
Verbal communication
Nonverbal communication
Channel
Noise
Receiver
Decoding
Circular/interaction-based
  models
Feedback

Field of experience
Transactional models
Physical needs
Social needs
Ego needs
Phatic communication
Formal structure
Informal structure
Human communication
Ethical communicator
Discourse ethic
Ethic of care
Ethic of resistance

From:	"Tay"
To:	"Shura" <vicentsx@futurenet.ab.net>
Sent:	Monday, September 4th 9:20AM
Subject:	WHERE ARE YOU?

Shura! Wake up! Where are you, Shura? Why aren't you answering your telephone? All I keep getting is your answering machine.

It's 9:20 now. I called at 7:30 to make sure you were up for 8:00 class. You weren't there and WE HAD A TEST! Did you forget? You need to call me as soon as you get this message.

Can't believe how drunk everybody got last night. Man, am I hung over! Did you get home OK? I know I was supposed to take you home, but you and Brian looked pretty cozy.

E-mail or call me as soon as you get this message. I'M NOT JOKING AROUND. If you're not in Chem class at 3:00, I'm calling campus police!

—Tay

Imagine sending an e-mail message to your best friend like the one Tay sent to Shura. Many of us don't have to think long or hard to imagine such a horrible situation. You may have been trying desperately to communicate with someone you love, but you couldn't find them. Or they may have been sitting directly in front of you, wearing an angry or hurt expression, but you couldn't get them to understand what you were trying to say, no matter how hard you tried.

From the moment we are born until the day we die, communication is the way we tell people we love them, empathize with them, or fear for their lives. It is the way we communicate our own personal fears, our attitudes, beliefs, and values, and the needs we have in order to survive. It is the way we cultivate lasting personal relationships. At a professional level, we communicate to get and keep a job, to ask for a raise or promotion, and to develop relationships in the workplace. And that short list is only the beginning!

How can you learn to communicate in ways that allow you to be successful in achieving these goals? How can increasing your sensitivity, knowledge, and skills about communication maximize the chances that you will be successful in life? For years, a close friend and colleague, Dr. Michael Smilowitz, has offered the following advice to his students—no matter what their major: "Almost everyone who has reached the age of 18 is an adequate communicator, by necessity. Otherwise, we never would have reached adulthood. But to be really good at communicating, you must study and practice effective communication."

To help you achieve your fullest potential as a communicator, this book is designed to provide you with the most current information available on human communication theory and research. Additionally, we present a number of basic principles in every chapter to aid you in mastering communication in a number of social settings. By increasing your sensitivity, knowledge, and skills regarding important communication principles, we hope to accomplish our primary aim: to help you become a more effective and successful communicator.

Before we move to a more complete discussion of the issues and problems we mentioned above, you need to gain a basic understanding of current communication perspectives and models. You also need to understand some basic principles of communication as well as the role that ethics plays in twenty-first century communication. To that end, we now move to a discussion of communication perspectives.

Communication Perspectives

Many different approaches have been used to explain human communication. Each perspective offers us a unique point of view and, thus, provides different information and insights about human communication. *Biological perspectives* view human communication as derived from genetic, biological, physiological, and neurophysiological processes. *Cultural/social perspectives* see human communication as a process that is learned via cultural and social influences. Finally, *systems perspectives* view human communication as a total process, in which biological and cultural/social variables both play a vital role. Because of the unique contribution that each perspective makes to our understanding of communication, let's take a closer look at each of them.

Biological Perspectives

Although we are certainly social creatures, we are also biological organisms. We are conceived, born, live, and die like all other biological organisms on Earth. Whether human beings are unique and superior to other animal species has been the subject of debate for centuries. However we answer this question, it is clear that our behavior, and especially our communication behavior, is a joint product of our biology and our culture (McCroskey & Beatty, 2000; Condit, 2000a; Beatty & McCroskey, 2000; Condit, 2000b).

For example, we also have biological structures that permit the production of speech (Bickerton, 1995). We have a complex set of muscles in our faces that, according to some estimates, enables us to produce more than a thousand facial expressions that are a part of our nonverbal communication system (Ekman, Friesen, & Ellsworth, 1972). We are born with a temperament that predisposes us to be nervous, sensitive, intelligent, energetic, excitable, or constrained, and to have good or poor memories (Bates, 1989; Cattell, 1946), which probably has an effect on the kinds of communication behaviors we subsequently produce (Horvath, 1995). We have a brain with the capacity both to create language we use to influence others and to interpret language produced by others (Bickerton, 1995).

Dr. Noam Chomsky (1957), a widely respected language scholar, has suggested that all babies are born "hard wired" to learn language and to be able to recognize the "deep structure" of language.

THE LAWS APPROACH.   During the early and middle 1900s, scholars in communication, social psychology, sociology, linguistics, sociobiology, anthropology, and political science began to examine human behavior using the logic and research methodologies of the biological and physical sciences. Just as in the physical sciences, they were interested in discovering broad *explanatory and predictive laws* from which theories could be generated to explain communication behavior. Finding a "law" meant finding the "causes" of our communication behavior. The search for absolute causes and consequences of communication continues today. However, because of the advances we have made in understanding communication, we no longer expect to find that communication is determined by simple, individual causal relationships.

COMMUNIBIOLOGY.   The *communibiological* perspective is an example of a laws approach, and suggests that certain communication behaviors are biologically and genetically determined. Its supporters posit a trait-based explanation for many communication behaviors, including communication apprehension, verbal aggressiveness, and communicator style (Beatty & McCroskey, 1997, 2000; Beatty, McCroskey, & Heisel, 1998; Bodary & Miller, 2000; Horvath, 1995; Valencic, Beatty, Rudd, Dobos, & Heisel, 1998). This paradigm emerged from work by psychobiologists, who view temperament and personality as biologically inherited traits (Bates, 1989; Eysenck, 1991), and recent research regarding the neurophysiological processes in our brain (Damasio, 1999a, 1999b; Gray, 1991). The communibiological paradigm suggests that genetics influence our temperament as well as many basic personality traits. For example, communibiologists are interested in how our brain responds to strong emotions, such as communication anxiety and hostility.

During the early and middle 1900s, scholars in communication and other disciplines began to examine human behavior using the methodologies of the biological and physical sciences.

Cultural/Social Perspectives

It is clear that our communication is shaped, enhanced, diminished, restricted, and altered by a multitude of environmental and cultural influences throughout our lives. Becker and Roberts (1992) suggested that we live in a "communication matrix" that influences us in a multitude of ways. For example, from birth, we are constantly bombarded by verbal and nonverbal messages. These messages affect us in varying degrees, but they most certainly affect us. Furthermore, they may bring about specific communication behaviors.

RHETORICAL APPROACHES.   The earliest approach to studying communication incorporated cultural and social factors. The study of communication can be traced to the work of early *rhetorical theorists and philosophers* around 500 B.C. These early theorists included Aristotle, Cicero, Plato, and Socrates. Early rhetoricians were concerned with the oral communication skills necessary to argue in legal courts, conduct business, educate citizens, and govern democratically. Reading and writing were primitive and difficult (Harper, 1979); however, the ability to persuade others was of central importance, both philosophically and pragmatically, within both public and personal relationships. "The Greek legal system required that each citizen be his own lawyer. For many years, the Athenian could not hire a professional to speak for him in court" (Harper, 1979, p. 17). Imagine what life would be like if your communication skills determined whether a jury of several hundred persons believed you.

Today, rhetorical theorists conduct research and teach about increasingly complex human messages.

One of the most influential books in the Western world to date is *The Rhetoric* by Aristotle. In it, Aristotle attempted to describe and prescribe the best ways to argue issues in public. *The Rhetoric* has been used as a textbook at many different educational levels for more than 2,500 years. It is still used today, probably because most of what Aristotle had to say still applies. Additionally, contemporary researchers are continuing to validate much of what he wrote.

SOCIAL LEARNING THEORY.   Another approach to studying the social and cultural influences on communication is social learning theory. In his book entitled *Social Learning Theory,* Bandura (1969) examined factors that determine the extent to which children model the communication behaviors of others. For instance, Bandura noted that a child who observes other children being punished for negative behavior is less likely to perform that same behavior than a child who sees the same behavior go unpunished. Some hypotheses derived from social learning theory have been challenged by communibiologists. For example, the explanation that communication apprehension might be caused by learned helplessness was challenged by Beatty, McCroskey, and Heisel in 1998.

RULES.   Another cultural-social approach to studying communication is the rules approach. The *rules approach* focuses on describing the culturally and socially generated knowledge of communicators that allows them to act with mutual understanding (Cronen, Pearce, & Snavely, 1979; Cushman, 1977; Pearce, Cronen, & Conklin, 1979). To illustrate, what behaviors do you use to show someone that you respect them, that you are committed to your relationship with them, or that you are determined? What behaviors are taken to "mean" that someone is angry but still cares for you? According to rules theorists, ***regulative rules*** tell us (1) to whom it is appropriate to communicate about certain topics, (2) when we may do so, and (3) how we should act during an interaction. For example, it might be acceptable in your family to interrupt your brother or sister but not your parents, or to talk about sex with your mother but not your father.

Rules vary in complexity. Some are explicit and easy to learn; others are intricate, implicit, and, thus, difficult to learn. Rules vary in the extent to which we can use them in a broad range of contexts. For instance, some rules apply only to our home setting, whereas others apply equally to bank, office, and casual settings. Some rules apply only to college students, and others apply to many kinds of people. Rules vary to the extent that they are understood. For example, we are offended when people break a rule that we expect most people to know, such as rules about not interrupting others who are talking. Finally, rules vary in degree of mutual understanding and our willingness to honor them (Cushman & Whiting, 1972). An excellent example is when someone tries to skip one or more "stages" in a romantic relationship. Saying "I love you" too early in a relationship places a demand on the other person to respond similarly, when, in fact, he or she may not be ready to do so. If the latter person says "I love you, too," because of the situation, rather than from his or her real feelings, the relationship may be jeopardized.

According to rules theorists, we learn these rules from our parents, friends, teachers, ministers, media, and culture. We also create new rules for special relationships with others. When two or more people interact, they must coordinate and manage the "meaning" of their rules. Each individual has a separate and somewhat unique system of rules. Achieving shared meaning means meshing our "rules" with the rules of the other person.

The *Coordinated Management of Meaning Theory* (Pearce & Cronen, 1980) suggests that we do so by enacting sequences of messages that we punctuate, or interpret, as *episodes,* or interpretable and meaningful patterns of behavior. For example, you might initiate an episode with a classmate, such as "asking for a romantic date." Your partner might confirm your episode with the desired communication behavior, or disconfirm it with a "let's just be friends" episode. In other words, the process might look something like this:

Sally: "Hi Jay, what are you doing this Friday night?"

Jay: "Not much."

Sally: "Would you like to go to a nice restaurant for dinner and then see a romantic comedy with me?"

Jay: "Sure, let's ask Mark, Trina, and Elizabeth if they want to go with us, too."

Do you think that Jay's response is what Sally had in mind?

Knowing the appropriate rules allows us to communicate efficiently and effectively. Additionally, when we share the same expectations, we are better able to coordinate our communication behavior in order to achieve our goals (Cushman, Valentinsen, & Dietrich, 1982). One of the major emphases in the rules perspective is that human beings are purposive. They make intentional choices when pursuing their goals, and their communication is "goal-driven" behavior.

Systems Perspectives

As scholars have achieved greater understanding of human nature and the communication process, they have become increasingly aware of multiple influences interacting together to produce our communication behavior as well as our "human nature." Although they may argue over the relative weights to assign to physical, biological, psychological, and cultural influences (de Waal, 1999; Condit, 2000a, 2000b; McCroskey & Beatty, 2000), it is clear to almost everyone that our cultural, social, physical, and biological selves affect the communication process. This more integrated approach to the study of communication has been accomplished through the systems perspective.

A *system* is an entity that is comprised of components (or subsystems) that interact with, or mutually influence, one another in ways that enable the entity to achieve a goal or goals (Emmert & Donaghy, 1981; Monge, 1977). Systems can be biological, physical, chemical, social, or philosophical in nature. Examples include the solar system, our bodies, the air transportation system, a fraternity or sorority, the ecological system, a hospital, a theme park, the McDonalds restaurant chain, your college or university, and the government of the state or nation in which you live, just to mention a few. We are surrounded by systems, we are part of systems, and we are systems ourselves. It should come as no surprise, then, that when we communicate with others, we comprise a *communication system.*

GOAL-SEEKING.   Since all systems are purposive, communication systems also are *goal-seeking* (Monge, 1977). We have many goals, both cultural and biological, that we achieve through communication. To illustrate, you can use communication to reduce uncertainty by seeking information from others (Berger & Bradac, 1982). If you want to ask someone for a date, or want your new college roommate to like you, you can make plans, either consciously or unconsciously, before using communication to achieve your goal (Berger & diBattista, 1992). When you are jealous, you can communicate to maintain the relationship, preserve your self-esteem, increase your certainty about the relationship with the other person, retaliate, find out more about your rival, or reassess the relationship (Guerrero & Walid, 1999).

Goals influence our choice of message strategies as well as our verbal and nonverbal behaviors (Samp & Solomon, 1998, 1999). Thus, one of the most important things we can do to improve communication effectiveness is to accurately define the goal(s) of our communication system. If we have accurately defined our goal, we can plan better messages and strategies. Additionally, by recognizing that others are also active and goal directed, we can adapt our communication behavior to help meet their goals (Slater, 1997).

COMMUNICATION SYSTEM ARE BOTH ENTROPIC AND ANTIENTROPIC.   One of the goals present in many systems, including communication systems, is survival of the system itself. A principle that came to us originally from physics is the **second law of thermodynamics,** which specifies that all systems have a tendency to develop entropy (Emmert & Donaghy, 1981; Monge, 1977). *Entropy* is the tendency for a system to become random, disorganized, or fall apart. If that system continues to experience entropy, ultimately it will cease to exist.

For example, as you are reading this chapter, your body is losing moisture and, thus, becoming biologically disorganized. You can directly combat entropy by drinking water. You can also use communication to ask someone to get you a glass of water. Thus, communication can be **antientropic,** since it can be used to combat entropy.

Entropy can also exist within the communication process. For instance, consider the word "broadcaster." If we were to use this term to refer to "a device that was used to sow seed," but the person with whom we were communicating interpreted the word in the context of radio or television, then our communication would experience entropy. In this situation, communication itself would become disorganized, or uncoordinated, in light of our two different meanings for the word.

Upon noticing that the other person seemed confused by our comments, we might ask what caused the confusion. The other person might share his or her meaning of the word "broadcaster," and this response would give us the opportunity to explain the original agricultural use of the word. Such an interchange would reduce the misunderstanding and, in turn, restore some order and coordination in the communication exchange. In this example, communication would be used to combat entropy created by the original message exchange. Thus, it is possible for communication to be both entropic and antientropic.

INTERDEPENDENCE.   Systems are comprised of many subsystems or components. This is true with communication systems as well. The components that make up communication systems will be discussed in the next section of this chapter. For now, we'll just say that these components are interdependent. *Interdependence* in a communication system means that all parts of a system affect every other part of that system (Emmert & Donaghy, 1981; Monge, 1977). Most people assume that a speaker affects a listener, but many are surprised to learn that the listener also affects the speaker. Other components that affect a communication system include time of day, the room in which the interaction takes place, preceding events, the people involved, and the verbal and nonverbal messages, to name a few. In other words, interdependence means that one part of a communication process cannot be changed without all other parts being affected.

THE WHOLE IS GREATER THAN THE SUM OF ITS PARTS.   Authors of books like this one are faced with having to discuss one topic at a time in some kind of order. That's the nature of a book. It's also the nature of a classroom discussion. If we try to consider all concepts at once, it becomes impossibly confusing for everyone. So we discuss topics individually, such as verbal messages, nonverbal messages, motivation, cultural effects, gender, and so on. However, such a linear approach to discussion creates the illusion that these phenomena exist in isolation.

The opposite is the case, however. When considering communication systems, it is important to keep in mind the principle of *holism,* or the idea that systems exist as whole entities rather than as isolated parts. For example, picture yourself trying to express your love to someone for whom you really care by using words without any nonverbal components (e.g., tone of voice, volume, pitch, eye contact, facial expressions, gestures, touch, etc.). You cannot do it because the production of a word requires the use of volume, pitch, and tone. However, even if it were possible to produce the words "I love you" in isolation, they would not convey the warmth and affection—the love—most of us would like to convey with those words. Thus, to understand communication, we are forced to study the parts separately. However, we should constantly consider how the components of communication relate to each other, and try to conceptualize a "whole" that is greater than the sum of its parts.

EQUIFINALITY.   The idea that there are many ways for a system to reach its goals is called *equifinality* (Emmert & Donaghy, 1981; Monge, 1977). In most communication situations, there is probably more than one way to reach our goal. For instance, if two people have a conflict over what restaurant to eat at, they could: (1) argue until one person gives into the other's wishes, (2) compromise, with one person choosing one night and the other person choosing the next time they eat out; (3) agree on a third restaurant that both people like; or (4) decide to stay home rather than to eat out at all. Such is the case with communication systems, whatever their goals. One of the implications of equifinality for every communication system is that we should never forget that we have *many* options by which to achieve our goals.

Communication Models

Knowing a communication model is like knowing the map of a city. Once you have a map in your hands (or memorized), you can find your way around and avoid making wrong turns. Similarly, when a relationship gets off track because someone makes a communication error, your knowledge of communication models can enable you to diagnose the problem and create solutions that work. Of course, the ideal use of both maps and models would be to plan your travels with them to avoid mistakes in the first place.

Think of a model as a generalized map of communication systems. Of course, a generalized map is just that—general. This limitation can make it less applicable in some situations than in others. However, just as a model airplane can teach us a great deal about flying, so can a communication model teach us about the dynamics of communication. Once we have mastered the general structure of a communication model, we can apply it to specific communication events and better understand them.

Before we continue, it is important to note: Different models offer us different vantage points from which to view communication. Thus, any single model by necessity is incomplete because it focuses on some aspects of communication and not others.

Linear Models

Linear models of communication focus attention on the sender's use of messages to influence other people. As such, they examine one-way communication exclusively (e.g., public speaking and mass communication). One of the earliest linear models was developed by Laswell in 1948, and focused on "Who? Says what? In what channel? To whom? With what effect?" To illustrate how Laswell's model helps us understand the communication process, consider the following scenario. When you are preparing a public speech, you determine what to say and what visual aids you plan to use. You analyze your audience and determine the effects you hope to achieve. If your presentation is outside the classroom, you might decide to send the message via radio, television, telephone, or the Internet. Depending on the choices you make, you might not know the effects of your message until long after it is delivered.

The *source* is the person (or entity) who originates the message and begins the communication process. When the source translates ideas, concepts, and intentions into verbal and nonverbal messages, the process is called *encoding.* The behavior that the individual produces is a *message. Verbal communication* is usually thought of as the words we use. *Nonverbal communication* includes behaviors such as facial expressions, tone of voice, gestures, body movement, and the clothing we wear. In linear models, the meaning of a message resides in, or is usually determined by, the speaker/encoder's meaning.

The source does not necessarily have to be an individual. Communication scholars use linear models to examine many communication events such as religious pageantry (Armstrong & Argetsinger, 1989), negative political advertising (Procter & Schenck-Hamlin, 1996), and the voices of marginalized groups in society (Huxman, 1997; Morris & Wander, 1990).

The *channel* is the conduit through which a message is sent. We may decide that it is better to deliver some news face-to-face rather than by phone or by e-mail. We may choose a public debate or a newspaper advertisement to convey our message. Our motives, goals, and familiarity with the channel may influence the one that we choose. Communication via one channel rarely produces the same effects as communication via another channel (Flaherty, Pearce, & Rubin, 1998). To illustrate, consider the difference that it makes when someone sends us a greeting card rather than an e-mail message wishing us a happy birthday.

There also may be *noise* or interference between the speaker's intended message and the listener's reception of that message (Shannon & Weaver, 1949). For example, if you have ever heard your voice played back on a recorder, you probably thought it sounded nothing like you. The explanation is simple: internal noise. The voice you hear when you speak isn't the same voice your receiver hears, because you are hearing vibrations conducted by bones and air. In contrast, your listeners hear vibrations conducted by air alone. External noise may enter the picture if you or your audience is distracted by sounds outside the room, or by someone who is talking in the audience.

The person or persons for whom the source intends his or her message are termed *receivers* in most communication models. A receiver receives a message as physical stimuli and then engages in *decoding,* or the process of interpreting or translating incoming stimuli into thoughts, ideas, and concepts. In linear models, the speaker's goal isn't shared meaning, but rather some overt behavior that allows the speaker to determine whether the message has influenced the listener in the desired manner.

Circular/Interaction-based Models

Circular or *interaction-based models* of the communication process include the concept of *feedback,* or a listener's response to a speaker's message, and the speaker's response to the listener's message (Schramm, 1955). They also highlight the notion of "mutual influence" and posit that "meaning" resides in both the sender/encoder and the receiver/decoder. If a speaker and listener's meanings are identical or nearly so, the result is "understanding." Interaction-based models have been used to examine a number of communication phenomena, including the verbal and nonverbal messages that communicators use to regulate conversational turn taking (Burgoon, Buller, & Woodall, 1996). They also have been used to examine the effects of various message characteristics on feedback.

In addition to contributing the concepts of feedback and mutual influence, interaction-based models have stressed the importance of overlapping fields of experience (Schramm, 1955). A communicator's *field of experience* includes his or her cultural and life experiences, beliefs, values, attitudes, language, and so on. To the extent that we share similar fields of experience, we will find it easier to understand each other and our respective messages. Conversely, we can use communication to create overlapping fields of experience. For instance, a friend tells you about losing a pet cat, and you share your story about losing a pet dog. As both of you share stories about the funny things your pets did and the times they comforted you when you were sad

American Sign Language is a form of verbal communication.

or ill, you are attempting to create a "shared experience." If you are successful, you will feel that you understand each other. If not, you may end the interaction angry that "anyone could possibly think that losing a dog is the same as losing my cat."

Transactional Models

Transactional models depict the simultaneous interaction of complex, multilayered elements of the communication process. These interdependent elements operate simultaneously and mutually influence one another during communication.

From a transactional perspective, every communicator is a "speaker/listener." Even as we encode messages, we decode incoming messages simultaneously. We also may engage in speaking and listening simultaneously. One of us once observed two men in a fast-food restaurant, both of whom were eating hamburgers. For several minutes, they spoke at the same time, each seeming to respond to the content of the other's message, each stopping to take a bite or drink at the same time. Although extensive simultaneous speech is somewhat rare in American culture, we do engage in mutual speech when arguing, expressing support for another, or asking questions while the other person is speaking.

Transactional models also reflect the changing nature of communication over time. Relationships change during single interactions, and over the many interactions that constitute those relationships. Additionally, through the process of mutual influence, we "construct" who we are with each other as well as how we relate to one another. For example, you might meet someone and dislike him immediately. However, as the two of you interact over time, you may come to like him. You also may feel that your interaction has changed the person you are for the better. Transactional models that describe complex communication phenomena such as these generally represent very complex systems models.

What We Believe about Communication Today

To this point, we have provided you with three major perspectives associated with the study of communication. We also have presented you with three major models. In this section, we will examine eight specific ideas about communication that many, if not most, communication scholars would accept today.

COMMUNICATING IS ACTION.   The fact that our communication abilities and behaviors are based partially in biology is obvious. Less obvious may be the fact that communication is *behavior*—precisely because it is biologically based. One of our daughters was asked in grade school what her father did at work. She responded that ". . . her father doesn't do anything. He just sits around and talks." Indeed, some people fail to recognize that talking *is* behaving, or performing some form of action. Communication is one of the most basic actions of all human behaviors.

When people talk, they are *doing something* that is essential to their mental and physical well-being. We will articulate this argument in greater detail in the sections that follow.

WE COMMUNICATE TO SURVIVE.   If a team of anthropologists were sent to Earth from another planet to study and explain human behavior, first, they would watch us long enough to determine our most frequently occurring behaviors. Doing so would be crucial because the actions that a species performs most often are the things that are most important to that species. Of course, it would become evident quickly that, other than breathing, the thing people do most often is communicate with each other.

Humans are constantly upgrading computers to refine, enhance, and expand their communication abilities.

Our alien anthropologists would observe people talking in groups of two or three; people talking in small or large groups; people reading; people writing; people watching and listening to television, radio, and movies; and people sending and receiving information through computers. They would observe humans spending most of their waking hours communicating with others. In fact, research suggests that college students spend about 61 percent of their waking hours communicating (Verderber, Elder, & Weiler, 1976) and about 99 percent of our time at work is spent in communication activities (U.S. Department of Labor, 1991). This activity is so important to us that, as a species, we devote large amounts of time, money, energy, and other resources to developing and refining machines to expand and enhance our communication behaviors.

The next task our alien anthropologists would probably attempt is explaining why humans spend so much time and effort communicating. Across the many disciplines in which human researchers work, most who study human behavior agree that communication serves to facilitate *survival*—both as a species and as individuals (Liska &

Cronkite, 1995). It is easy to see that humans respond to a baby's cry by feeding it, changing its diapers, cuddling it, or engaging in some other behavior that helps the baby survive. But "survival" is not that simple.

First, survival may be viewed from several different perspectives. We can talk about the survival of individuals, or the survival of a tribe, community, nation, or species. We can talk about the survival of DNA, which is passed from generation to generation. At the most basic level, many biologists, geneticists, and anthropologists maintain that the survival instinct is driven by genes or DNA. Consider the following statement offered by Richard Dawkins (1995), a widely published biologist and geneticist:

> From the point of view of the particular gene, the . . . causes of death will average out. From the gene's perspective, there is only the long-term outlook of the river of DNA flowing down through the generations, only temporarily housed in particular bodies, only temporarily sharing a body with companion genes that may be successful or unsuccessful. In the long term, the river becomes full of genes that are good at surviving for their several reasons . . . the genes that survive in the river will be the ones that are good at surviving in the average environment of the species. . . . (pp. 28, 29).

Clearly, Dawkins and many other natural scientists would say that the real survival concern is survival of DNA, or genes. Their view is entirely consistent with the argument that our primary concern is survival of the species.

Through communication, members of a culture create and maintain values and beliefs that are passed from generation to generation. These values and beliefs also function to facilitate the survival of our species. For instance, the old cliche, "women and children first," which has been communicated to sailors (and others) for generations, is clearly intended to preserve the future of our species.

Sometimes, cultural values or beliefs that are intended to preserve our species are in conflict with an individual's need to survive. The men on the Titanic who put women and children on lifeboats first were well indoctrinated: Their culture's emphasis on species survival took precedence over their individual survival needs. How we decide to engage in individual versus species survival behaviors is a complex process. Suffice it to say, that communication plays a major role in the creation, transmission, and inculcation of cultural values and beliefs that result in both kinds of behavior.

WE SATISFY NEEDS TO SURVIVE.   Our alien anthropologists would err, however, if they focused only on survival of the species. Humans have at least three individual needs: physical, ego, and social (Emmert & Emmert, 1984). Interestingly, each of these needs must be satisfied or individual survival will be threatened. People spend their lives trying to satisfy these needs, even though they may have no conscious awareness of the reasons for their behavior.

Sometimes we try to satisfy our needs directly and make no use of communication behaviors. For instance, while writing this paragraph in a home office, one of us became thirsty. He got up, walked to the kitchen, and got himself a glass of iced water. This behavior directly satisfied a *physical need.* Dehydration was slowed down, thus helping him to survive. However, while getting water, your author experienced no conscious thoughts about possible dehydration or his overall physical well-being. He simply got the water and drank it. Additionally, no communication was required to bring about need satisfaction. His behavior was a direct physical, nonsymbolic response to thirst.

People can directly satisfy many of their physical needs. We also can satisfy them indirectly through communication (e.g., asking someone to get us a drink of water). When we employ symbols (e.g., words) to change another person's behavior in order to satisfy our physical needs, we are using communication at its most basic level. Think about it for a minute. In many cases, humans use communication as a tool to satisfy their needs indirectly rather than directly. In doing so, they are physically manipulating their environment in some way to satisfy themselves. Of course, our messages can be counterproductive and fail to satisfy our needs if we misjudge a situation or communicate ineffectively. Such a misstep can result in injuries, and sometimes even death.

Our earlier example about the need for water is easy to understand, but we use communication to satisfy other needs as well. For instance, as part of the process of writing this chapter, your authors met several times over lunch to discuss the material. To be sure, we achieved work goals during those sessions, but we also enjoyed each other's company. In other words, we interacted socially, thereby meeting our *social needs.* Indeed, human communication is used to establish "connections" between people. When we talk about a favorite movie or CD, the surface content in the conversation may be about the film or music. However, the underlying content is associated with our relationship with the person to whom we are talking. If we cannot satisfy our social needs for extended periods of time, we become depressed, detached, and, ultimately, less interested in our own survival.

The human need to think well of ourselves, or *ego needs,* appears to be linked to our physical states as well. For example, people with extremely negative self-concepts are more likely to attempt suicide or behave in socially unacceptable ways, which could make their survival in society more difficult. Researchers also have suggested that instances of cancer, ulcers, and other physical ailments may be connected to ego needs as well. Whether or not these hypotheses are true, the more we receive messages that increase our self-esteem, the less likely we are to engage in self-destructive behavior. Additionally, it is more likely that we will communicate with, and behave toward, others in a positive manner.

In short, at the most basic level, we communicate to change other people's behavior so they will do something to meet our (survival) needs (Emmert & Emmert, 1984). Of course, to be successful, our message must show our receivers how a change in their behavior simultaneously meets their needs. This particular view of communication highlights the goal-driven nature of communication.

COMMUNICATION IS PURPOSEFUL.   We communicate for a reason! Consider the following. If you have ever been asked to make even a brief presentation, at the end of that presentation you probably felt very tired. Just having a quiet conversation with another person increases our blood pressure. However, biological organisms (including humans) do not waste energy or resources if they can avoid it. Although we may be unaware of our motivations to communicate, we are doing so for a reason either consciously or subconsciously (Liska & Cronkhite, 1995; Infante, Rancer, & Womack, 1990; Emmert & Donaghy, 1981).

We may be communicating to cause another person to do something for us. We may be trying to sell something to somebody. We may be trying to begin, build, or repair a relationship with someone for whom we deeply care. Even "small talk" over a cup of coffee with a friend has relationship elements, as will be discussed in Chapter 5. Small talk is often termed *phatic communication* (Emmert & Emmert, 1984), and is considered meaningless communication by many people. However, relationships can be reinforced and validated through this kind of talk. As you can see, communication is purposeful in each of these cases.

COMMUNICATORS MUTUALLY INFLUENCE ONE ANOTHER.   When most people think about communication, they think of an event that requires them to speak or listen. At best, this type of thinking reflects a linear approach communication. Perhaps, it's more accurate to think of communication as a system or a *process* rather than as a single event with clearly identifiable boundaries. The word "process" suggests a multidirectional interaction on the part of all parties involved. It also suggests the *transactional* nature of communication in which we mutually influence one another.

COMMUNICATION SYSTEMS HAVE STRUCTURE.   One of the more difficult ideas to grasp is the notion that communication can be studied—just as psychologists study mental illness, doctors study diseases, and civil engineers study bridge building. This is true of many phenomena, including food. For instance, when we are young, food is whatever our caretakers give us to eat. Food is simply food. As we get older, however, we begin to understand that food is comprised of simple and complex carbohydrates, proteins, fats, vitamins, minerals, and calories. There is a structure by which we can understand food, and that understanding can help us to eat more healthfully than we did when we were children.

Like food, communication is a process to which we have been exposed all of our lives. It is more or less taken for granted. Most of us fail to perceive the structure of communication, yet it is there for us to use in improving our communication with others (Emmert & Donaghy, 1981). The structure of communication can be either formal or informal. Think back to the city map we discussed earlier. Most of us who have lived in a city for an extended length of time know shortcuts that are not obvious to a newcomer— even if they have a map. Likewise, we "locals" know places in the city to avoid because of traffic congestion at certain times of day. The "official map" of the city is like the *formal structure* that exists in communication. In your college or university classes, the formal communication structure is dictated by the role of the teacher, students, and the arrangement of the room. Additionally, an *informal structure* exists in those same classes, which results from relationships that have formed. Variables that affect the informal communication structure of a university class (and other communication events) include the gender and ages of the students, their physical characteristics, the nature of their relationships, and whether or not the class is required or an elective.

Both formal and informal communication structures have a significant impact on the communication dynamics of a college classroom. This statement is also true for virtually every communication event. To increase your awareness of the true complexity of communication, think of communication as multilayered. If you ever have eaten a two-layer chocolate cake, then you have something of the idea. Think of one layer as the formal structure of a communication event, and the other layer as its informal structure.

From here our visual image gets more complex. Consider that everyone involved in any communication event has learned what is appropriate communication behavior in different families, in different educational systems, in the context of different relations, and in different parts of the country. Depending on their gender, age, ethnicity, educational level, and more, they will have more or less diverse expectations regarding communication behavior. This means that the second layer of our chocolate cake, the informal communication structure, is many times multilayered itself. Each communicator brings multiple perspectives (or layers) to every communication event, making for anything but the simple act of communicating.

COMMUNICATION SYSTEMS EVOLVE.   It has been said that the only permanent thing in the world is change. Eastern philosophies and religions remind us that we cannot put our hand in a river in the same place twice. The river is flowing and, thus, is never the same. Every second we grow older, and so does everyone else. This same is true of communication systems. As soon as one person begins the communication process, the system is different than it was before they spoke. Every movement, word spoken, and entrance or exit affects every other component in the system and, hence, the system itself. Additionally, systems like college classes and families *evolve*. For example, students who have been away from home for several months notice (if they are sensitive) that their families have changed while they've been gone. It is important to pay attention to such changes in communication and to adapt to them by making use of the principles and theories discussed in this book.

Communication Defined

Drawing on the preceding discussion, we define *human communication* as a biologically and culturally based, complex, continuing, and interactive process in which two or more people use verbal and nonverbal symbols to shape, reinforce, or change one another's behaviors, either immediately or over time, for the purpose of satisfying their respective needs and, in turn, ensuring the survival of both the species and the individuals. In addition to reflecting the previous comments, this definition includes some other notions that will be discussed throughout this textbook.

Ethical Considerations and Human Communication

Whenever we communicate with other people, we often do so without thinking about the ramifications of our messages for everyone concerned. That's because we've been communicating since the day we were born and have learned (through trial and error) how to influence other people, and hopefully to get what we want or need. Think about the first time you talked your parents into giving you the family car, or letting you go out on a date with someone who was two years older (or younger) than you. You probably thought carefully about what you would say and how you would say it before you approached them. You probably also made promises about being home before you really wanted to, but knew that making time concessions was an important part of the deal.

In the process, you may (or may not) have thought about the consequences of your request from their perspective. Your safety and welfare are ultimately their responsibility, at least until you are legally considered an adult. As such, the many questions they may ask are valid and important to ask, and yet we may respond to them with resentment and anger. To ensure that we get what we want, we may find ourselves considering some form of deception.

The interesting part about teaching our students effective human communication principles is that doing so inevitably poses an ethical dilemma for us. You see, every principle or strategy that you learn in this book (or any communication course) is amoral. In other words, the principles themselves are neither moral nor immoral, but may be used for good or evil purposes. Consider the possible outcomes. You could take a strategy that you've learned but never tried, and do anything—for example, persuade your parents that you are worthy of their trust.

The question is "Are you?" This question is important. No matter what form it takes, this and similar questions constitute your ethics as a human communicator, or the system of morals that you use to judge your own and others' human conduct. The extent to which you are an ***ethical communicator*** is the extent to which you create messages that are "right, proper, just, honorable, decent, upright, principled, fair, honest, good, and virtuous" (*Oxford Desk Dictionary and Thesaurus,* 1997).

This definition of an "ethical communicator" seems pretty straightforward, doesn't it? All you have to do is make sure that you are using communication for purposes that are good, not evil. The problem is that individuals define "good" and "evil" in different ways. Add to this problem the fact that different cultures vary regarding what constitutes "good" and "evil," and you have a new and bigger problem, one of cultural relativism. Consider, for example, the issue of using the death penalty as a means of practicing justice. In Saudi Arabia and other Middle Eastern countries, the issue is "black and white." Take someone else's life and your own will be taken. In the United States, the issue seems much less clear. For many people, taking the life of a convicted murderer also constitutes murder. Who is right? Who is wrong? Cultural relativists say "It depends on the culture you hail from."

So how can you decide what constitutes ethical and unethical communication? What questions can you ask to maximize the chances that you and others will perceive you to be ethical? There are no easy answers. However, an interesting model of communication ethics posed by Cooper in 1998 offers us some interesting insights.

According to ethicist, Martha Cooper, there are three (not one) dimensions of ethicality that we should consider when we communicate: a discourse ethic, an ethic of care, and an ethic of resistance. Associated with the ***discourse ethic*** is the art of questioning oneself and others before constructing a persuasive message. As Cooper (1998) noted,

> Questioning embodies an ethical guideline that advises communicators to subject all assumptions to scrutiny, to take nothing for granted without probing its implications. To ensure such an exercise of skepticism, communicators are advised, among other things, to avoid polemics [controversial discussions and attacks], to gain access to . . . data banks, and to construct an ideal speech situation in which any statement may be analyzed for intelligibility, truth, truthfulness and appropriateness.

In other words, we must deliberate, argue, and make careful judgments before ultimately proceeding. This means taking into account diversity, including both gender and cultural differences.

Just like anything can be taken to excess, so too can the logic of discourse. For that reason, Cooper recommended that we balance our discourse ethic with an ethic of care. An ***ethic of care*** emphasizes responding to the needs of the other person while we are communicating, and "counsels concern for human relationships that can be enacted by reaching out for, and responding, to an Other with compassion and love" (1998, p. 70). You may be wondering why you should always consider Others when you communicate, since what you have to say seems (at first glance) to require little or nothing from them. However, Cooper noted that communication (by its very nature) can introduce dominance and submissiveness into the communication event. While one person wins, the other person loses, thereby marginalizing rather than empowering the Other as a communicator. (Consider Jamie who likes to have her way in everything that she does. She will say or do anything to achieve her communication goals, even if it means rendering Others completely powerless.) Because communication has the power to marginalize or empower, Cooper advised that we create messages that reveal empathy for other people, and that allow them to "tell their side of every story" in every communication event.

The first two ethics (discourse and care) allow us to be responsive to others. However, we all know people who are too argumentative or too responsive. Consider the "jerk" in your history class who questions everything the instructor or other students say. In the process of deliberating, she winds up discouraging other students' opinions. Everyone walks out of class in agony, secretly wishing for a meteor to come out of the blue and "nail" her on the way to the student union building. In the case of the latter—being too responsive—one need look no further than the last time you met someone whom you came to perceive as a "clinging vine." Upon first meeting him, you may have been flattered that he seemed to "hang" on your every word. Over time, you realized that you were actually encouraging him to be too dependent, especially when he wound up calling you for advice before making a single move.

That's where the *ethic of resistance* comes into play. According to Cooper, "An ethic of resistance calls for maintaining a space for [ourselves and others] to position themselves as freely choosing [agents] even in the face of oppressive practices and discourses that threaten to marginalize or constrain them" (p. 71). In other words, we have to let people be who they are as people (and communicators); find ways to balance detachment from them and connection to them; and discover ways to both tolerate and empower them as unique communicators. In the process, we affirm ourselves and others by understanding "the importance of having a voice, and the ability to tolerate the opinions of others" (McPhail, 1996, p. 132; as cited in Cooper, 1998, p. 73).

"O.K. This little discussion has been just lovely," you may be saying, "But how can I use it in everyday communication?" Start by asking yourself the following questions every time you find yourself constructing a message that you know has a persuasive intent:

1. Have I examined the situation from my own and the other person's perspective? Have I brought to light all information (both good and bad) that should be examined in order for an informed decision to be made? Have I examined all possible responses that may be made as well as their ramifications for all parties involved?

2. Have I genuinely allowed the other person(s) to voice their concerns and tell their own stories? Have I truly empathized with their position?

3. Have I given both of us enough space to be who we really are (good or bad)? Have I detached myself from both the immediate response and ultimate outcome enough to maintain perspective? Have I recognized and honored the importance of my connection with the other person no matter what the outcome may be? Have I balanced my tolerance for the other person's opinion with a need to empower one or both of us during the process of communicating?

By consciously asking yourself these three questions whenever you attempt persuasion, you can assess the ethicality of each message you construct, increase your chances of creating and maintain healthy relationships, and continue your transformation into an effective and successful communicator. The process won't be easy. But neither is becoming a world-class athlete. To be a world-class communicator, you have to practice being a world-class communicator. That means increasing your sensitivity, knowledge, skills, and will to become a more effective communicator.

Communication can build both social and professional relationships.

Summary

Human communication is critical for many reasons, including survival, relationship building, and personal and professional success. For these and other reasons it is important to understand important communication perspectives, models, and principles.

Based on an extensive review of literature, three major communication perspectives are important to consider. The biological perspectives view human communication as a function of genetic, biological, physiological, and neurophysiological processes. The cultural-social perspectives see communication as a learned process with emphases on cultural and social influences. The systems perspective views human communication as a total process, in which biological, cultural, and social variables play an integral and integrated role.

The biological perspectives include the laws and communibiological approaches. Cultural-social perspectives include rhetorical approaches, social learning theory, and rules approaches. Systems perspectives include an emphasis on such concepts as goal seeking, entropy, interdependence, holism, and equifinality.

Communication models serve as road maps for understanding and diagnosing communication problems and developing solutions. Linear models focus primarily on the sender's use of messages to influence others. These models contributed to the literature such concepts as source, encoding, message, channel, receiver, decoding, and noise. Linear models also distinguish between verbal communication (i.e., words) and nonverbal communication (i.e., behaviors such as facial expressions, eye behavior, tone of voice, gestures, body movement, clothing, etc.). Circular or interaction-based models add to our understanding the concepts of feedback, mutual influence, and fields of experience. Finally, transactional models depict the simultaneous interaction of elements in a communication system. Every communicator is viewed as a speaker/listener. Additionally, this model focuses on the ever-changing nature of human communication.

Eight primary principles on which most communication scholars today would agree are as follows. Communication is action. We communicate to survive. We communicate to satisfy needs. We attempt to change other people's behavior to survive. Communication is purposeful. Communicators mutually influence one another. Communication systems have structure. And, communication systems evolve.

Based on these perspectives, models, and principles, we defined communication as a biologically and culturally based, complex, continuing, and interactive process in which two or more people use verbal and nonverbal symbols to shape, reinforce, or change one another's behavior, either immediately or over time, for the purpose of satisfying their respective needs and ensuring survival of both the species and the individuals.

Finally, communication ethics play an important role in the overall communication process. Because communication concepts themselves are amoral (i.e., devoid of moral or immoral material), we must develop a way of judging the extent to which we are ethical communicators. Martha Cooper (1998) proposed three dimensions of ethicality by which we may judge our messages: a discourse ethic, an ethic of care, and an ethic of resistance. A discourse ethic is associated with the art of questioning oneself and others before constructing a persuasive message. An ethic of care emphasizes responding to the needs of others while communicating with compassion and love. Finally, an ethic of resistance calls for maintaining a space in which we (and others) can position ourselves as free agents, even in the face of oppressive practices and discourses that threaten to marginalize or constrain us.

Exercises

GROUP EXPERIENCES

Breakdowns

DESCRIPTION   The human communication system is a complex process in which breakdowns can occur at any point. In this chapter, we discussed the following elements of communication (1) source, (2) message, (3) channel, (4) receiver, (5) feedback, (6) noise, and (7) overall system. The purpose of this activity is to identify the barriers that can occur at each stage in the communication process.

PROCEDURE   Think of an important message you want to send to another person. For example, you may want to tell your parents that you plan to complete an internship this summer. Whatever your message, identify the barriers that could occur at each stage.

DISCUSSION   Were you able to identify a potential barrier of communication at each stage of the process? By identifying various types of barriers, you should be able to better analyze communication problems that you experience daily. The next time you encounter a communication problem, attempt to determine how the breakdown occurred. Doing so will help you avoid unnecessary barriers to communication in the future.

Walk a Mile in My Shoes

DESCRIPTION   To a large extent, successful communication depends on how well the source encodes his or her message. In any communication interaction, both the source and the receiver have fields of experience that may or may not be shared. When the fields of experience are different for the source and receiver, special attention must be given to sending and receiving messages accurately. One effective method is to "walk a mile in the other person's shoes." This activity is designed to demonstrate (1) the importance of shared fields of experience between the source and receiver and (2) a method for dealing with the different fields of experience of the two parties.

PROCEDURE   There are two stages in this activity. The first stage involves role-playing in a situation in which the source and receiver do not share a field of experience. Although a sample situation is provided, you may wish to write your own. A three- to five-minute dialogue should take place between the following characters. Each character should be played in such a way that neither person shares fields of experience nor understands the other's point of view.

Source: A college freshman who wants his or her parents to sign a permission slip to allow him (her) to live in off-campus housing instead of in a dormitory.

Receiver: A parent who never went to college and who considers the purpose of college to be "education," not "socialization."

The second stage of this activity requires that the two role-players switch roles. In other words, the college freshman should play the parent, in an attempt to see the world through the eyes of the parent, and the parent should now be playing the college freshman. In this reversed role-playing, each person should attempt to understand the other's position based on his or her life experiences.

DISCUSSION   In the first stage of the role-playing situation, the characters had different fields of experience. Communication under these conditions is very difficult, if not impossible. In the role-reversal situation, each character tried to bridge the gap by seeing the world through the eyes of the other person. If you face a similar situation, try to step back and understand how the other person experiences the world.

Responding

DESCRIPTION   Feedback is an important element in the communication process. The three types of feedback include (1) negative feedback, conveying a lack of understanding; (2) positive feedback, indicating that the receiver has understood the source's message; and (3) ambiguous feedback, which is neither clearly positive nor negative. This activity will help you identify the different types of feedback.

PROCEDURE   After reviewing the example given, write a negative, positive, and ambiguous feedback response to each of the following three statements.

Statement 1: California girls are more feminine than girls from the Northeast.

Statement 2: If I had my choice, I'd always be my own boss.

Statement 3: I hate attendance policies. It seems to me that since I'm paying for my education with my tuition, I should decide whether to go to class or not.

Example

Statement: I would like to go to a private college. I have heard that you can get a better education there.

Positive Feedback: You might check into a private school and see how you feel about its educational program.

Negative Feedback: Private schools have poor athletic programs—why would you want to go there?

Ambiguous Feedback: I see.

DISCUSSION   A good communicator is always sensitive to feedback and constantly modifies his or her messages in response to feedback received. Feedback can be conveyed through both verbal and nonverbal channels.

PERSONAL EXPERIENCES

1. Is it true that one cannot *not* communicate? Gather evidence based on logic or personal experience that proves or disproves this statement.

2. Select a person with whom you spend a great deal of time. Observe the type of feedback this person gives you. Is it mostly positive, negative, or ambiguous? Do you tend to like people who give you positive feedback? How do you respond to negative feedback?

3. Are you an effective communicator? Take a day and find out. Determine your awareness of the various elements of communication by observing yourself. Do you listen and respond to both verbal and nonverbal messages?

Discussion Questions

1. What is communication? Identify the basic elements of communication.
2. How does communication today affect communication tomorrow? Discuss the possible effects on the communication process or on you as a communicator.
3. Explain the concept of fields of experience.
4. Contrast linear, interactional, and transactional models. What does each contribute to our understanding of communication?
5. How does feedback affect the communication process?

References

Armstrong, R. N., & Argetsinger, G. S. (1989). The Hill-Cumorah pageant: Religious pageantry as suasive form. *Text and Performance Quarterly, 2,* 153–164.

Bandura, A. (1969). Principles of behavior modification. New York: Holt, Rinehart & Winston.

Bates, J. E. (1989). Concepts and measures of temperament. In G. A. Kohnstamm, J. E. Bates, & M. K. Rothbart (Eds.), *Temperament in childhood* (3–26). New York: Wiley.

Beatty, M. J., & McCroskey, J. C. (1997). It's in our nature: Verbal aggressiveness as temperamental expression. *Communication Quarterly, 45,* 446–460.

Beatty, M. J., & McCroskey, J. C. (2000). Theory, scientific evidence, and the communibiological and the nature/nurture question. *Communication Education, 49,* 25–28.

Beatty, M. J., McCroskey, J. C., & Heisel, A. D. (1998). Communication apprehension as temperamental expression: A communibiological paradigm. *Communication Monographs, 65,* 197–219.

Becker, S. L., & Roberts, C. L. (1992). *Discovering mass communication* (3rd ed.). Boston: Addison-Wesley Longman.

Berger, C. R., & Bradac, J. J. (1982). *Language and social knowledge: Uncertainty in interpersonal relationships.* London: Edward Arnold.

Berger, C. R., & diBattista, P. (1992). Information seeking and plan elaboration: What do you need to know to know what to do? *Communication Monographs, 59,* 368–387.

Bickerton, D. (1995). *Language and human behavior.* Seattle, WA: University of Washington Press.

Bodary, D.L., & Miller, L.D. (2000). Neurobiological substrates of communicator style. *Communication Education, 49,* 82–98.

Burgoon, J. K., Buller, D. B., & Woodall, W. G. (1996). *Nonverbal communication: The unspoken dialogue.* New York: McGraw-Hill.

Cattell, R. B. (1946). *Description and measurement of personality.* New York: World.

Chomsky, N. (1957). *Syntactic structures.* The Hague: Mouton.

Condit, M. C. (2000a). Toward new "sciences" of human behavior. *Communication Education, 49,* 29–35.

Condit, M. C. (2000b). Culture and biology in human communication: Toward a multicausal model. *Communication Education, 49,* 7–24.

Cooper, M. (1998). Decentering judgment: Toward a postmodern communication ethic. In J. M. Sloop & J. P. McDaniel (Eds.), *Judgment calls: Rhetoric, politics, and indeterminacy* (63–83). Boulder, CO: Westview Press.

Cronen, V., Pearce, W. B., & Snavely, L. (1979). A theory of rule-structure and types of episodes and a study of perceived enmeshment in undesired repetitive patterns ("URPs"). In D. Nimmo (Ed.), *Communication Yearbook, 3,* New Brunswick, NJ: Transaction Books.

Cushman, D. P. (1977). The rules perspective as a theoretical basis for the study of human communication. *Communication Quarterly, 25,* 30–45.

Cushman, D. P., Valentinsen, B., & Dietrich, D. (1982). A rules theory of interpersonal relationships. In F. Dance (Ed.), *Human communication theory.* New York: Harper & Row.

Cushman, D. P., & Whiting, G. (1972). An approach to communication theory: A consensus on the rules. *Journal of Communication, 22,* 217–233.

Damasio, A. R. (December, 1999). How the brain creates the mind. *Scientific American, 281*(6), 112–117.

Damasio, A. R. (1999). *The feeling of what happens: Body and emotion in the making of consciousness.* New York: Harcourt Brace.

Dawkins, R. (1995). *River out of Eden.* New York: Basic Books.

De Waal, F. B. M. (1999). The end of nature versus nurture. *Scientific American, 281*(6), 94–99.

Ekman, P., Friesen, W. V., & Ellsworth, P. C. (1972). *Emotion in the human face.* New York: Pergamon.

Emmert, P., & Donaghy, W. C. (1981). *Human communication.* New York: Random House.

Emmert, P., & Emmert, V. J. L. (1984). *Interpersonal communication* (3rd ed.). Dubuque, IA: Wm. C. Brown Publishers.

Eysenck, H. J. (1991). Biological dimensions of personality. In L. A. Pervin (Ed.), *Handbook of personality* (244–276). New York: Guilford.

Flaherty, L. M., Pearce, K. J., & Rubin, R. B. (1998). Internet and face-to-face communication: Not functional alternatives. *Communication Quarterly, 46,* 250–268.

Gray, J. A. (1991). The neuropsychology of temperament. In J. Strelau & A. Angleitner (Eds.), *Explorations in temperament* (pp. 105–128). New York: Plenum.

Guerrero, L. K., & Walid A. A. (1999). Toward a goal-oriented approach for understanding communicative responses to jealousy. *Western Journal of Communication, 63,* 216–248.

Harper, N. (1979). *Human communication theory: The history of a paradigm.* Rochelle Park, NJ: Hayden Book Company, Inc.

Horvath, C. W. (1995). Biological origins of communicator style. *Communication Quarterly, 43,* 394–407.

Huxman, S. S. (1997). The tragicomic rhetorical "dance" of marginalized groups: The case of Mennonites in the great war. *Southern Communication Journal, 62,* 305–318.

Infante, D. A., Rancer, A. S., & Womack, D. F. (1990). *Building communication theory* (2nd ed.). Prospect Heights, IL: Waveland Press.

Laswell, H. D. (1948). The structure and function of communication in society. In L. Bryson (Ed.), *The communication of ideas.* New York: Harper & Row.

Liska, J., & Cronkhite, G. (1995). *An ecological perspective on human communication theory.* New York: Harcourt Brace College Publishers.

McCroskey, J. C., & Beatty, M. J. (2000). The communibiological perspective: Implications for communication in instruction. *Communication Education, 49,* 1–6.

McPhail, M. L. (1996). *Zen in the art of rhetoric: An inquiry into coherence.* Albany, NY: SUNY Press.

Monge, P. R. (1977). The systems perspective as a theoretical basis for the study of human communication. *Communication Quarterly, 25,* 19–29.

Morris, R., & Wander, P. (1990). Native American rhetoric: Dancing in the shadows of the ghost dance. *Quarterly Journal of Speech, 76,* 164–191.

Oxford desk dictionary and thesaurus: American edition. (1997). New York: Berkley Books.

Pearce, W. B., Cronen, V. E., & Conklin, F. (1979). On what to look at when analyzing communication: A hierarchical model of actors' meanings. *Communication 4,* 195–220.

Pearce, B., & Cronen, V. (1980). *Communication, action, and meaning: The creation of social realities.* New York: Prager.

Procter, D. E., & Schenck-Hamlin, W. J. (1996). Form and variations in negative political advertising. *Communication Research Reports, 13,* 147–156.

Samp, J. A., & Solomon, D. H. (1998). Communicative responses to problematic events in close relationships II: The variety and facets of goals. *Communication Research, 25,* 66–95.

Samp, J. A., & Solomon, D. H. (1999). Communicative responses to problematic events in close relationships II: The influence of five facets of goals on message features. *Communication Research, 26,* 193–239.

Schramm, W. (1955). *The process and effects of mass communication.* Urbana, IL: University of Illinois Press.

Shannon, C., & Weaver, W. (1949). *The mathematical theory of communication.* Urbana, IL: University of Illinois Press.

Slater, M. D. (1997). Persuasion processes across receiver goals and message genres. *Communication Theory, 7,* 125–148.

U.S. Department of Labor. (1991). *Skills and the new economy.* Washington, DC: U.S. Government Printing Office.

Valencic, K. M., Beatty, M. J., Rudd, J. E., Dobos, J. A., & Heisel, A. D., (1998). An empirical test of a communibiological model of trait verbal aggressiveness. *Communication Quarterly, 46,* 327–341.

Verderber, R., Elder, A., & Weiler, E. (1976). A study of communication time usage among college students. Unpublished manuscript, University of Cincinnati.

2

Verbal Communication

key concepts and terms

Language
Words
Labeling
Interaction
Transmission
Innateness theory
Imitative, learned behavior
Language acquisition devices
Infancy

Toddlerhood
Early childhood
Symbolic process
Semantics
Symbol
Sense
Referent
Concrete
Abstract

Ambiguity
Vagueness
Denotation
Connotation
Style
Non-identity
Non-allness
Self-reflexiveness
Linguistic stereotyping

From:	"Liliana"
To:	"Eileen" <parramem@futurenet.ab.net>
Sent:	Friday, October 20th 4:47 PM
Subject:	Am I just being overly sensitive?

Hey, girl! Just a note to check in and get your opinion on something. As you know, my boyfriend Enzo is a retail store manager, and was transferred last week from his store in the mall to a new store on the other side of town. I went by and saw Enzo on Monday and got the chance to meet both of his employees. They seemed nice enough. But now I wonder. And now I don't know whether I should phone Enzo there or not.

You see, I called him at the store two days ago and Sam, one of the guys, answered the phone. When I asked for Enzo, I heard Sam say, "Enzo . . . Telephone. It's your parole officer." I was really angry at first, Eileen. Sam doesn't even know me. How could he say that about me? Enzo says Sam was just kidding around, but I'm still a little miffed. I know I'm probably just being overly sensitive, but I can't seem to get it out of my mind. Tell me I'm just being stupid and I'll drop it. Hope all's well with you. Let's talk by phone on Sunday. I've missed you, girl!
—"Sensitive" in Santa Fe

For a moment, think back to when you were a child. Do you remember the old adage, "Sticks and stones can break my bones, but words can never hurt me"? If you're like us, you probably remember saying it (loudly or under your breath) to the class bully. He may have called you "four eyes" if you wore glasses, or "metal mouth" if you wore braces on your teeth. She may have made fun of your "athletic prowess" with a loud and nasty, "Loser!" Words *can* hurt us! They also can help. They can take us from the highest highs to the lowest lows, depending on who says them.

To understand why verbal communication has such power, this chapter will focus on the essence of language and how it operates in our daily lives. We will begin with a discussion of the functions of language and how people actually develop personal language patterns. We will then address the concept of meaning and some of the features of language that affect our everyday lives, including abstraction and concreteness, ambiguity and vagueness, denotation and connotation, and language style. Finally, we will discuss the relationship between language and behavior. In this section we will address how language is often used to stereotype individuals or their behavior and look at several ways in which we can begin to make our everyday language more effective.

Before we launch headfirst into a discussion of these topics, let's begin with a working definition of language. *Language* is the communication of thoughts and emotions by means of a structured system of symbols. In our language these symbols are known as **words**. The word *innovation*, for example, is just an arbitrary combination of letters that, over time, has come to be accepted as a *symbol* for the introduction of some object or process that is new and exciting. Our ability to use these symbols defines our level of language skill.

Functions of Language

We use language to fulfill three primary functions: to label, to interact with others, and to transmit information.

Identifying an object, act, or person by name so that she, he, or it can be referred to in communication is known as *labeling*. Once something is named, it takes on all of the characteristics and meanings that we associate with its label. For example, your meaning of the word "success" might include a $120,000-a-year salary and a new Porsche 911, while for someone else "success" might be defined as having a job outdoors to enjoy the fresh air and wilderness. The same is true of our respective names. They are badges of our identity and symbols in their own right. That is one reason why we become easily perturbed if someone calls us a "name" (like Liliana was when Sam referred to her as Enzo's "parole officer"). That is also why we dislike having our name misspelled or mispronounced or (worse yet) having someone make fun of our name.

In fact, names are so powerful that, according to Grant Smith, they actually may contribute to the outcome of political races. Smith, a U.S. English professor, conducted a study in 1998 to "determine the impact of language sounds in political elections" (p. 154). Results of his study suggested that the rhythm and ease with which political names are articulated may be associated with "a greater sense of comfort or reassurance as voters read or speak the names" (p. 155). To test his hypothesis, Smith developed an analytical model of language to determine the possible association between the language characteristics of politicians' names and the final outcomes of 42 U.S. presidential elections (1824–1992); 44 local elections in the state of Washington in 1995; and 34 U.S. Senate elections and 44 House elections in 1996. Results of the study provided support for his hypothesis. Try it for yourself. Can you guess which of the following politicians won their respective elections? (1) Fairchild or Sangmeiester. (2) Sanders or Pekelis. (3) Dellwo or Reilly. (4) Bernsdoff or Combs. (For fun, consider "Lincoln" or "McClellan" and "Bush" or "Gore.") If you guessed Fairchild, Sanders, Reilly, and Combs you are correct. Grant's conclusions about the power of names certainly are interesting, if not compelling.

The next function of language, *interaction,* focuses on the sharing and communication of ideas and emotions. Through language we can call out an array of emotional responses in others—from sympathy and understanding to anger and confusion. For example, if a friend is in the middle of suggesting an idea for a Saturday retreat, and you believe that you have a "better" plan of action, you can use language more effectively by "holding your fire," letting her finish the idea, and beginning your response in a diplomatic, nonemotional way. For instance, you might say, "That's a great idea. Or we could . . . (your idea) . . . Let's ask Latasha and Hosea what they think." In this way, language can serve as the basis for a positive rather than a negative interaction.

Through language, information also can be passed on to other individuals. This function of language is referred to as *transmission.* Consider for a moment all of the information that you send and receive daily, from the first "good morning" that you hear until the last sentence you read before turning off the light at night. From books, lectures, and electronic billboards to videodiscs and satellite transmissions, there is no end to the ways through which language can transmit information.

Researchers have argued that transmission of information is perhaps the most important function of language in the history of human civilization. For example, language connects the past, present, and future. It also ensures the perpetuation of our cultures and traditions. Older generations die but, through language, they are able to leave behind their ideas, accomplishments, failures, and plans for the future. Thus, later generations do not have to repeat the trials and errors of their predecessors but can adapt and constantly improve upon the successes of the past. Just think how little of your present knowledge comes from your own experience and how much is based on long-accepted facts. Indeed, language has enabled us to advance intellectually, psychologically, and culturally.

Language Development

Newborn babies have only a few ways to communicate—body movements, facial expressions, and sounds that are generalized to many needs. For example, a cry can mean fear, hunger, pain, or any number of other things. However, as babies grow, they discover language and its importance in ensuring their personal well-being and development.

Babies discover that language is useful for expressing and conveying feelings to others. Their first "mama" or "dada" evokes immediate smiles and caresses. Their later, more sophisticated expressions, such as "I love you" or "Go away," will continue the process of exchanging emotions through language. This aspect of language is quite important in creating psychological balance and adjustment.

During their early years, children also discover the meaning of "yes" and "no." No longer can they do everything they wish and still please others. Through spoken and, later, written symbols, they come to understand their culture and its expectations. Language thus serves as a means of socialization—teaching mores, norms, and accepted behavior.

Theories of Language Development

From childhood to old age, we all use language as a means of broadening our knowledge of ourselves and the world about us. When humans first evolved, they were like newborn children, unable to use this valuable tool. Yet once language developed, the possibilities for humankind's future attainments and cultural growth increased. Let's now look at three theories of language development: (1) innateness, (2) imitative, and (3) language acquisition devices.

Many linguists believe that evolution is responsible for our ability to produce and use language. They claim that our highly evolved brain provides us with an innate language ability not found in lower organisms. Proponents of this ***innateness theory,*** most notably Eric Lenneberg, say that our potential for language is inborn, but that language itself develops gradually, as a function of the growth of the brain during childhood. Therefore, there are critical biological times for language development—once the growth of the brain is complete (during the early teen years), it is much harder to learn language.

Current reviews of innateness theory are mixed; however, evidence supporting the existence of some innate abilities is undeniable. Indeed, more and more schools are discovering that foreign languages are best taught in the lower grades. Young children often can learn several languages by being exposed to them, while adults

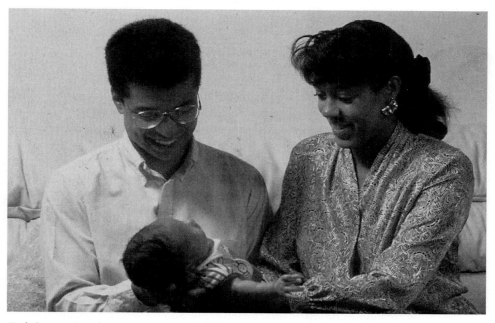

Early interactions between parent and child encourage language and intellectual development.

have a much harder time learning another language once the rules of their first language have become embedded.

Although some aspects of language are undeniably innate, language does not develop automatically in a vacuum. Children who have been isolated from other human beings do not possess language. This demonstrates that interaction with other human beings is necessary for proper language development. Some linguists believe that this interaction is more basic to human language acquisition than any innate capacities. These theorists view language as *imitative, learned behavior.* In other words, children learn language from their parents by imitating them. Parents gradually shape their child's language skills by positively reinforcing precise imitations and negatively reinforcing imprecise ones.

A third theory of language development borrows elements and truth from both the innateness and the imitative theories. Noam Chomsky said that we are all born with *language acquisition devices* (LAD, for short). This doesn't mean that grammar is somehow innately in our heads, but rather that these LADs help us sort out the language we hear and understand its grammatical rules. From listening to adults, American children learn, for example, that the usual sentence order is subject-verb-object. They will therefore begin to put words into this order. Children from another culture will learn the grammatical rules of their society. Thus, Chomsky's view suggests an interaction between innate (LAD) and learned aspects of language.

Children who, for one reason or another, have been isolated from speaking humans during the critical periods in which language usually develops find it very difficult, if not impossible, to acquire language abilities. Scientists explain that these children have passed crucial biological times in their neural development, critical periods during which language learning must occur. Once passed, these developmental stages can never be recaptured (Bohannon, MacWhinney & Snow, 1990).

Additionally, the quality of the language environment in which children are reared affects their overall language development. For example, research has suggested that children who come to school from homes in which many books and magazines are read, shared, or processed generally make the transition to literacy with greater ease than do children who come from low-print homes. As Geraldine Wallach (1990), one language researcher, has noted, this discrepancy results, in part, from the fact that children from high-print homes talk more like books and have already begun to learn what styles of language are appropriate for various situations. Thus, children who are reared by parents who rely heavily on an oral tradition, rather than on one that emphasizes the importance of reading, will find themselves at a disadvantage when they come to school, because teachers and schools rely more exclusively on literate or written modes.

As you can see, parents and teachers serve a vital role in language development. Thus, they (and we) must learn to create supportive, stimulating environments that are conducive to language learning. Only in this way can children successfully integrate innate and learned language skills, and become articulate, competent members of their culture.

The Process of Language Development

The developmental continuum for a baby's early achievements in language learning and communication may be divided into three periods of approximate length: infancy (birth through 12 months), toddlerhood (12 to 24 months), and early childhood (24 to 48 months) (Prizant & Wetherby, 1990, p. 6).

According to Prizant and Wetherby, achievements during *infancy* (birth through 12 months) may be classified into four major categories. Although these categories overlap, they generally include: (1) getting the attention of and interacting socially with principal caregivers; (2) participating in "joint activity routines" (for instance, diaper changing, eating, etc.); (3) early vocalizing and gesturing to regulate caregivers' behavior, attract and maintain attention, and share an object or event; and (4) comprehending words in routine interactions (p. 7).

From birth to nine months, infants' behaviors generally are confined to preverbal gestures and sounds. In fact, research shows that infants not only can make all of the sounds of their own language at this time, but also can produce sounds that constitute all the languages in the world. For example, American infants are able to make the distinct sounds of the French "r" and German "ü."

At 9 to 10 months, the infant begins to use sounds and gestures to communicate intentionally. Infants can point, use conventional words like "mama" as a general request for objects, mark predictable points in events (for example, say "bye-bye" when the babysitter puts a toy on a shelf), use gaze aversion or thumb sucking to help them cope with stress in the environment, and make decisions about their own behavior based on the facial expressions of caregivers (for example, whether to crawl across the room or put their hand in the toilet) (pp. 7–9).

Toward the end of the first 12 months, infants generally can communicate their intentions and signal for the attention of others. At this point, they generally enter the next stage of language development or *toddlerhood* (approximately 12 to 24 months in age). Toddlerhood is marked by (1) increasing frequency, perseverance, and intentionality in preverbal communication; (2) acquiring symbols to communicate about his or her actions and immediate world; (3) representing past events through internal, symbolic representations (for instance, remembering previous play with a truck, ball, or kitten); and (4) anticipating future events. As toddlers gain these abilities, they begin to reflect and make decisions based on prior experiences. For example, they learn to associate a loud, firm "No!" with pulling the dog's tail and, therefore, begin to make more "informed" decisions (pp. 7, 10–11).

Around 13 months of age, toddlers begin to form their first words, generally in the form of labels for objects (such as hat, book, or cat). During this "one-word stage," acquiring words is a slow process; however, between 12 and 18 months, children generally increase their rate of sounds and coordinating gestures. At 18 months, toddlers begin to show marked improvement in the growth of their vocabulary and produce several new words per day. Finally, between the ages of 18 and 24 months, they begin to use word combinations and to describe states and qualities about people, objects, and events (for example, "Daddy go?"). They also begin to ask for information and bring up events that are associated with other places and time (for instance, "Matthew get ice cream?"). In short, they begin to take part in real conversations (pp. 10–12).

During *early childhood* (approximately 24 to 48 months in age), a child's achievements normally include (1) an increasing ability to communicate about events and other people's actions; (2) symbolic interactions about past and future events; (3) the ability to comprehend conditional, causal, and other complex relationships; and (4) a basic level of communication competence. For instance, prior to or around 24 months, a child's thoughts may be represented by a single word ("hug" may mean "Daddy, I want a hug") or by several words that are run together (such as "mamagive"). From 24 to 36 months, children begin to grasp sentence grammar, including word and sentence organization. They are able to construct sentences (for example, "Me give mama a hug"), and they experience rapid growth in their vocabularies. They also begin to understand concepts like position, size, and time, and are able to better express their ideas because they can construct more complete and complex sentences. As this period progresses from 36 to 48 months, children start to express their goals, feelings, and thoughts. Additionally, their self-esteem and self-image begin to be significantly affected by their competence in play with other children (pp. 7, 12–14).

By the time children are six years old, they seem to know all the grammatical rules that enable them to speak correctly. However, the learning process never ceases. With every new experience, their vocabulary can continue to increase as long as they live.

Meaning

Semantics

Once you have acquired words and grammar, you still must learn to use them effectively to communicate. You gradually learn to combine your words in an infinite variety of ways to transmit an infinite number of messages. Still, transmission of messages is not enough. You also want them to be received and understood. Commonality of language between speaker and listener is obviously essential for this understanding. What is even more essential is commonality of meaning.

But what is meaning? To provide a starting point for understanding this complex phenomenon, consider the word "jaram." This word *means* nothing. Let's say, though, that you are now shown an object called a "jaram." Hereafter, the word *jaram* will bring to mind a picture of that object. Now the word has meaning for you. The use of words such as *jaram* as symbols representing objects and concepts is known as the *symbolic process.* The study of the relationship between these word symbols and their meanings is called *semantics.*

Semantics is quite a complicated area of study, since many symbols and dimensions of meaning exist. However, researchers generally agree that words have three dimensions of meaning: symbol, sense, and referent. The *symbol* refers to the word or nonverbal sign that represents an object in the real world, and the *sense* to subjective feelings we have about the symbol. The *referent* is the actual object as it exists in reality. Thus, your meaning of the word *football* is a function of the symbol (the word *football*), the sense (pleasant feelings brought on by the thought of last year's winning season), and the referent (an actual football). Of course, this analysis applies only to the linguistic level of meaning. We cannot forget that there are philosophical, psychological, and logical levels of meaning as well.

Language Features

At a minimum, meaning involves shared understanding or shared agreement regarding a symbol, its sense, and its referent. For example, we probably can all agree that an "office" is a place where business is transacted. However, the word "office" takes on a different dimension of meaning when it describes a large, beautifully decorated corner room with lots of windows—and when the word refers to a 6 × 6 windowless room located near an elevator. What features of language allow the same word to take on such a diverse set of meanings? Although the answer to this question is complex, semanticists have agreed on at least four factors that affect word meanings: (1) the extent to which words are abstract or concrete; (2) the amount of ambiguity and vagueness in a language; (3) the denotative and connotative dimensions of meaning; and (4) language style. Each of these topics will be addressed more completely in the following paragraphs.

ABSTRACTION AND CONCRETENESS.   Determining meanings is complicated when the words in question are not concrete. *Concrete* words symbolize objects or events that can be pointed to, touched, or directly experienced. Words like "hackeysack," "walleye," and "mango" are in this category. On the other hand, *abstract* words represent things that we cannot sense directly, such as "loyalty," "spirituality," "integrity," and "freedom."

No matter how difficult it may be to define abstractions, they are very important to the communication process. With abstract words, we are able to extend the level of our thoughts and speech beyond the concrete, everyday world. We can talk about the complicated concepts of right and wrong, discuss things that we cannot see, and consider the future as if it existed today.

AMBIGUITY AND VAGUENESS.   Two other language variables that affect understanding are ambiguity and vagueness. *Ambiguity* has been defined as the amount of doubtfulness or uncertainty in meanings. Generally, ambiguity arises for the simple reason that human language customarily assigns one symbol to several categories or

The quality of children's language environments significantly affects their language development.

things. To illustrate, consider the word *heavy.* One can have heavy luggage, a heavy yield of grain, a room heavy with moisture, a heavy odor, heavy gunfire, heavy food, a heavy date, and a heavy book, both in weight and in profundity.

Vagueness can present even greater problems for language users than can ambiguity. A word or phrase is said to be *vague* if it lacks precision or clarity of expression. In other words, vagueness occurs when the language we use is unspecific or imprecise. For example, if you have been asked by your boss to pick up a job candidate whom you have never met, and you are told to look for the tall man at the train station entrance, you may have difficulty locating the person because of imprecision in the description. The definition of "tall" for someone who stands 5′2″ may be different for someone who is 6′2″ in height.

Vagueness leads to trivial arguments, such as "I say it's green," which is countered by, "Well, I say it's blue." However, vagueness also may lead to more serious concerns, such as "Where does truth end and falsehood begin?" or "Where does business savvy end and corrupt practice begin?"

DENOTATION AND CONNOTATION.   Meaning is also affected by the denotation and connotation of particular words. *Denotation* is the objective reference of a word—that is, its factual, concrete meaning. Dictionary definitions present denotations. Some words are primarily denotative, but most words also possess less definable connotations. *Connotation* refers to meanings beyond the objective reference. The word *automobile,* for example, denotes a four-wheeled motor vehicle. Yet it may connote little or nothing to one person, anger to someone who has just been fired from an automobile factory, and pleasure to someone who has just bought a new sports car. Very specific words—*chair, desk, book,* and so forth—are usually without connotation for most people. Other words, such as *obsolete* and *respectable,* can fall either way, depending on context, while words such as *fantastic* and *horrible* are almost totally connotative in nature.

We acquire our connotations from social and personal experiences. The word *farm* means something different to a city dweller than to a country person. The more two people have in common—the more similar their backgrounds, past experiences, attitudes, and outlooks—the better chance they have of attaching the same meaning to a word or concept.

Consider the following situation. Ingrid is talking with her parents, and all is going well. They are communicating for a change. Then the conversation turns to the subject of drugs. Communication quickly comes to an end. Ingrid and her parents stop communicating because they have different connotations for the word *drug*. But the word is only a small part of a larger problem. Ingrid, her mother, and her father have different attitudes about many things, and this difference in attitudes influences the connotations they attach to words. The end result of these differing connotations is often a breakdown in communication.

STYLE. Another factor that influences meaning is *style,* or how we choose, organize, and use those features of the language that are open to individual selection.

The rules of our language that dictate the arrangement of words in sentences (subject-verb-object) and frequently determine which forms of words must be used (present or past tense, singular or plural verb) are not matters of style, but of grammar. Style, on the other hand, refers to an individual's characteristic tendencies to choose particular kinds of words (simple versus multisyllabic, factual versus descriptive), particular sentence constructions (short versus long, complete versus fragmentary), or even particular phrases ("you know," "I mean," or "right on").

Style is influenced by variables in the speaker as well as in the listener. Have you ever wondered why it seems difficult to talk with some people and easy to talk with others? Think for a minute about dates you've had, parties you've attended, or bus rides you've taken. Pleasant interactions are usually associated with people with whom you hit it off immediately. Even though you may have found commonalities, successful communication was probably based on more than just similar professions or common interests.

Personality differences do exist between communicators, and we tend to make positive and negative judgments based on specific communication styles. We often base first impressions more on how a person says something than on exactly what words he or she uses. This fact of communication life leads to statements like, "She turned me off with her sarcastic attitude," or "He really had a way of making people feel right at home." In fact, the first few minutes of interpersonal interaction often determine whether or not we will continue interaction. These minutes are also often the key to business achievement, social success, family harmony, and sexual satisfaction.

Another important variable associated with language style is the extent to which our talk is perceived to be powerful (or powerless). According to James Bradac and Anthony Mulac (1984), a powerless style is associated with "a relatively large number of hedges ("I sort of did."), intensifiers ("We really did."), hesitations

("I . . . uh . . . like this."), deictic phrases ("That man over there . . ."), tag questions ("It is, isn't it?") or declarative sentences with rising intonation and polite forms ("Yes sir . . .")" (p. 307). In contrast, powerful language is reflected by the use of "fluent, terse, and direct speech" with few of the elements previously listed.

As you can see, we need to be aware of our own style so that we can communicate more effectively with others. Additionally, when we understand our style of communication, we can more easily adapt to the styles of others. For example, effective communicators tailor their language for a particular audience, or base their language on the nature and purpose of their messages. An environmental scientist who uses scientific jargon with colleagues probably should avoid doing so with people outside the profession. Physicians often have a habit of talking with their patients as if the latter were familiar with the latest medical terminology. As a result, patients sometimes feel alienated, especially when Latin terminology seems to change their simple complaint into what sounds like a fatal illness. Asking a physician to speak in "lay language" will enhance a patient's understanding of the doctor's diagnosis.

Korzybski's Laws

Language is a highly complex, yet powerful, phenomenon. However, we can all strive to become more aware of the subtle but powerful influence of words in our lives. Alfred Korzybski, a pioneer in the area of general semantics—the study of the structure and function of speech and resultant behavior—observed that people often falsely identify with words. We sometimes respond to words as if the words themselves were the objects they symbolize. In fact, many individuals are tyrannized by words. For example, just hearing the word *snake* may cause someone with a fear of snakes to shiver. The snake itself does not have to be in sight; the symbol, not the referent, causes the response.

This observation led to Korzybski's law of ***non-identity,*** which says that a word is *not* the thing it represents. The word *cat* and the animal itself are not one and the same thing. (See Figure 2.1.)

Korzybski's second law, that of ***non-allness,*** reminds us that a word cannot symbolize *all* of a thing. *Cat* may bring to mind your own pet and the expensive show animal you saw on TV last night. However, *cat* may symbolize something quite different for an Ethiopian who has experienced cats of a larger and more ferocious variety than the string of "Fluffys" you have owned and loved. Neither you nor the Ethiopian, though, might think of an Egyptian god or a Canadian lynx. Clearly, language never conveys *everything* about *anything.*

Korzybski's third law concerns ***self-reflexiveness.*** It explains that a word can refer not only to something in the real world but also to itself. The word *cat* not only refers to a kind of four-legged animal in the real world but also to the word formed in English by the letters *c-a-t,* or to the word formed in Spanish by the letters *g-a-t-o.*

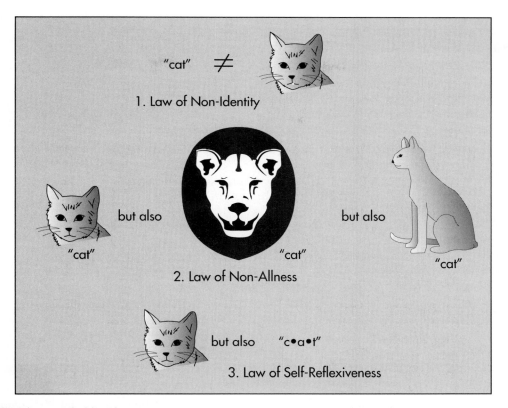

FIGURE 2.1 Korzybski's Three Laws

Language and Behavior

Our discussion of connotation and style revealed the effects of environmental and personal variables on an individual's language usage. It is also important to recognize that our language affects the attitudes and subsequent behaviors of others.

We know, for example, that listeners can accurately identify or estimate, on the basis of speech alone, various characteristics of speakers, including their age, sex, race, socioeconomic status, personality, specific identity, facial and body features, and height and weight. In addition, researchers have found that speech style contributes to a group's or culture's identity and cohesion (Maass, Salvi, Arcuri, & Semin, 1989). One illustration of this language principle is the use of "secret" rites (and their corresponding language) that groups such as college fraternities and sororities employ.

Language patterns also have an effect on the degree to which people are perceived to be credible or powerful. Interestingly, linguistic patterns typical of women

WORDS IN WONDERLAND

Lewis Carroll was an English mathematician and logician whose real name was Charles Lutwidge Dodgson. He is remembered, not for his contributions to mathematics or logic, but as the author of *Alice's Adventures in Wonderland* and *Through the Looking-Glass*. These great works are sometimes called "nonsense" literature, but from the excerpts that follow we can see that even in Wonderland Carroll was concerned with the logic of words and how they represent reality.

"Come, we shall have some fun now!" thought Alice. "I'm glad you've begun asking riddles—I believe I can guess that," she added aloud.

"Do you mean that you think you can find out the answer to it?" said the March Hare.

"Exactly so," said Alice.

"Then you should say what you mean," the March Hare went on.

"I do," Alice hastily replied: "at least—at least I mean what I say—that's the same thing, you know."

"Not the same thing a bit!" said the Hatter. "Why, you might just as well say that 'I see what I eat' is the same thing as 'I eat what I see!' "

"You might just as well say," added the March Hare, "that 'I like what I get' is the same thing as 'I get what I like!' "

"You might just as well say," added the Dormouse, which seemed to be talking in its sleep, "that 'I breathe when I sleep' is the same thing as 'I sleep when I breathe!' "

"It *is* the same thing with you," said the Hatter, and here the conversation dropped. . . .

Alice's Adventures in Wonderland

"I don't know what you mean by 'glory,' " Alice said.

Humpty Dumpty smiled contemptuously. "Of course you don't—till I tell you. I meant 'there's a nice knock-down argument for you!' "

"But 'glory' doesn't mean 'a nice knock-down argument,' " Alice objected.

"When *I* use a word," Humpty Dumpty said, in rather a scornful tone, "it means just what I choose it to mean—neither more nor less."

"The question is," said Alice, "whether you *can* make words mean so many different things."

"The question is," said Humpty Dumpty, "which is to be master—that's all."

Through the Looking-Glass

have been found to be less powerful than those associated with men. As suggested by research, women make greater use of indirect control strategies, as is reflected in their use of a significantly greater number of questions (for example, "What's next?"). Additionally, women use justifiers ("The reason I say that is . . .") more frequently, apparently perceiving a greater need to provide a rationale for their opinions. Furthermore, they use more intensive adverbs ("I really think X") than do men, perhaps to increase the strength of what they are saying. Finally, women talk more about people than objects, as exemplified in their greater use of pronouns ("We, you, they . . ."), and they employ a more indirect, qualified language style (for example, through the use of adverbs when beginning sentences, such as "Surprisingly, that test was a breeze") (Mulac, Wiemann, Widenmann, & Gibson, 1988, pp. 315–335).

Conversely, men have been found to use a more direct, or overt, control strategy through the production of more interruptions ("Let's move on; we can come back to that point later"). They also have a tendency to use a greater number of directives ("Why don't you finish this report before we talk?") and maintain longer speaking turns through the use of more conjunctions and/or fillers when beginning a sentence ("And another thing we need to consider . . .") (pp. 315–335).

What impact do these language differences have on the attitudes and behavior of other people? One answer seems to lie in the differential language patterns that women and men use when speaking in same-sex as opposed to mixed-sex groups. According to research, when women converse with other women, they are rated higher on sociointellectual status and aesthetic quality than men interacting with other men. In other words, when speaking to other women, females are perceived to be of high social status, rich, white-collar, and literate as compared to men speaking with other men. Additionally, women who interact with other women are perceived to be more "beautiful, nice, pleasant, and sweet" than are men when interacting with other men (pp. 331–332).

However, in mixed-sex groups (men interacting with women and vice versa), language patterns seem to change, and ratings of sociointellectual status begin to increase for men and decrease for women. Additionally, when interacting with men, women are no longer rated more highly than are men on aesthetic quality. Instead, men are perceived to be more "beautiful, nice, pleasant, and sweet" than are women. To their credit, women are perceived to be more dynamic than men when speaking in mixed-sex groups. In other words, women are perceived to be more strong, active, aggressive, and loud than men in mixed-sex communication situations (pp. 331–332).

One final note to remember about powerful versus powerless language is that using a powerful style is especially important when (1) we want to be persuasive, and (2) when we want to be perceived as dynamic and credible. Building on the work of Bradac and Mulac (1984), John Sparks, Charles Areni, and K. Chris Cox (1998) compared audience members' perceptions of a speaker and their attitudes toward his (her) recommendations when the speaker presented a powerful (or powerless) message in one of three forms: written, audio, and audiovisual forms. Power of language style had little effect on persuasion when the message was written. However, when the message took the forms of audio or audiovisual messages, persuasion was significantly influenced by power of language style. (For people who rely on the telephone as one of their primary communication channels, this finding is especially important.)

In her study of language and credibility, Laurie Haleta (1996) compared students' perceptions of university teachers who used powerful or powerless language. Haleta concluded that powerful language produces significantly greater perceptions of teachers' dynamism, credibility, and status than powerless language. Additionally, teachers using powerful language tend to produce significantly less uncertainty in the minds of their students than do teachers who use powerless language.

Linguistic Stereotyping

Assuming automatic relationships between particular linguistic styles and personal traits is known as semantic or *linguistic stereotyping*. Perceptions regarding the Amish people of the Pennsylvania Dutch area illustrate this point. Although the people of this region may share both similar cultures and beliefs, not everyone who speaks with a Pennsylvania Dutch accent prefers old-fashioned clothes and horse-drawn wagons. Likewise, many people unfairly underestimate the intellectual ability of people who speak slow and halting English. Conversely, linguistic stereotyping may also produce a perception of intellectual superiority for a speaker with a crisp Oxford accent.

As you may have guessed by now, most semantic stereotypes are negative. They are particularly harmful for individuals who share easily recognizable (yet nonstandard) dialects such as black English or Louisiana creole. Perhaps the greatest damage, however, comes when speakers of the standard or majority dialect of a culture believe that nonspeakers are somehow inferior. In fact, many employers in American businesses and industries are guilty of such perceptions. In turn, such instances of linguistic stereotyping have affected their hiring and firing and promotion policies.

The question then becomes: What can we do, given this knowledge concerning linguistic stereotypes? For "native" speakers, the solution seems to reside in concern

Awareness and appreciation of different cultures help eliminate linguistic stereotyping.

and awareness—awareness of the information we have presented and a concern for consistency in acting upon it, whether in interpersonal interactions or on the job.

For nonnative speakers, the solution is more complex and will involve a weighing of alternatives and their consequences. To disregard the importance of competence in using the dialect or style of the region in which you live or work may result in diminished opportunities and rewards. At the same time, individuals should be aware of the importance of their cultural identities, which are intimately tied to the language they speak.

Perhaps one answer lies in the individual's ability to achieve some degree of linguistic competence in both communities. Although such an attempt would be both difficult and frustrating, it could provide a means by which the "bilingual" or "bidialectical" person may communicate more effectively.

Making Language More Effective

When Clark Gable said "Frankly, my dear, I don't give a damn" in the film *Gone With the Wind* (1939), millions of people were either shocked or titillated. Times have changed. Four-letter words don't offend as they once did. New words come into the language almost daily, as they always have. As the norms and mores of a society change, so does its language. Both society and language reflect the "liberated" spirit of the twenty-first century.

Unfortunately, current language use often also means sloppy, imprecise language. Although people seem to be communicating *more* these days, they may be understood even *less*. As a student of communication (and now language!), you should be aware of the trend. You also can become a communication trendsetter by following these tips:

1. Try to speak clearly at all times (that is, use words with meanings that can be understood by those who are listening).

2. Relate to your listeners by being sensitive to their attitudes, beliefs, and experiences.

3. Avoid using slang and jargon (for example, computerese).

4. Minimize the use of regionalisms such as "y'all" or "you guys," especially in the professional world.

5. Converse without using habitual expressions, such as:

"you know what I mean?"
"uh-huh" (for yes)
"uh-uh" (for no)
"yeah"
"to be honest"
"truthfully"

Our social identities are inextricably tied to the language we speak.

6. Choose language that is appropriate to the purpose of the interaction and the communication setting—your language should be different when you are talking with a friend and when you are giving a presentation.

7. Avoid using vague and ambiguous language—learn to say what you mean and mean what you say.

8. Be careful not to overkill a subject by rambling. People especially appreciate others who KISS: "*Keep it simple and short.*"

9. Avoid "I-trouble," or talking too much about you. A conversation of indefinite length about your accomplishments or problems could be perceived as rude and selfish.

10. Finally, be "other-centered"—and learn to be an effective listener. You cannot learn anything new when you are talking.

Summary

Language is our most important tool of communication. It provides us with a means of labeling, or identifying by name, objects, acts, or persons. It is the basis of interaction, the sharing of ideas and emotions, and finally, the means by which we communicate information among ourselves and through the ages from one culture and generation to the next.

There are two major theories of language development: innateness theory and imitative theory. Innateness refers to the inborn ability to speak a language. The imitative theory holds that language is a learned behavior. While these are the two extreme viewpoints, many "middleground" theorists like Noam Chomsky draw upon both. Language development itself may be divided into three stages: infancy, toddlerhood, and early childhood.

Meaning is the essential part of any message. Understanding between individuals depends upon similarity of meaning. Semantics is the study of the relationship between our words and their meanings. Abstraction is the ability to give symbolic meaning to those things that cannot be sensed—concepts, ideals, and so forth. Ambiguity and vagueness arise because one word or symbol can have several meanings, and meaning itself is relative.

Words are also denotative and connotative. They may have concrete and factual meanings, or they may represent something beyond the objective reference.

Meaning is also influenced by style. All individuals have their own characteristic way of communicating. Style is influenced by our personalities, our purposes, and our communication settings. In short, these variables and the laws of self-reflexiveness, non-identity, and non-allness (and their use) may drastically affect communication outcomes.

The variables of language also affect our attitudes and behavior. We sometimes assume relationships between linguistic styles and personal or cultural traits. This process is known as linguistic stereotyping and usually has a negative effect upon communication. Linguistic stereotyping plays a large part in racism and causes individuals to react to words and symbols as if they were reality itself. In order to overcome linguistic stereotypes, we must be aware of their existence and concerned with their effects. In addition, each of us should strive to make language more effective. Speaking as clearly as possible, using words that can be understood by others, relating to our listeners, and using language that is appropriate to ourselves and others are only a few of the ways in which we may begin to be more concerned and effective communicators.

Exercises

GROUP EXPERIENCES
Meanings Are in People

DESCRIPTION The fact that a single word is used when referring to many different things (the example *heavy* was used earlier) points to the fact that people attach meaning to symbols; symbols have no meaning in and of themselves. This activity will focus on the multiple meanings we attach to words.

PROCEDURE Divide into groups of four to six. Each group should list as many different meanings as possible for the words given below. In listing the meanings, a phrase should be used to make clear the specific meaning of the word. Do as many as you can in five minutes. When the time is up, each group should read its list of meanings for each word. If a particular meaning is challenged, a standard dictionary or dictionary of slang should solve the argument.

Word List

crack	box	black
spirit	high	hot
lid	book	fly
jam	cool	ecstacy

DISCUSSION   What types of communication problems do multiple word meanings create? Do word meanings change with each generation? How can you use these and similar words in such a way as to make their meaning more explicit?

Do Your Symbols Convey Your Sense?

DESCRIPTION   Alfred Korzybski offered us three basic laws, the first of which is the law of non-identity. This law says that a word is not the thing it represents. We often forget how inadequate language is in describing our emotional feelings, for example. This activity will provide you with the opportunity to explore the limitations of language.

PROCEDURE   Divide into groups of four to six. Each group should take the following common phrases and attempt to state them in more precise or explicit language. In other words, you will need to describe what "love" is, for instance. After each group has completed the four phrases, a spokesperson should read the phrases aloud to the rest of the class.

Example

I *really like him.*

I wish he would *disappear.*

I *love you.*

My head *aches.*

I *have butterflies* in my stomach.

New Phrase

have a very positive feeling toward him.

DISCUSSION   Do the new phrases sound funny? Are they more explicit than the common phrases? What does the law of non-identity mean to you?

Who's Talking?

DESCRIPTION   How does language affect our behavior? When compared with various languages, English has a distinctive feature. We use the word *I* as a general referent for all the "roles" we play. What "I" do in one situation may not be the same action "I" would take in another situation. Eskimos avoid the direct identification of the term *I* with "self" by using phrases such as "this woman believes" or "this man feels." Eastern philosophy suggests that using phrases such as "I am" or "you are" can be very misleading, for they infer that "you" are the thing, and, moreover, that "you" do not change your basic personality. This activity will provide you with an opportunity to see how often you make use of pronouns such as *I* or *you*.

PROCEDURE   Divide the class into dyads (groups of two) and ask them to converse for 10 minutes. At no point during the interaction should they use the following words: I, you, he, she, they, we

Instead, you should replace these words either with formal statements or with an alternative referent. For example:

Normal: I think that . . . (*I* is unacceptable in this activity.)

Formal: It appears that institutions of education are not receiving the necessary financial support.

Alternate: This woman thinks that institutions of education are not receiving the necessary financial support.

In asking a question of your partner, you will also have to take special care with the wording. For example:

Normal: What do you think? (The use of the pronoun *you* is unacceptable in this activity.)

Formal: What are some alternative ways of viewing this situation?

Alternate: What does Karinda think? (In this case you would use the name of your partner to replace the personal pronoun *you*.)

DISCUSSION   Did you experience any difficulties during the conversation? Did the "meaning" of the conversation change with the use of your new referents? Did you find the conversation to be more depersonalized when you avoided using pronouns? Was it difficult for you to avoid using the word "I"?

PERSONAL EXPERIENCES

1. Sit alone in a quiet room. Very slowly begin saying your name over and over. Do this for 10 minutes and see if your name takes on a different meaning. Then consider whether or not you consider your "name" to be "you." Do you believe that a word in any language is not the thing but rather a symbol for it? Is your name simply a symbol for you?

2. Read the poem "The Jabberwocky" from *Through the Looking-Glass*. Then write your interpretation of this poem. Was Lewis Carroll making a comment on language in general? What do the words mean? Where did you find the meanings of the words (dictionary, context of the poem)?

Discussion Questions

1. What are the two main schools of thought on language acquisition in children?

2. Discuss the three stages of language acquisition. How does knowledge of the language development process contribute to an understanding of effective communication?

3. With the cultural diversity of our society broadening every day, what are the advantages and disadvantages of maintaining cultural speech patterns? Is there merit to stressing one "standard" of speech in a society composed of so many cultures?

References

Bohannon, J. N., III, MacWhinney, B., & Snow, C. (1990). No negative evidence revisited: Beyond learnability or who has to prove what to whom. *Developmental Psychology, 26*(2), 221–226.

Bradac, J. J., & Mulac, A. (1984). A molecular view of powerful and powerless speech styles: Attributional consequences of specific language features and communicator intentions. *Communication Monographs, 51,* 307–319.

Haleta, L. L. (1996). Student perceptions of teachers' use of language: The effects of powerful and powerless language on impression formation and uncertainty. *Communication Education, 45*(1), 16–28.

Maass, A., Salvi, D., Arcuri, L., & Semin, G. (1989). Language use in intergroup contexts: The linguistic intergroup bias. *Journal of Personality and Social Psychology, 57*(6), 981–993.

Mulac, A., Wiemann, J. M., Widenmann, S. J., & Gibson, T. W. (1988). Male/female language differences and effects in same-sex and mixed-sex dyads: The gender-linked language effect. *Communication Monographs, 55*(4), 315–335

Prizant, B. M., & Wetherby, A. M. (1990). Toward an integrated view of early language and communication development and socioemotional development. *Topics in Language Disorders, 10*(4), 6–14.

Smith, G. W. (1998). The political impact of name sounds. *Communication Monographs, 65*(2), 154–172.

Sparks, J. R., Areni, C. S., & Cox, K. C. (1998). An investigation of the effects of language style and communication modality on persuasion. *Communication Monographs, 65*(2), 108–125.

Wallach, G. (1990). Magic buries Celtics: Looking for a broader interpretation of language learning and literacy. *Topics in Language Disorders, 10*(2), 69.

3

Nonverbal Communication

key concepts and terms

Identification function
Relationship function
Emotion function
Delivery function
Repeating
Substituting
Complementing
Regulating
Turn-yielding cues
Turn-requesting cues
Turn-maintaining cues

Turn-denying cues
Accenting
Deception cues
Leakage
Kinesics
Emblems
Illustrators
Regulators
Affect displays
Body manipulators
Proxemics

Intimate distance
Personal distance
Social distance
Public distance
Territoriality
Paralanguage
Pitch
Resonance
Tempo
Voice quality

From:	"Katie"
To:	"Alphonso" <marcelax@futurenet.ab.net>
Sent:	Friday, November 15th 11:30PM
Subject:	I'm not a criminal!

OK. I've had it. I just lost my job at the pizza parlor tonight! Can you believe it? I always came in on time and got along great with the customers. And you know how incredibly responsible I am. (Worked for you three summers in a row and we always got along famously!) But since I got my eyebrow pierced last summer, everyone older than 21 treats me and my friends like criminals. My boss actually accused me of stealing money tonight. (It wasn't me! If he had just opened his eyes, he would have seen that it was his precious son!) And every time I go to the mall, the sales people watch me like a hawk. I'm the last person in the world who would steal anything from anybody!

Oh, well. Got to go. Parents just got home. They really ought to love this one. Just glad Dad understands. (Remember the story I told you about how he got his tattoo? I still laugh every time he tells it.) Mom's still not very happy with the look, so I'm bracing myself for an "I told you so." More later. . . .Katie

Since humans began walking on the earth, we have adorned ourselves with jewelry and clothing for protection, beauty, and identification. Additionally, we have manipulated our bodies to attract and impress, and mutilated them with tattoos and body piercings to express affiliation or individuality. No matter how hard we try to communicate a clear message about who we are or want to be, not everyone will understand or necessarily approve.

We agree with Katie! Wearing an eyebrow ring doesn't make you a criminal, just like wearing eyeglasses doesn't make you a "geek"! (We know! Both of your authors wear glasses and we're certainly not geeks!) However, to increase the chances that others will perceive us as we hope to be perceived, we have to take into account both the nature and nuances of nonverbal communication.

Although this chapter does not address tattoos, body piercing, or eyeglasses per se, it does address several related areas of interest—for example, the messages that we send to others through our facial expressions, eye behavior, body movements, gestures, clothing, and personal appearance. In addition, the chapter discusses the importance of touch, space, paralanguage, smell and taste, and environmental factors to communication. Because we acquire nonverbal behavior patterns early in life, we seldom have reason to think about them consciously. However, a great deal of information is communicated and can be learned from nonverbal expressions—both your own as well as those of people around you.

Before we continue, it is important to emphasize one point. No element of nonverbal behavior—be it a wink, a slouch, a tone of voice, or a gesture—can be interpreted in isolation. Verbal and nonverbal behavior are complementary; neither is really complete without the other. In addition, if we are to fully understand the nature of the nonverbal communication process, we must also consider the context, or the overall situation in which nonverbal behavior occurs, and its relationship to an individual's entire verbal and nonverbal behavior patterns.

Functions of Nonverbal Communication

Nonverbal communication plays a vital role in every communication event. From the clothes we wear during an important interview to the music we select for a romantic candlelight dinner, nonverbal cues convey messages that are frequently more compelling and eloquent than any words we could use. Although we are all aware to some degree of the impact of nonverbal communication, you may not be aware of the extent to which nonverbal messages function in our everyday lives. Specifically, there are four universal functions of nonverbal communication, no matter what culture from which we hail. They are the identification, relationship, emotion, and delivery functions.

Based on the work of world-renowned researcher Michael Argyle, Martin Remland (2000) offered the following distinctions among these four functions. The *identification function* is associated with the ability to distinguish humans from animals, males from females, and individual differences among people. Included in the list of nonverbal cues associated with this function are height, weight, skin color, body shape, facial features, hair color, voice quality, the use of clothing, cosmetics and perfume, and so on. For example, your authors have a friend who uses a very expensive, exotic perfume on a daily basis. The scent is intoxicating, but she never overuses it. You do know that she has entered a room seconds before you turn to greet her. Only Susan exudes the scent of exotic oriental flowers bathed in morning dew. Hers is a one-of-a-kind scent that results when her unique body chemistry intermingles with the aroma of the perfume.

The ability to identify our species, families, enemies, friends, and mates is necessary for human survival. So is the formation of relationships that allow us to survive and reproduce. According to Remland (2000), the *relationship function* of nonverbal communication is associated with two key variables: intimacy and control. "Intimacy involves questions of attachment and closeness; it includes courtship as well as companionship. Control is a matter of influence and deference; it becomes paramount under conditions of scarcity when individuals must compete for valued resources" (p. 42). To illustrate, consider the nonverbal behaviors that probably would be displayed if a leggy, "drop-dead-gorgeous" female (that nobody knew) walked in the door of a fraternity house and inquired about the next "Little Sister Rush." Upon first sight, the fraternity brothers would respond to her in one way (a "chest thrust" or broad swaggering walk), the "Little Sisters" in another (an uncompromising stare), depending on the level of attraction experienced by the former, and level of perceived threat sensed by the latter. All three of these nonverbal cues reflect the signal systems of animals and humans, which are associated with the creation and maintenance of relationships. The "chest thrust" is a common male courting behavior across a number of species, and "the stare" a universal threat display.

According to Remland (2000), the *emotion function* of nonverbal communication ". . . is a fundamental stimulus-response process that motivates an organism to engage in behavior that is essential for the survival of a species" (p. 54). Identified by Paul Ekman and Wallace Friedman in 1975, the primary emotions that are evoked, expressed, and experienced by humans are anger, contempt, disgust, fear, happiness, sadness, and surprise. Shame, guilt, and interest are also considered to be "candidates" for primary emotions (Remland, p. 59). Although these emotions are considered universal in terms of their experience by humans, *when* and *how* we express and evoke them are governed by cultural rules and norms. For instance, the expression of anger or contempt in public varies depending on the part of the world in which you live. Using nonverbal cues to express anger is considered more "taboo" in Asian cultures than doing so in Western cultures. However, there are also differences in the amount and appropriateness of their use for people in England versus France, the United States versus Canada, and other countries whose national borders meet.

Last, but not least, is the delivery function. For Remland (2000), the *delivery function* is associated with how humans use nonverbal cues for self-expression and the exchange of information about the outside world. The use of the human body to send messages through music, art, and dance are examples of self-expression. The use of (verbal and) nonverbal messages to convey information about our needs, wants, desires, as well as the world around us, are also part of the delivery function. Consider the plight of many African nations regarding the disproportionate spread of AIDS (ammuno-immune deficiency syndrome) in their countries, and we are talking about a delivery problem of the highest caliber. For many African villagers, the only means of communicating with the outside world is to travel on foot to the nearest village. So even if the people in one village learn ways to prevent the deadly virus, people in a village less than three miles away may learn nothing about the subject until virtually years later.

The four functions of nonverbal communication discussed here constitute a basic framework for *why* we communicate nonverbally. *How* nonverbal communication works involves a different but related set of functions. Specifically, nonverbal communication serves to repeat, substitute, complement, regulate, or accent our verbal messages. In addition, nonverbal cues often serve as a means for deception.

Repeating

When we communicate with one another, we use words and their nonverbal equivalents at the same time. For example, verbal statements of agreement or disagreement ("Right, right," "No way," "Are you kidding?") are often accompanied by a nod or shake of the head to indicate positive or negative feelings. We call these nonverbal gestures *repeating* messages because they convey the same meaning as the verbal message. Of course, either the words or the nods by themselves would be enough—but repeating messages are done almost without thinking. They are a very basic part of language behavior, occurring naturally, without conscious thought or intent.

Substituting

When hearing or speaking is impossible, nonverbal communication often replaces verbal messages. In such instances nonverbal messages are called *substitutes,* because they take the place of words. Thus, someone directing you into a tight parking space might substitute gestures for words when the car's noisy engine prohibits speaking. Another kind of substitution is made when someone with whom you've had an argument attacks you with "looks that could kill."

For nonverbal communication to act as a substitute, it must be recognized and, more importantly, interpreted in the same way by most of the people in a specific group, subculture, or culture. For example, people in the United States interpret the "thumbs down" sign to mean "no." Such well-known substitutes are so universal that they have been recorded in dictionaries of American gestures. Misunderstandings may occur, however, when we try to use our culture's nonverbal substitutes in another culture. Thus, Americans who say "I" by pointing to their chests would not be understood in Japan, where "I" is symbolized by pointing to one's nose.

Complementing

We also use nonverbal language to complement, complete, or accent explanations of how to do something or in descriptions of specific sizes or shapes. To understand how important these *complementing* actions can be, just try the following without using nonverbal behavior: Teach a new dance step, explain how to tie a slip knot, or describe the shape of an hourglass.

Complementing behaviors are also used to emphasize emotional feelings or attitudes. The same complementing gesture can accompany quite different emotions. Consider the following example.

> The gold, silver, and bronze medal winners skated out onto the ice and up to the podium to receive their medals. When the bronze medalist was announced, the silver and gold medalists applauded enthusiastically. When the gold medalist was finally announced, the silver medalist applauded, but as she did, a tear ran silently down her cheek.

In this example, the complementing gesture of applause was used in two instances, first to express a positive response (happiness) and then to accompany a negative one (disappointment).

Regulating

One of the most common purposes of nonverbal communication is ***regulating.*** Let's say that you and a friend are discussing a movie you saw the other night. Without regulating messages, you might sound something like this:

> "Hey, did you catch the movie at the Plaza the other night? O.K., I'm finished talking for the moment. You can speak."
> "Thank you. I wanted to answer your question. Yeah. Great. Especially that scene in the woods. . . ."
> "Can I talk?"
> "You want to talk again? Sure."
> "Thanks. I just wanted to say that I let out the biggest scream during that part!"

Fortunately, typical conversations don't require this kind of verbal permission to speak or respond. Instead, nonverbal cues keep the conversation flowing through our use of a conversational turn-taking system, or the rules of interaction that we learned early in life. This system is comprised of four major sets of nonverbal cues: (1) turn-yielding, (2) turn-requesting, (3) turn-maintaining, and (4) turn-denying cues.

Turn-yielding cues tell our listeners that we no longer wish to speak for the moment and want them to take a conversational turn. Turn-yielding cues include ending a turn with a question (such as, "What do you think?"), slowing our speech rate, and increasing our eye contact with the listener. On the other hand, we give *turn-requesting cues* when we want to take a conversational turn. For example, we may lean forward, take an audible breath, nod our head more rapidly, fill our pauses more often (for instance, "umm-hmm," "yeah"), or raise an index finger, as if to say, "I would like to take a turn."

Conversations also are regulated by turn-maintaining and turn-denying cues. We use *turn-maintaining cues* when we are speaking and do not wish to yield the floor to the listener. Cues that help us maintain the floor include increased speech rate, a raised hand, a touch on the listener's arm that says, "I'm not quite through talking yet," and averting our gaze away from the listener's eyes. ***Turn-denying cues*** are useful when we are listening, the speaker wants us to take a turn, and we do not wish to speak at that time. If we want to deny (avoid) a turn, we generally will remain silent, exhibit a more relaxed posture, lean slightly backward, and gaze directly into the speaker's eyes, as if to say, "Please continue." Or we may actually say, "Please go on. I would like to hear more."

Accenting

Another function of nonverbal communication is ***accenting,*** the use of gestures, such as nods, blinks, squints, and shrugs, to help emphasize or punctuate spoken words:

> Adrienne's cocker spaniel just won first prize in the dog show. As she leads him out of the ring, friends and family congratulate both Adrienne and the dog with warm words, but also with pats on the back.

Accenting can also be achieved by changing the pitch or stress on a word or group of words. In fact, our entire meaning often depends on which words are accented:

Did *you* go to the store today?

Did you go to the *store* today?

Did you go to the store *today?*

Deceiving/Revealing

"I'll see you and raise you five bucks," Kelly said with his usual poker face.

Sometimes we purposely deceive others or supply them with false information. You may not like a friend's new haircut, for example, but still say, "Your hair looks great!" to avoid hurting his feelings. At the same time that you are saying this and staring convincingly into your friend's eyes, you may be nervously pulling at your coat buttons. If your friend is sensitive to nonverbal behavior, he may pick up this contradictory message.

Deception cues (such as an overly exaggerated smile or a frown that is too severe) suggest possible falsehood but do not tell what information is being withheld or falsified. *Leakage,* on the other hand, implies "spilling the beans" about the withheld information. For example, biting a fingernail can leak nervousness, or a clenched fist can leak the desire to fight.

How good are humans at detecting deception? In a comprehensive review of the deception literature, researchers Thomas Feeley and Melissa Young (1998) concluded, "Over twenty-five years of research in behavioral lie detection has yielded one consistent finding: humans are not very skilled at detecting when deception is present" (p. 109). Although we are fairly good at identifying when people are telling the truth (70–80 percent of the time we are correct), we are much less accurate when detecting lies (35–40 percent of the time).

We mention this important distinction because deception researchers have identified (what is believed to be) eight nonverbal cues associated with deception. These are "greater pupil dilation, more blinking, decreased response length, more speech errors and hesitations, greater voice pitch, more negative statements, and more irrelevant information" (Feeley & Young, 1998, p. 111). The problem is, in much of the deception research to date, people are asked to judge lies that "bear little resemblance to the lies of everyday life" (p. 112). (Common examples of experimentally manipulated lies include participants cheating on anagram-solving tasks, mock thefts, etc.) Thus, we encourage you to proceed with caution when you believe you have detected a lie. According to Feeley and Young, your ability to do so accurately is affected by what you believe to be cues of deception, how close or familiar you are with the person whom you are observing, and the amount of formal training or life experience you have regarding deception detection.

Types of Nonverbal Communication

Many people consider body language to be the only form of nonverbal communication. However, nonverbal communication includes much more than just body language. Each day we nonverbally signal our attitudes, moods, and values to others. If you have ever dressed special for a certain date, consoled a friend with a hug, been late to a class, frowned as you looked over a test, you were communicating to others nonverbally. But we are often unaware of our nonverbal behaviors. In our attempt to increase sensitivity to different types of our nonverbal behavior, we will examine facial expressions, eye behavior, kinesics and body movement, personal appearance and clothing, touching, proxemics, paralanguage, smell and taste, and environmental factors.

Facial Expressions

Perhaps the most obvious vehicle for nonverbal communication is the face. It is a constant source of information to those around us. For example, a neuromuscular therapist uses nonverbal cues from a client's face to gauge the existence and subsequent release of "trigger points," or muscular tissue in which a great deal of tension has built up. Likewise, attorneys specializing in criminal law pay close attention to the face and eyes of future clients for clues to the latter's possible guilt or innocence.

How does the face send such nonverbal cues? When something makes you happy or sad or produces any other emotion, your nerves immediately send a message to the face, which causes the muscles to contract or relax. The feedback you get from these muscle movements is one of the cues that tells you what emotional feeling you are having. This process is a form of internal self-feedback in intrapersonal communication, which will be discussed in the next chapter.

Think of all the things your face can say about you without your saying a word. Things such as wrinkles, baldness, and coloring comment not only on your age but also on the kind of life you lead. For example, we suspect that people with dark tans spend a considerable amount of time outdoors. The length and style of your hair and the amount of makeup you wear suggest your economic status, interest in fashion, and sometimes even your politics. All of these things, plus the facial expressions that reveal emotion, can speak for you before you ever open your mouth.

Charles Darwin first argued that many of our facial expressions evolved from lower animals, and scientists are still debating this issue. On one side of the debate, some research has yielded support for Darwin's theory about universal behaviors. The research by Ekman and Friesen on emotion (mentioned earlier) provides a good example. However, contradictory results have emerged in several cross-cultural studies, and support an alternative theory of facial expressions and their origins: It is the context of the event that supplies the meanings for facial expressions, and one's culture is responsible for the ways in which its members encode and decode facial expressions.

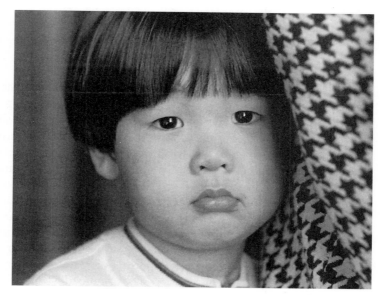

Faces tell us a lot about the emotions of others.

Although the debate concerning the origin of facial expression continues, some agreement exists regarding the universal ability of humans to encode and decode emotions via facial expressions. However, this "agreement" is qualified by the argument that cultures do differ in their uses of facial expressions and, hence, have a profound effect on how emotions are encoded and decoded.

It also is important to note that cultural rules and societal pressures often inhibit spontaneous facial expressions. At early ages children learn which expressions are acceptable and which are unacceptable by hearing things like, "If you keep frowning, your face will grow like that" or "A shot is nothing to be afraid of; you've got to act like a big boy now." We also learn how to adapt our facial expressions to meet the expectations of others. How many times have you smiled politely when receiving an unwanted gift, held back tears after a bitter disappointment, or avoided laughing when watching someone trip over a curb? We all adjust many of our natural facial expressions to those considered to be more appropriate.

Eye Behavior

For centuries poets and painters have paid tribute to our expressive eyes. Modern-day researchers, too, have been intrigued by the eyes and the many nonverbal messages they convey. Specifically, research has shown that eye behavior functions to:

1. provide information,

2. regulate interactions,

3. exercise social control,

4. express intimacy, and

5. facilitate goal achievement. (Kleinke, 1986).

Certain eye behaviors are associated with definite moods, reactions, and attitudes. In this way they provide us with information about people with whom we interact. For example, consider the common, negative traits that we associate with "small, beady eyes." For people who have the misfortune of being born with such eyes, they are often associated with cheating, lying, and general negativity. We also have certain beliefs and feelings about eye pupil size. Research indicates that our pupils dilate (grow larger) when we are presented with a pleasant stimulus (such as a picture of someone we love) and constrict when we are subjected to a negative stimulus (such as a grating noise or an unfamiliar touch) (Chaney, Givens, Aoki, & Gombiner, 1989). Additionally, people with large pupils are perceived to be happier and attractive, while those with small pupils are perceived to be angry or unattractive (Hess, 1965). However, it is important to realize that pupil variations occur in the context of other facial features. Thus, the child with eyes that have naturally large pupils and who seems to be innocent and sincere can be "caught" in deception if we attend to other nonverbal cues, such as facial expression.

Eye contact is another significant behavior that provides us with information. For example, public speakers who never look up from their notes while speaking send a message that they are nervous or highly formal. Speakers who do look at their audience during a speech are perceived to be more friendly, sincere, and relaxed. Likewise, listeners who do not look at a speaker send a message that they are distracted, are bored, or have little regard for the speaker. Perhaps this is why angry teachers or parents command, "Look at me when I'm talking to you." Although you may not be angered personally when others avoid eye contact while you are speaking, this eye behavior on a receiver's part may indicate a lack of interest in what you are saying.

A second function of eye behavior is to serve to regulate interactions. To substantiate this claim, one need look no further than the public speaking setting. When public speakers catch the eyes of listeners, they significantly increase the chances of catching the audience's attention as well. Effective public speakers use periodic "eye checks" to ensure that their listeners are still there and being attentive. Moving toward the audience (away from the lectern) and using more direct eye contact is an excellent strategy to use if you ever think you are "losing" an audience. In interpersonal communication, the principle is the same. Eye contact allows you not only to gain the attention of others, but also to direct the conversational turn-taking system overall.

Although we have pointed out certain commonalities in human eye behavior thus far, individual differences also exist when we converse with others. Depending on the speaker, gaze directed at other people can range in duration from 10 percent to more than 70 percent of the time. Such differences are often associated with social control, the third function of eye behavior. For example, research has shown that eye behavior is associated with patterns of dominance and submissiveness. Specifically, dominant and poised communicators tend to look more at others during conversations than do submissive, uneasy individuals, especially when they assume the speaking role.

Eye behavior also allows us to express intimacy, or our inner feelings to others, especially our interpersonal attitudes and the level of intimacy we are experiencing. Think for a moment about the last time you gazed into the eyes of someone you love. If he or she responded in kind, you probably felt the "connection" associated with mutual gaze. If the person diverted his or her gaze to somewhere else in the room or to the floor, you probably felt that something was amiss. This communicative/monitoring function of eye behavior allows us not only to collect information but also to regulate the level of interpersonal intimacy that we are experiencing. In short, the eyes, indeed, may be viewed as "the window of the soul." Through them we can communicate additional—and often more "meaningful"—information not in the verbal exchange.

The fifth function of eye behavior is facilitation of goals. This function is associated with our use of eye behavior to accomplish some action; for example, our use of gaze to encourage or discourage behavior on the part of others. We are all familiar with the ability of respected teachers to stop someone from talking with a simple, straightforward glare. Conversely, we also are able to encourage others when we offer a warm glance and an encouraging smile.

Kinesics and Body Movement

The human body is so incredibly versatile that it can send thousands of nonverbal messages. In fact, it is hard to know just how to classify all of these nonverbal communications. Ray Birdwhistell, a pioneer in the field of nonverbal communication, coined the word *kinesics* to describe the study of body movement. Early researchers categorized body expressions according to the part of the body involved—facial expression, trunk movements, hand gestures, and so forth.

Birdwhistell viewed body expressions as a language that, like French or Russian, could be studied, learned, and understood. Other specialists such as Ekman and Friesen (1969) have focused on the general classification of nonverbal communication, and have identified five classes of specific body expressions: emblems, illustrators, regulators, affect displays, and body manipulators.

EMBLEMS.   *Emblems* are commonly recognized signs that communicate a message that generally is unrelated to an ongoing conversation. They usually take the form of gestures. For example, if you and a friend suddenly realized that your animated conversation was disturbing the person at the next table in the library, you might hold an index finger to your lips. This indication to talk more quietly serves to reduce the volume of your conversation without interrupting its flow. We learn such emblems early in life through imitation and continue to use them throughout our lives (see Figure 3.1).

FIGURE 3.1 Can you identify these emblems?

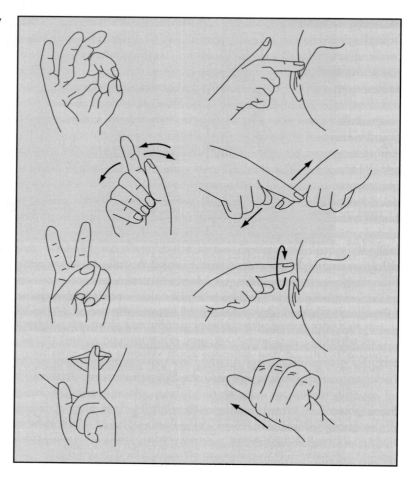

Beware of the man whose belly does not move when he laughs.

CHINESE PROVERB

ILLUSTRATORS. These body expressions illustrate the verbal language they accompany. *Illustrators* may accent or add emphasis to a phrase; show the direction of thought; point to an object or place; depict spatial relationships, rhythms, or bodily actions; or demonstrate shape. You are using an illustrator when you point to someone across the room while shouting his or her name, or when you use your hands to estimate the length of the fish that you almost caught.

REGULATORS. *Regulators* such as gazes, nods, and raised eyebrows assist in the exchange of listening and speaking roles among participants in a communication

Our bodies convey our emotional states.

setting. They provide smooth transitions in conversations as well as control verbal communication.

AFFECT DISPLAYS.   Body changes that convey our internal emotional states are *affect displays.* These emotional displays can involve facial expressions, such as angry stares or wide-eyed fear, or body movements, such as trembling hands or knocking knees. Affect displays are not always strictly tied to what we are saying at the time. For example, an airline ticket agent may be surprised by the deep sadness that lines the face of a man who has just asked for a ticket for the next plane to Pittsburgh, unaware that the passenger is going home to attend the funeral of a loved one. Because facial affect displays are easily simulated, they often can be used in deception. For example, we have all heard the expression, she was "smiling on the outside but crying on the inside."

BODY MANIPULATORS.   *Body manipulators* are movements that were originally associated with body functioning (such as rubbing the eyes when tired), that have come to be used unconsciously and independently of bodily needs. For example, twirling your hair during a test, rubbing your chin while you are thinking, and rocking yourself in the fetal position when you are upset are examples of body manipulators as we are defining them here. Other body manipulators involve touching an object or another person. Drawing "doodles" on a pad with a pencil while you are talking on the phone is an example of an object-focused body manipulator. Patting someone's hand while you are communicating with them is an example of an other-focused body manipulator.

We use our bodies to transmit messages about degrees of association and agreement.

All body movements that involve contact with some body part are not necessarily classed as body manipulators, however. Some of these movements may be emblems or illustrators, depending on their nature and purpose. For instance, placing a forefinger against your temple may act as an emblem for "thought." Likewise, tapping the top of your wrist may serve as an illustrator if you are asking someone for the correct time.

BODY MOVEMENT AND POSTURE.   Body movements fall into one of several categories. For instance, how you walk is often a strong indicator of how you feel. When you have a problem, you may walk very slowly with your head down and your hands clasped behind your back. You may even pause to trace your toe in the sand. On the other hand, when you feel especially proud and happy, you may walk with your chin raised, your arms swinging freely, and your legs somewhat stiff—with a bounce in your step.

We all know how to "read" such obvious nonverbal cues, but conscious and sustained effort can help you pick up even more subtle expressions of the nonverbal language. For example, you sometimes use your body parts to show that you are or are not associated with the people near you. Thus, crossing your legs in the same way the person next to you crosses hers may indicate identification with that person. Or, if you are standing and arguing with three other people, you may soon find yourself assuming the body posture of the person with whom you agree—both of you standing with your hands on your hips, for instance, while your two opponents may also assume like postures.

Other movements and gestures show openness and honesty. Holding the hands open while talking indicates sincerity; hands clenched into fists reflect the opposite.

Similarly, if someone unbuttons or even takes off his or her coat in your presence, this conveys openness and friendliness toward you.

In contrast to these gestures of openness are those that indicate defensiveness. The crossed-arms-on-chest position is perhaps the best-known defensive gesture. Charles Darwin argued that this stance is universal in all societies and that it strongly influences anyone who is observing. In fact, communication often comes to a complete halt when someone assumes this position, which says, in effect, "I have now withdrawn from this conversation." Of course, this is not true every time someone crosses his or her arms. However, if it happens during a conversation, you might examine what you have just said or done that would have prompted a withdrawal.

Even the way you sit communicates information. Someone who is speaking while his or her legs dangle over the arm of a chair might be saying, "I am not feeling cooperative. In fact, I am unconcerned or hostile to your feelings or needs." Similarly, people who sit backwards on chairs or put their feet up on a desk may be signaling their feelings of superiority, saying, "I am the dominant person here."

Such reflections of dominance seem to perpetuate sex role stereotypes. Men, for example, characteristically express dominance by taking up more space in a bed than a woman; crossing their legs at the thighs (which takes up a considerable amount of room); and looking into a woman's eyes while talking to her. Women, on the other hand, often use submissive gestures when they are with men: compressing their bodies into a small space in bed; crossing their legs at the ankles or sitting with uncrossed legs held tightly together (which takes up very little space); and looking down when talking to men. We shall explore such spatial relationships later in the chapter.

Personal Appearance

Each year Americans spend millions of dollars on cosmetics, weight control, and plastic surgery to increase their physical attractiveness. To become beautiful people, we starve ourselves to lose weight, spend countless hours in front of mirrors styling our hair and applying makeup, use special conditioners to halt thinning hair, and wear clothing to accent a bulge here and minimize a bulge there. We have been told that inner beauty is what counts in relationships, but research on first impressions suggests that physical attractiveness affects interpersonal outcomes. Physical appearance influences job interviews, blind dates, consumer buying behavior, grades in school, and even courtroom decisions.

Although the face usually determines beauty, we are also judged by our body shapes, skin color, and hair. Every time televisions are turned on, advertisements are stereotyping people according to their physical attributes. Can you remember ever seeing an overweight, unkempt, scar-faced doctor recommend a leading aspirin? Advertisers usually hire neat, clean, attractive models to sell their products. Unattractive individuals are usually used only in advertisements that feature before-and-after sequences, such as when methods for increasing bust size or achieving younger-looking skin are being advertised. To look just right, we are encouraged to change our skin color and texture by applying makeup and medications, getting a golden tan, or using special skin softeners. Society also influences our views on hair. Men want to keep their hair because it is masculine to have hairy chests, beards, and mustaches. Women, however, are constantly finding ways to get rid of their hair. Using laser technology, electrolysis, waxing and shaving, women eliminate unsightly hair under arms, on legs, over lips, and on eyebrows. Certainly, the way we look is important to ourselves and others. We manipulate our physical appearance so that we will be perceived as attractive rather than unattractive.

Clothing

It is often said that clothes make a person, but it may be more true to say that clothes *are* the person. Your clothes provide visual clues to your interests, age, personality, and attitudes. Even status information is gained from the clothes' age, condition, and fashion. Some of us are interested in clothing as a means of keeping up with the latest social changes. Others use clothing as a form of decoration and self-expression. T-shirt designs, for example, are a communication channel between the wearer and the world.

By a man's fingernails, by his coat-sleeve, by his boots, by his trouser-knees, by the callosities of his forefinger and thumb, by his expression, by his shirt cuffs—by each of these things a man's calling is plainly revealed. That all united should fail to enlighten the competent inquirer in any case is almost inconceivable.
SHERLOCK HOLMES

In her book, *Letitia Baldrige's New Complete Guide to Executive Manners,* Ms. Baldrige (1993) emphasizes the importance of clothing in the business community. She suggests that clothing determines a person's job success. Thus, dress is an influential variable in the total system of nonverbal communication. It can fulfill functions ranging from protection, sexual attraction, and self-assertion to self-denial, concealment, group identification, and the display of status and role. To illustrate, have you ever thought of the impact that clothing can have on evaluations of job performance?

Numerous studies have shown that clothing indeed affects how people perceive us. One team of researchers interested particularly in "fashion in the classroom" included Tracy Morris, Joan Gorham, Stanley Cohen, and Drew Huffman (1996). Focusing on the effects of clothing worn by male and female graduate teaching assistants (GTAs), the researchers asked students to rate GTAs on five dimensions of source credibility: competence, character, sociability, composure, and extroversion. The three types of clothing that the GTAs wore were *formal* (dark business suits, dress shoes), *casual professional* (casual slacks/skirt, sports shirt/sweater, leather shoes/pumps), or *casual* dress (faded, worn blue jeans, T-shirt or flannel shirt, sport/athletic shoes).

Results of the study revealed that formal dress was associated with higher levels of competence, particularly for female students evaluating female GTAs. A close second was casual professional attire, with the lowest ratings of competence reserved for casual attire. Male GTAs wearing casual professional attire were rated higher in competence than female GTAs in similar attire. In contrast, students' ratings of GTA sociability and extroversion were most positive in the casual dress condition, followed by casual professional, then business professional. In other words, students rated GTAs in *very* casual dress as far more sociable, extroverted, and interesting presenters than GTAs dressed in the other two types of attire.

Although we must be careful generalizing these results to other situations, they do support what we have known for some time. Dress up and you will be perceived as higher in competence, status, power, poise, and success. Dress down and you will be perceived as more friendly, likable, sociable, and enthusiastic.

Touching

Do you often reach out to touch other people? Although ours is not a "high-contact" culture, touching is nonetheless the most basic form of nonverbal communication.

We all use touch at times. To emphasize a point or to interrupt another person, for instance, we may grab the speaker's elbow and interrupt with, "But you don't understand." Touching can be used as a calming gesture, too. We frequently try to comfort someone with a pat on the back and a "I know." In other situations, touching provides reassurance. Not only do we reach out to reassure ourselves of the presence of people we are fond of, but we sometimes do the same with objects—stroking the smooth leather of our gloves, for instance.

These behaviors suggest the importance of touching to human beings. In fact, physical contact with other humans is vital to healthy development. Lack of such contact in childhood may contribute to physical and psychological problems later in life. To understand the significance of this statement, consider how parents touch and teach their children about touch. A child who is reared in a high-contact family will have a high touch orientation. As a result, he or she generally will see and share touch in different ways than a child who is reared in a low-contact family. If parents teach their children through words or deeds that touch is something to be given generously, in turn, their children will see and give touch in this way. Conversely, children who are taught that touch is "dirty"—or, at best, should be minimized—will grow up to view touch as their parents did.

Proxemics

Just as we communicate with words, gestures, and facial expressions, we also can send messages by placing ourselves in certain spatial relationships with other people and objects. The study of these spatial factors is called *proxemics;* it focuses on how we react to space around us, how we use that space, and how our use of space communicates certain information. For example, the amount of space in which a person must live or work communicates a message about the status of that individual. Consider a North American family comprised of a single parent and three sons, but whose house has only two bedrooms for the children. In recognition of the eldest son's status, chances are that he will have a room to himself, while the two younger children share the second bedroom.

SPATIAL ZONES.   Edward T. Hall, a pioneer in the study of proxemics, specified four spatial zones of interpersonal communication: intimate distance, personal distance, social distance, and public distance.

Intimate distance stretches from actual contact to 18 inches. A parent and child, two intimate friends, or other close pairs would have contact in this zone. Of course, even strangers can be thrown into this zone (such as on a crowded elevator). However, such forced closeness is usually countered by silence, averted glances, and other nonverbal messages that say, "O.K., this is fine for now, but it's only going to last for a minute, because I don't really know you."

Personal distance, from 1 1/2 to 4 feet, is the zone we use for casual interactions. You would probably assume this distance when talking with a friend at a cocktail party. In contrast, *social distance,* from 4 to 12 feet, is used by people meeting for the first time or by people conducting business. *Public distance,* from 12 to over 25 feet, is most often used in formal address; for example, by a teacher lecturing students or by a politician speaking at a rally.

We also adapt our behavior when forced to interact in a different zone. For example, when even close friends are farther than 12 feet apart (public distance), they often speak in more formal phrases. On the other hand, casual acquaintances placed in an intimate distance usually whisper and use small, rather than expansive, gestures. Compare the gestures you use when sitting next to a friend with those used to shout a greeting to your neighbor across the street.

Also consider how people will talk before they enter a crowded elevator, but will stop abruptly once the doors close. The reactions that you receive are interesting if you do choose to continue a conversation after the elevator begins to move. Others who are in the elevator cannot help but overhear the conversation, but they will often turn away or lower their heads and pretend not to listen. It is even more interesting (despite the risk of some strange looks) to watch the response of others when you laugh out loud to yourself in this quiet atmosphere.

It is important to note that these spatial zones, though common for white, middle-class Americans, are by no means universal. Each culture has its own spatial needs. Thus, Arabs stand so close to each other while talking that they can easily touch and perceive body odors and heat—very different from the "noncontact" culture that characterizes the majority in the Western world.

Intimate distance.

TERRITORIALITY.   Scientists have long observed the territorial habits of animals but have only recently begun to understand that humans exhibit similar territorial needs and controls. In fact, all of us carry our own personal space around with us. This *territoriality*—the need to call space *our* space—is another facet of proxemics.

Territoriality implies a desire to possess or give up space or objects around us. For example, different body parts permit us to claim temporary possession of an object. Thus, we often use our hands to reach out and grab an object (as in straightening someone's tie or holding another person's hand). Or, we employ our whole bodies as spatial indicators. Standing with hands on hips and elbows extended, for instance, claims all of the space around our bodies and says, "Don't come any closer to me than my elbows, or else!" On the other hand, when we are kissing, we close our eyes, perhaps to break down spatial barriers. "It's okay," we imply. "Your closeness is not infringing on my territory." We also use objects to define our territory. Have you ever used books, paper, pencils, sweaters, and other objects to stake out your space at a library table? Such markers say, "This area is mine."

SEATING ARRANGEMENTS.   Did your father always sit at the head of the table in your house? The person who sits at the head of a table will usually be designated the "leader," whether or not that designation is appropriate. Have you ever avoided taking a chair at the head of a table for this very reason? The two ends of a table and the middle seats on the sides are "hot seats" in which people either do, or at least are expected to, talk more.

These examples illustrate the effects of seating arrangements on interpersonal interactions. Some spatial arrangements, such as a round table, encourage us to face each other and to communicate. Other arrangements—for example, a row of chairs

Personal distance.

in a theater or classroom—force us to face away from one another. These arrangements naturally produce less interaction.

Thus, different seating arrangements are desirable for different types of interactions. If two people are having a friendly conversation, they might prefer seats at the corner of a rectangular table. When working together on a task, they might sit side by side. During competition (playing cards, for example) they would prefer to sit across from one another, thereby making it more difficult to see each other's hand and easier to establish strong eye contact.

Similarly, spatial relationships in the classroom can influence student–teacher interactions. The three most popular ways to arrange classrooms are in rectangular, horseshoe, and modular arrangements (see Figures 3.2, 3.3, and 3.4). Most classrooms in North America are rectangular, with desks arranged in straight rows. This arrangement is best for information dissemination or straight lectures. Horseshoe and modular arrangements are frequently used with smaller classes. Courses in disciplines such as home economics, architecture, horticulture, and speech communication would be likely to use these arrangements. Both the horseshoe and modular arrangements increase student participation. The grouping of the modular design allows for maximum interaction and is especially effective for teachers who need to work with groups and individual students.

Most of us also have preferences about where we sit in classes. Have you ever been disappointed, on the first day of class, to find that you couldn't sit in the back row, in front of the teacher, or by the blackboard? A variety of factors, such as wanting to sit by the best-looking student, or wanting to be able to see the board, determine seating preferences. Investigations of seating arrangement and interactions in classrooms indicate that students who sit in front rows may actually receive higher grades than those who sit farther back (Holliman & Anderson, 1986). Additionally,

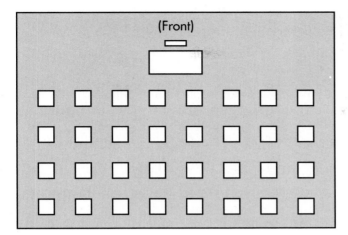

FIGURE 3.2 Rectangular Seating Arrangement

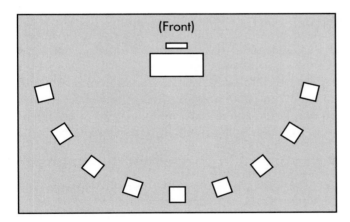

FIGURE 3.3 Horseshoe Seating Arrangement

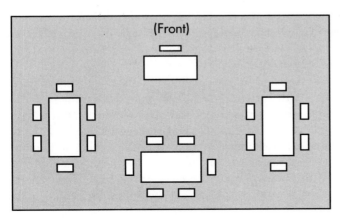

FIGURE 3.4 Modular Seating Arrangement

proximity or closeness to the teacher is related to student enjoyment, motivation, interest, and feelings of inclusion (Millard & Stimpson, 1980).

Paralanguage

The next time you turn on the TV, close your eyes and listen to the actors' voices. What emotions are they portraying? Are the speakers male or female, British or American? How old are they? Try the same experiment while listening to a radio talk show. Is the caller nervous, tired, angry? *Paralanguage,* or variations in the voice, allows us to answer these questions. Paralanguage is "a language alongside of language" and includes vocal characteristics such as pitch, range, resonance, tempo, and quality, and various vocal sounds such as grunts, groans, and clearing of the throat.

Although paralanguage is closely tied to verbal expression, it is quite unlike the signs and symbols we know as language. Consider voice *pitch.* Some people use a wide variety of changes in their pitch while others make few pitch changes or even talk in a monotone. For instance, we generally drop our voices (pitch) at the end of a statement and raise our pitch level at the end of a question. Ask yourself the question, "May I have some water?" and notice how your voice rises on the word "water." Pitch changes like these are part of your paralanguage.

Other paralanguage cues relate to *resonance,* the variations from a thin and quiet voice to a loud and booming voice. For example, shyness or embarrassment can affect the voice. Have you ever begun an introduction to a large group of people only to find that nervousness has made your voice fade to a mere whisper?

I understand the fury in your words but not the words.

WILLIAM SHAKESPEARE

Some people speak so quickly that it is hard to pick up all their words; others speak very slowly. This paralanguage quality is called *tempo.* Good public speakers know that the ability to pause at the proper time and to draw out words for emphasis creates color and interest in what is being said. The nervous orator's short, choppy phrases and monotonous style are a real giveaway to the audience that the speaker is ill at ease and probably inexperienced.

Paralanguage cues are also revealed by the quality of a speaker's voice. *Voice quality* is most often associated with variations of harshness and breathiness in the voice. Quality also involves smoothness of delivery and other similar factors.

Although paralanguage may seem to focus only on subtle nuances, paralinguistic expressions need not be subtle. For example, sounds such as sneezing, coughing, or crying all serve well-recognized purposes. Similarly, if you walk into a room in which two of your friends are deeply involved in a conversation, rather than standing there until one of them notices you, you might clear your throat. This simple noise communicates your presence and says, "Hey, look at me. I'm here."

Paralanguage conveys information about age, sex, emotional states, personality variables, and other common attributes. Thus, it should not surprise you to learn that words in themselves account for a relatively low percentage of the communication of feelings. Consider a typical conversation. The speakers start out quite friendly but slowly build to a heated argument. As anger increases, voices become louder (intensity), the range of voices increases (pitch), and the speed of the exchange quickens (tempo). Even if you couldn't understand the speakers' angry words, their paralanguage would immediately tell you that the two people were quarreling.

Smell and Taste

Every day we use our senses of smell and taste to receive information about the world around us. However, we also use the mediums of smell and taste to send out such information about ourselves. Think, for example, about the last time you were getting ready to go out with a very special person. After getting out of the bathtub, where you showered with deodorant soap and washed your hair with scented shampoo, you probably put on deodorant or antiperspirant and adorned yourself with after-shave lotion or perfume. You then proceeded to brush your teeth with a fresh-tasting toothpaste and, perhaps, gargled with a "germ-killing" mouthwash. Finally, you put on fresh-smelling clothes and odor-free shoes, the former having been washed in a freshly scented detergent and rinsed in a fabric softener, and the latter "freshened" with "odor-eating" talcum powder or foot pads.

Environmental factors influence our behavior.

A North American's perceptions of smells and tastes differ, however, from the perceptions of members of other cultures. For example, many North Americans have been conditioned to be ashamed of natural body odors. Have you ever kept your distance from someone for fear that the garlic on your breath would be offensive? Such a feeling of self-consciousness concerning a potential message such as this is only one example of how the U.S. culture differs from other cultures. Members of several cultures would feel quite insulted if you deprived them of your breath!

The sense of smell, however, is not the only "silent" sense that sends and receives messages. Our sense of taste allows us to receive messages of pleasure as well as warning and has the ability both to influence and to reflect our physical needs as well as preferences and attitudes. Do some smells and tastes make you happy, depressed, or nostalgic? If you do not believe in the communicative power of these two senses, consider what Billy Crystal did on the set of one of his movies. The scene was an Italian kitchen and the set had been dressed to resemble a full kitchen. But the mood was not right for some reason. So Crystal had his crew spend the night sautéing onions, garlic, and vegetables on the set. The next day, as actors and crew walked in, many began to cry, and explained that the set now reminded them of their mother's or grandmother's kitchens.

Environmental Factors

ARCHITECTURE AND OBJECTS.   Have you ever walked into a room and immediately felt at home, calm and relaxed? Or avoided a building that made you feel nervous and insecure? Nonverbal messages from architectural structures and other objects around us indeed can influence our behavior. For this reason dentists have comfortable chairs and pleasant decors in their waiting rooms—all to make us worry a little less. Nightclub, bar, and restaurant owners have also learned that interiors can greatly influence their customers. They realize that dim lighting, a quiet atmosphere, and soft music lead to greater intimacy, which encourages their patrons to stay longer.

These informal observations are supported by scientific studies. One classic experiment, for example, used three rooms: an "ugly" room, designed like a janitor's storeroom; a "beautiful" room, with carpeting, draperies, and other decorations; and an "average" room, decorated like a professor's office. While located in these different rooms, subjects were asked to rate a series of photographs of faces. Those in the beautiful room gave higher ratings to the faces than did those in the ugly room. While the beautiful room was found to stimulate feelings of pleasure, comfort, enjoyment, and the desire to continue the activity, the ugly room caused fatigue, headaches, discontent, sleepiness, irritability, and hostility. Subsequent measures of recall and problem solving in these rooms showed better performance in the beautiful surroundings (Maslow & Mintz, 1956).

COLORS.   We all recognize cliches of color and emotion—"tickled pink," "feeling blue," "green with envy," and "seeing red," to name a few. It is well known that specific colors are associated with particular human moods. As one early study demonstrated (see Table 3.1), we tend to describe some moods in terms of a specific color, while other moods are associated with two or more colors. Additionally, research on achievement motivation has shown that highly motivated people prefer cool or somber colors and tend to be in a hurry, while people who are less motivated prefer warm or brighter colors, like red and yellow, and are generally less time-conscious. To support these earlier findings, Charles and Carlota Salter (1982) investigated automobile color as a predictor of driving behavior. Specifically, they focused on color of car and propensity of the driver to speed at great velocities and to run red lights and stop signs. Results of their study revealed that drivers of cars with higher-achievement colors (such as blue and black) tended to speed at higher rates and to run red lights more often than drivers of cars with low-achievement colors (such as red or yellow). However, they did not tend to run stop signs more often.

The difficulty with such research, of course, is in discerning whether people pick colors that are truly associated with specific moods or whether their choices actually reflect learned stereotypes. Do you respond to different colors in different ways? What colors are you wearing at this moment? Do they reflect the mood you were in when you dressed? Answering these questions may give you some interesting insights into your reactions to particular colors. What about color combinations? Are there certain color combinations, say orange and red, that you would *never* wear? Why not? What nonverbal messages do you think you send by wearing such combinations?

TABLE 3.1 Association of Moods and Colors

MOOD	COLOR
Exciting, stimulating	Red
Secure, comfortable	Blue
Distressed, disturbed, upset	Orange
Tender, soothing	Blue
Protective, defending	Red, brown, blue, purple, black
Despondent, dejected, unhappy, melancholy	Black, brown
Calm, peaceful, serene	Blue, green
Dignified, stately	Purple
Cheerful, jovial, joyful	Yellow
Defiant, contrary, hostile	Red, orange, black
Powerful, strong, masterful	Black

From L. B. Wexner, "The Degree to Which Colors (Hues) Are Associated with Mood-Tones," *Journal of Applied Psychology*, 38 (1954), 432–35.

"We want it done in tattletale gray."

TIME.   North Americans are preoccupied with time, unlike people from many cultures. Just observe the many timepieces around us—clocks in our homes, schools, and workplaces; church bells chiming every quarter-hour; banks lighting up the time, second by second; radio stations announcing the time after every commercial; and almost everyone wearing a wristwatch. Time also plays an important part in our everyday oral discourse. We "kill time," "waste time," and "use time wisely," depending on the situation. We also use expressions like "it's high time," "time is of the essence," and "now is the time to. . . ."

Time is significant in nonverbal communication as well. In the United States, time is a valued commodity. Time is money—we are paid for the time we spend at work, and we pay for the time we go to class. Time is power—the more time someone gives you, the more important you are. Time is status—we are more punctual for an important business meeting than for a casual get-together. In short, we are compulsive clock-watchers—bound to our watches, time clocks, agendas, and timetables. Time keeps running on . . . running us.

Scientists have discovered that perceptions of time provide important nonverbal cues, cues that vary from culture to culture. Western industrialized cultures, for example, think of time in linear-spatial terms related to past, present, and future. Thus, North Americans think of moving "through" time, with the present as the intermediate point between past and future. In contrast, other cultures stress "felt time," the "now" of living for each day and not for the past or future. Greeks, for instance, see themselves as stationary. Time comes up behind them, overtakes them, and then becomes the past. Many Native Americans have the same concept. Indeed, the Sioux (comprised of the Dakota and Lakota tribes) in the United States have no words for "time," "late," or "waiting."

We also make certain assumptions about other people based on their time-consciousness. Those on time for appointments are considered most sociable and composed; those who are early are seen as least dynamic; and latecomers are usually viewed as least sociable, composed, and competent. Bringing time closer to home, consider how someone else's time conceptions affect you. If you discover that your boss or professor is very time-conscious—keeps track of tardiness, absenteeism, and so forth—how might you modify your behavior? How would use of time affect such a boss or instructor?

MUSIC.   Have you ever put on soft music to set the mood for a special date or wondered why some restaurants play classical music and others play light rock? Maybe you haven't thought about the reasons behind the music selections, but whether you know it or not, music affects us and our interactions with others.

Music also plays a major role in our society. North Americans spend more money on MP3 players, CDs, and cassettes than they do on textbooks for schools. The power of the music industry can be attributed to its diversity. With access to both radio stations and the Internet, we have the freedom to tune into anything from rap to jazz to classical. Tastes in music communicate information about others. Personality characteristics are often associated with the types of music to which people listen. However, to assume that intellectuals listen to classical music, truck drivers enjoy country-and-western music, and long-haired liberals get into grunge rock is to engage in dangerous generalizations. Just as there is diversity in the sounds of music, there is diversity in what people appreciate and like to listen to in music.

Awareness of Nonverbal Communication

While the previous sections have described some of the meanings attached to specific gestures, body language, expressions, and environmental stimuli, we must assert that these nonverbal messages cannot be viewed in simple, black-and-white terms. Like words, nonverbal communication has connotations as well as denotations. Just as each of us responds differently to a given word, term, or concept because of our different experiences, attitudes, and beliefs, so, too, do we respond differently to nonverbal messages.

Awareness of your own nonverbal behavior and that of others can increase your sensitivity in social interactions. We are usually attentive to nonverbal stimuli—we purposely wear clothes that evoke a particular response (positive or negative), and we reach out and touch a friend who is unhappy to let him or her know that we are there. At other times, we overlook or misread nonverbal cues that might enrich our understanding of interpersonal communication. Similarly, just as we may misinterpret the nonverbal behavior of others, they may do the same with us. Thus, you should consider questions such as, "I know what my facial piercing means to me, but what does it mean to my parents or boss?" "Do my cartoon ties influence how others view my work?"

In the following section we will discuss the factors that affect our interpretation of nonverbal messages.

Context

Context influences our own nonverbal communication as well as our responses to other people's nonverbal messages. For example, when you are at home watching a movie via satellite, you probably prop your feet up on the coffee table or curl them under you on the sofa. You might noisily dig to the bottom of the potato chip bag, ignoring the crumbs that miss your mouth and fall to your chest. And, if the beer or soda you've been drinking should make you burp—so what? But what if you were watching the same movie in a crowded theater? Your behavior might differ considerably. Even if you wanted to slouch, the stiff theater seats might prevent it. If you insisted on potato chips rather than a less noisy snack, you would probably be more careful not to rattle the bag or scatter the crumbs. And, if the soda had the same effect on you it has at home, you would probably suppress the burp or let nature have its way—discreetly.

We learn appropriate context behaviors by negative reinforcement during childhood. How many times were you told as a child, "Don't put your feet on that table! You're not at home now!" Or, did you ever get stern looks because you talked too loudly in a movie theater or popped your gum in a library? After much scolding and some praise, we learn to vary our nonverbal behaviors according to whom we are with, where we are, and whether or not the situation is defined as formal or informal.

Just as context modifies our own nonverbal behavior, so too it affects our response to nonverbal messages in our environment. For example, a simple gesture can have several different meanings, depending on the context in which it occurs. Let's say you are driving your car down the road and you spot someone hitchhiking. In a matter of seconds, you must decide whether to stop. What you do is based on contextual variables—first, consider your mood. Are you feeling helpful, or do you want to be bothered? Are you in a hurry or on a leisurely drive? Are you afraid of all hitchhikers, never pick them up, or do you usually give them a lift? And what about the environment? Would it make a difference to you if it were daytime or night? On a crowded highway or on a country road? In the summer or during a snowstorm? What about the person himself . . . or herself? Would it matter to you if the hitchhiker were a man or a woman? Or perhaps a man *and* a woman—or a man with his pet German shepherd?

Would the hitchhiker's age and weight influence you? Or clothing, hairstyle, and other gestures? Finally, if and when you do pull over, would you take a few more seconds to change your mind after studying facial expressions, voice, and general demeanor?

Stereotypes

As you can see, the same gesture—"Hey, I need a ride. Please pick me up."—can be interpreted in many different ways, depending on the context and, of course, our stereotypes.

Like it or not, most of us do have stereotypes about people and the way they act. These stereotypes play a large part in first impressions. Whether or not the stereotypes bear any resemblance to reality, they do exist and we must consider them when analyzing interpersonal behavior.

As our hitchhiking example demonstrated, we often make judgments about the personality and behavior of individuals just by observing their physical appearance or superficial actions. In fact, we sometimes make important decisions based on voice alone: "I didn't like the sound of his voice, so I. . . ." or, "As soon as she started to talk, I knew I could trust her." Researchers have verified this reliance on voice characteristics. In one experiment, students listened to two tape recordings of the same speaker. On one recording the speaker used a conversational delivery pattern—that is, a smaller range of inflections, a greater consistency of rate and pitch, less volume, and generally lower pitch than in the second recording, in which the speaker used a more dynamic delivery pattern. The students in this study did not realize that they were hearing the same speaker with two different vocal approaches. Instead, they rated the speaker who used the conversational delivery as honest and person-oriented, while the dynamic delivery elicited descriptions of tough-minded, task-oriented, self-assured, and assertive (Pearce & Conklin, 1971).

Of course, we all have stereotypes about many aspects of behavior other than voice. Do you have certain beliefs about the way people should or shouldn't walk, smile, sit, stand, eat, laugh, sneeze, or cry? Ask yourself *why* the next time you jump to a conclusion based solely on some aspect of another person's behavior. Chances are your conclusion doesn't reflect the facts of the situation. Herein lies the danger of stereotypes: Too often they turn out to be assumptions completely unrelated to objective facts.

However, the main point of this chapter is awareness: You cannot eliminate your stereotyped response to nonverbal messages, but you cannot disregard those stereotypes either. Thus, if you know, for example, that someone has a negative stereotype about blue jeans, either you will not wear them when you are with that person or you will not be surprised or offended by the person's behavior when you do. In short, awareness improves understanding, and understanding improves communication—be it verbal or nonverbal.

Summary

In addition to our spoken and written language, all of us communicate on the nonverbal level of body movements, gestures, facial expressions, tone of voice, and other related signs. Our interpretatin of such nonverbal messages is a function of both their context and their relationship to the sum of the communicator's verbal and nonverbal behavior patterns.

Four basic functions of nonverbal communication are identification, relationship, emotion, and delivery. These constitute the "whys" of nonverbal behavior. The "hows" include repeating, substituting, complementing, regulating, accenting, and deceiving. The body expressions that serve these functions are limitless. The language of facial expressions, eye adjustments, and related movements is responsible for a significant part of all human communication. In addition, specialists have organized body expressions into classes such as kinesics and body movement.

Classes of body expressions include emblems, illustrators, regulators, affect displays, and body manipulators. These expressions and the functions they serve are the subject of the scientific discipline known as kinesics, or body language.

In addition to kinesic messages, we communicate through our personal appearance and our choice of clothing. Likewise, touch, the most basic form of nonverbal communication, is an important part of our communication system and contributes to our overall sense of well-being.

In addition to these forms of nonverbal behavior, we communicate by our relationship to the space about us and our use of that space. Proxemics, the study of these spatial factors, specifies several distinct zones of interpersonal communication that are affected by our territoriality.

The last three areas of nonverbal communication we discussed are paralanguage, our senses of taste and smell, and environmental factors that surround us.

It is important to become aware of these factors and of the context in which nonverbal messages occur. We also must recognize the perceptual stereotypes that always affect our interpretation of both verbal and nonverbal messages. This heightened awareness can help ensure understanding of others and improve communication on all levels.

Exercises

GROUP EXPERIENCES

How's Your Sign Language?

DESCRIPTION   As children, we used nonverbal communication as our direct statement of what we wanted, while verbal communication was the complement. As we grew older, this process became reversed, so that our nonverbal communication no longer served as a direct statement but as a complement to what we said verbally. Children depend a great deal on sign language (gestures that replace words, numbers, and punctuation). Research shows that children are easily able to send and interpret 12 frequently used gestures. Try this activity and see if your sign language is as good as a child's.

PROCEDURE   Divide into groups of four to six members. Each member should try to send a short phrase nonverbally. The following list of phrases is offered only as a beginning—these are the phrases mentioned above that children are able to use quite easily.

Go away	Be quiet	Shape (round or square)
Come here	Give me attention	I don't know
Yes	How many	Goodbye
No	How big	Hi

The first person to accurately guess the message becomes the next sender. This process continues until all members have had the opportunity to create at least two messages.

DISCUSSION   How well do you send and interpret nonverbal messages? Consider this question in light of the activity you have just completed. If you have trouble sending messages nonverbally, you may need to work to improve your communication. On the other hand, if you have trouble interpreting messages, you may be misinterpreting people. Problems with either sending or interpreting nonverbal messages may lead to communication breakdowns on an interpersonal or group level.

How Others Stereotype You

DESCRIPTION   Are you aware of how others stereotype you on the basis of your behavior and personal appearance? Not many people are. This activity will provide you with information about how others view you and should also help you understand your own nonverbal behavior.

PROCEDURE   Divide into groups of four to six members. Each member should make a list of everyone in the group and put his or her name on the top of the list. Across the top of the paper, three categories should be written: books, dogs, and adjectives. Starting with yourself, select one choice from each category that most closely reflects you or the person for whom you are making the choice. When you are selecting, try to determine the specific behaviors that cause you to view a person in a particular stereotyped way.

Category A. Which book would you most likely find (insert name) reading?

a. *How Managers Make Things Happen*

b. *How to Read the Stars*

c. *The Wild, Wild West*

d. *One Hundred Ways to Improve Your Golf Swing*

e. *The Koran*

f. *How to Eat Better and Spend Less*

g. *How to Be Your Own Best Friend*

Category B. What type of dog does (insert name) remind you of?

a. Poodle

b. German shepherd

c. Sheepdog

d. Cocker spaniel

e. Dachshund

f. St. Bernard

g. Chihuahua

Category C. Which group of adjectives most closely describes (insert name)?

a. Open, optimistic, energetic

b. Meticulous, nervous, punctual

c. Soft-hearted, good-natured, loving

d. Competitive, dominant, authoritative

e. Closed, pessimistic, quiet

f. Fun-loving, ambitious, talkative

g. Introspective, spiritual, analytical

DISCUSSION   There are two ways to assess the results of this activity. Either start with a category and discuss each group member in the category, or start with a particular group member and discuss him or her in each of the three categories. Whichever method you choose, keep in mind that meanings are in people, not in words. Try to provide information on *why* you made a particular selection. Focus on the personal appearance of the person and consider whether you stereotyped hairstyle or clothing in a particular way. If you find that the impressions others have of you are inconsistent with the way you view yourself, then observe your own behavior and personal appearance to understand what you are nonverbally conveying to others. The expansion of nonverbal awareness begins with understanding how you project impressions to others.

It's Not What You Say, It's How You Say It!

DESCRIPTION   This activity can be conducted either in small groups of four to six members or as a demonstration activity in which the majority of the class serves as an audience while four or five individuals play roles in selected situations. Two partners will be needed for each role-playing scene. Two scenes are offered as examples of the type of drama that can be reenacted to illustrate the effects of pitch, rhythm, intonation, intensity, and other vocal qualities. The purpose of this activity is to clearly demonstrate that it's not *what* you say, but *how* you say it!

PROCEDURE   Two partners will be needed for each role-playing activity. Each team can either invent a scene they would like to portray or use one from the following list. In each scene only numbers are to be used—absolutely no words are permitted. For example, practice by reading the following numbers tenderly, angrily, and sadly: 42, 567, 3, 356, 8. Once you get a feel for this, try one of the following scenes. After a team plays a scene, the group should discuss the emotions and feelings that were being conveyed.

Scene 1: Husband and Wife

The wife comes home from work and the husband is irritable after spending the day watching the children and cooking. He displays his irritability the moment she walks through the door. The wife at first tries to be supportive, but then fights openly with her husband.

Scene 2: A Couple

In this scene the couple has been dating for a long time. Finally, after waiting for months, he pops the question. The scene is tender and romantic.

DISCUSSION   Are you aware of the subtle nonverbal cues that are sent through the voice? Consider how, even if the words are identical, a change in pitch, intensity, or even pause rate can dramatically alter the meaning of a message. After participating in this activity, you should be able to listen to your own vocal characteristics to see how you alter messages. Also consider the extent to which the vocal characteristics of others influence your interpretation of their messages. In other words, is it *what* they say or *how* they say it that counts?

Body Expressions

DESCRIPTION   The body and the face convey many emotional meanings in both speaking and listening. Most of us learn to convey emotions through our facial expressions but have difficulty conveying emotions with other parts of our bodies. The following activity will provide you with an opportunity to determine how well you send and interpret the nonverbal display of emotions through the use of facial expressions and body movement.

PROCEDURE   Write each of the following body areas and emotions on separate cards.

Body Areas	Emotions
Whole face	Hate
Whole body	Love
Hands only	Anger
Face only	Surprise
Mouth only	Happiness
Eyes and eyebrows only	Distrust
Feet only	Disgust
Dyad (whole body with another person)	Contentment

Divide into groups of six to eight members. (Each group needs one set of cards.) The first person should select one card from the "body area" category and one card from the "emotion" category. The person should then try to portray the selected emotion with *only* the body area designated on the card. The rest of the group has three guesses to determine both the correct body area and the emotion. If the group guesses correctly, the person receives one point. If the group does not guess correctly, the person loses one point. After the first person has finished, the cards should be returned to the appropriate deck. Go around the group until each participant has had three turns. The number of turns may be modified depending on the number of participants in the group and the amount of time available for the activity.

DISCUSSION   As a group, identify which emotions were most difficult to convey and which were easiest. Identify which body areas most accurately sent the emotional states and which least accurately. Which was more difficult—the creation of nonverbal messages or the interpretation of them?

Conversation and Space

DESCRIPTION   Particular spatial arrangements may either aid or inhibit interactions. We are constantly readjusting our distance from other people and objects to match the nature of our conversations. The following activity provides you with the opportunity to experience the relationship between conversational topic and distance.

PROCEDURE   Divide into dyads. The members of the dyad should stand directly opposite one another at a distance of 10 feet. Engage in a conversation on any topic you choose, but while you are talking, maintain the distance of 10 feet between you and your partner for three minutes. After three minutes reduce the distance to five feet and continue to talk. You may change topics as many times as you wish. After another three minutes reduce the distance to two feet, then 12 inches, and finally six inches. Each distance should be maintained for a minimum of three minutes.

DISCUSSION   Discuss your reactions to the various conversational distances you maintained with your partner. Did the topic of the conversation or the intensity with which you discussed the topic vary with the different distances? Did certain topics seem inappropriate at particular distances? What types of topics do you consider to be appropriate at the following distances: ten feet, five feet, two feet, one foot, six inches?

PERSONAL EXPERIENCES

1. Strike up a conversation with a stranger while you are waiting in line, sitting in a bus, or walking on campus. After a couple of minutes, ask if he or she would be willing to participate in an experiment requiring no more than a few minutes. If the person is willing, ask him or her to relate the first impression of you. Stress the need for an honest appraisal of your personal appearance, nonverbal behaviors, and conversational qualities. Is the impression accurate? What was your reaction to the description of you? How aware are you of the nonverbal impression you create?

2. Select a person in one of your classes for observation. Watch your subject over a period of several days and see if you can classify his or her nonverbal behaviors as (a) regulators, (b) illustrators, (c) emblems, (d) affect displays, or (e) adaptors. What does this classification tell you about the person? For example, does the absence of the use of regulating nonverbal behavior suggest that the person may not provide adequate listening response for a speaker?

3. Watch television with a friend, but at separate locations. Have your friend watch the same program so that you can compare notes later. When you watch the program, however, turn off the sound completely. Watch the body movements and facial expressions very carefully and try to understand the story line. After the program, tell your friend what happened—describe the emotions, the drama, and the interaction between characters in the program. Then listen to your friend's description. What were the major differences in your descriptions? Did the absence of sound produce more information on the nonverbal level while reducing the content of the information, which is obtained through the verbal medium?

4. The next time you have a telephone conversation with someone you have never seen (a telephone operator, a salesperson), try to determine information about that person on the basis of vocal cues. For example, try to guess age, height, weight, race, sex, and the area of the country he or she is from. After you have made some tentative guesses, check your results by asking your telephone partner to verify the information. Try this several times and see how vocal cues help, hinder, or do not affect the identification of background and personality characteristics of an individual.

5. Observe yourself for a day to determine how you see "time." Record the number of times you look at a clock, ask for the time, or refer to time in any manner. Next, go a step further and determine whether you live in present time, future time, past time, or linear time (no past, present, or future). How well can you relate to people who have a different time orientation?

6. Pick a task that takes approximately two hours to complete. Work on the task for one hour in an "ugly" room and one hour in a "beautiful" room. What effect did the difference in environment have on your productivity? Did you experience different physical feelings in each room? Are you sensitive to your environment?

Discussion Questions

1. What is the difference between nonverbal communication and nonverbal behavior?
2. What are some of the ways (functions) in which we use nonverbal communication?
3. How is the formation of first impressions related to stereotyping?
4. Can you describe your nonverbal behaviors during speaking and listening?
5. What nonverbal behaviors do you use to defend your territory and personal space?
6. To what extent do nonverbal behaviors reflect our attitudes or emotions?
7. Do cultural norms regarding the use of space tell us anything about a given society?
8. How important do you consider paralinguistic cues to be in verbal communication?

References

Baldridge, L. (1993). *Letitia Baldrige's new complete guide to executive manners.* New York: Scribner.

Chaney, R. H., Givens, C. A., Aoki, M. F., & Gombiner, M. L. (1989). Pupillary responses in recognizing awareness in persons with profound mental retardation. *Perceptual and Motor Skills, 69,* 523–528.

Ekman, P., & Friesen, W. V. (1969). The repertoire of non-verbal behavior: Categories, origins, usage, and coding. *Semiotica, 1*(1), 49–98.

Freeley, T. H., & Young, M. J. (1998). Humans as lie detectors: Some more second thoughts. *Communication Quarterly, 46*(2), 109–126.

Hess, E. H. (1965). Attitude and pupil size. *Scientific American, 212*(4) 54.

Holliman, W. B., & Anderson, H. N. (1986). Proximity and student density as ecological variables in a college classroom. *Teaching of Psychology, 13*(4), 200–203.

Kleinke, C. L. (1986). Gaze and eye contact: A research review. *Psychological Bulletin, 100*(1) 78–100.

Maslow, A. H., & Mintz, N. L. (1956). Effects of esthetic surroundings: I. Initial effects of three esthetic conditions upon perceiving "energy" and "well-being" in faces. *Journal of Psychology, 41,* 247–254.

Millard, R. J., & Stimpson, D. V. (1980, April). Enjoyment and productivity as a function of classroom seating location. *Perceptual Motor Skills, 50,* 439–444.

Morris, T. L., Gorham, J., Cohen, S. H., & Huffman, D. (1996). Fashion in the classroom: Effects of attire on student perceptions of instructors in college classes. *Communication Education, 45*(2), 135–148.

Pearce, W. B., & Conklin, F. (1971). Nonverbal vocalic communication and perceptions of a speaker. *Speech Monographs, 38,* 235–241.

Remland, Martin S. *Nonverbal communication in everyday life.* Boston, MA: Houghton Mifflin.

Salter, C. A., & Salter, C. D. (1982). Automobile color as a predictor of driving behavior. *Perceptual and Motor Skills, 55,* 383–386.

Listening and Intrapersonal Processes

key concepts and terms

Hearing
Listening
Active Listening
Attending
Perceiving
Interpreting
Assessing
Responding
Cognitive dimension
Affective dimension
Behavioral/verbal dimension
Behavioral/nonverbal
  dimension
Behavioral/interactive
  dimension
Listening preferences
Long-term memory
Retrieval
Recognition

Recall
Sorting
Assimilation
Emotional processing
Physiological processing
Gestalt
Biofeedback
Transmission
Self-feedback
Content-oriented listener
Action-oriented listener
People-oriented listener
Time-oriented listener
Focusing
Tracking
Reflecting
Digging
Dampening
Redirecting

Intrapersonal processes
Intrapersonal
  communication
Stimuli
Internal stimuli
External self-feedback
Internal self-feedback
Interference
Values
Attitude
Belief
Opinion
Prejudices
Traits
Locus of control
Manipulation
Dogmatism
External stimuli
Overt stimuli

Covert stimuli	Sensory storage	Projection
Threshold of consciousness	Short-term memory	Insulation
Reception	Tolerance of ambiguity	Reaction formation
Selective perception	Self-esteem	Identification
Intensity	Maturity	Repression
Cognitive processing	Defense mechanisms	Self-awareness
Memory	Rationalization	

From:	"Tripp"
To:	"Robyn" <sanderrx@futurenet.ab.net>
Sent:	Friday, December 23 1:30AM
Subject:	Why can't parents just listen?

Hey, Robyn—

Can't believe we've been out of school for less than a week and I'm already missing the place. Since the minute I got home, Mom and Dad have been dogging me about what I'm going to do with my life. I'm only a first-semester sophomore but they're sure I should know by now what I want to do when I graduate, and how my major is going to get me there. I keep telling them what my advisor said about the importance of exploring my options right now, but they won't listen. Mom won't let me finish a sentence without interrupting. And Dad keeps criticizing everything I say and telling me my advisor isn't paying for my education. He's right! With the exception of half my tuition, I'm paying for everything—books, my apartment, food, gas, electricity, water—everything!

Can't take much more of all this "holiday good cheer." Hope things are better at your end. Let me know if you have any sage advice. Will be out shopping tomorrow (oh boy!), but will be home by around 6:00 tomorrow night! "Haaaaaapppppy Holidays!" Bah-humbug—Tripp

---

Listening and intrapersonal processes are the bases for effective communication. As Tripp shared with Robyn, it's difficult to communicate when nobody is listening and everyone is talking. It's even more difficult when we think we are listening, but we aren't. One way to help ensure more effective communication is to examine the challenges and difficulties associated with listening. Another is to understand the complex intrapersonal processes that take place inside our heads as we communicate with ourselves and others.

This chapter is designed to help you accomplish these two primary goals. In the first half, we will define listening, present five stages associated with listening, and

Listening effectively is a complex and challenging task.

discuss five dimensions of listening that all of us must master in order to be competent communicators. We also will talk about the contributions of listening preferences to communication outcomes, and discuss six major ways to improve your listening skills.

Once we have discussed listening, we will turn to our attention to intrapersonal processes that take place during communication. Specifically, we will focus on ways that we process information cognitively, emotionally, and physiologically; the effects of three major intrapersonal variables on communication outcomes; and a means by which you can increase your own self-awareness and, in turn, your competence as a communicator.

Defining Listening

As described in the communication model in Chapter 1, listeners are not isolated from speakers during the communication process. *Hearing,* which is only one part of the listening process, refers to the physical act of receiving sounds. It is a passive process that occurs even when we're asleep. *Listening,* on the other hand, is hard work and is a dynamic, interactive process involving both speakers and listeners. *Active listening,* therefore, is a series of interrelated processes that includes attending, perceiving, interpreting, assessing, and responding. For successful communication to occur, listeners and speakers must take mutual responsibility. In active listening, the role of listeners is to plan strategies to help themselves listen more effectively, and the role of speakers is to plan strategies to help others listen more effectively.

The Listening Ladder: A Five-Step Approach

One way to help ensure more effective communication is to examine the challenges and difficulties listeners face at each step of the listening process. Visualize the active listening process as a listening stepladder and refer to Figure 4.1 as you read the descriptions for each step along the way. The ladder represents the five steps listeners go through when communicating with others. At the top of the ladder is our goal: successful communication. To reach our goal we must make appropriate listening choices at each step. Keep in mind that listening is not easy. Therefore, we frequently miss steps, lose our balance, and/or slip down the ladder.

Attending Level

The initial step of the listening process, which affects the success of all the other steps, is *attending.* At this level we show differing degrees of involvement in verbal and nonverbal environmental stimuli. We demonstrate conscious efforts to listen to others through attending behaviors such as eye contact, forward lean, appropriate facial expressions, and concentration on the message. Unfortunately, many listeners begin with focused attention and find themselves getting distracted. When we get distracted, we unconsciously allow objects, speakers, or events to divert our attention. On many occasions it is our inner voice that hinders our ability to concentrate and to climb steps on the listening ladder. For example, when worrying about a test we are to take next class, we often fail to hear a teacher's last minute assignment.

Hearing is only one stage of the listening process.

Perceiving Level

The next step of the listening process is *perceiving.* At this step, listeners use one or more of their basic senses to receive verbal and nonverbal messages. Mistakes in listening occur when one of the senses does not receive a message or receives one in a distorted fashion. In most cases perception and listening involve hearing, but hearing is only one of the senses involved in the listening process. Although information can be gained from using all of the senses, the primary senses involved in listening are hearing and seeing. It is not unusual for us to miss information when our senses are required to do more than one thing at a time. Friends often miss important bits of information when trying to listen to conversations either in a room with loud music playing or during a football game when the crowd is screaming for the home team. Our perceptions are also influenced by our personal interests, past experiences, knowledge, and skill levels.

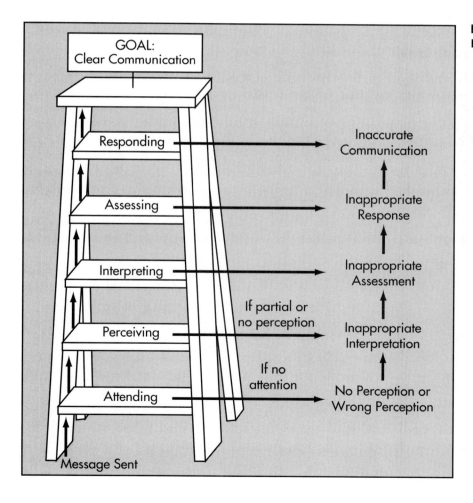

FIGURE 4.1
Listening Ladder

Interpreting Level

After you attend to and perceive a message, the next step is *interpreting* what you perceived. Listeners try to understand the meanings of messages at the interpreting level. Unfortunately, because we each differ in our experiences, knowledge, and attitudes, most communication breakdowns occur at this step of the listening process. There are numerous examples that illustrate how this can happen. For example, an American manager worked for a Japanese import firm. One day while discussing a problem with a Japanese accounting manager, the American thought they had come to an agreement and remarked, "It looks like we're thinking on parallel lines." She was surprised two weeks later when the problem surfaced again. She stormed into the accounting manager's office and said, "Didn't we agree we were thinking along parallel lines?" The Japanese manager looked puzzled, held up his hands, and said, "Parallel lines never meet." In essence, he had agreed to disagree. To ensure accurate communication, we must be sure that we interpret each other's messages correctly.

Assessing Level

After we interpret a message, we begin to make judgments about the message and its importance to us. There are two different ways of *assessing* information. The first deals with the perceived accuracy and credibility of the message. At this level of evaluation, the listener determines whether or not to believe the message, agree with the speaker, and/or retain the information. The second type of assessment occurs when the listener evaluates the relative importance of the individual parts of a message and the message as a whole. These assessments are based on the listener's perceptions of what the speaker believes is important as well as on the listener's personal value system.

Without effectively assessing what is said, most people make hasty evaluations. To ensure accurate communication, we should delay our evaluations until the message has been received completely. Probably one of the most dramatic assessing errors that has received international attention occurred with the space shuttle *Challenger* disaster. Engineers warned officials that the O-rings were defective and needed further inspection. Tragically, the information was evaluated as not critical enough to stop the launch. It was not until later that a full investigation discovered that the deaths of Christa McAuliffe and all the *Challenger* crew could have been avoided if someone had made a different evaluation.

Responding Level

The last step of the ladder is *responding*. Listening is not complete until there has been some kind of response. During this stage, we react to the message and/or sender. The completion of this stage is critical because it is the only step in which responses are actually seen and/or heard. While the responding level is the one most frequently blamed for listening errors, in actuality if listening has been successful up to this point, listening is likely to continue to be successful. When speakers perceive listeners' responses, they can check for understanding and test the accuracy of their interpretations. Even if we don't send verbal responses, we always send nonverbal responses. In fact, a nonverbal response such as the "silent treatment" can actually speak louder than words.

The chance for a responding-level error increases when the person listening is not necessarily the person responsible for acting on what was said. You have probably used the drive-thru lane of a fast-food restaurant. Most people have preferences about what goes on their hamburgers or chicken sandwiches. Think of the times you have ordered a sandwich without mayonnaise, had your request repeated back accurately, and then opened the sandwich to find a glob of mayo. In this particular example, chances are that more than one person was involved in responding to your request. When there are intermediaries between the person you communicate with and the person who gives a response, the chances for errors at the responding step increase substantially.

The steps of the listening ladder are hierarchical. Listeners cannot skip steps or proceed effectively to other steps and hope to reach the goal of successful communication. Of course, all these steps may take place in a fraction of a second, so for practical purposes they are not separate or independent. The arrows on the left on the ladder in Figure 4.1 show the process an effective listener takes in attending to, perceiving, interpreting, assessing, and responding to a message correctly. The arrows on the right depict where breakdowns in communication occur on steps of the listening ladder. If listeners fail to attend to messages, there is little or no chance that listeners can progress to other levels. Remember, however, that speakers often don't find out that errors have occurred until it is too late to correct the situation. Figure 4.2 provides a simple exercise to enhance your listening effectiveness.

Now that we've discussed the five stages of effective listening, go back and reread Tripp's e-mail to Robyn. At what stage of the listening process did communication break down between Tripp and his mom? Between Tripp and his dad? We would argue that Tripp's mom failed to actively attend to his messages and leaped directly to the assessing or responding stage. By cutting Tripp off in mid-sentence, she bypassed the opportunity to accurately perceive or interpret Tripp's words. In contrast, Tripp's father attended to and perceived what was said, but failed to interpret Tripp's message correctly. Tripp's dad also rushed to the assessing and responding stages, but without checking the accuracy of his interpretation. As you can see, this approach to listening provides us with useful information about the listening process. It also offers us a way to analyze listening problems and to overcome them in the future.

To increase your awareness of the listening environment around you, take a few minutes to follow some simple instructions:

1. Set a timer on your watch or microwave for 30 seconds.
2. Close your eyes and just listen with your ears.
3. For these 30 seconds, listen to all the sounds in your environment.
4. After 30 seconds, get a sheet of paper and write down every sound that you heard.
5. Now, put down the book and begin listening for 30 seconds.

Welcome back. You should have been able to list at least five different sounds. Your list may have included air conditioning or furnace fans, outside traffic, a plane overhead, rustling of paper or clothing, footsteps in the hall, doors shutting, elevators dinging, your own breathing, telephones ringing, printers or machinery sounds, voices, music, or birds or crickets chirping.

You probably were not aware of most of these sounds prior to this exercise, but they were there all the time. By focusing your awareness on such sounds, however, you were able to identify them and classify them as important or inconsequential. But let's look more closely for a moment at some of the items on the list of what we heard during the 30 seconds.

While you were taking the above test, were there any other sounds that you may have overlooked? Did you, for example, list your own inner voice? Some of you may have had your voice listed first, but most of us fail to acknowledge the loudest sounds of all—our inner voices. During the day our inner voices never stop talking to us. During the preceding exercise, your inner voice probably made comments such as "This is a long 30 seconds, "Why would the authors ask us to do something like this?" "There are more sounds than I thought," or "I don't hear anything." In actuality your inner voice was and is the loudest sound in your world and does more to hinder your reception of messages than other interference.

It is our inner voice that:

- hinders us from remembering names during first introductions;
- causes us to rush to a response ("The great comeback") before people finish their thoughts;
- fades in and out of conversations by jumping to other topics and thoughts because of emotional trigger words or associations.

And while it is our inner voice that helps us monitor our interactions with ourselves and others, sometimes our inner voice screams when it needs to whisper, interrupts when it needs to wait, or argues when it needs to reflect.

FIGURE 4.2 Sounds of Silence

Five Dimensions of Listening

Information about the five stages of listening provides a useful foundation on which to build your knowledge about listening. So too does understanding the five major dimensions (or components) of listening, each of which contributes uniquely to your listening competence. Since the early 1950s, listening researchers have attempted to identify the ways that we process information. In the process, they have uncovered five major dimensions of listening: cognitive, affective, behavioral/verbal, behavioral/nonverbal, and behavioral/interactive.

According to Halone, Cunconan, Coakley, and Wolvin (1998), the ***cognitive dimension*** of listening is associated with the extent to which we

1. work hard at listening and actively concentrate on what a speaker is saying;

2. think about, mentally summarize, and attempt to remember the speaker's main ideas;

3. know why we are listening, and recognize and evaluate the speaker's biases;

4. "catch [ourselves]" when we stop focusing attention and attempt to refocus;

5. listen to only one message at a time and quickly determine the speaker's purpose;

6. listen "between the lines" to what is not being said;

7. listen for something of value when the speaker is uninteresting;

8. ignore distractions and motivate ourselves to listen;

9. differentiate between a speaker's relevant and irrelevant points; and

10. concentrate on what is being said rather than waiting for an opening so we can express our ideas (p. 18).

How well do you accomplish these tasks when you are listening to other people? Your ability to do so definitely affects your communication competence as well as others' perceptions of you as a "good listener."

In contrast, the ***affective dimension*** of listening is associated with the extent to which we enjoy listening to others; listen effectively to whomever is talking no matter who they are; care about how our listening behaviors affect other people; maintain emotional control during an interaction; listen freely and with an open mind; and accept responsibility for contributing to the success of an interaction (Halone et al., 1998, p. 20). As you can see, this dimension is associated with how you feel when you are listening to other people. It also is related to how motivated we are to listen at a given time.

The actual behavior that we exhibit when we are listening was termed by Halone's research team as the ***behavioral/verbal dimension.*** Rating high on this dimension means knowing when and when not to speak; using an appropriate tone of voice given the speaker, subject, and occasion; asking questions to increase understanding or to check the accuracy of our interpretation; refraining from giving advice or telling our own stories when someone is sharing a problem; giving appropriate feedback without having to be asked; and apologizing for any necessary interruptions that you make. If you return for a moment to Tripp's e-mail to Robyn, you can see that Tripp's mom could easily improve on this dimension. Interrupting and talking while someone else is talking are two of the biggest listening errors that many of us make.

The *behavioral/nonverbal dimension* of listening is reflected in how well we use nonverbal language when we are listening. Included in this dimension are being aware of and using eye contact and body movements that encourage communication; being sensitive to the nonverbal cues of the speaker and taking them into account when interpreting a message; being aware of the nonverbal messages you are sending as a listener; *not* doodling, grooming, or engaging in other tasks while you are attempting to listen (like watching television, working on the computer, writing, or reading); and taking notes when appropriate (e.g., during an interview or while listening to an oral presentation) (Halone et al., 1998, p. 21).

Finally, Halone and colleagues (1998) suggest that the *behavioral/interactive dimension* emphasizes our awareness of the relational elements associated with listening. How effectively do you use the following behaviors when you are listening to others?

1. Trying to make time to listen when someone wants to talk

2. Staying actively involved in the conversation rather than daydreaming

3. Allowing the other person to completely express her thoughts

4. Using listening skills that are appropriate for the reason you are listening

5. Avoiding interruptions and stopping your message if someone else begins to speak while you are talking

6. Refraining from behaviors that imply that the speaker is wasting your time

7. Avoiding nonverbal cues that signal impatience

8. Eliminating external distractions that interfere with listening

9. Keeping a pen and pad nearby so you can take down important notes when necessary

As you can see, research in this area has contributed useful information about the nature of listening. Additionally, it offers us some excellent guidelines through which we can improve our overall communication competence.

Listening Preferences

Before attempting to change your listening behavior, it is important to get an even clearer picture of yourself as a listener. The goal of this section is to help you glean additional insights into your listening behaviors and habits. Habits are important to observe because they develop so slowly that you often fail to notice them. The first step toward increasing your awareness is to identify your *listening preferences* and to observe your listening activities and habits in your immediate environment.

Listening habits and preferences do not develop in the same ways for all people. Some people prefer to hear from only credible sources, others want to be entertained, some focus on the other person's needs, and others want a speaker to get to the point as quickly as possible. Listening preferences develop over a lifetime as a function of socialization and reinforcement patterns.

Based on our preferences, unknowingly, we make judgments and decisions that may hinder our communication effectiveness. Similarly, our own preferences influence how we present information to others. The following paragraphs provide general descriptions of the four listener preferences: content-, action-, people-, and time-oriented (Watson & Barker, 1992).

CONTENT-ORIENTED.   *Content-oriented listeners* have a tendency to critically evaluate everything they hear. At times it is as if they are looking under a microscope to determine weaknesses or inconsistencies in information. While they willingly give time to listening, they prefer to listen to experts and highly credible sources. Content-oriented listeners have the ability to see both sides of issues, enjoy listening to challenging or complex information, and elicit high-quality ideas. Because content-oriented listeners carefully question information, in extreme cases, they may intimidate other people. Used in roles of authority, such as parents, teachers, or bosses, this listening style may hinder spontaneous discussions and creative exchanges of ideas.

ACTION-ORIENTED.   *Action-oriented listeners* are very time-conscious when listening and encourage others to be time-conscious as well. They often prefer to listen in outline form and find it difficult to listen to speakers who are disorganized. Action-oriented listeners are appreciated members of most meetings because they encourage others to stay on task, to keep meeting time to a minimum, and to present information in a logical, organized way. At times, however, because they appear to be in a rush, action-oriented listeners come across as impatient and not very interested in building relationships with others.

PEOPLE-ORIENTED.   *People-oriented listeners* are most concerned with how their listening influences their relationships with others. They listen to understand both the content and emotional states of others, willingly take time to listen, and usually remain nonjudgmental. When confronted with personal problems or crises, we seek out people-oriented listeners. Since they are open to all types of people and topics, they can get overly involved with others. In fact, at times people-oriented listeners can lose their objectivity when listening.

TIME-ORIENTED.   *Time-oriented listeners* are clock-watchers and encourage others to be the same. They are direct in how they value time and often get impatient with others who waste it. While they encourage efficiency and time management, their self-imposed time constraints can limit creativity. Time-oriented listeners must be careful not to interrupt or discount relationships with others. It is interesting to note that "Type-A Personalities" tend to endorse the content, action, and time orientations. (Sargent, Fitch-Hauser, & Weaver, 1997). (As you probably know, Type-A Personalities are aggressive, hurried, and competitive and, hence, more prone to heart disease than Type-B Personalities.)

Preferences affect the way that we listen.

After reading about these listening preferences, identify your own listening preferences. Think about how it might affect the information you receive and your interactions with others.

Improving Your Listening Skills

Our listening behaviors usually go unnoticed until something goes wrong. It is only when we are reminded that we missed an important meeting or forgot to return a call that we realize that a change in our listening behaviors is necessary. Even so, when our friends and family members confront us about our poor listening skills, it is often human nature to make excuses. If we want to reach our goal of successful communication, however, then we must take responsibility for the process.

Just as a speaker's role is to connect with and help the listener, the listener's job is to reach out to the speaker. As we climb the listening ladder, we must have confidence that each progressive step of the ladder will hold and that the next step will be as steady as the first. At times, listeners must test for the sturdiness and stability of the ladder to ensure successful communication. The following examples and suggestions are designed to help listeners climb the listening ladder successfully (Barker, Johnson & Watson, 1991).

Focusing

If we want to get the most from a listening situation, we must prepare ourselves to listen by *focusing*. Effective listeners make sure that they have an adequate energy supply and use the energy to concentrate on what a speaker is saying. Paying attention to others requires effort, but most listeners have not practiced the skills necessary to stay involved when others are talking. It does little good to attend to others as listeners if the message doesn't have a chance of getting through. The following suggestions provide a basic foundation for taking responsibility for the success of communication and for getting ourselves ready to listen.

1. Remove or reduce distractions by turning off TVs, closing drapes or blinds.

2. Sit or move closer to the speaker.

3. Minimize interruptions by unplugging the phone and closing the door.

4. Ask the speaker to speak louder.

5. Focus attention and concentrate.

6. Prepare for the speaker, topic, and situation in advance.

7. Look at the speaker.

8. Be rested.

Tracking

Most of us have been guilty of interrupting or discouraging others from talking. The *tracking* strategy encourages others to keep talking and us to keep listening. Especially when we listen to people who have a different point of view, it is easy to begin evaluating their message before they finish talking. We all have been guilty of "planning the great comeback" or "rehearsing a response." Rather than jumping to conclusions, it would be best to mentally note or jot down points we'd like to clarify—and keep listening. The following suggestions should help us in following what others have to say.

1. Avoid interrupting.

2. Withhold or defer judgment.

3. Remain objective with minimum bias.

4. Be aware of the speaker's biases.

5. Show nonverbal encouragement through head nods, eye contact, etc.

6. Ask about priorities of requested actions.

Reflecting

Listeners may need to test their understanding. Listeners can clarify messages by *reflecting*—using such questions as, "So are you suggesting that we wait until next week to go to the mountains?" or "Do you want me to come to the meeting at 9:00 or 9:30?" Remember, listeners are put at a disadvantage if they fail to get involved with the speaker throughout the communication interaction. Listeners need to ask questions or to take control of the communication situation to make sure that they have interpreted messages correctly. When listening:

1. Summarize key points.
2. Describe the emotional state of the speaker.
3. Repeat ideas or paraphrase to the speaker.
4. Identify words with multiple meanings.
5. Analyze and adapt to the speaker's point of view.

Digging

Most of us have, at one time or another, tried to hide what we were thinking or feeling from someone. Perhaps we didn't want to hurt their feelings, or we were afraid of what they would think of us. But keeping our thoughts or feelings hidden interferes with accurate communication. Therefore, most of us would like to know what is going on within a person before we make important decisions. *Digging* is a strategy to help listeners discover underlying issues and concerns. Digging clarifies verbal and nonverbal messages by reflecting on the emotions and thoughts of speakers. To get additional information:

1. Ask open-ended questions that require more than a yes or no answer.
2. Ask for examples.
3. Ask clarification questions.
4. Use preliminary closes to check for feelings.
5. Ask for additional evidence or supporting material.

Dampening

In some listening situations, one person's need is so great that the appropriate way to listen is to say little or nothing. The person may be angry, depressed, excited, or happy. *Dampening* is a listening strategy we can use to calm a person when he or she is in a negative emotional state. When a person is angry, for example, he or she may begin to take the anger out on others. As listeners we can choose to "punch back" or to "take the blow." If we respond in anger or punch back, we usually intensify negative emotions. If, however, we choose to become a pillow and take the punch, the person usually begins to calm down and may begin to respond less emotionally. When trying to calm the speaker:

1. Refrain from rehearsing a response.
2. Use encouraging remarks to keep the other person talking.
3. Use empathetic responses to demonstrate understanding.
4. Avoid interrupting the speaker.
5. Summarize the speaker's feelings to show understanding.

Redirecting

Speakers sometimes get sidetracked during meetings or conversations. While digressions can be appropriate, many are not; as a listener you may need to get the person back to the topic or task at hand. When diversions occur, the listener's *redirecting* helps the speaker get back on track by using comments such as: "Now that we've discussed . . ., How can we use the information to. . .?" or "Since this topic wasn't on the agenda, why don't we table this until our next meeting?" To get a person back on the subject:

1. Restate the original topic or issue.

2. Make statements that clarify the message.

3. Ask questions to get the person back on track.

4. Summarize what has been said to provide feedback.

5. Explain how the topic changed direction.

To sum up, you can improve your listening behavior by being aware of your listening energy and habits. The trick is to actually behave appropriately in actual listening situations. Some of the more desirable listening behaviors are listed in Table 4.1.

TABLE 4.1 **Tips for Effective Listening**

1. When listening to "uninteresting" subject matter, look for benefits and opportunities by asking "What's in it for me?"

2. Judge content—not the appearance or delivery of a speaker.

3. To avoid getting overstimulated by some part of a message, hold your reaction. Wait until the message is complete to make a judgement.

4. Listen for cental themes and ideas, not just facts.

5. Be flexible when taking notes; take fewer notes and use different systems of note-taking depending on the speaker.

6. Assume an active listening stance (for example, lean forward, make eye contact with speaker). Don't fake attention.

7. Resist distractions by fighting or avoiding them; learn how to concentrate.

8. Seek out difficult material rather than avoid it; use "heavy" material as an exercise for the mind.

9. Keep an open mind when confronted with an emotional word with which you are uncomfortable.

10. Use the thinking–speaking time differential to summarize mentally, weigh evidence, and listen "between the lines."

Source: Adapted from L. K. Steil, L. L. Barker, and K. W. Watson, *Effective Listening: Key to Your Success* (Reading, Mass.: Addison-Wesley, 1983), 72–73.

Intrapersonal Processes

Fourteen years after Dr. James Black began his highly experimental project, little did the Welwyn Research Institute in England know that their chief of pharmacology would eventually bring to market the most successful drug in the twentieth century. The drug that was developed at Welwyn for Smith, Kline and French Laboratories (SK&F) was Tagamet, a drug that heals ulcers quickly and painlessly. Tagamet became the first billion-dollar drug in pharmaceutical history and changed the course of SK&F from "the senior citizen of the drug business" into one of the world's foremost pharmaceutical research and development firms. However, the drug probably never would have emerged had it not been for Black's vision, scientific persistence, and defiance of the institutions for whom he worked. As a result of his argument that pharmaceutical researchers could move away from blending chemicals "like medieval herbalists" and could actually solve problems by designing combinations of atoms, Black and a handful of SK&F "baton carriers" eventually introduced Tagamet to the world and ultimately moved their pharmaceutical company into the twenty-first century (Nayak & Ketteringham, 1986).

How does this story relate to intrapersonal processes? *Intrapersonal processes* may be defined as the complex activities that take place inside the human brain whenever we evaluate and react to internal and external stimuli. *Intrapersonal communication,* a related term, has been defined as the sending and receiving of messages within ourselves. To illustrate intrapersonal processes, return for a moment to our Tagamet story. Dr. Black worked for more than 14 years on this single project. To see his vision through to the end, Black had to deal with trillions of stimuli: from frustrations that must have mounted as he worked on the project, to physical, mental, and emotional fatigue, to outside input regarding his success or failure.

The discussion in this chapter will focus on just such intrapersonal processes and variables that ultimately affect communication outcomes. We also shall touch briefly on intrapersonal communication when we present our model of intrapersonal processes in the paragraphs that follow.

Intrapersonal processes are the foundation upon which every other form of communication rests. Therefore, it is necessary to understand these processes before you can optimally communicate with others. The model presented in Figure 4.3 may help you to visualize communication from an intrapersonal perspective. The elements that set the process in motion are called *stimuli.*

Internal Stimuli

The brain is made aware of the state of the body by nerve impulses, *internal stimuli* that can prompt you to respond by communicating. Let's say you have the flu. Your muscles ache, your fever is high, and you are depressed. Such a miserable state may prompt you to call a doctor to relieve your physical ills and a friend to relieve your depression. The internal stimuli in this situation have resulted in communication.

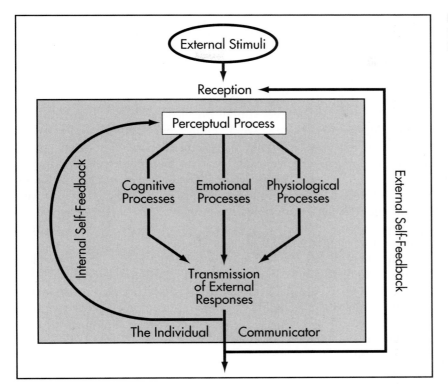

FIGURE 4.3
Intrapersonal Processes

External Stimuli

External stimuli are, of course, those stimuli that originate in the environment outside of your body. There are two kinds of external stimuli. *Overt stimuli* are received on the conscious level. They are picked up by the sensory organs and then sent to the brain. More than one overt stimulus usually affects a person at any given moment. For example, the pizza being advertised on TV and the sounds and aromas coming from the kitchen can prompt an eager, "What's for dinner?"

Covert stimuli are external stimuli that are received on the subconscious level. Let's say you are getting dressed for school. One of your favorite songs comes on the radio, so you turn the volume up. The song ends and the news begins, just as you discover a gaping hole in your sock. You find another pair and finish dressing, but you are running late. Is it too cold for your lightweight jacket? You suddenly realize that the weather report has just ended, but you have no idea what was said, despite the blaring volume.

The stimulus of the weather report was received and stored in your brain, but it was below the *threshold of consciousness*. Thus, you were not consciously aware of *what* was said, even though you recognized that you were hearing the weather report. Such covert stimuli have been shown to affect behavior and communication. Subliminal presentations of the words, "Drink Pepsi" can indeed make a movie-goer feel thirsty.

Reception

The process by which the body receives stimuli is called *reception.* From an intrapersonal processing perspective, both external and internal receptors send information to the central nervous system. External receptors for the five senses—sight, sound, smell, taste, and touch—receive stimuli that are changed into nerve impulses and then sent to the brain. These external receptors are located on or near the body's surface and react to physical, chemical, and mechanical stimuli to provide you with information about the environment. Internal receptors such as nerve endings, on the other hand, convey information about your interior state—the dryness of your mouth or the fullness of your stomach, for example.

Although your body receives every stimulus present in a particular communication setting, you could not possibly communicate in response to every one of them. The process that helps you to cope with this jumble of stimuli is called *selective perception,* the screening out of a huge number of stimuli present in your environment, which permits attention to just a few. What determines which stimuli we do perceive? The main factor is *intensity:* Loud sounds, bright colors, sharp smells, and so forth are often perceived when less intense stimuli are not.

Processing

Processing of internal and external stimuli occurs at three levels: cognitive, emotional, and physiological. At each level of processing, some stimuli receive more conscious attention than others. This attention is a function of the particular stimulus and of the context in which it is presented. Some stimuli are perceived with full awareness (traffic lights, sirens, TV programs), while others may not be consciously noticed (background noise during a lecture, the hum of fluorescent lights in a room). Stimuli that are perceived consciously, or at least with some awareness, are the first to be processed. Stimuli that are perceived subconsciously are usually "stored" in your memory for later processing.

COGNITIVE PROCESSING. *Cognitive processes* are associated with the storage, retrieval, sorting, and assimilation of information. We don't know exactly how such processing occurs; our goal here is simply to describe these processes on both the conscious and subconscious cognitive levels.

Memory. The storage of information that we choose to remember is called *memory.* There are three forms of memory: (1) sensory storage, in which the information is held for only an instant; (2) short-term memory, in which the information is stored for several seconds; and (3) long-term memory, in which the information is stored indefinitely. *Sensory storage* refers to our ability to hold some information for a fraction of a second after the stimulus disappears. For example, you are unaware of the gaps between frames when you watch a movie because each frame is held in sensory storage until the next appears. The major difference between sensory storage and *short-term memory* is that in the latter, data are analyzed, identified, and simplified so that they can be conveniently stored and handled. Short-term memory is a kind of "holding device" in which you keep information until you are ready to use or discard it. If such information seems useful, you may transfer it to the permanent storage of *long-term memory* for future reference.

Retrieval. Information is stored so that it can be used to help establish the meaning of later incoming stimuli. However, stored information is relatively useless unless it can be retrieved from memory. Such *retrieval* takes the form of either recognition or recall. *Recognition* involves awareness that certain information is familiar, having been experienced previously. *Recall* is more difficult, in that it requires reconstruction of the information that has been stored. For example, while we may recognize a certain word whose meaning we looked up last week, we may be unable to recall its definition.

Sorting. Your brain processes countless bits and pieces of information. In any particular processing situation, you must first select or *sort* the most relevant information from your entire storehouse of knowledge. Here again we know very little about the actual workings of our individual selection systems. We do know, however, that such selection processes occur. For example, when we read, we sort the letters until we are able to make words of them.

Assimilation. Cognitive processing is not simply the sum of memory storage, retrieval, and sorting functions. Rather, it involves *assimilation,* the process of incorporating some aspect of the environment into the whole set of mental functionings in order to make sense out of what goes on around us. To continue our reading example, your ability to read was first learned, then stored in long-term memory. Whenever you open a book or view a computer screen, you retrieve this information, use it to sort the letters on the page (or screen) into words, and then assimilate the words into sentences and ideas that have meaning for you.

EMOTIONAL PROCESSING. As mentioned at the beginning of this section, intrapersonal processing also involves *emotional processing,* or the nonlogical response of an organism to a stimulus. Variables, ranging from attitudes and beliefs to opinions and emotions interact to determine our response to any particular communication.

PHYSIOLOGICAL PROCESSING. The third type of processing occurs at the physiological level. Although *physiological processing* is of obvious importance in staying alive, its significance to communication is only beginning to be recognized. Some of the subconscious variables in this process are heart rate, brain activity, muscle tension, blood pressure, and body temperature.

Brain wave activity has been given considerable attention by researchers as an aid in monitoring information processing. Have you ever wondered what parts of your brain process certain types of information? Research with an electroencephalograph (EEG) suggests that we alternate between our right- and left-brain hemispheres to process stimuli (Sellers & Stacks, 1990). Generally, if you are working on a carburetor, following a recipe, or working on a computer, you will be using your left hemisphere. The left hemisphere processes information logically and is concerned with speech and with mathematical and analytical tasks. The right hemisphere, in contrast, processes information abstractly and is involved with imagery and with spatial, musical, and *gestalt* (viewing an object or event as a whole rather than looking at its individual components) tasks. When you listen to your favorite CD, draw a sidewalk chalk picture, or imagine how a date will go, you are using the right hemisphere of your brain.

Monitoring physiological variables makes it possible to control internal processes. First, we must be aware of what our states are. Awareness is much more developed in some people than in others. For most people, conscious physiological awareness is limited to sensations of pleasure, pain, tension, and relaxation. Some people use *biofeedback,* a form of external self-feedback, to help themselves become more aware of their physiological processing. Subjects are attached to instruments that provide information about physiological parameters such as pulse rate, muscle tension, and skin temperature. In some manner, this information helps individuals to alter these levels. For example, biofeedback has been used to teach control of bodily functions such as heart rate, blood pressure, and seizures. In addition, through the power of positive imagining, biofeedback has been shown to create confidence, increase self-control, and establish enhanced and peak performance in athletic, educational, and psychophysiological endeavors (Norris, 1986).

Transmission

The process by which messages are sent from a source to a receiver is called *transmission.* In intrapersonal communication, the source and the receiver are the same person. Thus, transmission takes place through nerve impulses in the brain rather than through sound waves in the air or words written on a page. The intrapersonal communication cycle is completed when the brain reacts to these nerve impulses by transmitting a message to smooth muscles, which regulate the movements of the body. Putting a hand on a hot pan causes the individual's touch receptors to send a neural transmission to the brain, saying, "It's hot," which causes the brain to transmit a message to the muscles in the hand, ordering, "Move away from the pan immediately."

Feedback

We usually think of feedback as information from another person. In intrapersonal communication, however, there are two kinds of *self-feedback*—external and internal.

External self-feedback is the part of your message that you hear yourself. This kind of feedback enables you to correct your own mistakes. For example, you would surely backtrack if you heard yourself say something like "external felf-seedback."

Internal self-feedback is usually picked up through bone conduction, nerve endings, or muscular movement. For example, you might perceive an awkward facial gesture without actually seeing it—simply by feeling the muscle tension in your face. Again, perceiving this information enables you to correct yourself.

Interference

Interference is another important variable in the communication process. *Interference* refers to any factor that negatively affects communication. It can occur at any point along the communication network and at any level of communication. For example, the blast of your roommate's DVD or a splitting headache might make it impossible for you to read.

A special form of interference occurs intrapersonally when stimuli are processed at one level, although another level is better suited to dealing with them. For example, many people react emotionally to information that should be processed on a cognitive level. Have you ever started crying or gotten angry in response to a teacher's comments on your paper, when if you had remained calm, you might have been able to analyze and profit from the information? On the other hand, some individuals insist on processing information on the cognitive level when an emotional response would actually be more helpful. Often a good cry can relieve the pressure of a bad day better than a careful rehash of the day's events.

The Effects of Intrapersonal Variables on Communication

Even though a particular message may focus on the here and now, your personality and past experience influence your interpretation of it. Thus, it is important to consider the intrapersonal factors that influence communicators. For example, the experiences of someone who has recently lost a close friend will no doubt affect that person's communication on the subject of death.

Personal Orientation

The way you react to the following situation will be determined by your personal orientation.

Warren and Jerry are interviewing for the job of advertising copywriter in a large advertising agency. Neither of them has had any experience, but both come to the interview prepared to show samples of the kind of work they are capable of producing. Jerry's samples represent many hours of hard work and a little talent, while Warren's show much talent but very little effort—he lifted them almost word for word from a textbook.

Self-feedback helps us to correct mistakes.

How do you feel about Jerry and War-ren? Do you respect Jerry for his honesty and hard work, or do you appreciate Warren's craftiness in trying to get the kind of job he wants? Your reaction to this situation reflects the values, attitudes, beliefs, and opinions that make up your personal orientation.

VALUES.   Each of us maintains a set of *values*—moral or ethical judgments of things we consider important. Values can be a source of conflict within an individual as well as a barrier between people of opposing standards. Fearing a malpractice suit, for instance, a doctor who comes upon an accident victim may be reluctant to offer assistance. The doctor's values will determine what action is taken. Sometimes an individual will voice one set of values and be guided by another. For example, parents may scold their children for dishonesty but think nothing of cheating on their income tax.

ATTITUDES.   An *attitude* is a learned tendency to react positively or negatively to an object or situation. It implies a positive or negative evaluation of someone or something. Attitudes operate at three different levels: (1) cognitive, (2) affective, and (3) instrumental. The cognitive level involves a particular belief, the affective level involves a particular feeling, and the instrumental level involves overt behavior or action.

Let's examine a specific situation. Carlotta Ramirez, a member of the state board of higher education, is a strong opponent of free tuition. Her negative attitude toward the topic can be broken down in this way:

1. *Cognitive (belief):* People who value a college education should be willing to pay for it, even if it means going to work to get enough money for tuition.

2. *Affective (feeling):* People who try to get something for nothing make me angry.

3. *Instrumental (action):* I vote no on the proposal for free tuition at state universities.

BELIEFS, OPINIONS, AND PREJUDICES.   A *belief* is anything accepted as true. Note that this definition does not imply either a positive or negative judgment. For example, you may believe that there is life on other planets, yet this belief does not indicate a positive or negative attitude toward that idea. However, if you were to take your belief one step further to say that since you believe there is life on other planets, it would be in our best interests to increase space exploration programs, you would then be voicing an *opinion.* An opinion lies somewhere between an attitude

Our attitudes, beliefs, opinions, and prejudices influence our communication with others.

and a belief. It implies a positive or negative reaction.

Not all our beliefs and opinions are well founded. Sometimes they are based on preconceived ideas and not on our own actual experiences. In this case they are, in fact, *prejudices*—preformed judgments about a particular person, group, or thing. None of us is free from prejudice, but certain prejudices are more harmful than others. Think for a moment about your own experiences with prejudice, when you were either guilty of prejudice or were its victim. Or consider this example of how foolish our prejudices can be:

Although it was against her principles, Ruth had agreed to help a good friend out of a tight spot by accepting a blind date with the friend's cousin from Louisiana. Ruth, who had never been south of Philadelphia, just knew that an evening spent with this hick was going to be one of the most boring of her life.

He arrived, and, sure enough, his accent was unlike anything Ruth had ever heard. By evening's end, however, she had changed her mind. Full of admiration for the most interesting and beautifully mannered man she had ever met, Ruth eagerly awaited their next date.

He never called again. A few weeks later, Ruth learned from her friend that he had returned to New Orleans and, before leaving, had announced: "All Yankee women are alike—hard to please!"

Think about the groups toward which you may be prejudiced. Does this example suggest ways in which you may be oversimplifying to the point of prejudice?

Personality Traits

Personality *traits* are those qualities that distinguish one personality from another. As the following examples indicate, some personality traits aid communication, but many are barriers to communication.

LOCUS OF CONTROL. One important personality trait that affects the communication process is *locus of control*. Locus of control can be internal, or perceiving reinforcement as contingent upon our own efforts or actions. External locus of control is perceiving reinforcement as a result of forces beyond our control and due to chance, fate, or situational contingencies (Canary, Cunningham, & Cody, 1988). A difference in communication patterns emerges for those who believe that they control events and those who believe that their desired outcomes are affected by the beliefs, desires, or attitudes of people who have power over them. The former person, with a more internal locus of control, would be more straightforward upon presenting new plans to an upper-level supervisor, while the latter person's communication (the person with an external locus of control) would be more indirect, vague, and ambiguous.

MANIPULATION.   Related to the locus of control that a person exhibits is the degree to which he or she attempts to manipulate others. People vary with regard to the characteristic of *manipulation,* or the degree to which they attempt to achieve goals by dominating and controlling others. However, research has shown that people who have an external locus of control (that is, who believe that the world is ordered and controlled by others) often desire that control for themselves and tend to exhibit greater manipulative behaviors than do people who have an internal locus of control. People with an internal locus of control believe that they control their own fates, and do not generally manifest excessive degrees of manipulation.

DOGMATISM.   One of the most difficult personality traits encountered in a communication situation is *dogmatism.* Dogmatic individuals have closed minds and are reluctant to accept new ideas and opinions. Yet they may accept without question the word of certain authorities and expect the same kind of blind acceptance from those they consider their inferiors. Dogmatic individuals often remain steadfast to ideas or opinions in spite of contradictory evidence.

TOLERANCE OF AMBIGUITY.   While some people can live with shades of gray, others insist on things being clearly defined and unambiguous. This varying *tolerance of ambiguity* frequently affects the communication process. Consider the following example:

> Ahmed and Rita go to the theater to see *Miss Saigon.* After the play, both agree that the production was extremely well done. However, Ahmed is bothered by several inconsistencies that Rita didn't seem to notice. Ahmed points out three areas in the script that he thought were ambiguous. When he asks Rita what she thinks, Rita admits that she can't explain the confusing aspects of the play.

Rita's tolerance of ambiguity is greater than Ahmed's. Rita was able to ignore the ambiguities, while Ahmed found them troublesome. Perhaps you have experienced a similar situation when reading a complex book or when trying to analyze a particular communication interaction.

SELF-ESTEEM.   Communication is also affected by the self-esteem of the sender and the receiver. *Self-esteem,* which is your enduring evaluation of yourself, often determines your confidence in what you are saying and your readiness to accept the view of others. Therefore, in the communication process, it is important to use your perception of another person's self-esteem as a means of evaluating certain messages. For example, individuals with high self-esteem may state an opinion confidently even without sufficient evidence. You might be quicker to question their veracity than that of speakers whose low self-esteem would prevent them from supporting unproven viewpoints.

MATURITY.   Of the many personality variables, the one that most strongly affects communication is level of *maturity.* It is difficult to pinpoint the stage at which a person matures psychologically, but we usually judge a person as mature when he or she is able to function independently in a social setting. One measure of such maturity is the individual's ability to satisfy psychological needs for things such as independence, approval, affection, and so forth. What this means in a communication setting is the absence of intrapersonal conflicts that might intrude on objective transmission and interpretation of messages.

Defense Mechanisms

We all suffer from varying degrees of anxiety. For most of us, anxiety stems from intrapersonal conflicts—conflicts between inner psychological needs and external realities. If severe enough, anxiety can distort your perception of yourself and your environment and thus act as a barrier to communication with others.

The self must find various ways to resolve the anxiety produced by such intrapersonal conflict. These methods, known as *defense mechanisms,* help us accept things that might otherwise cause emotional pain. Defense mechanisms, when used in moderation, aid our personal adjustment to the environment. If used to excess, however, they can become a crutch that distorts reality.

RATIONALIZATION.   Defense mechanisms take many forms. Perhaps the best known is *rationalization,* an attempt to justify our failures or inadequacies. Most of us rationalize from time to time. For example, when Regina was not hired for a job she wanted very badly, she rationalized her failure by claiming that the man who would have been her boss was threatened by her abilities. Pedro rationalized his rejection by a vet school by telling everyone that he really didn't want to go anyway.

PROJECTION.   Sometimes we ignore certain traits, motives, or behaviors in ourselves and attribute them to others. This defense mechanism is known as *projection.* Eleanor, who has a weight problem and is constantly dieting, goes to lunch with her friend Tatiana, a perfect size 8. When the women finish eating, Eleanor remarks, "I can tell you're still hungry." Actually, Tatiana is quite full. It is Eleanor who is still hungry.

INSULATION.   One way to resolve conflicts caused by contradictions is to isolate contradictory feelings and information. This defense mechanism is known as *insulation.* For example, a member of a radical group who protests abortions by killing

Increasing self-awareness is a key to successful communication.

the clinic doctor has clearly insulated contradictory behaviors. This person is able to oppose "murder" on the one hand and commit "murder" on the other.

REACTION FORMATION.   Sometimes people deal with "undesirable" urges or behaviors with a defense mechanism known as *reaction formation.* This process involves denial of what you or society consider unacceptable feelings or behaviors, coupled with extreme advocacy of the opposite position. For example, someone who is easily aroused by pictures of nudes may deny this tendency by becoming an outspoken opponent of pornography.

IDENTIFICATION.   We have discussed the importance of identification in developing self-concept. The *identification* process can also be used as a defense mechanism against insecurity or inadequacy. Thus, adolescents, who often feel uncertain about themselves, may seek security by identifying themselves with stars of the entertainment or sports worlds. Such identification accounts for much of the popularity of personalities such as Dr. Dre, Madonna, Eminem, and Michael Jordan.

REPRESSION.   Some people deal with unpleasant or unacceptable feelings, desires, or experiences by repressing them. *Repression* is a defense mechanism that keeps certain thoughts and feelings beneath the conscious level. Thus, children brought up in overly strict homes, where outbursts are severely punished, often learn to repress anger.

Awareness and You

One way to improve your communication effectiveness is to increase your knowledge and understanding about the topics we've discussed in this chapter. (By study-

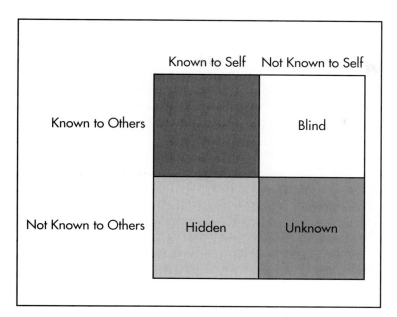

FIGURE 4.4 The Johari Window

ing the chapter, you will have achieved that goal.) Another way is to increase your *self-awareness,* or the extent to which you are cognizant of (and open to) incoming information about yourself and the world around you. To aid communicators in achieving this goal, Joseph Luft and Harrington Ingham developed the Johari Window, which compares aspects of open versus closed communication relationships (Luft, 1969). (See Figure 4.4.)

The "open" section in the diagram represents self-knowledge that you are aware of and are willing to share with others. The "hidden" section represents what you are aware of but are not willing to share. The "blind" section represents information of which you yourself are unaware but which is known to others. The "unknown" section represents what is unknown both to you and to others.

Although each section of the Johari Window is conceptually the same size in Figure 4.4, in "real-life" situations different proportions would be drawn for each relationship that you are in, depending on the amount of information that you share with that individual. In a close relationship, for example, your open area might be considerably larger than the hidden area. When communicating with a casual acquaintance, your hidden area would be the largest part of the window.

Let us see how this window applies to a particular communication situation:

Linda and Tony are reunited after a two-month separation. Linda lets Tony know how much she missed him (open), but does not tell him that she has started to date someone new (hidden). Tony senses that Linda is upset, although she claims that she is fine (blind). The unknown in this situation is a whole range of feelings that are not clear to either of them. For example, both individuals are probably unsure about Linda's feelings toward Tony.

Again, you can use the concept of the Johari Window to increase your self-awareness. This, in turn, should improve your communication with others. As you strive to shrink the blind and unknown segments, you may begin to discover a self you only partially knew before, a self that may or may not resemble the concept you've always had about that person you call "me." The more information you can bring into the open from the hidden, blind, and unknown areas, the better your interpersonal communication will be.

Summary

Listening is an active process involving five distinct, hierarchical steps: attending, perceiving, interpreting, assessing, and responding. For successful communication to take place, listeners and speakers must take mutual responsibility for the outcome. Five dimensions of listening also have been identified by researchers: cognitive; affective; behavioral/verbal; behavioral/nonverbal; and behavioral/interactive. We also have one or more listening preferences, depending on the type of information we prefer. The four listening preferences are content-, action-, people-, and time-oriented. Listening skills can be improved. Six important strategies to use to improve listening include focusing, tracking, reflecting, digging, dampening, and redirecting.

The most basic level of communication is intrapersonal, involving the sending and receiving of messages within one individual. This is the level on which you communicate with yourself. At the same time, internal and external stimuli affect the cognitive, emotional, and physiological processing of communication.

An individual's intrapersonal processes must be considered in any analysis of interpersonal communication situations. For example, personality variables such as manipulation, locus of control, dogmatism, tolerance for ambiguity, self-esteem, and maturity—and personal orientations, values, attitudes, and beliefs—all intrude on the objective sending and interpreting of interpersonal messages. Communication is further hampered by the many defense mechanisms that people use to minimize anxiety.

One way to improve your communication skills is to increase your self-awareness. The Jahari Window provides an excellent vehicle for exploring your open, hidden, blind, and unknown areas of the self.

Exercises

GROUP EXPERIENCES
Do You Really Understand What I Am Saying?

DESCRIPTION   We use the word *understand* very loosely. Most of the time we mean that we are "hearing" something and translating it into the way we perceive the world—and then we call this phenomenon "understanding." The following experience is an opportunity to see how well you understand another person and how well he or she understands you.

PROCEDURE   Divide into groups of three. Persons A and B should discuss an issue they find controversial. Person C should observe the interaction and report on it after the exercise is completed. After each communication between Person A and Person B, the listening partner should attempt to paraphrase the speaker's position until the speaker accepts the paraphrase. An example of this interaction would be as follows:

Person A: I think that war is a waste in general. On the other hand, George Kennan claims that war can clear the path for a new form of government to emerge.

Person B: What I heard you say is that war isn't bad as long as it serves to clear the way for better forms of government.

Person A: I will not accept your paraphrase.

This process will continue until Person B provides an acceptable paraphrase for Person A. The person doing the paraphrasing should try to use different words than those of the speaker. The interaction should take from 15 to 20 minutes. At the end of that time, Person C should offer an appraisal of what occurred.

DISCUSSION   When you have completed this activity, ask yourself these questions: How long did it take you to provide accurate paraphrases for your partner? How long did it take your partner to provide accurate paraphrases of your position? Was your verbal message clear? What are the implications of this activity? Does it suggest that most of the time we do not truly understand what another person is saying?

Did You See What I Saw?

DESCRIPTION   Our psychological makeup causes us to attend selectively to different stimuli, but we do not necessarily select the same stimuli as another person. We truly see the world through our own set of filters. The following activity demonstrates this idea.

PROCEDURE   Have one person arrange approximately 30 different items on a tray, such as a can opener, a lipstick, a pen, a paperclip, and so on. Include (1) items that most people would not know the name of, such as a special tool; (2) items that are typically used by one sex as opposed to the other (pipe, lipstick); and (3) items that are "taboo," such as underwear, a sanitary napkin, and so on.

Each individual may take 20 seconds to look at (not touch) the items on the tray. Immediately after you view the tray, try to list everything you saw. (Afterwards you may wish to check your list against a complete list of the items on the tray.)

DISCUSSION   The most obvious finding of this experiment is that people will remember different things. Were the first five items you remembered different from the first five items others remembered? Did you remember the "male" items? the "female" items? Did you attempt to describe the items for which you did not have a particular name? By comparison, did you remember more, less, or the same number of items as other people did? Do you selectively attend in listening as well as in seeing?

Silence Is Golden

DESCRIPTION   Most of us are poor listeners. We are usually thinking about what we want to say rather than about what the other person is saying. Try the following experiment, and check out your own listening behavior.

PROCEDURE   Divide into dyads (groups of two). Person A should begin the conversation by describing a peak experience—a high point in his or her life. Person A should talk in short stretches, no more than 30 seconds at a time.

Person B must then wait 10 seconds before continuing the conversation. Person B should either respond to A or describe a peak experience of his or her own. The same guidelines of length applies to Person B.

This process continues with each person waiting 10 seconds before speaking.

DISCUSSION   Does it feel awkward to wait before talking? At which point in listening do you begin to think about what you are going to say? Do you usually try to avoid these silent spaces? By the way, are you a good listener?

PERSONAL EXPERIENCES

1. Sit in a public area, such as a pizza pub, bus station, or park, and close your eyes for 10 minutes. Listen to the different sounds around you and try to determine what you are hearing. Would you normally be hearing these sounds if you had your eyes open? How aware are you of different sounds? Do you selectively listen during everyday activities?

2. Observe yourself during a class of your choice—particularly one in which there is a lecture presentation. Watch the number of times your attention wanders—and for how long.

3. Keep a diary for a week. At the end of each day, record the feelings you experienced during the day. For example, you might write that you felt angry for most of the morning, but by the end of the day you felt very calm. At the end of the week, reread your log to determine if (a) you have experienced highly intense feelings that may properly be called emotions and (b) if those feelings were predominantly positive or negative. How does your inner world of feelings affect your communication with others?

Discussion Questions

1. How do we distinguish *listening* from *hearing?*
2. What qualities does a good listener possess?
3. To what extent can you achieve effective communication with another person without understanding his or her values, attitudes, and beliefs?
4. How do you use the various defense mechanisms in your daily activities?
5. How would you draw the Johari Window for (a) an intimate relationship, (b) a casual relationship, and (c) an initial interaction with another person? Remember that you can change the proportions of any square.

References

Barker, L. L., Johnson, P. M., & Watson, K. W. (1991). The role of listening in managing interpersonal and group conflict. In D. Borisoff & M. Purdy (Eds.), *Listening in everyday life* (139–162). New York: University Press of America.

Canary, D. J., Cunningham, E. M., & Cody, M. J. (1988, August). Goal types, gender, and locus of control in managing interpersonal conflict. *Communication Research, 15*(4), 430.

Halone, K. K., Cunconan, T. M., Coakley, C. G., & Wolvin, A. D. (1998). Toward the establishment of general dimensions underlying the listening process. *International Journal of Listening, 12,* 12–28.

Luft, J. (1969). *Of human interaction.* Palo Alto, CA: National Press Books.

Nayak, P. Ranganath, & Ketteringham, J. M. (1986). Tagamet: Repairing ulcers without surgery. In *Breakthroughs: How the vision and drive of innovators in sixteen companies created commercial breakthroughs that swept the world* (102, 129). New York: Rawson Associates.

Norris, P. (1986). Biofeedback, voluntary control, and human potential. *Biofeedback and Self-Regulation, 11*(1), 1–20.

Sargent, S. L., Fitch-Hauser, M., & Weaver, J. B., III. (1997). A listening styles profile of the type-A personality. *International Journal of Listening, 11,* 1–14.

Sellers, D. E., & Stacks, D. W. (1990). Toward a hemispheric processing approach to communication competence. *Journal of Social Behavior and Personality, 5*(2), 45–59.

Watson, K. W., & Barker, L. L. (1992). *Personal listening preference profile.* New Orleans, LA: SPECTRA, Inc.

5

Interpersonal Communication

key concepts and terms

Interpersonal communication
Dyad
Functional communication
  theory
Linking function
Mentation function
Regulatory function
Dominance
Affiliation
Involvement
Coordinated management
  of meaning theory

Constitutive rule
Regulative rule
Self-disclosure
Trust
Feedback
Feedforward
Attraction
Initiating
Experimenting
Intensifying
Integrating
Bonding

Differentiating
Circumscribing
Stagnating
Avoiding
Terminating
Alternating monologue
Stimulus—response
  interaction
Interaction with feedback
Interaction with empathy
Conflict management

From:	"Jae"
To:	"Matt" <sandertx@futurenet.ab.net>
Sent:	Tuesday, November 20 1:30PM
Subject:	American girls

Just had lunch with Stephanie. You will never believe what she wants to fight about now! Remember I told you she invited me to meet her parents last weekend? Now she says I must not really care about her, or—get this—I wouldn't have wanted to "spend more time with her parents than I did with her." How could she ever think that?

I love this country, Matt. The freedom is incredible. What I don't understand is the lack of respect that American kids have for their elders. In Japan, I learned to be respectful of people who are even a couple of years older than I am. Even more so my parents (and the parents of someone I care about). I just don't know if this relationship is going to work, but I'm crazy about her, Matt. Any advice you could offer at this moment would be more than appreciated.

—Jae

When was the last time you had an argument with someone you loved? What was the topic of communication that drove the conflict? What role did talking with a good friend like Matt in the e-mail message above play in helping you to deal with the conflict? All of us have had moments like Jae's when we felt frustrated and confused. Love relationships are difficult sometimes, and talking with others can help us sort things out. At times like these, we feel the need to reach out to others and to share our feelings and ideas. This sharing of experiences—both positive and negative—is known as *interpersonal communication.* It is the extension of ourselves to other people and their extensions toward us.

An Interpersonal Communication Model

Interpersonal communication can occur in any environment, be it formal (the lecture hall) or informal (the checkout line), face to face or via the Internet. Most interpersonal messages are informal, however, and stem from everyday, face-to-face encounters. Think of your own communication. From your first "Good morning" to your last "See you tomorrow," your interpersonal communication is usually spontaneous, unplanned, and loosely organized, probably even ungrammatical. With the exception of telephone and Internet conversations, most of this communication involves people close enough to see and touch each other. This makes sending and receiving messages much easier and eliminates the need for the kind of formal rules followed in business meetings, debates, news conferences, or other public speaking situations.

Dyadic Versus Small Group Communication

Most interpersonal communication involves a *dyad,* or two people in close contact. As a result, the potential for sending, receiving, and evaluating messages is divided between the two halves of the dyad (see Figure 5.1). That is, both participants alternate from one role to the other—sometimes originating messages, at other times responding to them. Both roles provide a means for exchanging information, but neither is complete in itself; if one participant only listened, and the other only spoke, communication would soon break down. Thus, communication in a dyad is very much a shared responsibility. This equally shared responsibility differentiates a dyad from a small group. In small groups, the balance of communication shifts. Because each participant has a different role and status in the group, the potential for sending and receiving messages is not evenly divided. Furthermore, group members not only serve as sources or destinations of messages, but they also function as channels to relay the messages of others.

Another difference between interpersonal and group communication is purpose. Many groups are problem-centered; that is, members are working together for a defined purpose, usually decision making or problem solving. In contrast, interpersonal communication in dyads focuses on the *sharing of meaning.* Although interpersonal dyads may also solve problems or make decisions, their messages convey a wider range of feelings and emotions. The information they exchange is not just the dry, factual material common in a sales meeting, for example. Rather, it consists of meanings derived from personal experiences and observations. These interpersonal messages have a significant psychological impact: The process of translating thoughts into verbal and nonverbal messages increases a sender's awareness of his or her feelings and self-concept. In turn, the listener's responses confirm or alter these feelings. With effective interpersonal communication, this process becomes reciprocal; both participants strengthen themselves and each other through the sharing of the meanings and emotions.

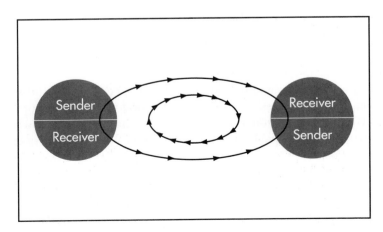

FIGURE 5.1 Dyadic Communication

This chapter will focus on various interpersonal communication theories as well as on variables that affect interpersonal relationships. A variety of factors affect interpersonal relationships, including time, physical, social, cultural, emotional, and intellectual factors. Additionally, we will examine the growth and decline of interpersonal relationships and discuss how we can more effectively manage interpersonal communication. By the time you have completed this chapter, we hope you will have taken the time to examine your own interpersonal behaviors. Such self-analysis is critical to the development and maintenance of healthy interpersonal relationships.

Theories of Interpersonal Communication

Interpersonal communication may be viewed in a variety of ways, each of which can help us to better understand the overall communication process. Although the study of interpersonal communication may seem relatively straightforward when you first consider it, perusal of the many different approaches to its study reveals the true complexity of the subject. For example, some communication theorists are interested in the functions of interpersonal communication, while others focus solely on dimensions of interpersonal relationships. Still other communication specialists are interested in how meanings are created and interpreted, while others address variables that affect interpersonal communication.

To introduce you to the study of interpersonal communication, the following sections will focus on three specific theories of interpersonal communication: functional communication theory, which addresses the functions of interpersonal communication; relational communication theory, which focuses on dimensions of interpersonal relationships; and the theory of the coordinated management of meaning. This final theory addresses meanings in interpersonal relationships and the rules through which we construct interpersonal communication.

Functional Communication Theory

According to the *functional communication theory,* we use interpersonal communication for a variety of reasons. For example, through interpersonal communication, we are better able to understand our world. Talking through a problem with a friend or business associate in order to better understand a situation is an illustration of this function. At other times, we communicate interpersonally in order to think and evaluate more effectively. For example, when managers ask for input from their staffs in order to help make more informed decisions, they are illustrating another interpersonal function. We also communicate interpersonally in order to change behavior in some way, whether that behavior is our own or someone else's.

As we mentioned in Chapter 1, for communication specialists Frank Dance and Carl Larson (1976), interpersonal communication serves precisely these three functions. More specifically, it (1) provides a *linking function* between a person and his or her environment; (2) allows us to conceptualize, remember, and plan, each a part of the *mentation function;* and (3) serves to regulate our own and others' behavior, the *regulatory function.*

To illustrate the importance of these three functions, first imagine a world in which communication would not allow you to relate to the outside world, but instead would only let you communicate with yourself—intrapersonally. Then imagine a world in which you could not relate to other people. Not only would a world such as this be a very lonely place in which to live, but you also would probably be unable to survive for much longer than an hour. Through interpersonal communication, we are nurtured as infants—physically, emotionally, and intellectually. In addition, we develop cultural, social, and psychological ties with the world through interpersonal communication. In short, interpersonal interactions allow us to *function* more practically in life.

Relational Communication Theory

Based on more than 65 years of research in psychology and communication, researchers believe that there are three important dimensions of every interpersonal relationship: dominance, affiliation, and involvement.

According to interpersonal experts James Dillard, Denise Solomon, and Mark Palmer (1999), *dominance* is "the degree to which one [person] attempts to regulate the behavior of another" (p. 53). As such, dominance is associated with attempts to control another person's behavior and ultimately the course of the relationship. In Jae's e-mail to Matt at the beginning of this chapter, Jae provided a perfect example of an attempt by Stephanie to establish relational dominance. By complaining that "he must not care about her" or else he wouldn't have spent so much time with her parents, Stephanie was using emotional blackmail to control both the relationship and Jae's future behavior. (Note: Jae was focused more on cultural than interpersonal aspects of their relationship and didn't notice this dimension of her message . . . yet.)

The second dimension of interpersonal relationships, *affiliation,* is associated with the feelings of regard that we have for another person. Such feelings range from liking to respect, and are associated with the amount of solidarity we perceive to exist in a relationship. To illustrate, take a moment to reread Jae's e-mail. To what extent would you guess that Jae and Stephanie were experiencing similar levels of affiliation? We could surmise that Jae is experiencing greater liking and respect for Stephanie than she is for him. If such a difference in their affiliation levels indeed exists, the couple will have to overcome more than cultural differences in order for their relationship to grow.

Affecting both our perceptions of dominance and affiliation in a relationship is our level of involvement with the person in question. *Involvement* is associated with the level of intensity we are experiencing in a relationship, as reflected in how attentive or distracted, interested or indifferent, and "involved" or "uninvolved" two friends or partners are when it comes to their behavior. According to Dillard and his colleagues, involvement drives both the amount of dominance and affiliation (or liking) that are reflected in the relationship. If you think about Jae and

Stephanie's situation, Dillard's argument makes perfect sense. While Jae perceived that he was acting appropriately when he was visiting with Stephanie's parents, she perceived that he was being inattentive and disinterested. In response, her feelings of affiliation (may have) decreased, and her need to dominate Jae and their relationship increased.

As you can see, relational theorists offer us a lot when it comes to a better understanding of the nature and dimensions of interpersonal relationships. We now turn to a third theory that offers us some unique insights: the coordinated management of meaning.

The Theory of Coordinated Management of Meaning

Unlike the two theories of interpersonal communication we have already addressed, the *coordinated management of meaning theory,* CMM for short, is a meaning-centered theory of communication. In other words, its primary focus is on meanings in interpersonal communication, and on how we coordinate and manage meanings in everyday life.

Perhaps one of the most compelling arguments that CMM theorists make is that all communication is best viewed as the coordination of rules for interacting with others (Pearce & Cronen, 1980). For example, if we were to meet for the first time, we both would bring to that initial meeting certain rules about interactions. To illustrate, my rules might include the following:

1. When meeting someone for the first time, I should smile and say, "hello."

2. When meeting another person, it is generally considered polite to shake hands.

3. If I am interested in that person, I should maintain a fair amount of direct eye contact.

In turn, you also might bring these rules to our initial interaction. Once we move through the behaviors that are guided by these rules, however, what should we say to each other next? Should I inquire about your health? Your background? Whether you have read the latest edition of *Communication?* What meanings should I assign to your words and should you assign to mine?

According to Pearce and Cronen, the two primary developers of CMM theory, two sets of rules help to answer these questions and allow us to coordinate the interaction. The first of these rules, or *constitutive rules,* define what a given act or behavior should "count as" and allow us to decide what each other's behavior "means." Using CMM notation, this type of rule could be written something like this:

$$\boxed{\begin{array}{l} \text{initial meeting} \\ \hline \text{smile} \longrightarrow \text{sign of friendliness} \end{array}}$$

Or, "In the context of an initial meeting, a smile may be taken to count as a sign of friendliness." As you can see, the symbol ⌐ simply designates the situation or context, while the arrow → is used to designate what the given behavior (in this instance, a smile) should "count as."

Regulative rules, on the other hand, tell us how we should behave in a given situation. For example, the following regulative rule might apply during our initial interaction:

initial meeting

| other person smiles | ⊃ | I should smile in return |

Or, "In the context of an initial interaction, if the other person smiles, then I should smile in return." At this point, the only unfamiliar symbol in this rule is the symbol ⊃, which says, "If you do *x*, then I should respond with *y*."

Although these examples are exceptionally simple, very complex acts may be described in a similar fashion. In addition, CMM theory allows us to see how these rules actually mesh—in other words, how we actually coordinate meanings. To illustrate this coordinated management of meaning, Figure 5.2 describes a potential sequence that might occur during our (same) initial meeting.

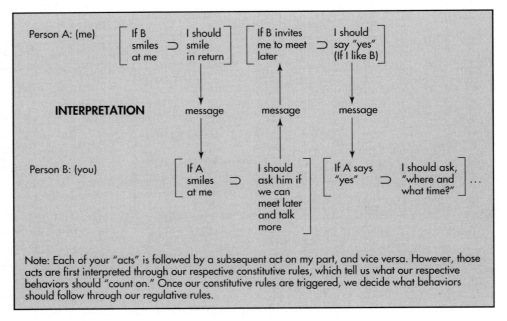

Note: Each of your "acts" is followed by a subsequent act on my part, and vice versa. However, those acts are first interpreted through our respective constitutive rules, which tell us what our respective behaviors should "count on." Once our constitutive rules are triggered, we decide what behaviors should follow through our regulative rules.

FIGURE 5.2 Coordinated Management of Meaning

Source: Adapted from W. B. Pearce and V. Cronen, *Communication, Action, and Meaning* (New York: Praeger, 1980), p. 174.

As you can see, communication indeed may be defined as the coordination of individual rules and the meanings that we attribute to resulting behaviors. In short, for CMM theorists, effective communication is viewed as a function of two components: (1) a mutually shared system of rules and (2) the coordinated management of meanings that results.

Variables Affecting Interpersonal Relationships

We have identified three theories of interpersonal communication in order to show you how communication theorists currently conceptualize interpersonal communication. We hope that this discussion has helped to reveal the complexities associated with interpersonal communication and ways in which you can observe and improve relationships in your own life.

This section will focus on variables that affect interpersonal relationships, including self-disclosure, trust, feedback, nonverbal behavior, and interpersonal attraction. Our success or failure in addressing these variables in our own interpersonal communication determines how satisfying our interpersonal relationships are at a given moment in time.

The uttered part of a man's life, let us always repeat, bears to the unuttered, unconscious part a small unknown proportion. He himself never knows it, much less do others.

THOMAS CARLYLE

Self-Disclosure

Self-disclosure lies at the heart of the process of interpersonal communication. It is the vehicle by which others know what is going on inside us, what we are thinking and feeling, and what we care about. In addition, appropriate self-disclosure can reduce anxiety, increase comfort, intensify interpersonal attraction (Lazowski & Andersen, 1990), and increase marital satisfaction (Finkenauer & Hazam, 2000).

Knowing these facts will not always make self-disclosure any easier. For example, how do we know whether or not a given self-disclosure is "appropriate"? Our natural tendency is to hide feelings of incompetence, loneliness, guilt, anxiety over love and rejection, and conflicts based on anger and resentment. According to Hornstein and Truesdell (1988), these feelings are natural and are reflected in the limited number of private and personal disclosures that we make during the early stages of a relationship. However, as the relationship progresses and greater trust is established, we usually begin to share information that is private and personal.

Even when feelings such as anxiety and guilt are not involved in a relationship, self-disclosure may still be difficult because of well-learned habits that help us to avoid emotional pain. We all learn these evasive strategies as part of our socialization process. They are so rewarding that it becomes difficult to know when to put them away. Many people in our society are accustomed to hiding what they really want, think, or feel. For this reason, self-disclosure becomes a rare and valued gift. Confiding in others and receiving their confidences is, therefore, one of the most effective interpersonal communication tools we possess.

Because of the importance of self-disclosure to the development of interpersonal relationships, communication researchers have explored the nature of self-disclosure and its relationship to other important interpersonal concepts. Psychologist Steven Broder (1987) summarized research findings from a number of studies and found that people often reveal personal information in response to another person's disclosure, even when they do not like the other person very much. Such reciprocity plays an important role in social interaction. Additionally, Broder found that we disclose to people whom we like, but also that we like people more when they disclose to us. Thus, liking plays an important role in disclosure. Finally, Broder looked at the trust—disclosure relationship and found that research also documented this relationship. In short, we share intimate aspects of our lives with those whom we trust, despite the personal risk and feelings that accompany being "open." Generally, we do so because expressing ourselves gives us a sense of relief and improved psychological functioning. Despite the fear associated with "getting something off our chests," we self-disclose in order to be closer to people about whom we care.

As Broder's research demonstrates, self-disclosure is a vital component of interpersonal communication. However, the work of these scholars should perhaps be qualified in at least two ways. First, as Caltabiano and Smithson (1983) have noted, self-disclosure should increase in scope and intimacy as a relationship develops, in order for self-disclosure to be seen as appropriate. Second, during the acquaintanceship stage, positive disclosure of information (in contrast to negative disclosure) is seen as more appropriate, with positive disclosures viewed as more adjusted and emotionally stable than negative disclosures.

Trust

Just as self-disclosure affects the nature of interpersonal relationships, so too does trust affect the quality of our interactions. We all have experienced the satisfaction that results from learning that we can trust a new acquaintance. Likewise, we know the importance of being trustworthy in return. According to Rogers-Millar and Millar (1976), both of these trust dimensions must be in operation before interpersonal trust can develop in a relationship. Thus, *trust* may be best defined as an interaction between trusting and trustworthy behaviors. More specifically, it involves (1) an *admission* of dependency on each other by all parties involved, and (2) the *acceptance* of an obligation not to exploit control in the relationship.

As you know, however, trust does not just happen. Trusting another person develops over time. According to Gamble and Gamble (1982, pp. 226–228), trust is established in four major ways:

1. The individuals who are involved must be willing to disclose themselves to the person of interest—trust precipitates trusting behaviors in others.

2. We must be willing to let the other person know he or she is accepted and supported—reducing threats to another's ego increases trust.

3. We must be willing to develop a cooperative rather than a competitive orientation; working to win in a relationship can destroy it.

4. Finally, we should trust people when trusting them is appropriate; taking inappropriate risks can be as destructive as not taking risks at all.

In short, the "bottom line" regarding trust in relationships is threefold. First, trusting others generally encourages their trust in you. Second, you must be cooperative and supportive of the other person. Finally, trusting behavior may be appropriate or inappropriate, depending on the context or situation. Only you can decide when and how to trust another person.

Self-disclosure is vital to healthy interpersonal communication.

The highest compact we can make with our fellow is—"Let there be truth between us two forevermore."

RALPH WALDO EMERSON

Feedback and Feedforward

Another variable that influences interpersonal interactions is the extent to which we share feedback and feedforward with one another. We now turn to a brief discussion of these concepts.

Feedback, a term borrowed from computer technology, originally referred to a self-regulating mechanism that keeps machines running smoothly and efficiently. You provide this feedback by *paraphrasing* (thereby confirming or correcting your understanding of a message), by *asking questions* (thereby demonstrating your interest and your desire for more information), or by *responding with feeling statements* (thereby showing that you care about your partner). The following dialogue illustrates all three of these forms of feedback.

Andy: My trip to Paris last summer was the most interesting experience of my life.

Angelina: You really enjoyed your stay in Paris. What did you like best?

Andy: Well, I lived in a dorm for foreign students, and I got to meet people from all over the world.

Angelina: I can appreciate your pleasure in meeting people from different backgrounds. Two years ago my family hosted an exchange student from Zambia, and I really grew a lot from knowing him.

We often require feedback from others to shape our own behavior. This is especially true in social situations, in which we tend to monitor our own actions to conform to the behavior of the group. Social cues are the feedback that allows us to monitor our behavior. For example, at a party, high self-monitors are acutely aware of their behavior and model the actions of other guests. They talk quietly when others talk quietly, and they laugh at jokes that seem to amuse the other guests. In contrast, low self-monitors disregard this situational feedback and follow their own inclinations. They start dancing while other people are engaged in serious conversation or drink too much when others are drinking very little.

Concern about the ramifications of social feedback also can help (or hinder) you in planning effective communication strategies. For example, how have you communicated with a friend or romantic partner in the past when you were experiencing jealousy in the relationship? According to Laura Guerrero and Walid Afifi (1999), the messages we send in these instances serve important goals or functions: "They can help maintain one's relationship, preserve one's self-esteem, reduce uncertainty about the primary relationship, reduce uncertainty about the rival relationship, re-assess the relationship, [or] restore equity through retaliation" (p. 216).

In response to a written questionnaire distributed by Guerrero and Affifi, 266 respondents who defined their romantic relationships as "exclusive" reported using the following communication strategies when they were experiencing jealousy: (1) negative nonverbal behavior (acting anxious in the presence of their partner and rival, appearing hurt, crying); (2) openly sharing jealous feelings, asking questions, trying to understand; (3) accusing, being sarcastic, yelling, or arguing; (4) giving their partner the "silent treatment" or distancing themselves physically; (5) avoiding or denying jealous feelings; (6) threatening or enacting violent behavior; (7) spying or finding ways to decrease the chances that their partner and the rival could get together; (8) finding ways to improve the primary relationship (e.g., sending flowers or gifts, or attempting to be more attractive); (9) attempting to make their partner feel bad or testing their partner's loyalty; (10) communicating with their rival in an attempt to learn more about or terminate the relationship; and (11) displaying violent behavior toward objects (e.g., breaking dishes, slamming doors, or throwing their partner's possessions out a window or onto the lawn) (Guerrero & Afifi, 1999, p. 222).

How many of these communication strategies have you employed in the past when you were feeling jealous? What goals were you attempting to achieve? Guerrero and Afifi argued that your goals probably predicted your strategies. Thus, creating more effective communication strategies in the future will require greater awareness of the ultimate goals you wish to achieve, and more conscious selection and use of the appropriate strategies through which to achieve your goals.

Nonverbal Behavior

Nonverbal behavior plays a strong, necessary role in interpersonal relationships. So much can be "said" by a smile, hug, or handclasp that words are often not needed.

As we mentioned in Chapter 3, eye behavior is especially important in interpersonal situations. For example, studies have suggested that eye contact between close couples is much greater than that between casually dating couples. Besides showing interest and caring, eye contact also can express hostility or the desire for dominance. Indeed, competing athletes use staring as an aggressive gesture and an indication of their confidence level. In contrast, the avoided glance often signifies submission.

Touching is another important nonverbal factor in interpersonal relationships. Touching usually communicates intimacy: Couples walk down the street with their arms around each other; a father caresses his baby; a child hugs her dog. Touching can also communicate status and power. Ask yourself who would be more likely to use a patronizing pat on the head or an aggressive poke in the chest: professor or student; policeman or detainee; physician or patient; boss or subordinate. Status differences related to gender are also revealed in touching behavior. Who is usually the first to hold the other's hand or to demonstrate physical affection in a male-female relationship? Women have come a long way, but it is still rare for them to make the first move by putting an arm around a date in a dark movie theater.

Interpersonal Attraction

Self-disclosure, trust, appropriate feedback, and nonverbal behavior all work together to increase your interpersonal effectiveness. Interestingly enough, this increased effectiveness somehow improves interpersonal attraction, the "strong vibes," "magnetism," or "invisible force" that somehow draws people together.

Attraction is a positive attitude, movement toward, or liking between two people. What causes this attraction is rarely "love at first sight." Rather, the cause can be found in the complex mix of variables within ourselves and within the other individual. Research indicates that many of the factors that determine attraction relate to interpersonal communication. For example, in their summary of the attraction literature, Neimeyer and Mitchell (1988) discuss several precursors to interpersonal attraction, including the need to feel close to someone, shared preferences for activities (such as athletics, cooking, or travel), physical attractiveness, and attitude similarity. Geographical (physical) proximity and closeness also affect our feelings of attraction and, hence, our interpersonal relationships.

One question that all of us have asked at one time or another is, "Why don't Laura and Isaiah get together? I know they say they're just good friends, but they're made for each other!" If you have ever walked in Laura or Isaiah's shoes, you probably know. If you haven't, research by Susan Messman, Daniel Canary, and Kimberly Hause (2000) has shed some interesting light on the subject of opposite-sex friendships. According to these researchers, at least six major reasons are given by university students for maintaining "purely platonic" relationships: a wish to safeguard the relationship as it is, lack of attraction, disapproval of other significant people in their lives, the potential of hurting a third party who is involved, fear of being disappointed or hurt, and lack of desire to date or become involved with anyone at this time.

Physical proximity positively affects interpersonal attraction.

Development of Dyadic Relationships

Thus far, we have examined several skills that are important in interpersonal relationships. But where and how do relationships begin? What factors cause relational growth or disintegration? Recent popular literature suggests that individual personalities evolve over time through life experiences, acquired knowledge, and environmental factors. Interpersonal relationships also evolve in this way. Cultivating a lasting friendship can take months or even years. However, time is relevant. Two people also may experience love "at first sight." Ultimately, relationships progress through five different stages of development. These phases of relationship development will be discussed in the following section.

Phases of Relationship Development

Think for a moment about the types of relationships you have in your family, school, and community. Each relationship has unique qualities that set it apart from others, even though the characteristics may be positive or negative. If we look back to the beginning of each of our relationships, we see that there are a variety of reasons for the involvement. Maybe at one time you needed special care (mother), information (teacher), service (postal carrier), or a lover (girlfriend or boyfriend). According to Mark Knapp (1984), relationships follow characteristic patterns of development (coming together) and disintegration (coming apart). His five phases of relationship development are initiating, experimenting, intensifying, integrating, and bonding.

INITIATING. During the first stage of relationship development, we make conscious and unconscious judgments about others. Although we are cautious at this stage, we have usually sized up the other person within 15 seconds. David entered a singles' bar and scanned the room for prospective dancing partners. He stereotyped and classified available women according to personal preferences. After narrowing the field to two women, David determined his approach strategies. Finally, he began a conversation by asking, "Would you like a drink?" "Are you waiting for someone?" "You look like you need company," or "It was nice of you to save me this seat." Sometimes we *initiate* communication nonverbally. In the same situation, the girl at the bar could easily signal for David to leave by looking away, turning her back to him, or moving to another stool.

EXPERIMENTING. After making initial contact, we begin *experimenting* with the unknown. This stage is known as the "do you know" period of interaction. Most relationships do not develop beyond this superficial point. We all can remember situations in which we used small talk to establish a friendly atmosphere. For example, after being introduced to her blind date, Renee attempts to find common interests by asking about Philippe's major, family, favorite bars, job, and so on. Renee may not even be interested, but she asks questions to make the situation more comfortable. If initial interaction goes well, each person probes to determine whether pursuing the relationship is worthwhile.

In interpersonal communication, participants strengthen themselves and each other through the sharing of meanings and emotions.

INTENSIFYING. As relationships develop into friendships, participation and awareness are *intensified.* Gradually, steps are taken to strengthen the bond by asking for and reciprocating favors. Through self-disclosure and trust, the two personalities begin to blend. Statements such as "I've never told anyone this . . ." or "There is something you need to know: I was arrested when I was eighteen . . ." become more common. The verbal relationship usually changes, with the couple using nicknames, pet names, and slang. More time is spent sharing expectations, assumptions, and experiences. Nonverbal behaviors begin to communicate just as effectively as verbal ones. As a relationship intensifies, you notice mutual winks, nods, touches, and so on.

INTEGRATING. At the *integrating* point in relationship development, we agree to meet the expectations of the other person. Two people begin to share many commonalities, such as interests, attitudes, friends, and property. At this stage they do not completely lose their identity; however, there is a need to please the other person by giving in to his or her way of life. Not only do the individuals treat each other differently, but the two are now seen as a unit. In a dating relationship, Julia and Stefan would tend to dress for each other. Stefan is interested in sailing, so Julia subscribes to a sailing magazine. Julia is health conscious and watches fat grams in her diet. For support, Stefan agrees to eat fat-free foods when they go out. When friends have parties, Julia and Stefan are invited together, rather than individually.

BONDING. In the final stage of relationship development, serious commitments and sacrifices are made. In today's society, "commitment" involves marriage or a verbal commitment to live together. Sacrifices usually include a willingness to help with even the most difficult of personal problems and to give gifts or favors that require a substantial expenditure of time, money, and energy. The *bonding* of any relationship can become a powerful force in making the relationship better or worse. Marriage is the most common form of commitment and usually gains social and institutional support. However, the couple also usually has to agree to the rules and regulations of the contract.

Phases of Relationship Disintegration

Just as with relationship development, relationship disintegration may take years—or it can take a few seconds. For example, after their children were married, Bill and Sang found that they had nothing left in common after 36 years of marriage. Tom and Sam, identical twin brothers, never spoke to each other again after Tom saw Sam with his girlfriend.

Thus far we have examined five patterns of relationship development. We will now look at patterns of disintegration. The five phases of relational disintegration are differentiating, circumscribing, stagnating, avoiding, and terminating.

DIFFERENTIATING. Integration in a relationship signifies a union, and *differentiating* signifies a separation. Differences occur at every stage of relationship development, but with differentiating there is increased interpersonal distance. At this stage, differences become more and more apparent. The partners usually begin to want freedom and individuality. Both parties begin to play games that test the relationship and the other person's involvement. After Bob and Kathy had been dating for seven years, friends and relatives expected them to get married. During the last few years, however, the couple began experiencing different lifestyles, and they began to want different things out of life. At one time each knew what the other person wanted, but now they weren't so sure.

CIRCUMSCRIBING. When relationships begin to disintegrate, there is less communication. Topics of conversation are controlled or *circumscribed* to reduce conflict and tension. On the surface everything appears to be all right, but underlying difficulties are evident. The presence of others increases interaction, and socially the relationship seems unaltered. Sally wondered, after having so much fun at her friend's party, why she and Harry sat in silence all the way home. At this stage of disintegration, there also tends to be less expression of commitment verbally and nonverbally. Affection is given only occasionally, and loving remarks are almost nonexistent.

STAGNATING. During the *stagnating* stage, all efforts to communicate are abandoned. The interpersonal atmosphere is cold. Nonverbal messages are often the only feeling states expressed. As Marcella got home from her dance recital, she was met with a cold stare from her husband. We wonder why individuals would continue a relationship that is so unrewarding. Many people stay in relationships because they want to punish the other person, they hope for reconciliation, or they want to avoid the pain of ending the relationship. Sandy was afraid she could not pay the rent on her own, so she continued to live with Angela, even though doing so was like having two roommates because Angela was living with Ron.

AVOIDING. At this stage, one or both parties act as though the other person does not exist. Each person tries to find ways to *avoid* interaction. Meetings are often arranged so that there is someone else around, or excuses are made for not being able to be with the other person alone. Toward the end of this stage, one or both people seek a permanent state of separation. Natasha called Nikita on the phone because they had not communicated in two weeks. She said, "Nikita, we need to talk this thing through. Can we get together this weekend? How about Monday? Do you have a test on Tuesday? Okay, then you tell me the next time that you are free, and I will change my plans."

TERMINATING. The *termination* of a relationship can be immediate or delayed. A friend may die of a heart attack, a marriage may dissolve because of an affair, or your company may transfer you to another city. Termination is dependent upon the type of relationship, perceived status of the relationship, effects of dissociation, and timing. As with relationship development, the final stage of relationship disintegration can occur suddenly with heated words over a poker game, or slowly and unobtrusively by failing to make plans to get together. Methods of termination are usually dependent upon future goals and expectations.

The stages of relationship development and disintegration can occur in the order in which we have just presented them, or they can start at any phase of development. In a crowded bar, a fight might end a relationship that was a minute old. If a person breaks into a concert ticket line, you quickly make a judgment to avoid this person.

Managing Interpersonal Relationships

To this point, we have emphasized the processes involved in interpersonal communication. In this section, we turn our attention to the people involved and how we may best "manage" interpersonal relationships.

Types of Relationships

Just as individuals are emotionally healthy and productive, or sick and ineffective, so too are interpersonal relationships. Manipulative involvements are a prime example. In such relationships, one or both members try to satisfy psychological needs by smothering the individuality or potential of the other. In manipulative relationships based on dependency, for example, one or both partners may be so "addicted" to the other that he or she drops all outside interests, activities, and friends. Just as the single-minded pursuit of a drug addict destroys his or her life, so can the dependency relationship destroy self-identity, self-respect, and all chances for growth and development.

So what do healthy friendships and marriages look like? Carol Bruess and Judy Pearson, two interpersonal communication scholars, conducted a fascinating study in 1997 about rituals associated with intact friendships and marriages. Friendship rituals that emerged in their study were (1) "social/fellowship" rituals (sharing recreational activities or pastimes, getting together on a regular basis, scheduling trips or vacations together, and planning escapes from daily activities); (2) "idiomatic/symbolic" rituals (celebrating birthdays or holidays together, joking, kidding around and being silly, doing everyday things like watching soap operas together); (3) "communication" rituals (regular phone calls, e-mails, or exchanges of greeting cards); (4) "sharing/supporting/venting"; (5) doing "tasks/favors" for one another; and (6) establishing "patterns/habits/mannerisms" that are associated only with them as friends (sitting in the same place at Barnes and Noble every time you meet and getting coffee together) (pp. 37–41).

Married couples reported similar rituals, with an additional element of intimacy: (1) "couple-time" rituals (traveling, attending sporting events, sharing hobbies, playing games, and going to movies together); (2) "escape episodes" (rendezvousing at their favorite hideaway once a month); (3) "idiosyncratic/symbolic" rituals (saving Thursday nights for pizza together in front of the television, sharing special words and pet names, intimately teasing and playing with one another, and

Empathy means sharing others' joy and pain.

creating private games that only they play); (4) "celebration" rituals (birthdays, anniversaries, and holidays); (5) "daily routines and tasks" (housework, meal preparation, kisses goodbye before leaving for work); (6) "intimacy expressions . . . physical, symbolic, and verbal expressions of love, fondness, affection, or sexual attraction"; (7) "communication" rituals (specific times for talking and sharing); (8) "patterns/habits/mannerisms" (always curling up together in front of the television, "spooning" their bodies around each other before falling asleep); and (9) "spiritual" rituals (praying, worshiping, and sharing other forms of spiritual fulfillment) (Bruess and Pearson, 1997, pp. 33–37).

Levels of Social Interaction

Depending on the type of interpersonal relationship, different forms of communication or social interaction will take place.

ALTERNATING MONOLOGUE.   The least productive and least fulfilling kind of communication, often seen in manipulative relationships, is the *alternating monologue.* Each individual knows that the other is speaking but does not listen openly to what is being said. Each person is so preoccupied with his or her own concerns that there is no sharing or understanding of ideas. The end of one statement merely signals the beginning of an unrelated reply:

Will: You wouldn't believe what I had to do at work today.

Grace: Oh, yes. Tonight I have to go over to school and take that exam.

Will: I almost quit, I was so angry at the boss.

Grace: I cannot believe how hard I've studied for this test.

Will: Maybe I'll quit—get away from it all and have some fun.

Grace: Hey, now you're talking. Have some fun. That's what I'll do tonight after the exam.

STIMULUS–RESPONSE INTERACTION. *Stimulus–response interactions* are no better. In these interactions, the speaker proceeds in a set manner, independent of any responses the listener may make. The librarian who requests information to issue a card or the salesperson who wants to know what size hiking boots you wear is participating in this type of interaction. They already know what questions to ask, and the responses do not change them.

INTERACTION WITH FEEDBACK. Alternating monologues and stimulus–response interaction are alike in their neglect of feedback. *Interactions with feedback* are more common and more productive. For example, a political canvasser bases her comments on the responses she gets from the voter.

Scenario 1:   Canvasser: Excuse me, are you going to vote for Raymond Charles?

           Voter: That idiot? No way would he have my vote!

           Canvasser: Perhaps you received some wrong information about our candidate. Let me tell you a little about him.

Scenario 2:   Canvasser: Excuse me, are you going to vote for Raymond Charles?

           Voter: I don't know. But I do know I don't want to be pestered.

           Canvasser: Excuse me. I'll just leave this information with you, so you can read it at your leisure.

Even in these feedback situations, responses may be based as much on habit or learning as on interpersonal factors. Because the canvasser has had many similar experiences in the past, his or her answers may be automatic, requiring no feedforward or feedback.

INTERACTION WITH EMPATHY.   The most productive form of communication is *interaction with empathy.* Empathy means deep understanding of other people, identifying with their thoughts, feeling their pain, sharing their joy. Such empathy is typical of strong, healthy relationships. Indeed, empathic communicators know each other so well that they can predict the responses to their messages. For example, Mario says to himself, "I know if I tell May that I'm not crazy about her new dress, she'll be hurt. So instead I'll say, 'May, that dress looks great on you, but I think the green one is even more becoming.' " This illustrates the special feedback that empathy can produce.

Managing Interpersonal Conflict

People who care about each other will get angry, but their intimacy should ensure healthy, productive conflict and the use of words, not to hurt, but to find out what is bothering each person. Then, bottled-up tensions can be released.

There is a big difference between this type of arguing and the destructive variety. Whereas healthy conflict stresses the facts, destructive conflict aims for the ego, with statements such as "You're ridiculous," and "Me? You should see yourself." The goal of an argument should be **conflict management,** not character defamation. Better to say, "I don't like your behavior choice" than to say "I don't like you right now."

Gamble and Gamble (1982, pp. 322–328) proposed six principles for managing interpersonal conflicts effectively and efficiently.

1. *Recognize that conflicts can be settled rationally.* A conflict has a better chance of being resolved if you do not pretend it doesn't exist, withdraw from discussing it, surrender to the other person, try to create distractions, find fault or lay blame, or attempt to force the other person to take your view.

2. *Define the conflict.* Ask yourself: Why are we in conflict? What is the nature of the conflict? Which of us feels more strongly about the issue? Then try to figure out a way that all can "win."

3. *Check your perceptions.* Perceptual distortions of the other person's behavior, position, or motivations can take place. At this time, attempt to determine whether you understand one another.

4. *Suggest possible solutions.* The goal at this stage is to put your heads together and come up with a variety of solutions. However, neither you nor the other person(s) should evaluate or condemn the suggested solutions at this time.

5. *Assess the alternative solutions and choose the best one.* Determine which solutions will let one party "win" at the other's expense, which solutions would allow both parties to lose, and which solutions will let both parties win. Then choose the one that allows both people to win.

6. *Try out the solution and evaluate it.* Determine to what extent the selected solution is working or not working. Then make appropriate alterations in the plan.

As you can see, interpersonal conflict can be managed successfully. However, doing so means taking the time and expending the necessary energy to talk through the conflict.

Summary

Interpersonal communication is the sharing of feelings and ideas with other people. Most interpersonal messages are informal exchanges in dyads—that is, between two people in close contact. The potential for sending, receiving, and evaluating messages is shared between the members of the dyad. The purpose of their communication usually focuses on the sharing of meaning as well.

Successful conflict management aims at facts—not egos.

Three specific theories of interpersonal communication can help us better understand the complexities of interpersonal communication. Functional communication theory addresses the functions of interpersonal communication, while relational communication theory focuses on three specific dimensions of interpersonal relationships. These dimensions are dominance, affiliation, and involvement. Finally, the coordinated management of meaning theory focuses on meanings in interpersonal communication, as well as on the concept of coordination.

Skills related to self-disclosure, trust, feedback and feedforward, nonverbal communication, and interpersonal attraction combine to determine how successfully meaning will be conveyed in such dyadic communications.

Another important topic in the study of interpersonal communication concerns the phases of relationship development. Of the 10 stages, initiating, experimenting, intensifying, integrating, and bonding represent the growth in relationships. The five phases of relationship disintegration are differentiating, circumscribing, stagnating, avoiding, and terminating.

Managing interpersonal relationships involves a number of factors. For example, the people involved often bring personality and environmental factors into the interpersonal setting. The variables also influence the success or failure of the communication process. For example, individuals with manipulative needs often destroy opportunities for communication that might aid personal growth and development of friends and associates. Similarly, certain types of messages also limit effective social interaction. For instance, both alternating monologues, in which the speakers seem not to hear each other, and stimulus–response interactions, in which the speakers' set messages are unaffected by their listeners' replies, hinder effective communication. In contrast, interactions characterized by feedback and empathy build strong, healthy relationships.

Finally, managing relationships necessarily involves the management of conflict. Six principles that can help with this often difficult aspect of relationship management are the following: (1) Recognize that conflicts can be settled rationally; (2) define the conflict; (3) check your perceptions; (4) suggest possible solutions; (5) assess alternative solutions and choose the best one; and (6) try out the solution and evaluate it.

Exercises

GROUP EXPERIENCES
Positive-Negative

DESCRIPTION   One aspect of interpersonal attraction is the extent to which another person shares your attitudes and beliefs. Simply stated, we are more attracted to people who share our attitudes than to those who do not. Consider some of the relationships you have had with others. Relationships that you remember as positive probably were ones in which your ideas were readily and willingly accepted or at least supported. When you have a falling out with another person, you may both have reevaluated each other and may consider the attitudes of the other person to be strange. Because nobody wants to be considered strange, you leave the situation. The purpose of this activity is to magnify the emotional feelings a person has when his or her ideas are positively and negatively reinforced.

PROCEDURE   Divide into groups of four to six persons. Choose one person as the subject. Select a controversial topic of discussion or a topic that requires preparation (such as planning a picnic). During your discussion, accept and support all ideas suggested by the subject on the topic. Listen carefully to everything he or she has to say. After five minutes, select another subject. Then for the next five minutes, reject all comments presented by the second subject. Avoid listening. Let the subject know that you consider his or her beliefs to be strange, wrong, and worthless. The final part of this activity is a report from the subjects about the emotional states they experienced during the activity. The subjects should indicate how much they liked other group members, along with their reasons for liking or disliking them.

DISCUSSION   Most people surround themselves with people who agree with and reinforce their ideas. Let's face it—people who like us can't be all bad! The two subjects most likely had very different feelings about the group. Creating the actual emotional condition that you would feel in a real-life situation was probably difficult, because in the back of everyone's head is a little voice saying, "It's just an activity." However, the next time you are in a group that evaluates you either positively or negatively, watch your emotional state. Do you tend to gravitate more toward people who like you?

Perfect Partner

DESCRIPTION   Everyone has varying opinions as to what they regard as attractive. During different periods of time, being pleasantly plump was "in" and looking excruciatingly thin was definitely "out." In fact, history records periods of time when women were sent to "fattening schools" to prepare for marriage. Today everyone runs to a gym to lose those extra 10 to 15 pounds. Even within a given period and culture, people simply have different ideas about beauty. This activity will provide you with the opportunity to identify what characteristics of attraction you want in your Perfect Partner.

PROCEDURE   As a group, list characteristics of the perfect mate. Don't evaluate, just list. Then, from the list of characteristics, write the ones that you agree are important. Are there others you would add? Are there some you disagree with and would not include? Are there some characteristics based on gender? On physical appearance? What does this say about our culture?

Write an ad for your "Perfect Partner." Be brief and concise, as want ads are, but include all the traits you consider really important—you may get what you advertise for.

DISCUSSION   You probably found some of the ads funny—maybe even ridiculous; the question is, "Would you have been attracted to the same characteristics others wrote about?" Discuss the sayings, "Beauty is in the eye of the beholder," and "Love is blind." Are they true? Do you ever see couples that you think are physically mismatched? The final question to consider is this: "What do you really want in a Perfect Partner?"

PERSONAL EXPERIENCES

1. Make a list of three people whom you like and three people whom you dislike. Consider each person separately and determine how they respond to you. Are they enthusiastic about your ideas? Do they share similar attitudes and beliefs with you? After you have answered these questions, reflect on this one. Do you tend to like people who positively reinforce you, and dislike those who negatively reinforce you?

2. Using Knapp's 10 phases of relational growth, chart the growth and decline of a relationship that you were a part of in the past. Then compare it with a chart of some relationship in which you are currently involved. How are the two relationships alike? How are they different? What factors affected the former relationship? How can you avoid those events in your current relationship? Does "knowing" the phases of growth and decline help in any way? If so, how?

3. Make a list of communication strategies that you can use to make your interpersonal communication more effective. Which suggestions do you find easy or difficult to practice? How can you be more aware of the communication strategies that you use each day? How can you learn to practice effective strategies more consistently? How can you learn to avoid detrimental communication strategies?

Discussion Questions

1. What role do quarrels or arguments play in an interpersonal relationship?
2. How can theories of interpersonal communication help you in your day-to-day activities?
3. Explain how phases of development and disintegration evolve in interpersonal relationships.
4. What methods can be used to manage interpersonal conflict?

References

Broder, S. N. (1987). Helping students with self-disclosure. *School Counselor, 34*(3), 182–187.

Bruess, C. J. S., & Pearson, J. C. (1997, March). Interpersonal rituals in marriage and adult friendship. *Communication Monographs, 64,* 25–46.

Caltabiano, M. L., & Smithson, M. (1983). Variables affecting the perception of self-disclosure appropriateness. *Journal of Social Psychology, 120,* 119–128.

Dance, F. E. X., & Larson, C. E. (1976). *The functions of human communication.* New York: Holt, Rinehart & Winston.

Dillard, J. P., Solomon, D. H., & Palmer, M. T. (1999, March). Structuring the concept of relational communication. *Communication Monographs, 66,* 49–65.

Finkenauer, C., & Hazam, H. (2000). Disclosure and secrecy in marriage: Do both contribute to marital satisfaction? *Journal of Social and Personal Relationships, 17*(2), 245–263.

Gamble, T. K., & Gamble, M. (1982). *Contacts: Communicating interpersonally* (226–228, 322–328). New York: Random House.

Guerrero, L. K., & Afifi, W. A. (1999). Toward a goal-oriented approach for understanding communicative responses to jealousy. *Western Journal of Communication, 63*(2), 216–248.

Hornstein, G. A., & Truesdell, S. E. (1988). Development of intimate conversation in close relationships. *Journal of Social and Clinical Psychology, 7*(1), 49–64.

Knapp, M. L. (1984). *Interpersonal communication and human relationships.* Boston: Allyn & Bacon.

Lazowski, L. E., & Andersen, S. M. (1990). Self-disclosure and social perception: The impact of private, negative, and extreme communications. *Journal of Social Behavior and Personality, 5*(2), 132.

Messman, S. J., Canary, D. J., & Hause, K. S. (2000). Motives for remaining platonic, equity, and the use of maintenance strategies in opposite-sex friendships. *Journal of Social and Personal Relationships, 17*(1), 67–94.

Neimeyer, R. A., & Mitchell, K. A. (1988). Similarity and attraction: A longitudinal study. *Journal of Social and Personal Relationships, 5,* 131.

Pearce, W. B., & Cronen, V. (1980). *Communication, action, and meaning.* New York: Praeger.

6

Small Groups and Teams

Contributed by Eileen M. Perrigo

key concepts and terms

Group	Global team	Democratic leader
Small group	Intercultural team	Laissez-faire leader
Team	Virtual global team	Transactional leader
Study group	Face-to-face group	Transformational leader
Support group	Cultural diversity	Problem-solving group
Focus group	Ingroup	Cohesion
Work team	Outgroup	Conformity
Task team	Gender diversity	Intergroup conflict
Management team	Leadership	Intragroup conflict
Technology-based group	Leader	Constructive conflict
Chat room	Leadership style	Destructive conflict
Teleconferencing	Autocratic leader	Bypassing

From:	"Lindsey"
To:	"Erla" <krisjanea@futurenet.ab.net>
Sent:	Wednesday, July 17 10:35 PM
Subject:	Soccer Rules!

Hi, Erla!

Did you see the game? You had to have seen the game! Wow, did the U.S. women kick butt or what? I can't wait to hear what the other women on our team have to say about it. We meet tomorrow night to review our films from last week's game, and have a big one coming up this Saturday. Wish we could get it together like the U.S. women did against China!

How's everything going with your team at State College? I know your team stats, but is Cameron emerging as the leader you thought she could be? How's the team coming together? E-mail me when you get a chance and we can catch up on the latest gossip. Take care, E!

—Lindsey

More than 90,000 people flocked to the final game of the Women's World Soccer Cup between the United States and China in 1999. According to the July 19, 1999 *Newsweek* article, "Learning What 'Team' Really Means," "American women are the best team athletes in the world. They rock. They rule. And they're good sports (p. 55)." They knew how to compete, they knew how to lead, they knew how to bond, and they knew how to take risks. They listened to their team leader and to each other. They were focused.

What the U.S. women's soccer team experienced was teamwork at its highest potential. The two best women's teams played a tight match for everyone in the world to see. Both teams exhibited characteristics of strong team members that you will learn about in this chapter.

As we enter the twenty-first century, it is becoming increasingly obvious that we must cooperate and collaborate with other people in order to accomplish our personal and professional goals. Unless you plan to live the life of a hermit, more than likely you will be involved in groups and teams both socially and professionally.

With the explosion of communication technology, we are able to connect with each other 24 hours a day, 7 days a week, 365 days per year. No longer do we have to interact face-to-face with each other in a small group or team. Technology-based groups using the Internet, e-mail, teleconferencing, and videoconferencing have changed the way we communicate with each other.

In this chapter, you will learn principles that can assist you in communicating effectively in small groups and teams. Following a brief overview, we will provide some working definitions and team guidelines. Then we will discuss responsibilities of team members, taking into consideration culture, gender, and technology. After we cover the process of team building and leadership, we will talk about problem solving. We also will examine personality, cohesion, and conformity as variables affecting team performance. Finally, we will conclude by addressing group conflict.

Communicating in Small Groups and Teams: An Overview

Think for a moment about all of the different groups to which you belong, whether they are social, political, educational, spiritual, occupational, or special interest groups. Now think about the teams to which you belong that are sports, work, professional, or volunteer teams. From the moment we are born until the day we die, we all participate in groups or teams. Today, it is virtually impossible to exist independently of all groups and teams. In fact, as Vangelisti, Daly, and Friedrich (1999) have noted, the small group is "probably the most important social formation where individuals and collectives are made and remade" (p. 99). People join and leave groups and teams for many reasons. For example, you may join a social group such as a fraternity or sorority to meet other people who share similar likes and dislikes. You may choose to stay in the group because group members satisfy your social needs. Or, you may elect to leave the group due to financial constraints, lack of time, or a change in the behavior of group members. In order to understand the concept and nuances of groups and teams, let's look at some definitions.

Definitions

A *group* is any number of people who share a common goal, interact with one another to accomplish their goal, and see themselves as part of a group. Members of a sorority or fraternity constitute a group because they exhibit all of these characteristics. Another example of a group would be individuals who share a common interest in some type of dancing. They may enjoy swing dancing, country western dancing, square dancing, clogging, tap, ballet, or jazz. Each person in the group interacts with others who want to learn and perform dance for the purpose of enjoyment or entertainment of others.

A *small group* is "a system of three to fifteen individuals who think of themselves as a group, are interdependent, and communicate by managing messages for the purpose of creating meaning" (Socha, 1997a, p. 11). Given this definition, think of the many small groups to which you belong. Perhaps you are part of a student organization on campus, or you play an integral role in a group project in class, or maybe you are actively involved in a study group. Each of these groups has a different meaning for you and serves a specific purpose in your life.

Certain generalizations can be made about small versus large groups. For instance, small groups tend to be more informal and less structured, while large

Effective teams collaborate to achieve a common goal.

groups may have to adopt formal rules to maintain order. A small group can function effectively without a designated leader, but a large group may need a leader to maintain order and ensure that the group performs efficiently. Theoretically, an increase in size means an increase in the group's resource pool, since the addition of people means more information, ideas, and opinions. However, the larger the group, the less chance for individual participation; likewise the tendency is greater for dominant or aggressive individuals to monopolize the discussion. This type of behavior causes the shy person to withdraw from interaction and experience a sense of frustration. After a large group has functioned for some time, a number of cliques tend to develop, which often hinders the overall group effort. Therefore, as a group becomes larger, greater difficulty arises in accomplishing a particular task.

A *team* is a group of people working together in a collaborative effort to achieve a common goal. In many cases, teams evoke feelings of camaraderie and friendship, whether in a social or professional environment. Effective teams are synergistic because their senses are heightened, performance is enhanced, and the connection between team members is strong (Elledge & Phillips, 1994, p. 5). When teams are in this state, members learn from each other and benefit from team experience, regardless of the outcome. For example, when the U.S. women's soccer team played China for the 1999 World Soccer Cup, both teams were in synch. Each team member played her best game with one goal in mind—to win the World Cup. Even though the United States won the game, both teams played synergistically and experienced a sense of "oneness" as a team.

Now that you know the definitions of "small group" and "team," you may be asking yourself, what is the difference? A discussion of types of groups and teams may shed some light on the distinctions.

Types of Groups and Teams

Throughout your life you will take part in many groups and teams. Let's take a look at the purpose of some of the more distinctive ones.

A *study group* is a gathering of people who get together to learn new information or skills. They may assemble as a group only one time or may come together periodically. Perhaps you are a member of several different study groups whose members help you review material to pass your exams.

A *support group* focuses on learning to cope with situations to meet the needs of its members. In the future, you may find that you need a support group to help you through a crisis in your life. Examples of organizations that sponsor support groups are Alcoholics Anonymous, American Cancer Society, Alzheimer's Family Association, and Students Against Drunk Drivers (SADD), just to name a few.

As part of your college career, you may be asked to participate as a member of a *focus group*. A focus group is comprised of members of a certain target audience that uses a particular product or service. Group members are asked questions by a "neutral" third party about that product or service. For example, during an election year, you may see a group of people interviewed on C-SPAN about their views on presidential candidates. A professional facilitator usually leads focus group discussions.

In addition to various types of groups, there are many different types of teams. According to Kinlaw (1991, pp. 10–12), groups and teams are functionally and qualitatively different. A team starts out as a group but reaches a new level of quality, develops special feelings among its members, creates a critical work process, and reflects leadership that encourages team development and performance (Lumsden & Lumsden, 2000). Groups can become teams over time. Three types of teams that are found in many organizations are work teams, task teams, and management teams (Aranda, Aranda, & Conlon, 1998, p. 7).

A *work team* is a collection of individuals who form natural work groups within an organization. For example, a self-managing creative team in an advertising agency may conduct research and formulate ideas about a specific product to present to the management team. Another example is a health care team. For instance, if a patient is admitted for third-degree burns over 85 percent of her body, the "burn team" assigned to her might include a burn surgeon, physical therapist, occupational therapist, social worker, plastic surgeon, pulmonologist and various nurses, depending on her individual needs. All of these professionals will work together to diagnose and treat the patient. Team members experience camaraderie as they work together toward a common goal. Figure 6.1 identifies characteristics of effective work teams.

A *task team* is a group that is formed for a specific period of time to work on a particular problem or issue. Usually such teams are comprised of people with a wide variety of skills, experiences, and ideas. For example, you may be asked to serve on a temporary task team to plan a fundraising event for a nonprofit organization such

---

The following chart examines feelings of effective work teams. Use this guide to assist you in determining your level of inclusion, commitment, loyalty, pride, and trust as a team member (Aranda, Aranda, & Conlon, 1998).

Inclusion
- Team members get information that affects their jobs and their lives in the organization.
- New ideas are encouraged and treated with respect.
- Team members receive quick responses from other team members when they ask for help.

Commitment
- Team members make personal sacrifices to make sure the team succeeds.
- Team members care about team results.
- Team members are determined to succeed.

Loyalty
- Team members go out of their way to ensure the success of their peers.
- Team members give their colleagues the benefit of the doubt when they have apparently failed to fulfill a commitment.

Pride
- Feedback is sought out and taken seriously as a chance to improve.
- Team members believe that what they do is important and tied to organization goals.
- Team members have a strong orientation toward the future and expect to exceed their own current levels of performance.

Trust
- Team members do what they say they are going to do.
- Team members never conceal information from one another.
- Team members are willing to listen to one another and defer to one another because they expect reliable information and good ideas from one another.
- Team members view one another as having the knowledge and skills to perform.

FIGURE 6.1 **Characteristics of Effective Work Teams**

as the American Humane Society. Your team may consist of someone who plans the event, another person who promotes the event, and yet another who keeps accurate records of incoming funds. You also will need a volunteer coordinator who is well connected in the community and who asks people to volunteer to work the event. Other names that task teams may be called are "task forces," "project teams," and "quality circles."

A *management team* is a collection of managers who meet on a regular basis to make decisions and determine the future direction of a unit or organization. Management teams have meetings during which members report on the work, problems, and achievements in their departments. Sometimes team members make operational decisions that affect the departments and organization as a whole. For example, when a company is undergoing restructuring, the management team usually provides synthesis to organizational goals and activities. They develop the timeline for reorganization and notify employees of impending changes. They also may assemble temporary task teams to assist with the process of reorganization. In summary, these three types of teams (i.e., work, task, and management) have different purposes and needs. In order for any of them to work efficiently and effectively, it is best to continuously evaluate their performance.

Technology-Based Groups

The twenty-first century has been marked by significant growth in the use of technology-based groups. What separates members of *technology-based groups* from face-to-face groups is the members' dependence on technological communication. As part of your educational, social, or work environment, you probably have communicated online with members of one or more computer-based groups.

One example of technology-based groups would be people who regularly participate in Internet *chat rooms* where they take part in real-time conversations online. Chat room topics include anything and everything from discussing the latest fashions to sports equipment to the best places to visit in the world. You can communicate online with people from all over the world simultaneously any hour of the day.

Another example of technology-based groups involves the use of *teleconferencing.* During a teleconference, three or more people talk via telephone at a prespecified time and date. (At the time of this writing, one of your authors was asked to participate in several hiring interviews via teleconferencing.) Timing is one of the biggest challenges for a global teleconference if participants are located in different time zones (e.g., Europe, the Americas, and Asia). If you and your teammates find yourself in this situation and must communicate via teleconference over an extended period of time, "rotate" the time of day during which calls are made so that the same person isn't inconvenienced every time. Participants may enter the meeting via telephone from an office, home, or a cellular phone anywhere in the world. Teleconferencing can be used to call people locally, regionally, nationally, or internationally. Teleconferencing flourished in the 1990s and will continue to play an important role for many groups in the foreseeable future.

As the amount of technology-based group communication increases, so too will the number of global teams. *Global teams* may be divided into two distinct categories: *intercultural teams,* in which people from different cultures meet face-to-face to work on a project, and *virtual global teams,* in which individuals remain in their separate locations around the world to conduct meetings via different forms of technology (Solomon, 1998, p. 12). To illustrate, assembled are Jazeri from Pakistan, Maaji from Finland, Mohammed from Egypt, and Liliana from Mexico, along with Stephen and Katie from the Sloane-Kettering Foundation. They are working together in Europe for the next six months to raise money for children around the world who need specialized medical care. This group of caring people is an example of an intercultural team.

Let's compare an intercultural team with a virtual global team. In an intercultural team, people from different countries assemble in one geographic location (i.e., Europe). In contrast, virtual global team members can meet online or via satellite while working in their respective countries. For example, U.S. Navy instructors conduct distance learning courses around the world. The courses are taught "live" at the Naval Air Station in Pensacola, Florida. They are transmitted via satellite to Americans in Italy, Saudi Arabia, Japan, and other foreign countries. People in distance learning classrooms learn the same information from the same instructor simultaneously. In sum, members of virtual global teams are generally located in places around the world.

Benefits and Pitfalls of Technology-Based Group Interaction

In all likelihood, you have already experienced the benefits and pitfalls of group computer interaction. In *face-to-face groups,* you are able to see and hear the participants and get a better sense about them based on their nonverbal cues. Technology-based groups are different, and have their own particular advantages and disadvantages.

One of the benefits of computer technology is increased accessibility to group members. Geographic distance and time constraints are virtually nonexistent when group members meet for online discussions. Group members save time because members do not have to travel to group meetings (Galinsky, 1997).

A related benefit of technology-based group meetings is convenience. Since participants can meet at any hour of the day, group members can chat any time that is convenient for all participants. Of course each person would have to agree on the best time for all concerned. Time management is essential for effective online group discussions.

A number of studies indicate that computer groups have more equal participation among group members than groups who work together face-to-face (Bonito & Hollingshead, 1997). For instance, research suggests that people feel less inhibited when interacting via computers because they are less aware of social differences.

One of the disadvantages of technology-based groups is the inability of members to send and receive nonverbal messages. Important information may be lost due to the fact that participants cannot see each other. In turn, some group members may feel isolated. Participants can only read words on the screen rather than receiving the complete message.

In addition, interruptions and distractions at home or at work can inhibit participation. For example, the television or stereo may be blaring, or family members or coworkers may need your immediate attention while you are online, which is very distracting. Confidentiality may be threatened because others may gain access to information. Third parties may view correspondence that is intended for group members only.

In today's fast-paced world, technology-based groups offer an alternative to face-to-face small groups and teams. By identifying the benefits and pitfalls of each type, you may select the one that best fits the parameters and needs of your own group or team.

Effective Team Members

From time to time you will be called upon to serve as a team member, whether in a class, as part of your sorority, fraternity, or church group, or in your work environment. In order to function as an effective team member, you need guidelines to follow. Figure 6.2 provides one useful set of guidelines for you and your team to review.

Group and Team Diversity

If a small group is to function successfully, its members must possess certain attitudes and behaviors. Your first responsibility as a group participant is to keep an open mind about problems and issues. You should try to remain objective during the course of the discussions and evaluate information and ideas independently. This means being aware of your own personal biases to make sure they do not interfere with your willingness to listen.

Think of a team that you are currently involved in. Then, check each guideline that you meet or exceed when it comes to qualifications of team members whom everyone wants on their team. By reviewing these guidelines, you will have a better understanding of the elements of a successful team member.

- Commits to the achievement of the team's goals.
- Establishes high standards and challenges others to meet those standards.
- Voices disagreements and views differing opinions as new sources of information rather than sources of conflict.
- Thoroughly analyzes problems, explores all possible alternatives, and evaluates each before deciding on a plan of action.
- Encourages a full and open discussion of issues and pursues consensus in decision making.
- Has a feeling of team cohesiveness.
- Listens and provides useful feedback to others.
- Shares all relevant information, ideas, and concerns with the team.
- Recognizes individual team members for the contributions they make.
- Assists others when necessary to ensure the successful completion of team goals.
- Attaches a high value to new and creative approaches to problems.
- Is flexible and open to influence by others.
- Attends all meetings promptly and participates fully.
- Completes all work assigned in the time agreed upon and with a high level of quality.
- Seeks to find solutions to problems when they occur rather than placing blame.
- Honestly discusses areas of difficulty and concern about the team, its goals, the team members, and task completion (Elledge & Phillips, 1994, p. 120).

FIGURE 6.2 Team Member Guidelines

In the twenty-first century, diversity plays an integral role in the composition of groups and teams. Valuing diversity means accepting differences and ensuring equal rights, no matter where you are from (Schreiber, 1996, p. 462). Two types of diversity that are evident in teams are cultural and gender diversity. *Cultural diversity* is the sum total of the different ways of life, behaviors, and beliefs reflected by the individuals who constitute a particular group or team. In their book, *Riding the Waves of Culture,* Trompenaars and Hampden-Turner (1998) note that cultural diversity involves more than differences in behavior and outward appearances. Diversity is reflected in how people view individualism versus collectivism; outwardly express emotions; get involved; accord status to other people; manage time; and relate to nature (i.e., if we see nature as something to be controlled or allowed to take its own course).

In turn, individuals from different cultures influence the overall behavior, attitudes, and values of a group or team. Unfortunately, as part of socialization into our respective cultural groups, we often are taught to interact with, or to avoid, members of other groups because of their ethnic heritage, religion, political views, social class, gender, skin color, or dress. People with whom we are taught to associate are referred to as *ingroups.* Groups of people with whom we are taught to avoid association are referred to as *outgroups* (Gudykunst & Kim, 1997).

Several consequences can result from the formation of ingroups and outgroups. First, we tend to expect members of our ingroups to behave and think like we do. Second, we experience less anxiety about interacting with ingroup than outgroup members. Third, we have a tendency to cast ingroup members in a more favorable light (Gudykunst & Kim, 1997). When we do these things, and members of either group surprise us either positively or negatively, we may not know what to think or to say. At such moments, we have the chance to grow as human beings and communicators.

Invariably, misunderstandings can result from cultural differences. For example, Italians are famous for being verbally and nonverbally expressive, especially when compared to the Japanese, who tend to avoid expressing emotions. North Americans require greater "space" in interactions when compared to people from Middle Eastern cultures. When people from such different cultures get together, they may be surprised and "turned off" by each other's behaviors. However, to participate effectively in small group communication, we must be aware of such differences and work harder to understand why people behave and communicate in the ways that they do.

In sum, understanding cultural differences plays an integral role in the effectiveness of small groups and teams. Cultural diversity tends to increase the number of fresh ideas and approaches to problems, and contributes to overall group effectiveness.

Gender diversity involves masculine and feminine socially learned behavior. Men and women grow up with two different sets of attitudinal and behavioral norms. As a result, they may react to situations differently. Gender differences and their effects on team performance have been the subjects of some interesting small group research (Watson, Johnson, & Merritt, 1998). For example, researchers have found that, in conversations between North American men and women, women tend to ask questions to keep the conversation going whereas men do so to gain information. Also men tend to focus on obtaining facts, while women are interested in building relationships. Interestingly, all of these goals are necessary to achieve when attempting to increase team effectiveness.

Let's take a look at some other gender differences. According to gender expert Deborah Tannen, women are socialized to view talk as important to developing and maintaining relationships. In contrast, men use talk to assert their dominance and demonstrate their independence (Tannen, 1990). As a result, if you were completely asexual and observing from Venus or Mars, women would seem to be playing by one set of rules, and men by another. In fact, misunderstandings do occur as a function of misinterpretation. Another example of gender diversity emerges when men and women discuss problems. Often, when women discuss problems, they are simply looking for reassurance from other group members. In contrast, men may interpret the desire to discuss a problem as a request for help in developing a solution. These are just a few gender differences that researchers have found to exist between men and women. Since they are socialized differently, men and women often learn different rules for interpreting group interaction (Tannen, 1990).

So how do we maximize our strengths to deal with different types of diversity in teams? Being open-minded about various differences will contribute to the overall effectiveness of the team. So will showing sensitivity to the moods of others and the emotional tone of the group as a whole. Sometimes what people say and mean are two different things. If you are sensitive to this fact, you may be able to "read" people more effectively. For example, a different tone of voice, change in posture or body position, and other nonverbal cues may reinforce or contradict what group members are verbally communicating.

Individual members have an obligation to make sure that everyone participates in the group process. For example, a newcomer to the group may feel somewhat intimidated by the other members, particularly if they all know one another and have worked together for a long time. As a sensitive group member, you should try to make new persons, especially people from different cultures, feel at ease and draw them into the discussion.

Participation in a group often requires preparation or homework. Sometimes group members may agree to think about a problem or complete research on a particular subject before the next meeting. Following through on such assignments is essential. If not, time will be wasted at the next group meeting, and those who have done their work will be frustrated and annoyed. For example, when a local chapter of a statewide public relations association was deciding which nonprofit organization to work with for their community outreach program, seven members were tasked with researching a different organization. When only three of the seven members arrived at the meeting prepared, the group's work was set back at least a week. As part of a group, you have an obligation to other people as well as to yourself.

Most of the benefits and pitfalls of technology-based groups apply here. In addition, global teams may experience language difficulties and different manners of speaking in cross-border teams. Members must realize that people need to understand each other's differences before they can come together as a group.

Basic Communication Skills

No matter what type of group or team you are involved in, the basic communication skills of speaking and listening are of paramount importance. Whether you are face-to-face or across the world, your speaking and listening skills are essential components of good communication.

SPEAKING. Because the group process depends on interaction among members, you must communicate your ideas and opinions as accurately and concisely as you can. Here are some ways to increase the effectiveness of your communication in face-to-face groups and teams.

1. If you find yourself mumbling or rambling, you may be saying something that is unimportant. Avoid speaking unless you have something to contribute.

2. Address your comments to the group as a whole. Involving everyone is essential to group success.

3. Organize your remarks whenever possible. Although group interaction is spontaneous by nature, you can prepare the information you are presenting before you arrive.

4. Relate your ideas or opinions to what others have said. Make connections clear whenever possible.

5. State only one point at a time so that the group can digest what you have said. Doing so will keep the discussion on track and allow the group to respond to individual points.

6. Ensure that everyone understands your comments by speaking clearly and using language to which the group can relate.

7. Avoid "sidebar" conversations. For example, as the leader you may be addressing an entire group of people and, while you are talking, two of the participants are having their own conversation. It is the leader's responsibility to discourage this type of behavior in a group setting.

LISTENING. As a group member, you must be both a speaker and a listener. Listening effectively is as important as speaking effectively. To become a better listener, review and practice the following listening habits.

1. *Limit your own talking.* It is virtually impossible to talk and listen at the same time. Take time to listen to the other person's viewpoint before making a decision.

2. *Ask questions and clarify.* You may feel you misunderstood the concept your team member was attempting to explain.

3. *Paraphrase a complex or emotion-laden message back to the speaker before you respond.* Sometimes speakers may be disgruntled or in a negative mood for whatever reason. Repeating the message you thought you heard clarifies the information.

4. *Avoid interrupting at all costs.* It is best to let the speaker finish the sentence before you respond.

5. *Concentrate intently on what the speaker is saying.* Try to block out anything else that comes into your mind and focus on the content of the message.

6. *Make positive comments.* Let the person know you are listening by making such comments as, "I see" or "now I understand what you are saying."

7. *Listen for the feelings behind the facts.* In face-to-face groups, you will have the advantage of reading nonverbal cues of group members. A participant may be verbally telling you one thing and feeling something different.

8. *Maintain control over your emotions.* Sometimes you may have negative feelings about one or two group members or you may find yourself disagreeing with others' comments. It is best to keep your emotions in check as you listen attentively.

9. *Always make an effort to listen.* Sometimes the subject matter may be difficult or the speaker may be boring. Try to look for new points of view or new information as you listen.

10. *Challenge yourself.* Identify a person with whom you have a difficult time listening. Change your behavior to accommodate the listener. Was the speaker aware of any notable changes in your listening behavior? (Gaut & Perrigo, 1998, pp. 51–52)

Even though people try to listen carefully, sometimes a certain amount of misunderstanding takes place. Sending feedback is one way to help reduce such misunderstanding. The use of questions can improve communication throughout the group process. At the outset, it helps members to ask questions about the goals and objectives of the group as well as the purpose of the meeting. Once these goals are established, questions about procedures should be asked. Even when conclusions have been reached, carefully thought-out questions can often refine decisions to a considerable degree.

How Does a Group Become a Team?

If you play sports or know someone who plays sports, you are familiar with the team concept. Usually the coaches and star players get all the recognition for the team's success. But it takes an entire team working together to win in any sport. The most effective teams take time to build team spirit. Let's take a look at the process of how to build a team.

The Process of Team Building

What does the concept of team building mean to you? It could represent an after-work social hour, a weekend getaway at a beach resort, or practice to improve the team's ratings. Team building varies with the size, function, culture, and structure of the group. In order for team development to take place, some essential elements must be present.

1. *Commitment,* the willingness to place the group's goals above your personal goals.

2. *Trust,* a feeling of confidence and support from each other.

3. *Purpose,* an understanding of the team's mission.

4. *Communication,* the ability to handle conflict, make decisions, and interact on a day-to-day basis.

5. *Involvement,* or partnership and ownership in the team's mission.

6. *Process orientation,* or the tools, activities, processes, and structures for dealing with the daily operation of the team (McEwan, 1997).

Let's take a look at a hypothetical team, a task force that is being formed to investigate the need for providing additional parking spaces on your campus. The team will consist of students, faculty, and administrators who all share a *commitment* to the goal of the team. Every one of the members of the team has stories to tell about missed appointments or coming into class late due to a lack of parking spaces. Therefore, each team member *supports* the others because they all share the same *purpose.* When the team is formed, they will get to know each other by *communicating* their findings to each other in planned meetings. If a conflict should arise, the group will take appropriate action and move on to the next topic of discussion.

The group leader has the responsibility to help build the team by keeping members *focused on the team's mission.* Each team member plays an integral role for completing the task of finding a solution to the parking problem on campus. When the task is complete, the leader will communicate the teams' findings to the vice president of administrative affairs, who in turn will provide recommendations to the president of the college or university. Hopefully, the parking problem will be resolved and everyone on campus will have additional parking places. Of course, this is a hypothetical situation. In Box 6.1, you will read about one company whose members are rewarded through the process of teamwork.

QuickBreak 6.1

THE ADVANTAGE COMPANIES

Chris Smith and Tim Handley, co-owners of the Advantage Companies in Pensacola, Florida, know about teamwork. Chris and Tim played tennis together before starting the Advantage Companies, a group of companies that assist businesses with consumer credit, employee assessment, and web-based applications. An excerpt from the company mission statement says, "The company's rapid growth requires dedicated employees who understand that their greatest opportunity for personal reward is through *teamwork* that supports the company's mission."

Tim compares Advantage employees to an athletic team. "You get the team to buy into your objective and everyone understands they each play an integral role. People on a sports team always try to do their best. They have one goal, and they're going for it together. We're tapping into that athletic synergy."

One payoff of synergistic teamwork is demonstrated in team members' paychecks. To reward team members for their hard work, Chris and Tim give a crisp $100 bill to each employee at the end of the year. Periodically, they award outstanding employees stock in the company for loyalty and stellar performance. Handing out cash awards to team players is one of Tim's favorite duties.

Leaders and Leadership

In the study of group dynamics, *leadership* is any kind of behavior that helps the group toward its goals. A *leader* is any person who influences the group in this way. How do leaders emerge in small groups? Research suggests that the amount of member participation affects leadership development in small groups. For example, Bonito and Hollingshead (1997) found that the person who speaks the most is often identified as the group leader. These researchers also examined the relationship between the amount of speaking time and what is being said. Surprisingly, they found that group members who were perceived as "high participants," regardless of the quality of their contributions, were ranked as more competent, confident, and influential than people who were perceived as "low participants."

Styles of Leadership

A number of approaches have emerged over the years to study leadership behavior. One approach that has played an important role in what we know about leadership involves an understanding of leadership style. *Leadership style* is most often associated with the means by which a person motivates others to accomplish goals. Early in the study of leadership, three primary styles were identified: autocratic, democratic, and laissez-faire. These three styles comprise what is termed the "traditional" leadership styles. More recent studies have revealed two additional styles: transformational and transactional leadership. We'll begin with a discussion of traditional leadership styles, and then turn to the two "contemporary" styles.

Autocratic leaders are more direct in their approach. They are extremely goal-oriented and have firm opinions on how to achieve these goals. If group members respect their competency, the group works well and efficiently. If not, group conflict is likely to arise. Autocratic leaders view tasks as paramount in importance, and relationships as playing a secondary role. They feel little responsibility for maintaining strong interpersonal relationships, since relationships can interfere with the task at hand.

You probably have been influenced by an autocratic leader at some time in your life. Can you identify an autocratic leader who is successful and one who is not? What makes the difference?

Democratic leaders guide rather than direct a group. Receptive to group members' suggestions, these leaders leave most of the actual decision making to the group itself. While this style of leadership is very popular, less-experienced groups may feel lost when left on their own to make a decision. The effectiveness of democratic leadership depends on the amount of power the leader has, the nature of the task, and the interpersonal relationships that exist between the leader and the group members.

From what you know about democratic leaders, can you identify a successful and an unsuccessful democratic leader? What makes the democratic approach work for one person and not the other? Generally, groups with a democratic leader are more creative and consistent than groups with other types of leadership. On the down side, groups with democratic leaders are less efficient when compared to groups with autocratic leaders.

The third leadership style is that of the *laissez-faire leader* (a French word meaning "leave them alone"). Laissez-faire leaders avoid directing the group at all. Seeing themselves as potential sources of information and feedback only, they function as observers and recorders and are available for advice when the group wants it. This kind of leadership is especially appropriate for groups engaged in creative activity, where more direction limits or stifles creativity.

Have you been in a group with a laissez-faire leader? What did and didn't work well under his or her direction? Why?

As you will recall, our two "contemporary" styles are transactional and transformational leaders. *Transactional leaders* control the team through negotiation, or exchanging rewards for performance. For example, he or she might reward group members for reaching a required number of sales per month, as a group. All members would receive the same reward, regardless of individual sales.

In contrast, *transformational leaders* empower and develop personal leadership in individual team members. In other words, he or she works to create future leaders by giving participants maximum freedom for self-direction. The leader changes or "transforms" members by personal example and demonstrates how to envision the future. Individual members are rewarded for maximizing the highest sales possible in their own way and time. Individual (rather than team) rewards and future promotional opportunities await those who thrive under transformational leadership.

It should be noted that transactional leadership produces a positive climate but less productivity and commitment to the group than transformational leadership (Bass, 1990, p. 24). Regardless of leadership style, however, positive evaluations of group performance ultimately result when a task is performed well and relationships are optimized. Beyond that, it's up to you to determine the style of leadership that fits you, both as a group leader and participant. After reviewing the five leadership styles again, ask yourself which style is most appealing to you.

Characteristics of Effective Leaders

Take a moment to think about leaders whom you admire. These leaders may be famous, dead or alive, or someone you see every day. What makes these leaders appealing to you? What characteristics do they have that make them stand out from all the others? Let's take a look at some of the many attributes of successful leaders.

• **Credibility.** Certainly credibility ranks high on the list. A credible person is one who is valued as a person, and is trustworthy and believable. Example: Oprah Winfrey

• **Competence.** The person must be qualified for the job as a leader. He or she must possess the intelligence necessary to fulfill the leadership role. Example: Madeline Albright, Secretary of State during Bill Clinton's second term

Successful leaders empower others to make contributions.

- **Trustworthiness.** A leader must be honest and reliable. Followers must have total confidence in the integrity of the leader. Examples: Reverend Billy Graham and the Dalai Lama

- **Visionary.** A good leader shares a vision with the rest of the team members. He or she must communicate that vision to the rest of the members of the team. Example: Bill Gates, founder of Microsoft

- **Interactive.** Communication skills, especially listening and feedback, are extremely important for leaders. Team members must feel that the leader is approachable. Example: Steven Jobs, computer guru

- **Empowering.** The ability to delegate tasks and authorize team members to carry out responsibilities is another quality of an effective leader. Example: Elizabeth Dole during her tenure with the American Red Cross

After reviewing the qualities of an effective leader, ask yourself if you or someone you know possesses these leadership attributes. You may already be a leader in some facet of your life. If not, you may have the potential to become a leader in the future.

Problem Solving through Group Discussion

We have all experienced the frustration that arises when a group of people cannot solve a problem that an individual could solve relatively quickly (such as four people trying to decide what type of pizza to order). Communication researchers have noted that the relative effectiveness of group decision making depends on the nature of the problem itself.

Groups are more effective in situations in which the pooling of data is necessary, or in which increased knowledge and a variety of approaches are required. In policy decisions, group participation leads to wider acceptance and better understanding of the solution. However, the group decision-making process is prone to problems that arise from any process involving human interaction. For some group members, winning an argument may become more important than finding a solution. Other group members may try to dominate the discussion, while others may habitually give in to win group acceptance. Our four friends who cannot decide which pizza to order may actually be arguing about social dominance and not about food at all.

A *problem-solving group* is a group of people who work together to solve a problem by collecting information about the problem, reviewing that information, and making a decision based on their findings. While we may ordinarily think of decision making as an unexciting or private process, problem-solving groups play a central and public role in our lives. If you are sensitive to the fact that problem solving is a *process*, you can improve your own participation in group discussions and also contribute to the effectiveness of the overall group effort.

A Standard Agenda for Problem Solving

When we are confronted with a problem, we often forget that problem solving is a process that takes place over time. Studies have shown that people tend to respond to problems in an ordered series of steps. The following eight-step plan is a guide to effective problem solving.

STEP 1: DEFINING THE PROBLEM. If a group has been given a specific and clearly defined problem, this step becomes unnecessary. In many cases, however, a group finds itself in the middle of a difficult situation, and a clear definition of the problem becomes an important part of the problem-solving process.

Consider the following example. One of the most universal problems on a college campus is parking. Many students live off-campus and have to vie for a limited number of parking places close to the buildings where classes are held. A group of students concerned with this situation meets to share complaints. The students are aware of the situation, and some have vague ideas as to possible solutions, but they need to define their problem more clearly. At this stage they have two goals. They want to frame their definition of the problem to increase its "solvability," and in a way that will promote discussion and effective interaction. Clearly, posing the question in a "yes-no" format does little to define the problem.

The most effective definitions are problem-centered rather than solution-centered. "How can we convince the university administration to add more parking spaces?" focuses on the problem and does not limit the range of possible solutions.

STEP 2: LIMITING THE TOPIC. After the problem has been defined, limits to the discussion must be set based on relevance to the group, the importance of specific issues involved in the larger problem, and the amount of time available for discussion. For example, our hypothetical group is interested in adding more parking spaces on or near the college campus. They should probably limit the discussion to on-campus parking since they would have little control over neighboring properties in close proximity to the college campus. The group's definition of the problem will also depend on the amount of time group members have available to dedicate to the problem. Do they have only a few hours, or will they meet over a period of weeks or months?

STEP 3: ANALYZING THE DATA. At this stage the group goes through its evidence, distinguishing relevant from irrelevant material, finding important details, searching for causes of the problem, and working out the dynamics of the situation. Our group might evaluate parking space availability, possible removal of old buildings, or the addition of a multilevel parking garage. They should also consider the increased parking fees that students and faculty are willing to pay for additional parking spaces. You may be interested to note that one of your authors pays more than $400 per year for a license "to hunt" for a parking space on campus.

STEP 4: ESTABLISHING CRITERIA FOR POSSIBLE SOLUTIONS.   The group must determine in advance what they expect from their proposed solutions. For example, our group might decide that its solution should meet the needs of as many students as possible by creating ample parking at a price they can afford. However, they must also consider different price ranges for students, faculty, and administrators. During this stage, group members must keep from judging which of the proposed criteria are acceptable until all suggestions have been heard. The group then selects criteria that are acceptable to the majority.

STEP 5: SUGGESTING POSSIBLE SOLUTIONS.   During the "brainstorming" stage the quantity rather than the quality of proposed solutions is important. Again, the group must not try to come to a decision until all possible solutions have been heard. Numerous approaches to the problem should be identified and discussed. For example, your group could negotiate with the university to add a multilevel parking garage or remove old buildings to make room for additional parking; talk to students about the additional parking price increase; discuss fundraising ideas to offset the cost of the parking garage; and so forth.

STEP 6: EVALUATING INDIVIDUAL SOLUTIONS USING THE ESTABLISHED CRITERIA.   How well does each solution satisfy the standards the group has established? Do some of the proposed solutions satisfy the criteria better than others do? At this point the group will throw out those solutions that fail to meet the established standards, and will evaluate the remaining solutions in light of the needs of the problem. In this stage the group must keep its discussion focused on issues, not personalities. Any proposed solution must be judged on its own merits—not on the popularity or loudness of its sponsor.

STEP 7: CARRYING OUT THE SOLUTION.   The group must decide how its solution may be carried out within the limitations of its authority, facilities, and budget. If the university administration agrees to build a multilevel parking garage, are the students willing to offset the cost by paying increased parking fees? Are current students willing to sacrifice their time to assist in fundraising efforts to help offset building costs, even though the parking garage will not be available until after they have graduated? The group must choose the most efficient and effective means of carrying out their solution.

STEP 8: EVALUATING THE EFFECT OF THE SOLUTION.   After the possible solutions have been discussed, various questions must be asked. Did we convince the university administration that additional parking spaces are needed? If we add a multilevel parking garage, will ample parking spaces be available to off-campus students? Will the increased student parking fees offset the cost of the new multilevel parking garage?

The standard agenda that we have described is only a guide. It is useful only insofar as all group members are aware of and accept it as a useful and organized way to approach the problem-solving process. Despite the orderliness of the standard agenda, its use does not guarantee effortless solutions. Several other factors affect the operation and outcomes of problem-solving groups.

Other Factors Affecting Group Performance

Personality

There are many variables that influence group interaction, but the primary one is the different personality of each group member.

Each person contributes his or her own experiences, values, attitudes, and personality to the makeup of the group. For example, some people are shy and tend to sit back in a group situation, while more aggressive individuals may use the group as an audience for their assertiveness. While some people try to avoid conflict in a group, other people like to provoke conflict and enjoy the combative interaction that often follows. Perhaps you have participated in a group that you felt could have functioned more efficiently if two members had been less argumentative or if someone had been more dominant.

Undoubtedly, you have heard the expression "personality conflict" used to describe the irreconcilable clash of personalities. Such a difference in personalities can sometimes cause a group to lose sight of its goal and remain unproductive. Yet differences in personality can have a positive effect on group interaction. For example, a person who is particularly task-oriented may counterbalance a member who is concerned with the satisfaction of the group. Similarly, a humorous individual can offset someone who is extremely serious or tense. The group is a complex entity because of the combination of different personalities. The next time you participate in a group or observe one in action, remember that the group is at least equal to or greater than the sum of the individual personalities of its members.

Cohesion

Groups develop personalities all their own. For example, some groups always seem to work smoothly and achieve their goals easily, while others are marked by conflict. Highly publicized mountain climbs such as those up Mt. Everest provide an example of this second type of group. For example, you may have read Jon Krakauer's (1997) riveting best-seller, *Into Thin Air*. If not, we encourage you to get to your local library and check it out. In his personal account of the most publicized disaster on Everest to date, Krakauer described step-by-step how he and a team of eight other climbers made their fateful climb in May 1996. Out of nine climbers on their team, five ultimately reached the top. However, four of the five, including their leader, Rob Hall, perished in a storm while descending the mountain. This elite group of climbers lost track of team goals and broke team rules. They separated from each other on the ascent and failed to follow the directions of the guide. As a result, they lost their lives.

A communication expert would diagnose one problem of Krakauer's team as a lack of group cohesion or solidarity. *Cohesion* is the degree to which group members identify themselves as a group or team, rather than merely a collection of individuals. Cohesion arises from and reinforces shared values, attitudes, and standards of behavior. Cohesion is a crucial factor in a group's success. Highly cohesive groups are more likely to be productive, their members are more likely to feel personally satisfied by the group process, and their interpersonal communication is more effective.

Interaction in highly cohesive groups has several special characteristics. First, because individuals feel secure in these groups, they can tolerate some degree of productive conflict. Specifically, they feel free to offer both rewarding and punishing feedback to other group members.

Second, cohesive groups offer their members greater returns, or rewards, for their personal investment in the group. For example, in an academic situation, a professor may give the same grade to all students working on a group project, regardless of their individual contributions to the project. As a rule, students will work harder to get a better grade. However, we have all experienced "social loafers," people who ride on the coattails of others in the group to get a better grade. Every effort must be made for all students in the group to be cohesive.

Third, cohesive groups offer psychological rewards—feelings of belonging and the friendship and respect of other people. Cohesive groups also offer their members the reward of prestige, which comes either from the social status of the group or from some group accomplishment. In either case, group members share the reflected glory of the group. Finally, participation in a cohesive group allows each member to experience achievement rewards, the satisfaction that comes from productive work, and the fulfillment that comes from contributing to a valuable cause or goal.

Conformity

Another important variable that influences groups is pressure to conform within the group. *Conformity* occurs when all the members of the group agree to abide by the outcome of the group decision. In and of itself, conformity is not a negative force. Sometimes, however, when consensus inhibits dissent, the pressure to conform, or "groupthink," can cause serious errors in decision making (Janis, 1982).

Pressure to conform is sometimes so subtle that a group member may be totally unaware of it; at other times, the pressure can be quite oppressive. Group members may be pressured to conform, even when conformity means going against their better judgment. This sort of overt pressure can result in dissonance, which can erupt in open conflict or defiance.

Some group members are more susceptible to group pressure than others. The following are personality characteristics of people who are most vulnerable to group pressure:

1. *Level of confidence.* The better one's self-concept, the more resistant one will be to group pressure.

2. *Regard for authority.* A closed-minded person, defined as one who relies on the accuracy and correctness of authority, will be more apt to conform to group pressure.

3. *Intelligence.* The greater one's intelligence, the less likely one is to conform.

4. *Need for social approval.* The greater one's need for approval, the more apt one is to conform.

To illustrate this concept, Eve is attempting to win Jack's attention because she wants him to ask her out for the New Year's celebration. Since Jack is an intelligent, self-confident team leader and Eve needs social approval from Jack as well as the rest of the team members, she agrees with Jack and the rest of the group and conforms to their way of thinking. As a bonus, Eve wins Jack as her date for the New Year's celebration. However, the group loses because Eve has valuable information that could have assured a positive outcome, had that information come to light.

Other variables that influence conformity are situational in nature. Situational variables include:

1. *The size of the group.* Conformity usually increases as the size of the group increases, but only until there are four members; thereafter, conformity decreases as group size increases. For example, a group of four professors is trying to determine which deserving student should be awarded a $1,000 scholarship. The criteria have been established and three students qualify. By outlining the criteria and comparing the accomplishments of each student, a clear winner is determined based on unanimous agreement.

2. *Group structure.* Group structures that permit a great deal of interaction between members produce more conformity than those that limit interaction.

3. *Difficulty of the task.* Conformity usually increases as the task becomes more difficult.

4. *Degree of crisis or emergency.* The old adage that there is safety in numbers may account for the increase in conformity during a crisis situation. For example, a group of shipwrecked survivors floating on a raft in the middle of the ocean would probably exhibit a high degree of conformity since deviation from the norm could mean disaster.

Group and Team Conflict

The ideal group is highly cohesive, but like most things in life, groups are rarely ideal, and conflict often emerges from group interaction. Conflict between groups—*intergroup conflict*—often benefits the groups involved by increasing goal-oriented activity and causing group members to value their work more highly. An extreme example is war, in which conflict strengthens ingroup bonds by providing an outlet for tension and focusing a group's goals. Conflict usually occurs when there are two or more competing or incompatible responses to a single event. Thus, conflict may occur both within the group itself, when individuals experience differing needs or values, or between groups, when the groups have competing interests over the accomplishment of a cooperative goal. Another example of intergroup conflict is when one group member works toward making a grade of "C" as part of a group project whereas the others want to make an "A." It might be that the person who wants a "C" out of the project is taking the class as an elective, and the other members of the group want to make an "A" since the course is one of their major courses.

In the past, researchers believed that *intragroup conflict* (conflict within a group) had the opposite effect—that it had a negative influence, reduced cohesion, decreased productivity, and caused group members to discredit their own achievements. They now believe that some degree of intragroup conflict is useful and productive. It is possible that when appropriately channeled, conflict can contribute to more effective results. Of course, this kind of conflict is not a pitched battle but an issue-centered form of open discussion and confrontation that uses group problem-solving methods to achieve better solutions. For example, Shannon feels an online discussion of group members is counterproductive. On the other hand, Jason suggests other group members will be more open online than they would in face-to-face discussions. When Jason persuades Shannon to try the online group meeting, she finds he is absolutely correct in his assumption. Indeed, two of their most shy group members open up and contribute their individual thoughts to all group members in an online session. The intragroup conflict is resolved and everyone benefits from the outcome.

What applies to intergroup conflict and intragroup conflict also applies to conflict in teams. Conflict is a natural part of the human experience. "From the roots of conflict come the fruits of innovation" (Caudron, 1998, p. 48). Knowing the difference between constructive conflict and destructive conflict is important in team building and problem solving. *Constructive conflict* leads to innovation in the group whereas *destructive conflict* leads to disharmony that often damages relationships. Without this framework, it is easy to believe that all conflict is negative. For example, how many times have you been in a group meeting when people nodded affirmatively about an idea that was presented? Then, as you left the meeting, you began discussing the idea with others and found out they didn't think the idea was that good after all. Such behavior indicates that conflict is considered taboo. In retrospect, when people are willing to disagree publicly, you have constructive conflict. When people are allowed to speak their minds, resentment does not build up. Disagreements can lead to well-rounded discussions and innovative solutions.

Asking questions is an excellent way to overcome barriers to communication in small groups and teams. One such barrier is called *bypassing,* a situation in which people are actually talking past each other. In such a situation, people argue or reach an impasse when, in fact, they are in agreement.

A major cause of bypassing is ambiguity or vagueness on the part of one or more group members. Questions relating to interpretation or calling for explanation can help bring out the intended meaning. On the other hand, sometimes a person will use stigma words or phrases, such as four-letter words that are emotionally loaded. The person who uses this type of vocabulary can provoke the rest of the group and cause conflict. Without accusing or intimidating the member who uses such language, other members should quickly ask for clarification.

So how do you foster constructive conflict in a group or team? First, you must respect individuals and individual differences. Create the kind of culture that supports diversity of all kinds, including diversity of thought and opinion. Model the kind of behavior that shows a comfort level with conflict. Second, agree to disagree. By doing so, you have given permission to team members to demonstrate an alternate opinion. Third, reward the behavior you want to encourage. Publicly praise a team member for speaking out and providing a diverse opinion. If team members are to work through difficult problems, they will take the initiative to find alternative solutions to the problem.

When you decide to become a member of a group, you and others have elected to pursue certain objectives. Whatever the mechanisms affecting a particular group—personality, cohesion, conformity—each group member is responsible for making the most of the positive potential of these forces. When goals are kept firmly in view, individual differences can often be recognized as the stumbling blocks they are and can be temporarily shelved while the solution is sought in an open-minded way.

Summary

Understanding how groups and teams function will assist you in group participation, whether you are a leader or a team member. Knowing the basic differences in types of groups and teams allows you to function well as you work through problem solving and group dynamics.

In the twenty-first century, technology plays a major role in global, cultural, and diverse groups. Being aware of the benefits and pitfalls of technology-based groups will give you the edge and make you more technologically savvy.

Although many people seem to be good leaders by nature, specific leadership characteristics can be learned. Effective leaders possess such attributes as credibility, competence, and trustworthiness, to name a few.

The three basic styles of traditional leadership are autocratic, democratic, and laissez-faire. Two contemporary leadership styles are transactional and transformational. Each leader possesses specific traits characteristic of the individual leadership style.

When approaching a problem, it is best to use the eight-step plan as a guide to the decision-making process.

Other factors affecting group performance are personality, group cohesion, and conformity. In some cases, conflict emerges from group interaction. Knowing the difference between constructive conflict and destructive conflict is important in team building and problem solving.

Exercises

GROUP EXPERIENCES

What Makes Teams Effective?

DESCRIPTION   In this chapter, you have reviewed the qualities of effective team members. You may want to brainstorm additional characteristics to add to the list based upon your own experiences with groups and teams. In this exercise, you will rate the effectiveness of a specific team of your choice, using information you learned in the chapter as well as other traits team members may identify.

PROCEDURE   Divide the class into five or six members. Identify a leader and recorder in each team. The leader will ask a series of questions and the recorder will write the responses for the team to share with the rest of the class.

1. When you think about successful teams, what teams come to mind? Why?
2. What characteristics of these teams stand out?
3. What makes you feel good about participating on a team?
4. What makes you dread being part of a team?

After the team identifies at least ten positive characteristics, ask team members to rank the traits from 1 to 5 using the following scale:

1 = Not at all characteristic of the team
2 = Only slightly characteristic of the team
3 = Somewhat characteristic of the team
4 = Mostly characteristic of the team
5 = Absolutely characteristic of the team

The leader will ask each team member to rate their team as a whole, using the characteristics of effective team members they have identified.

DISCUSSION   Would you have rated the qualities of an effective team the same way one year ago? Three years ago? In what areas has your idea of an effective team changed? To what do you attribute the change? Do the members of the teams on which you are currently serving exhibit the positive characteristics of effective team members? If not, what can you do to implement change?

Are You a Potential Leader?

DESCRIPTION   You have learned about the characteristics of effective leaders and five leadership styles in this chapter. This exercise will help you personally identify leadership qualities in yourself and other people.

PROCEDURE Divide into teams of three to four people. Brainstorm three great leaders whom your team members feel exhibit superior leadership qualities. The leaders you select should be familiar to other class members. They can be historical figures, political figures, corporate executives, and so on, who are living or dead. Do not reveal the names of the individuals until your instructor tells you to do so.

When you have finished brainstorming, your instructor will ask you to identify one- or two-word characteristics that make these leaders successful. These traits will be listed on the board. Compare the traits listed with the leaders your team selected. When your instructor asks, identify the leaders your team suggested. Compare your list with other teams.

DISCUSSION Did your team have an equal number of male and female leaders? Why, or why not? Do you think men or women make better leaders? Why? Do you think you have the potential to become a leader? Why, or why not? How did you measure up to the leadership characteristics listed on the board? How can you develop leadership attributes while you are still a student?

References

Aranda, E. K., Aranda, L., & Conlon, K. (1998). *Teams: Structure, process, culture and politics.* Upper Saddle River, NJ: Prentice-Hall.

Bass, B. M. (1990, Winter). From transactional to transformational leadership: Learning to share the vision. *Organizational Dynamics, 18*(3), 19–31.

Bonito, J. A., & Hollingshead, A. B. (1997). Participation in small groups. In B. R. Burleson (Ed.), *Communication Yearbook, 20*(227–261). Thousand Oaks, CA: Sage Publications.

Caudron, S. (1998, September). Keeping team conflict alive. *Training & Development, 52*(9), 48–52.

Elledge, R. L., & Phillips, S. L. (1994). *Team building for the future: Beyond the basics.* San Diego, CA: Pfeiffer & Co.

Galinsky, M. J. (1997, August). Connecting group members through telephone and computer groups. *Health and Social Work, 22*(3), 181–189.

Gaut, D. R., & Perrigo, E. M. (1998). *Business and professional communication for the 21st century.* Needham Heights, MA: Allyn & Bacon.

Gudykunst, W. B., & Kim, Y. Y. (1997). *Communicating with strangers* (3rd ed.). New York: McGraw-Hill.

Janis, I. L. (1982). *Victims of groupthink: A psychological study of foreign policy decisions and fiascoes* (2nd ed.). Boston, MA: Houghton Mifflin.

Kinlaw, D. C. (1991). *Developing superior work teams: Building quality and the competitive edge.* Lexington, MA: Lexington Books.

Krakauer, J. (1997). *Into thin air.* New York: Villiard.

Lumsden, G., & Lumsden, D. (2000). *Communicating in groups and teams: Sharing leadership* (3rd ed.). Belmont, CA: Wadsworth.

McEwan, E. K. (1997). *Leading your team to excellence: How to make quality decisions.* Thousand Oaks, CA: Corwin Press (A Sage Publication).

Nelson, M. B. (1999, July 19). Learning what "team" really means. *Newsweek, 55.*

Schreiber, E. J. (1996, October). Muddles and huddles: Facilitating a multicultural workforce through team management theory. *The Journal of Business Communication, 33*(4), 459–473.

Socha, T. I. (1997). Group communication across the life span. In L. R. Frey & J. K. Barge (Eds.), *Managing group life: Communicating in decision-making groups.* Boston, MA: Houghton-Mifflin.

Solomon, C. M. (1998, November). Building teams across borders. *Workforce, 3*(6), 12–17.

Tannen, D. (1990). *You just don't understand.* New York: Ballentine.

Trompenaars, F., & Hampden-Turner, C. (1998). *Riding the waves of culture: Understanding diversity in global business* (2nd ed.). New York: McGraw-Hill.

Vangelisti, H. L., Daly, P. A., & Friedrich, G. W. (1999). *Teaching communication: Theory, research, and methods* (2nd ed.). Mahwah, NJ: Lawrence Erlbaum.

Watson, W. E., Johnson, L., & Merritt, D. (1998, June). Team orientation, self-orientation, and diversity in task groups. *Group and Organization Management, 23*(2), 161–188.

chapter seven

Organizational Communication

key concepts and terms

Organization
Principles of scientific
  management
Time and motion studies
Bureaucracy
Hawthorne effect
Participative management
Regulation and policy
  messages
Task messages
Maintenance messages
Formal communication
  structure

Informal communication
  structure
Channels
Media richness
Networks
Downward communication
Upward communication
Lateral or horizontal
  communication
Informal network
Professional
Networking
Office politics

Interview
Employment interview
Appraisal interview
Exit interview
Directive interview
Nondirective interview
Business meeting
Formal presentation

From:	"Nick"
To:	"Amy" <andersax@futurenet.ab.net>
Sent:	Tuesday, March 28 9:15PM
Subject:	Real world to ivory tower! Come in, over!

Hey, Amy—

Can't believe it's March already. Seems like graduation was just the other day. Really feels weird knowing you're back in school and I'm finally out working in the "real world."

My new job has had its ups and downs during these first two months. I've had to do a lot of "figuring things out on my own" since some of my responsibilities used to be handled by people who recently have left the company. I'm gaining a lot of experience—mostly learning the "rules of the game" and ways to deal with so many different personalities. Arraganset is a huge company. There are 10 locations in northern California alone. More later. How's your job search going? (Remember you graduate in less than two months so stay on top of it!)—Nick

Effective communication is the key to success in any organization or workplace. From learning the rules of the game, as Nick mentioned in his e-mail to Amy, to actually constructing everyday messages, your competence as a communicator will help you to get and keep the job of your dreams. In fact, research by the U.S. Department of Labor has revealed five areas of competence most needed to excel in the American workplace: (1) *resource management*—ability to allocate time, money, material, facility, and human resources; (2) *information management*—ability to acquire, process, interpret, organize, and evaluate information; (3) *interpersonal communication*—ability to participate in teams, teach others, serve clients and customers, exercise leadership, negotiate, and work well with gender and cultural diversity; (4) *systems-related skills*—ability to understand social, organizational, and technological systems, monitor and correct performance, and improve and design systems for better products and services; and (5) *technology*—ability to evaluate and select technology to produce desirable results, appropriately apply technology to tasks, and maintain and troubleshoot technology (Secretary's Commission on Achieving Necessary Skills, 1991; as cited in Boyett & Boyett, 1995). If you look closely, all of these competencies involve the use of effective communication.

Given the importance of maximizing your own competencies in each of these areas, this chapter is designed to help you better understand the nature of organizational communication. At the same time, we hope to increase your sensitivity, knowledge, and skills associated with success in the twenty-first century workplace.

A Brief History of Organizational Thought

Organizations are collected groups of people that are created to achieve specific goals that cannot be met by individuals alone. Think about what the world would be like today if Microsoft or Apple had never existed—if Bill Gates and Stephen Jobs had had only themselves to realize their dreams. Additionally, what would the world be like with no governments, hospitals, police departments, grocery stores, car manufacturers, airlines, retail malls, mass media outlets, musical groups, and so on? Wow, the list could be endless!

Organizations like these have grown and changed over time in many significant ways. If you could journey through time from 1800 to the present, the time period during which organizations have been studied formally, you would see an evolution in thought of monumental proportion. You also would see how four major groups have shaped twenty-first century organizational life: the classical/scientific management, human behavior, integrated perspectives, and postmodern, critical, and feminist schools of thought.

Classical/Scientific Management

Suppose you indeed were planning a journey through organizational thought. You definitely would want to begin in Europe during the 1800s and meet up with Frederick Taylor (1856–1915), Henri Fayol (1841–1925), and Max Weber (1864–1920). These three early pioneers championed *principles of scientific management,* including the importance of selecting workers based on objective criteria (e.g., education or training), providing them with training to improve efficiency, establishing clear chains of command, and dividing labor equally between managers and employees. Frederick Taylor, an American engineer, was an avid believer in approaching work and management from a scientific perspective. He was especially interested in the value of *time and motion studies* to reveal the "one best way" to design and implement tasks. If you are interested in going into management some day, you may be interested to note that Taylor also is credited with establishing "management" as a distinct profession (Taylor, 1911).

Around the same time that Taylor's ideas were gaining international prominence, a French engineer named Henri Fayol was gaining fame for his work as chief executive officer (CEO) of a French mining firm. Fayol and his company had made substantial contributions to the war effort during World War I. Later as a consultant, Fayol promoted 14 principles of effective organizational management. These included the importance of division of labor (specializing in a single area of the organization); authority over workers on the part of management; discipline and a clear chain of command; formal structure within an organization; subordination of individual interests to those of the company; a fair day's pay for a fair day's work; a specific (centralized) way of communicating organizational messages; vertical versus horizontal message exchange; order (everyone has a place to work and clear responsibilities to achieve); equity, or kindness and justice for everyone in the organization; a stable workforce across time; initiative, or the ability to think through and execute plans; and *esprit de corps* or the need for organizations to establish and exhibit a singular union of purpose (Fayol, 1949). As you can see, Taylor and Fayol contributed many organizational principles that are still employed by twenty-first century organizations.

A contemporary of Fayol and Taylor, Max Weber was a German economics professor who later became known as "the father of bureaucracy." A *bureaucracy* is an organization that relies heavily on rules, regulations, and policies to establish authority, rather than on a single charismatic leader (e.g., Bill Gates) or more traditional forms of authority (e.g., authority that is passed from generation to generation like it was at Ford Motor Company before they went "public"). Weber formally presented his ideas in 1947 as a response to abuses of authority that he saw in organizations that were inherited by family members. Like Taylor and Fayol, Weber also was publicly supportive of the need for division of labor and a clear chain of command.

Human Behavior

If you journeyed back from Europe to the United States during the early and mid-1900s, you would find some very different ideas emerging about organizations from Elton Mayo (1880–1949), Douglas McGregor (1906–1964), and Rensis Likert (1903–1981). Mayo was a Harvard University professor of business who is credited with discovering the *Hawthorne effect,* the (now generally recognized) fact that work productivity increases when workers are given attention as human beings. Mayo and his team of researchers drew this conclusion while conducting a series of experiments at Western Electric Company's Hawthorne plant near Chicago, Illinois. Prior to Mayo's arrival, Western Electric had been attempting to determine the best lighting levels for optimum performance in their plant. Management was perplexed. They couldn't figure out why productivity increased whether lighting was increased, decreased, or remained constant. So they invited Mayo and his Harvard colleagues to investigate the matter further. After conducting a number of experiments on their own, Mayo and his research drew a surprising conclusion: *the workers were more productive because of the attention they were receiving from the researchers.* In short, Mayo (1945) was one of the first to go on record about the role that human factors play in the workplace. In the process, he launched what later would be termed the human behavior school of thought.

By the late 1950s, human behavior principles had made their way into many organizations around the globe. Managers were becoming more interested in what motivated workers, human interaction, and how these and related variables affected organizational events. Douglas McGregor, a management professor at the Massachusetts Institute of Technology (MIT), took the approach one step further. Interested in assumptions that managers (seem to) make about their workers and influenced by the work of Abraham Maslow, McGregor (1960) penned *The Human Side of Enterprise,* in which he laid out his now-famous Theory X and Theory Y.

For McGregor, managers who were advocates of scientific management principles seemed to view their workers as lazy, irresponsible, not highly intelligent, incapable of organizational creativity, unconcerned with organizational needs, unable to use human resources, and (at best) tolerant of work. He labeled these assumptions "Theory X" assumptions, and observed that Theory X managers tend to use control and intimidation as a result of these assumptions. In contrast, McGregor believed managers who espoused human behavior principles viewed their workers as ambitious, self-directed, responsible, internally motivated, self-motivated, creative, capable of organizational creativity, and able to use human resources effectively. He labeled these assumptions as "Theory Y" assumptions, and observed that Theory Y managers rely more heavily on ways to encourage employees as a result. At first, McGregor was criticized for drawing "either/or" distinctions about managers that polarized them and their approaches. In response, he explained that the two management approaches were best viewed as ranges of behavior, which could vary between two possible extremes (X and Y). If managers became more aware of their assumptions and used that knowledge to make better decisions, both "theories" could aid them in increasing productivity and job satisfaction.

The third key player to whom your journey through the human behavior school might take you is Rensis Likert. During his tenure as professor of sociology and psychology at the University of Michigan, Likert (1961) wrote the now-classic *New Patterns of Management,* a book in which he articulated his theory of participative management. Still employed by many twenty-first century organizations, ***participative management*** was Likert's employee-centered approach to management that encourages the creation of interlocking participative groups (or teams), each of which has multiple group memberships. Employees throughout the organization make decisions and communication flows in all directions. Likert believed that increased participation, trust, mutual support, and more effective communication would yield creative, motivated, and productive employees.

How many characteristics associated with the scientific management and human behavior schools of thought are reflected in the way your college or university operates? See if you can name at least three for each!

Integrated Perspectives

If you are aware of the extent to which mass communication technologies began to pervade our world in the 1950s, you would have to plot a course through the United States and Britain, and the work of many important writers. According to Pamela Shockley-Zalabak (1999), a noted organizational communication scholar, the theorists who are most often associated with the integrated perspectives school are generally divided into those who emphasize process and environment (Herbert Simon, Eric Trist, Kenneth Bamforth, Joan Woodward, Daniel Katz, Robert Kahn, Peter

Senge, Gareth Morgan, and Margaret Wheatley, to name a few), and those who emphasize culture (Terrence Deal, Allen Kennedy, William Ouchi, Thomas Peters, Robert Waterman, Edgar Schein, and Karl Weick, again to name a few).

Overall, theorists associated with the integrated perspectives school were critical of the limitations of classical/scientific management and human behavior approaches to organizations, specifically their "failure to integrate organizational structure, technology, and people with the larger environment in which organizations exist" (Shockley-Zalabak, 1999, p. 108). As Shockley-Zalabak noted, the former (classical/scientific management) concentrated on structure and work design and minimized the value of people and the environment; the latter (human behavior) focused on people but tended to ignore what was going on outside the boundaries of the organization.

That's where integrated perspectives entered the picture and theorists began to study how people, technologies, and environments work together to influence organizational outcomes (Shockley-Zalabak, p. 108). Focusing on process and environmental issues, Herbert Simon (1957) studied decision-making behavior in organizations with an emphasis on how those processes influenced the organization as a whole. Trist and Bamforth (1951) were interested in understanding the delicate balance between human needs and organizational goals, and how that balance could be achieved by optimizing social and technical systems. In the 1960s, Joan Woodward (1965) argued that there was no "one best way" to organize tasks, rather that organizations were required to adapt to changing needs and environments. Daniel Katz and Robert Kahn (1966) applied systems theory and concepts to organizations in their ground-breaking book, *The Psychology and Sociology of Organizations.* More recently, Gareth Morgan (1997), Margaret Wheatley (1992), and Peter Senge (1990) have focused on applications of quantum physics, self-organizing systems, and chaos theory to our understanding of organizations.

Cultural approaches to organizational theory focus on "how organizational members collectively interpret the organizational world around them in order to define the importance of organizational happenings" (Shockley-Zalabak, 1999, p. 117). In their seminal book, *Corporate Cultures: The Rites and Rituals of Corporate Life,* Terrence Deal and Allen Kennedy (1982) set the organizational field on fire with their discussion of what constitutes an organizational culture. William Ouchi (1981) contrasted Japanese (Type J) and American (Type A) organizations and proposed the value of a Theory Z organization, which would combine the best of Japanese and American thinking about how organizations should work. In their best-selling book *In Search of Excellence,* Tom Peters and Robert Waterman (1982) identified eight cultural themes that characterize "excellent companies": a bias for action, staying close to the customer, autonomy and entrepreneurship, productivity through people, a hands-on/value-driven philosophy, doing well what you do best, developing a mean and lean staff, and balancing centralization and decentralization. Edgar Schein (1985) took the literature another step forward by proposing a model of culture that focused on artifacts and creations, values, and basic assumptions, and how organizational cultures begin and grow. More recently, Karl Weick (1995) has helped us to understand individual and organizational sense making. (We bet you can see some of these ideas reflected in your own college or university and the way it does work on a daily basis!)

Postmodern, Critical, and Feminist Theories

The last three stops on your journey through organizational thought would take you to the 1990s and early 2000s. Proponents of *postmodern theories* of organizations focus primarily on characteristics of present-day organizations, including organizational flexibility; workers who are fast, life-time learners with multiple skills; the importance of marketing niches rather than mass consumption; decentralization of power; flattening of organizational hierarchies; organizational cultures based on trust and respect for differences; and the contribution of groups to organizational life (Shockley-Zalabak, 1999; McCauley, 2000).

Critical theories address how power, domination, and political influence are used in both organizations and society at large. Perhaps, the most unique characteristic of critical theorists is that they offer actual critiques of organizations that abuse power and control. As such they go beyond description, prediction, or explanation of organizational phenomena, the goals of most organizational theorists. Discussions of workplace democracy also have emerged from this school of thought, as reflected in the work of Cheney, Mumby, Stohl, and Harrison (1997) and Russell (1997).

Perhaps the most recent theories that have emerged in the organizational literature are *feminist theories,* which generally are perceived to be a type (or extension) of critical theories. However, rather than offering more general critiques associated with power and domination, feminist theorists have focused specifically on gender relationships in the workplace, assumptions about the varying roles and contributions of men and women, and the need for recognizing and valuing multiple voices and perspectives (Shockley-Zalabak, 1999, p. 129).

It is incredibly important to note how much we've learned about organizations in the past 200 years, and the extent to which each of these major schools of thought have contributed (and continue to contribute) to the evolution of organizational life as we know it today. If you believe that you should receive fair wages, should have a stable job, and should be treated fairly, then you can thank the classical scientific management school. If you believe that morale and job satisfaction are as important as productivity, you have the human behavior school to thank. If you believe that every organization has its own unique culture and that organizational excellence is a major key to success, you will want to applaud the integrated perspectives school. Finally, if you believe organizations have no right to abuse their power and that men, women, and the cultures they represent contribute uniquely and equally to organizations, you can thank postmodern, critical, and feminist theorists.

And so, there you have it—a brief history of organizational thought. We hope you have enjoyed the journey. We now turn to an equally important topic associated with organizational communication: dimensions of communication in organizations.

Dimensions of Organizational Communication

Think for a minute about the different organizations you've come in contact with in the last week. Now try to remember all the different channels of communication you used to get your message across to them. You may have called the power company to have electricity turned on, written a letter to a personnel director to ask about a summer internship, told a salesperson nonverbally that you are just looking and don't want any help, ordered a hamburger and french fries at a fast-food restaurant drive-thru, or e-mailed someone about a computer problem.

You can probably think of a variety of other situations, but consider for a moment the kinds of communication that take place among managers and employees that comprise that organization. Organizations have structured ways of operating efficiently and effectively. At a supermarket, for example, a sign over the door reads "Customer Satisfaction Guaranteed." A customer gets home with a carton of milk and finds that it is sour. The customer returns the opened carton to a cashier, who refunds the money and tells a supervisor, who, in turn, tells the dairy manager, who tells the assistant store manager, who notifies the general store manager about the spoiled product. Organizations have different ways of communicating to ensure that everything functions smoothly. To help you better understand communication in organizations, the next section will examine (1) the types of messages sent in organizations, (2) formal and informal communication structures, and (3) communication networks.

Types of Messages Sent in Organizations

Communication in organizations takes a variety of forms. Generally, these messages may be classified into one of three types: regulation and policy messages, task messages, and maintenance messages.

REGULATION/POLICY MESSAGES.   *Regulation and policy messages* play a key role in organizational survival. These messages take the form of policy statements, organizational procedures, agendas, schedules, orders, and control measures that ensure that the organization will function properly. Regulation and policy messages also are associated with many formal and informal rules of the organization. For example, in many organizations, nepotism (the hiring of relatives) is discouraged as a rule.

TASK MESSAGES.   Messages that focus on the products, services, and activities of an organization are called *task messages.* Examples include messages about improving productivity, increasing sales, and the quality of goods or services. Task messages are necessary in order for members of an organization to complete activities associated with their jobs. Thus, messages associated with training, orientation sessions, and goal setting also qualify as task messages.

Other task messages focus on the growth and development of the organization. These include messages associated with the creation of new products or services, including planning sessions, the use of focus groups, and brainstorming sessions. For example many companies have annual retreats for their employees in order to plan for the company's future. This retreat, its agenda, and the messages associated with it primarily will take the form of task messages.

MAINTENANCE MESSAGES.   Messages that focus on the relational element of the organization are termed *maintenance messages.* These messages are associated with the relational aspects of communication in the workplace, including the growth (and deterioration) of peer friendships; discussions of attitudes, values, preferences, likes, and dislikes; rumors, gossip, and jokes; conflict management and praise; and the informal rules of conduct Nick mentioned in his e-mail at the beginning of the chapter. Maintenance messages are shared throughout the day at lunch and during breaks; around the water cooler, the coffeemaker, and the copy machine; face-to-face; through personal notes, greeting cards, gift giving; birthday gatherings and celebratory lunches; and via phone, fax, and e-mail. They are the force that often helps an organization weather crises and a major contributor to a company's organizational culture.

Formal and Informal Communication

Messages that are sent through organizations may be classified as formal or informal. As we mentioned earlier, an organization's *formal communication structure* functions through rules, regulations, and procedures, and is characterized by more "formalized" channels of communication (see Figure 7.1).

At most universities, for example, students must petition for grade changes. Students first go to their instructor, the instructor then goes to the department chair, the department chair sends a memorandum to the dean of academic affairs, the dean sends notification to the records department, and the records department finally notifies students about appropriate grade changes. Failure to properly follow the steps results in confusion, no grade change, and, ultimately, no action through the normal channels. Other organizations work similarly, with office workers reporting to supervisors, supervisors reporting to managers, and so on.

On the other hand, the *informal communication structure* of an organization is created wherever and whenever people meet and interact. It emerges on its own from interpersonal relationships within the organization. Social groups such as the coffee drinkers, the lunch-time basketball bunch, and the meditation-break clan do not appear on any organizational chart. However, they do serve at least eight vital organizational functions (Han, 1983):

1. Providing employees with a sense of belonging, security, and recognition.

2. Providing a way for employees to discuss their concerns in an open, friendly manner, thereby reducing stress and pressure.

3. Maintaining a sense of personal integrity, self-respect, and free choice.

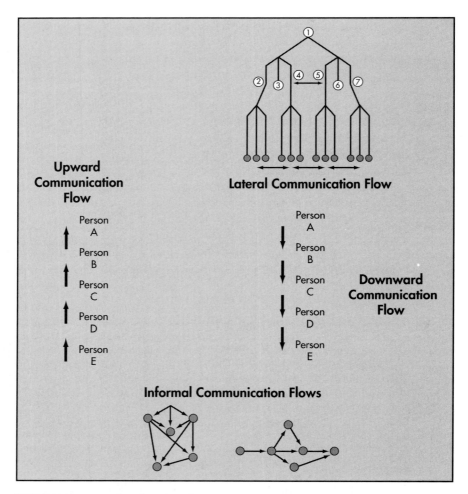

FIGURE 7.1 Networks Showing the Various Flows of Communication

4. Facilitating formal communication.

5. Providing an informal network of interpersonal and group communication.

6. Providing an opportunity for social interactions.

7. Providing a source of practical information for managerial decision making.

8. Producing future organizational leaders from within the ranks.

In short, formal and informal communication structures work like the blades of a pair of scissors. Without both, an organization could not function effectively. The following section will explain how channels are used specifically to disseminate information in both formal and informal communication structures.

Communication Channels in Organizations

Organizations are linked through a series of communication *channels.* AT&T, MCI, and Sprint would have consumers believe that the telephone is the most effective channel of communication, when, in actuality, those organizations also use face-to-face interaction, letters, memoranda, and computerized messages to get information to others. Communication channels are often taken for granted, and we usually use the channel that is most economical and convenient. Currently, in order to save time, many people use the telephone and the internet to check facts like product prices, locations of businesses, and whether or not an establishment stays open on weekends; in the past, many people hopped into their cars and actually drove to the business in question.

Thoughtful consumers and organizations are becoming more aware of how channels affect the reception of messages. The channels we use to transmit messages send cues to receivers about how sources view the receiver and the message.

According to Ronald Rice, John D'Ambra and Elizabeth More (1998), how a message is sent is a "question of choice and effectiveness" and differs in *media richness,* or the extent to which it can "(a) overcome various constraints of time, location, permanence, distribution, and distance; (b) transmit the social, symbolic, and nonverbal cues of human communication; and (c) convey [shared understanding]" (p. 4). To make sense of media richness as an important communication concept, think about the last time you tried to decide how to cancel a date, inform a teacher that you would be absent from class, or borrow money from a family member. You probably debated about whether to write, phone, e-mail, or talk with them in person. You probably also considered how each message would be interpreted, depending on the channel you selected. Questions about media richness are equally important in organizational communication. For example, should you phone or e-mail your boss about a problem you are having with a colleague in your department? Should you write a formal letter or take a client to lunch (or both) to apologize for an error you made in an important press release that you developed for his or her company?

To determine precisely how people perceive the richness of various media and how often they prefer to use one medium over another, Rice, D'Ambra and More (1998) asked 561 managers in Hong Kong, Singapore, Sydney (Australia), and the United States to respond to a written questionnaire about these issues; 401 people returned the questionnaire. The managers who responded to the survey ordered the following five media from high to low in media richness: (1) face-to-face (highest); (2) regular telephone; (3) voice mail; (4) electronic mail; and (5) business memo (lowest). In terms of their preferences for using these five media, managers ranked them as follows from high to low: (1) face-to-face (highest); (2) electronic mail; (3) regular telephone; (4) business memo; and (5) voice mail (lowest).

It is interesting to note that no major differences existed across the four cultures when it came to perceptions of media richness or preferences for their use. The only exceptions were that American and Australian managers rated the business memo lower and the telephone higher in media richness than did managers from Hong Kong

Informal communication.

and Singapore. However, the latter two groups of managers preferred to use the telephone more often than did the Americans and Australians, especially when dealing with uncertain situations. It would seem that the American managers preferred to rely more heavily on the written word when dealing with uncertain circumstances—an unusual finding, given their lower ranking of the memo (than other forms of communication) in media richness, and their implicit understanding of the potential for vocal cues to add to or clarify their messages.

Networks

Channel selection and organizational network usage affect communication effectiveness. *Networks* are the interconnected channels or lines of communication used in organizations to pass information from one person to another. The flow of communication operates in downward, upward, lateral, and informal networks (again see Figure 7.1).

Downward communication directs information messages to subordinates. Messages include job instructions, individual expectations and evaluation (feedback), organizational procedures, training, and company-directed propaganda. Downward communication is solicited by employees who want feedback about their job performance, similar to the ways students seek results from tests, papers, and projects. Problems occur when information doesn't filter down to appropriate organizational levels. In addition, messages are often distorted and disrupted before they reach lower levels of the organization. For example, information may become distorted when the word "leaks out" that a company is planning layoffs, or when the chairperson of the board is abruptly asked to resign by the board of directors.

Because downward communication is also seen as potentially threatening to employees, open communication between supervisors and subordinates becomes essential to organizational effectiveness. For example, when a supervisor calls and asks you to come to her office, you usually will feel anxious because you are unsure of what issues are involved (job evaluation, promotion, and so on). Top management should also be selective in choosing the types of messages they send to subordinates. A personnel director who calls departmental meetings every Monday morning for the same pep talk will eventually be tuned out. Employees get bored with redundant information and tend to listen more carefully when meetings are scheduled only when necessary.

Additionally, research by Virginia Richmond and James McCroskey (2000) indicated that supervisors who effectively use nonverbal communication to signal liking, positive evaluation, and positive affect for their subordinates will be perceived as more credible and attractive (from both task and social perspectives) in the eyes of their subordinates. Additionally, the latter will express more positive attitudes toward their supervisors as well as supervisor-subordinate communication.

Upward communication is defined as any message sent from a subordinate to a supervisor or manager. As such, these messages may take the form of comments and suggestions about regulations and policies, tasks (e.g., work updates, potential problems, opportunities for cost savings and increased production, business trends, etc.), or the maintenance of the supervisor-subordinate relationship. Jaesub Lee (1998) reported some interesting research conducted by Waldron (1991), Tepper (1995), and Lee and Jablin (1995) on the topic of supervisor-subordinate relationship maintenance strategies.

For example, Waldron (1991) noted four major tactics that subordinates use to develop and maintain relationships with their supervisors: (1) *personal tactics*—joking, information sharing, and social conversation; (2) *contractual tactics*—conforming to formal requirements, expectations, and general communication conventions associated with the subordinate's roles; (3) *regulative tactics*—limiting or managing the amount of contact, communication, or emotional displays with (or in the presence of) their supervisors; and (4) *direct tactics*—revealing personal views, opinions, expectations, and perceptions of injustice present in the workplace. Tepper (1995) observed a fifth major tactic, *extracontractual,* which reflects a subordinate's willingness to go beyond organizational and supervisory expectations or requirements regarding flexibility or the task at hand.

Lee and Jablin (1995) went one step further and noted the types of strategies subordinates use in supervisor-subordinate relationships that are escalating (moving to a higher or closer level than the subordinate is comfortable with), deteriorating (degenerating to a level with which the subordinate feels uncomfortable), or routine. When the relationship is *escalating,* Lee and Jablin noted that subordinates generally respond in one or more ways: avoid interactions entirely; change the subject of the conversation directly or indirectly; procrastinate when it comes to interacting with the supervisor; or openly express their positions, feelings, and opinions. When the relationship is *deteriorating,* they may approach their supervisors directly and openly with their concerns; work to increase feelings of closeness; deceive or distort their own views about the situation; use caution during interactions; or make attempts to raise their "stock" in the eyes of the supervisor. Finally, if the relationship is perceived to be *routine* (i.e., neither escalating or deteriorating) and they are comfortable with its status, subordinates will attempt to maintain the relationship in one or more ways: avoid negative interactions; approach their supervisors with caution; show encouragement, concern, and interest; engage in positive interactions; or create small talk whenever it's possible or appropriate.

As you can see from the previous discussion, managers need to encourage open and honest (upward) communication because it is an important indication of how effectively their (downward) communication is perceived by subordinates. Additionally, through the use of effective upward communication, subordinates can keep their supervisors and managers informed; increase openness and feel freer to comment both positively and negatively; increase trust in the supervisor-subordinate relationship; and contribute to a greater sense of organizational cohesiveness.

Lateral or horizontal communication takes place between peers at the same hierarchical levels. Its primary functions are task coordination, problem solving, information sharing, and conflict management. Lateral communication often acts as a substitute for upward and downward communication when organizational members are frustrated or angry. Other factors that limit the frequency and effectiveness of lateral communication are rivalries, employee specialization, and lack of motivation. In instances such as these, lateral communication actually can become destructive. For example, employees may complain among themselves about an assembly line inspector who fails to check safety equipment. Over time they may even begin to sabotage his efforts. In contrast, as the quality of lateral communication increases, a number of positive outcomes occur. Problems can be solved, tasks can be coordinated, and overall conflict can be managed or avoided.

As we stated earlier in the chapter, *informal networks* also exist in organizations. Generally, they operate in the form of elaborate "grapevines." The grapevine was once thought to be characterized by disorganized, poorly defined lines of communication. However, research has

A classroom situation reflects both upward and downward communication channels.

shown that grapevines are faster and more accurate than formal lines of communication. During periods of excitement and insecurity, the grapevine becomes exceptionally active. For example, the installation of word processors in a secretarial pool may be perceived as a threat to overall job security. At times such as these, the grapevine will buzz with activity, and should be fed by managers with accurate information to keep the situation from getting out of hand. Should the situation become explosive, the results could be poor employee relations, decreased production, and employee layoffs.

The boundaries of all human organizations are defined and limited by the reach and efficiency of their communication networks.

OTTO LERBINGER

Professionalism and the Organization

In the first part of this chapter, we offered you a brief history of organizational thought and examined the types of communication that exist in the organizational setting. We now turn to a consideration of professionalism in organizations. This section will examine "office politics" and the concept of networking. In addition, we will address the contribution of personal appearance.

Professionalism

When we hear the word *professional* to describe an athlete, we often think of the differences between amateurs and pros. Amateurs are those who are less experienced and knowledgeable than the pros, for example, high school or college ball players. Additionally, amateurs generally receive no formal payment for competing in sporting events, while professionals make astronomical amounts of money.

However, in most organizations there is more to making money that makes us professionals. There is a commitment to the standards of excellence established in most fields of work. In medicine, the Hippocratic oath guides physicians in life and death decisions. In many other fields, codes of ethics or standards of practice are established and followed by practitioners. To illustrate, consider the many attorneys, appraisers, engineers, surveyors, negotiators, relocation experts, and people from related fields who are responsible for building and maintaining roads, bridges, dams, waterways, power lines, telephone lines, telecommunication links, and pipelines around the world. For more than 50 years, many of these "professionals" in the United States and Canada have shared membership in, and adhered to the code of ethics of, an organization called the International Right of Way Association (IRWA). Other "chapters" of the organization that emerged in the 1990s included Mexico, Puerto Rico, and South Africa.

Being a member and adopting IRWA's code of ethics means maintaining a commitment to honesty, courtesy, high-quality service, and fair dealing; building good will and the confidence of the public and your employer; conducting yourself in the most ethical and competent manner when testifying as an expert witness; accepting responsibility for, and a commitment to, public service; striving to express sincerity in such a way that you enrich human contact with others; and "practice of the golden rule" (IRWA, 1999, p. 170). For these people, professionalism is associated with the way they conduct business on a daily basis. By necessity, that means knowing who they are and what they value as individuals and human beings, communicating in such a way that they meet or exceed the standards and ideals they have set for themselves, and "encouraging and fostering high ethical standards" on the part of anyone participating in their profession.

Given this definition of professionalism, many of the following (may) qualify: the quarterback of the Miami Dolphins, the president of your college or university, an FBI agent, a CNN news anchor, an assistant editor for a publishing house, an herbalist, or a dental hygienist. No matter what their line of work, professionals share one common characteristic: a commitment to high standards of conduct and excellence in their fields.

Although new graduates often perceive themselves to be ready to join the professional world, developing and maintaining a professional attitude and set of behaviors are challenging at best. Success means knowing yourself (your strengths, weaknesses, and values) and understanding what being a "professional" means to others in your field. Success also means understanding how decisions about personal appearance, networking, and "office politics" contribute to being perceived as a professional. Each of the latter three subjects will be addressed in the pages that follow. We hope this discussion will spark your interest and help you begin (or continue) your life as "a professional" in the field of your choosing.

PERSONAL APPEARANCE.   The contribution of personal appearance to perceptions of professionalism cannot be overestimated. First impressions serve a public relations function for you and your organization because appearance sends signals to others about attitudes, feelings, and personality. For many years IBM salespeople were required to wear dark suits or dresses, which stereotyped them as conservatives. Most companies no longer have stringent dress requirements for their employees, but clothing remains an important aspect of an organization's image. Thus, appropriate appearance is necessary for upward mobility within an organization. Observing people in higher management positions will indicate what attire is considered appropriate. When deciding what to wear to your first major job interview, find out the dress of others who work in the position for which you are applying. Regardless of your size or sex, clothing should be coordinated in terms of color, line, texture, and style.

NETWORKING.   Another vital dimension of professionalism is reflected in the concept of networking. *Networking* is the process of developing internal and external contacts for the purposes of sharing information, advice, and support. Male members of organizations have used informal networks for years to grow professionally. These networks have taken the form of social clubs, civic organizations, and athletic groups. Recently women have begun to take the concept of networking one step further. As DeWine and Casbolt (1983) have noted, women have begun to deliberately formalize the activity by establishing "freestanding networks," or networks that link women with other women in an attempt to expand organizational contacts. The major objectives of such networking are (1) to provide women with opportunities to make organizational contacts, (2) to provide successful role models for women, (3) to generate solutions to problems, and (4) to effectively disseminate information.

Whether you are male or female, just getting started or well underway in a professional career, networking with other professionals is important. Networking has become an important key to promotion and professional growth in organizations. As such, it is a vital concept to the professional.

OFFICE POLITICS.   We have all heard statements like: "She got the job because her father is a golfing buddy of the president," "He didn't deserve a promotion, but the top brass was snowed," or "There's no need to work hard, it's all political anyway." Like it or not, office politics exist, and many bright, highly capable people become jaded because of their inability to cope with the situation. According to Michael and Deborah Singer Dobson (2000), authors of *Managing Up: 59 Ways to Build a Career-Enhancing Relationship with Your Boss*, **office politics** "is simply the name we use to describe the informal and sometimes emotionally driven process of working out goals among people. The question is not *whether* you play office politics; it's *how* you play. You have to use positive strategies, while avoiding those negative behaviors often called 'political' " (p. 124).

Professionals succeed in managing office politics by understanding the nature of power and credibility in an organization. According to Michael and Deborah Dobson, organizational power is a function of eight factors:

1. Assertiveness—being willing to speak up and ask for what you want,

2. Accomplishment—establishing a track record of successes,

3. Knowledge—knowing what you're talking about,

4. Relationships—a function of networking and seeking out mentors,

5. Initiative—being willing to take risks and take charge,

6. People skills—working and playing well with others,

7. Communication—articulating your goals and desires positively and persuasively, and

8. Understanding—determining how you and your work fit into "the big picture" (pp. 125–126).

Credibility is established by respecting and learning as much as you can from others. In fact, we recommend that you listen a lot (and talk very little) during your first three to six months in a new position. This recommendation is especially important when it comes to suggesting significant changes in your department. Credibility also is enhanced by perceptions that you "play well with others," and may be improved (or destroyed) by the relationships you cultivate in the workplace.

Patricia Sias and Daniel Cahill (1998) offered an interesting discussion about the development of peer friendships in the workplace. In a mini-study of 19 peer friendships in a variety of organizations, Sias and Cahill observed that peer friendships can go through three major stages of growth: "coworker/acquaintance-to-friend, friend-to-close friend, and close friend-to-almost-best friend" (p. 273). According to the researchers, coworkers generally move from "coworker/acquaintance" to "friend" when they work closely together in physical proximity, share common ground, and socialize together outside the organization. Their communication becomes "broader" but still "remains relatively superficial." During the second stage of relationship development, from "friend" to "close friend," coworkers begin to disclose information about "personal and work experiences" and solicit advice about problems they may have with a supervisor, coworker, or change in organizational procedures. As Sias and Cahill noted, "Communication at this transition [becomes] broader, more intimate, and less cautious" (p. 273). Finally, the change from "close friend" to "almost-best friend" is associated with "extra-organizational socializing, life events and work-related problems" (p. 288). In the almost-best friend stage, communication is "even less cautious" regarding work-related frustrations and "more intimate" than it was in previous stages.

Communication Situations

As a professional, you also must be aware of three additional communication situations associated with success in organizations. While managing workplace relationships indeed is important, so too is mastering interviews, business meetings, and formal presentations.

The Interview

If you have answered survey questions for a public opinion firm, tried to get information from a local politician about foreign policy, answered questions when applying for a job, or talked about job preferences with a career planning counselor, you have participated in an interview. *Interviews* are the most common form of planned communication and are often defined as "a process of dyadic communication with a predetermined and serious purpose designed to interchange behavior and involving the asking and answering of questions" (Stewart & Cash, 1983). Although interviews take place for a variety of purposes and in a variety of situations, we are most concerned with interviews in organizations.

TYPES OF INTERVIEWS.   There are several different types of interviews, each requiring its own skills. During an *employment interview,* or series of interviews, the employer tries to gain as much pertinent information about the applicant as possible. This kind of interview is usually broad in scope and deals with all areas of the interviewee's background and personality. The interviewer wants to find out about the applicant's work history, work habits, ability to relate to others, health, and other areas not covered extensively in the résumé or application form. Interviewees, however, do not become merely answer-producing machines. They have their own interests in mind and ask about things such as the organizational culture, benefits and salary, and opportunities for advancement. Thus, information is given and sought by both participants.

In most companies employees are given *appraisal interviews* on a regular basis. In such an interview the worker's past performance and future potential are discussed. The discussion may cover a variety of topics, such as salary, job improvement, or the need for additional training. The objective is clear—to let employees know how they are doing, how they need to improve job performance, and where they are headed. If conducted properly, appraisal interviews also let employees know that their employer cares about their work and their well-being.

When employees plan to leave their jobs, they are often given an *exit interview,* which is designed to find out how they feel about the company, the working environment, and other job conditions. The company can use this information to assess itself and make changes where necessary.

APPROACHES TO INTERVIEWING.   Be it an employment, appraisal, or exit interview, the participants can adopt one of two possible communication strategies: directive or nondirective. As an interviewer in a *directive interview,* you must have not only a general plan of what you wish to accomplish but also a step-by-step outline to follow. Although this type of interview has the advantage of being thorough, it may be so abrupt and impersonal that the interviewee is uncomfortable. As the following dialogue between the manager of a men's clothing store and a job applicant illustrates, when you are conducting a directive interview, you use frank, matter-of-fact questions, which give you complete control over the discussion. In this case, the store manager is seeking to fill a vacant sales position. (For a more complete discussion concerning preparation for job interviews, see Appendix A.)

> Interviewer: By looking at your résumé, I can see you already have experience in the retail business. What exactly did your job entail at the department store?
>
> Interviewee: At first I was a cashier, and later I assisted customers.
>
> Interviewer: What did you enjoy most about the job?
>
> Interviewee: I like people and especially helping them out. So, I really enjoyed giving them some help with their purchases and answering any questions they had.

Gaining pertinent information is one major goal of employment interviews.

Interviewer: Is there any particular reason for your leaving the job?

Interviewee: Since the store was so large, it was sort of impersonal. I want to work in a smaller place where I can deal more with the customers. The department store is often self-service.

Interviewer: Do you have any plans beyond salesperson?

Interviewee: Yes, I hope to advance to store manager some day.

In a *nondirective interview,* you give interviewees a great deal of leeway in their responses. This kind of interview is not entirely unstructured, however. If an interviewee strays from the subject, he or she is redirected back to the topic. The conversation may run freely, but the major points are developed by the interviewer. The disadvantage of this approach is that you may not obtain all the needed information. The advantage is that an informal atmosphere relaxes the interviewee and encourages him or her to speak freely. Here is an example of a nondirective exit interview:

Interviewer: John, I'm sorry to see you leave, but I hear you have a good job offer.

Interviewee: Yes, B&G Steel Company hired me as their foreman.

Interviewer: So, tell me all about it.

Interviewee: Well, I'll be managing about fifty people and getting a lot more money. This will help the problems with the family.

Interviewer: Problems?

Interviewee: Yeah, you know how it is with two teenage kids . . . braces, sports, and school supplies. I liked this job and I really don't want

A business meeting.

to leave, but I didn't see any chance of promotion. And I couldn't wait any longer. Oh, and the new place is located pretty close to home, so I don't have such a long drive. The car is getting pretty run down, and just last week I thought it was a goner—couldn't start it up for hours!

Interviewer: You said you liked your job here. Why?

Interviewee: Well, the people in the shop are friendly, and the shop foreman is a good guy.

This sample shows both the strengths and weaknesses of the nondirective interview. Although the interviewee certainly feels relaxed, the interviewer has learned a lot about his personal problems but relatively little about working conditions at the shop. The ability to communicate effectively can obviously pay off in an interview situation.

The Business Meeting

After you join the workforce of an organization, business meetings may be your most frequent formal communication interaction. *Business meetings* usually involve information giving and small group discussion, and generally include five to ten people who interact about organizational concerns. Meetings are usually designed to disseminate information or to develop solutions to current organizational problems. A union spokesperson may explain to a small group of automotive-employee leaders the latest features of their negotiated contract, while management personnel get together to discuss methods of dealing with union demands. The business meeting is essential to every organization.

The Formal Presentation

Another structured form of organizational communication is the *formal presentation.* The responsibility is placed on one person to create interest and to motivate the audience to listen. The speaker sends a message orally with the aid of visual or audiovisual materials. A young civil engineer presenting a proposal for a new technology park to more established engineers in the city will carefully plan a verbal presentation explaining commercial potential, landscape design, acreage available, utilities, and so on. Most likely, the presentation will include a computer-generated audiovisual materials to ensure clarity and receptivity of the message.

As an employee, you may be asked to explain new organizational policies, teach other employees about the proper use of technical equipment through demonstration, attempt to persuade employees to accept new ideas, and try to motivate employees to greater productivity. Individuals in organizations are unique, and you must understand them before preparing a message to meet their needs. Chapter 8 explains methods of audience analysis that should make your job easier. For a formal presentation you will also be concerned about your delivery, types of communication purposes, organization of messages, and how to secure the information to be included in your presentation. Careful consideration of the principles in Chapters 9, 10, and 11 should help you improve your formal presentation skills.

Visual aids can be an informal part of a formal presentation.

Summary

Organizations are groups of individuals constructed to achieve specific goals that could not be met by individuals alone. They are influenced by more than 200 years of organizational thought.

Scientific management principles that heavily influenced the way we do business today were postulated by Taylor, Fayol, and Weber. Taylor championed a scientific approach to work and management that included an emphasis on time and motion studies. Fayol offered us 14 principles of organizational management, while Weber proposed bureaucracy as the most rational and logical approach to leadership and management.

Mayo, McGregor, and Likert were three major contributors to the human behavior school. Mayo presented us with information about the Hawthorne effect, and the importance of paying attention to human factors at work. McGregor contrasted Theory X and Theory Y styles of management and discussed their ramifications for motivation in the workplace. Likert proposed participative management as a more employee-centered approach to organizational management.

The integrated perspectives school emerged in response to the two previously mentioned schools. Proponents of this perspective brought discussions of organizational processes, environments, and cultures to the table. They were interested in studying how people, technologies, and environments work together to influence organizational outcomes. They were also interested in how organizational cultures emerge.

More recently, postmodern, critical, and feminist theories have emerged in the literature. These theories focus on characteristics of present-day organizations, how power, domination, and political influence are used in organizations, and the role that gender and diversity play in organizations. The latter two go beyond other theoretical approaches in that they serve as critiques of postmodern organizational life.

Organizations also are characterized by three types of messages: regulation/policy, task, and maintenance. These messages are affected by the structure of communication used in the organization. Formal structures function through organizational rules and regulations, while informal structures function through interpersonal relationships among employees. How messages are sent in organizations is a question of both choice and effectiveness. Media that are available for us to use differ in "richness." Face-to-face interaction is considered to be highest in media richness, while business memos are perceived to be lowest.

Networks are the channels used to transmit messages from one person to another. Communication networks operate in downward, upward, lateral, or informal modes.

After you have familiarized yourself with an organization's communication patterns and structures, it is important for you to understand professionalism and its role in the organization.

Professionalism is associated with the extent to which you honor and live by the code of ethics and standards of conduct associated with the field in which you work. It is also affected by perceptions of your personal appearance, ability to network, and knowledge and ability to manage office politics effectively.

Maintaining a "professional" personal appearance contributes to others' perceptions of you as a professional.

Networking is also a valuable tool for professionals' growth in organizations. Networking involves the development of contacts for information, advice, and moral support.

Knowledge of office politics should help remind you to select group affiliations carefully. Professionals succeed by establishing a power base and developing a set of strategies for implementing ideas and change.

Office politics is usually part of the informal communication structures, but for upward mobility, the formal, structured situations are most important. The most common formal communication situations are interviews, business meetings, and formal presentations. Knowing what to expect and guidelines to follow should help you perform effectively.

Exercises

GROUP EXPERIENCES
Organizational Networks

DESCRIPTION   Organizations use a variety of networks to communicate with employees. Supervisors use downward communications to give instructions. Subordinates send upward communications to offer ideas about working conditions. Peers communicate laterally to establish interpersonal bonds, and at times everyone communicates at once in haphazard informal networks. Networks are essential for interdepartmental coordination, but networks are often used inappropriately. This exercise is designed to provide experience in dealing with communication networks within organizations.

PROCEDURE   Divide into groups of five to seven persons. Within the groups, come up with a topic that could be used in the four communication networks. For example, each network is used in training programs in which new employees are instructed on the proper use of copying equipment, regulations, and so on. After the groups decide on topics, get group members to line up in rows (like a train). Exchange topics between the groups. With downward communication, the first person in the row should pass detailed instructions through channels until they reach their proper destination: person seven. (No feedback should be given, and all communication must move downward.) Next, divide the row into groups of two to three persons and discuss the message laterally; but again, remember that no interactions should take place with others in the chain. After a few minutes, form the rows again and send upward communication about the initial interaction. Finally, let members discuss the topic with whomever they wish.

DISCUSSION   Which communication network was the most satisfactory? You probably found that each situation contained unique problems. What problems were encountered with the networks? When would the use of one network be most effective? How could organizations improve their internal communication? What organizational network would you like to work in when you graduate?

Meeting Compatibility

DESCRIPTION   One of the most important formal communication situations within an organization is the business meeting. Interaction patterns during meetings are affected by the purpose of the meeting, the methods of control during the meeting, and the group membership. This exercise shows how people participating in meetings affect communication outcomes.

PROCEDURE   Divide the class into male and female groups of five to seven people. Select a controversial topic that encourages active discussion (such as ethical treatment of animals or medically assisted suicide). Each group should discuss the topic for five to ten minutes. Finally, change groups so that there is only one member of the opposite sex per group; again discuss the selected topic. After the second group discussion, have each member choose the group in which he or she felt most comfortable.

DISCUSSION   Share individual group selections with the rest of the class. What differences were there between the first and second group interactions? Why were there differences? How was the atmosphere affected by different-sex participants? How did your responses change with different group members? What does this exercise tell you about organizational meeting effectiveness?

PERSONAL EXPERIENCES

1. Find a campus organization to observe for one day. Try to analyze the formal and informal communication structures. Determine the purposes and power structure of the organization. How would you fit into this organization? After you've decided whether or not you would feel comfortable in this organization, make a list of personal criteria that organizations must meet to satisfy your needs.

2. Set up an interview with someone in middle management in an organization. During the interview, ask that individual to discuss the concept of professionalism from his or her point of view. What is a professional? What behaviors does he or she elicit? What examples does this person give of nonprofessional behavior? Then, examine your behavior in light of the talk you've had. How do you see your own behavior? How could you improve?

Discussion Questions

1. How can organizations improve their formal and informal communication structures?
2. What communication channels exist in organizations, and what role does immediacy play in their effectiveness?
3. Think about a job you have had in the past. Based on your reading in this chapter about upward communication, which relational maintenance strategies did you use with your boss? If your relationship was escalating or deteriorating at any time, how did you feel? Did the strategies you used work effectively? Why, or why not?
4. Why is it important to understand office politics?

References

Boyett, J. H., & Boyett, J. T. (1995). *Beyond workplace 2000: Essential strategies for the new American corporation.* New York: Dutton.

Cheney, G., Mumby, D., Stohl, C., & Harrison, T. M. (1997). Communication and organizational democracy: Introduction. *Communication Studies, 48*(4), 277–278.

Deal, T., & Kennedy, A. (1982). *Corporate cultures: The rites and rituals of corporate life.* Reading, MA: Addison-Wesley.

DeWine, S., & Casbolt, D. (1983). Networking: External communication systems for female organizational members. *The Journal of Business Communication, 20,* 57–58.

Dobson, M., & Dobson, D. (2000). *Managing up: 59 ways to build a career-advancing relationship with your boss.* New York: AMACOM/American Management Association.

Fayol, H. (1949). *General and industrial management.* (C. Storrs, Trans.) London: Pitman & Sons.

Han, P. E. (1983). The informal organization you've got to live with. *Supervisory Management, 28,* 27–28.

International Right of Way Association (1999). *IRWA membership directory and information guide, 1999–2000.* Torrance, CA: IRWA.

Katz, D., & Kahn, R. (1966). *The social psychology of organizations.* New York: Wiley.

Lee, J. (1998). Maintenance communication in superior-subordinate relationships: An exploratory investigation of group social context and the "Pelz effect." *Southern Communication Journal, 63*(2), 144–159.

Lee, J., & Jablin, F. M. (1995). Maintenance communication in superior-subordinate work relationships. *Human Communication Research, 22,* 220–257.

Likert, R. (1961). *New patterns of management.* New York: McGraw-Hill.

McCauley, L. (Ed.). (2000, October). Unit of One: Learning 101. *Fast Company, 39,* 101–136.

McGregor, D. (1960). *The human side of enterprise.* New York: McGraw-Hill.

Mayo, E. (1945). *The social problems of an industrial civilization.* Boston: Graduate School of Business Administration, Harvard University.

Morgan, G. (1997). *Images of organizations.* Thousand Oaks, CA: Sage.

Ouchi, W. (1981). *Theory Z.* Reading, MA: Addison-Wesley.

Peters, T. J., & Waterman, R. H., Jr. (1982). *In search of excellence.* New York: Harper & Row.

Rice, R. E., D'Ambra, J., & More, E. (1998). Cross-cultural comparison of organizational media evaluation and choice. *Journal of Communication, 48*(3), 3–26.

Richmond, V. P., & McCroskey, J. C. (2000). The impact of supervisor and subordinate immediacy on relational and organizational outcomes. *Communication Monographs, 67*(1), 85–95.

Russell, R. (1997). Workplace democracy and organizational communication. *Communication Studies, 48*(4), 279–284.

Schein, E. H. (1985). How culture forms, develops, and changes. In R. H. Killman, M. J. Saxton, & R. Serpa (Eds.), *Gaining control of the corporate culture* (17–43). San Francisco, CA: Jossey-Bass.

Secretary's Commission on Achieving Necessary Skills, U.S. Department of Labor. (1991, June). What work requires of schools: A SCANS report for America 2000.

Senge, P. (1990). *The fifth discipline.* New York: Doubleday/Currency.

Shockley-Zalabak, P. (1999). *Fundamentals of organizational communication: Knowledge, sensitivity, skills, values* (4th ed.). New York: Longman.

Sias, P. M., & Cahill, D. J. (1998). From coworkers to friends: The development of peer friendships in the workplace. *Western Journal of Communication, 62*(3), 273–299.

Simon, H. A. (1957). *Administrative behavior.* New York: Macmillan.

Stewart, C. J., & Cash, W. B. (1983). Interviewing: Principles and practices (3rd ed.). Dubuque, IA: Wm. C. Brown.

Taylor, F. W. (1911). *Principles of scientific management.* New York: Harper & Brothers.

Tepper, B. J. (1995). Upward maintenance tactics in supervisory mentoring and non-mentoring relationships. *Academy of Management Journal, 38,* 1191–1205.

Trist, E. L., & Bamforth, K. W. (1951). Some social and psychological consequences of the longwall method of coal-getting. *Human Relations, 4,* 3–38.

Waldron, V. R. (1991). Achieving communication goals in superior-subordinate relationships: The multi-functionality of upward maintenance tactics. *Communication Monographs, 58,* 289–306.

Weber, M. (1947). *The theory of social and economic organization* (A. Henderson & T. Parsons, Trans.). New York: Free Press.

Weick, K. (1995). *Sensemaking in organizations.* Thousand Oaks, CA: Sage.

Wheatley, M. (1992). *Leadership and the new science.* San Francisco, CA: Berrett-Koehler.

Woodward, J. (1965). *Industrial organization: Theory and practice.* London: Oxford University Press.

chapter eight

Intentions, Ethics, and the Speaker-Audience Relationship

key concepts and terms

Public speaking
Public communication
Speech to inform
Speech to persuade
Speech to entertain
Universal audience
Particular audience
Composite audience
Audience analysis

Demography
Beliefs
Values
Instrumental values
Terminal values
Casual audience
Passive or partially oriented
   audience

Selected audience
Concerted audience
Organized audience
Polarization
Social facilitation
Circular response

From:	"Antonio"
To:	"Daniel" <silkodx@futurenet.ab.net>
Sent:	Wednesday, April 23 1:30AM
Subject:	Give the guy a microphone!

You're not going to believe this one. I hardly believe it myself. Remember I told you about my area manager and his total lack of competence? Well, we had our monthly meeting yesterday, and I guess I had finally had it. It was the same old thing. Couple of managers came in late. Couple of others sat in the back and talked the entire time the AM was talking. I knew it was all over when the AM stuck a videotape into the VCR and, low and behold, it was a three-week-old clip from corporate. We needed half the stuff on that videotape three weeks ago, not yesterday.

Here's the amazing part. When he asked if we had any questions, I stood up and had my say. I talked about the "who-gives-a-crap" attitude that most of the managers in our area have, how that attitude was spilling over into sales and dropping our numbers to some of the lowest in the nation, and then I asked the AM if he was going to do anything about it anytime soon. (Otherwise I planned to submit my resignation on the spot!)

You could have heard a pin drop. I almost looked around to see for myself who had been talking. I was flippin' Ralph Nader. Guess that's what happens if you let things build up too long. I'll tell you more when we get together this weekend. What happened after that was the real show-stopper. But I'm still employed. More later.

—Tony

Public speaking situations can present themselves at the most amazing moments. It might be at a fraternity or sorority meeting or during an SGA meeting. It might be at a political or church conference or during a public speaking class. It even might be over lunch at D-Hall or while you're giving out flyers on the Quad. Although, as a rule, you want to be as prepared as possible when you speak, the situation may call for more immediate action, much as the situation did for Antonio in the scenario he described for Daniel.

A compelling speech doesn't require great oratory. What it does require is an understanding of effective public speaking. Fortunately, for Antonio, his public speaking training and three years on the university debate team really paid off. How can you gain the kinds of skills that will allow you to speak in public like a pro? The *information* that you need is contained in the following pages. However, as we mentioned at the beginning of this textbook, knowledge is only the beginning. To actually gain the requisite communication skills, you have to *practice!*

Public Communication: An Overview

Communication theory is relatively new, but the study of public speaking dates back to ancient Greece, when Aristotle and his contemporaries defined and practiced the principles of rhetoric. While these principles still provide the foundation of public speaking theory, modern styles of public speaking and public speaking situations are much less formal than they were in Aristotle's time. Even with less emphasis on formality, however, public speaking situations can intimidate people who are usually very talkative and outgoing. Although public speaking includes many of the same communication skills as other speaking situations, some people who are comfortable while talking in small groups feel anxious and experience communication apprehension in public speaking settings.

President Clinton angrily shakes his finger as he denies any improper behavior with an intern. "I did not have sexual relations with that woman," Clinton said. "I never told anybody to lie." (AP Photo/Greg Gibson)

Perhaps these difficulties arise because *public speaking* differs from other forms of communication in two ways. First, a public speaking situation includes two distinct and separate roles: speaker and audience. Second, in this speaker-audience relationship, the speaker carries more responsibility for the communication interaction than does the audience. In other communication situations, speakers and listeners exchange roles and share this responsibility.

A public speaking presentation does not have to be overly formal and imposing. It doesn't require a stage separating the speaker from the audience. All of us participate in public speaking when we contribute to a class discussion, when we make a suggestion at a club meeting, or when we tell a story at a party.

Like other forms of communication, *public communication* serves several purposes. When a kick-boxing instructor gives a demonstration, she uses public communication to instruct. When a member of Greenpeace speaks on the need to monitor whaling off the coast of Alaska, he uses public communication to advocate his point of view. The president of a college or university who delivers an annual speech on Martin Luther King Day uses the opportunity to stir feelings about the need to celebrate cultural diversity. Public communication can also be used to praise and to blame, to accuse and to defend. For example, when a political candidate speaks to a community group, he or she may use public communication to blame the current officeholder for everything that's wrong with the community. In contrast, a native American tribal chairperson may use the same form of communication to praise community members for helping the tribe move toward greater self-determination and economic development. The prosecuting attorney who addresses a jury uses public communication to accuse the defendant of a crime. To accomplish the opposite end, President Clinton used his testimony before Congress as a means of defending himself against charges of improper conduct with Monica Lewinsky.

Since public communication is such a useful tool for accomplishing a wide range of purposes, it is important to clear up some popular myths about speech making of any sort. The first is that the ability to make speeches is natural and cannot be learned. While some people do have a talent for it, effective public speaking can be learned through training and practice. Students who take speech courses generally improve their speech-making ability and increase their self-confidence.

A second myth is that good intentions are enough when it comes to making a speech. Good intentions do not guarantee an effective presentation. Effective public speaking depends on content and delivery. Even if someone has something valuable to communicate, if the delivery is poor, the message will be lost. Another myth is that it is not what you say that is important, but how you say it. The most eloquent delivery cannot save a meaningless message. Both content and delivery are important in achieving effective communication.

Finally, effective public speaking requires that the speaker be responsible for the message he or she presents. Although people who "speak their minds" are often praised for their stamina and courage, the effective speaker knows that, by virtue of gaining the opportunity to speak, she or he also acquires the chance to influence others. Reckless, irresponsible, or unethical speakers can cause great harm both to the members of the audience and to subsequent decisions they might make.

Although we have offered you a general distinction between public speaking and public communication, perhaps the best way to conceive of the two concepts is to view public communication as the broader of the two concepts, and public speaking (or "speech making") as a subset of public communication. Luckily for us, the principles for becoming an excellent "public communicator" and "public speaker" are the same. Given the overlap in meanings, we will use the words interchangeably for the sake of simplicity. Let's begin with the three major purposes of any form of public communication: to inform, to persuade, and to entertain.

Purposes of Communicating in the Public Setting

General Purposes

To be successful in public communication settings, you must have a clear purpose in mind. Although the purposes of speaking often overlap, you must decide if you intend to inform, persuade, or entertain your listeners.

INFORMATION EXCHANGE.   The exchange of information is basic to public communication, and all of us have participated in this type of communication situation. The *speech to inform* can take place in a variety of locations: on a lacrosse field, in a band room, or in a pool hall. Similarly, the speech to inform can use a number of formats. Instructions, reports, lectures, and demonstration talks are but a few examples. The coach explaining the strategy and tactics of a particular play informs the team through instructions. The surgeon informs colleagues about a new heart transplant technique by delivering a report on the subject. Airline attendants inform passengers how to prepare for an emergency by demonstrating lifesaving equipment. All of these examples represent public speaking situations in which the speaker's main purpose is to inform.

Since the informative speaker's goal is to successfully transmit information, he or she must present the information in a way that holds the attention of the audience. Perhaps you know teachers who could put you to sleep even though they were talking about a topic that interested you. Or perhaps you have had the opposite experience, in which a professor brought to life a subject you had previously considered fatally boring.

The success of an informative speech depends on how well the material is understood. Even if the audience is motivated to listen and the speaker is dynamic, the final evaluation of success must be based on what was learned by the audience. A brilliant speech on new advances in genetic engineering can be a failure if the audience cannot understand it.

Therefore, you must organize your speech to aid audience learning and aim for clarity and accuracy in your presentation.

PERSUASION.   The purpose of persuasion is to influence an audience's behavior or way of thinking. The art of persuasion has been a subject of interest throughout history; it is a powerful tool that can be used for both good and evil. In defining persuasion as a means of bringing about behavior change, Aristotle said that a speaker could accomplish his or her end by using *logos* (logic and reasoning), *pathos* (an appeal to the emotions), and *ethos* (proof of the speaker's morality and credibility). We will define the *speech to persuade* as a deliberate attempt to reinforce or change the attitudes, beliefs, or behavior of another person or group of people through communication.

ENTERTAINMENT.   We can define the *speech to entertain* as one that is intended to bring the audience pleasure. Such a speech is usually humorous, or at least characterized by some degree of humor. A humorous speech may be gently amusing or boisterously funny. The effect depends upon the speaker's personality, delivery, and brand of humor. A speaker can use exaggeration, sarcasm, witticisms, or burlesque humor when presenting a speech to entertain.

Listeners expend much less effort during a speech to entertain than during an informative or persuasive speech. The very nature of the entertainment speech creates speaker-audience rapport. Usually, such a speech is considerably more informal than other forms of public speaking.

Whatever your reason for giving a public presentation, you should begin and end by considering the ethical issues associated with public speaking. You will recall that we talked at length about communication ethics in Chapter 1. Everything that we shared with you at that time holds for public communication.

The Speaker and the Audience: Audience Analysis

Once you have determined your general purposes and have begun to consider the ethicality of your message, it's time to take a look at your audience. Two communication scholars who have made some interesting and important observations about audiences are Alan Gross and Frank Myers. Gross (1999) posited two primary audiences based on the work of well-known rhetorician, Chaim Perelman: universal and particular audiences. Gross (1999) and Myers (1999) added a third audience to the mix: composite audiences.

Before we present the distinctions among these three audiences, first we need to highlight two important assumptions on which we are basing this discussion. First we agree with Perelman and Gross that all audiences are *constructed* by the speaker. In other words, the term "audience" may best be defined as the speaker's "best guesses" about the people who ultimately will be listening, including the facts, values, and views of what is "real" and "preferable" associated with them (Gross, 1999). Second, our construction of "the audience" (i.e., our "best guesses") will change from the time we begin a speech or presentation until the time we end it. Our ability (or inability) to make assessments about "the audience" throughout a presentation, and our skill at adapting the message accordingly, ultimately determine the outcomes of that presentation.

To illustrate, consider your most and least favorite professors in college thus far. Your favorite teacher probably begins each term by treating her new class as a group of individuals, each of whom has varying levels of apprehension, skill, and interest in the subject. She starts there with her "best guesses" about the class, makes an effort to get to know everyone, and then adapts her material as best she can throughout the term. She slows down, speeds up, and allows sidebar discussions, based on her "best guesses" about the class on a given day. At the end of the term, her "construction" of the audience is different from the one she had at the beginning of the term. That's because, throughout the process of the course, they have changed and grown—just as she hoped they would do. How does your least favorite college professor stack up when it comes to his or her construction of "the audience"? We bet that construction has something to do with negative perceptions about college students in general, lack of interest in being in the classroom at that moment, and level of burnout as a teacher. Instead of getting to know your class, and constantly assessing his "best guesses," his perceptions remain the same from the beginning to the end of the term. As a result, he and your class become victims of a self-fulfilling prophecy. You `become" everything be believed your class to be at the outset: "disinterested," "unmotivated," "angry," and "critical of authority."

Although our example involves two speakers who create messages across months rather than minutes, we believe that Perelman's assumptions are relevant for speakers, no matter how long the presentation. Given the articulation of our assumptions, we now move to a brief discussion of universal, particular, and composite audiences.

According to Perelman and Gross, a ***universal audience*** is one to which you speak as "rational human beings." As such, you are interested in presenting themes associated with universal "facts" or "truths." In contrast, a ***particular audience*** constitutes "one segment or another of humanity" such as Americans, Republicans, Democrats, Catholics, Protestants, SAE's, Delta Chi's, Habitat for Humanity, the Outdoor Adventure Club, and so on (Gross, 1999, p. 210). With particular audiences, you focus on themes associated with "that which is valued" or "preferred" (pp. 206, 210). Note that the difference between the two lies in both your construction of them as well as the arguments with which you wish to approach them.

You should note that both universal and particular audiences are always ***composite audiences,*** or heterogeneous in terms of demographics, attitudes, beliefs, values, and attitudes toward the speaker, subject, and purpose of the presentation. As such, no matter how you construct an audience in terms of the forces and arguments that drive you to speak, you must deal with the realities of audience members as *individuals*. (That means you must adopt the approach and behaviors of your favorite professor in order to become more than just an average speaker.)

As you can see, communication in the public setting is much like that in other settings: It too involves both a listener and a speaker. A speaker's ideas, speaking style, and nonverbal behavior are only a part of successful delivery—the listener is equally important. How do you determine the type of composite audience to whom you will be speaking? The answer lies in the concept of ***audience analysis,*** or the act of acquainting yourself with your listeners before giving a speech.

For of the three elements in speech making—speaker, subject, and person addressed—it is the last one, the hearer, that determines the speech's end and object.
ARISTOTLE

Of course, it is impossible to know everything about the members of your audience, but you can aim for a realistic assessment of the overall situation. First, try to learn about those aspects of the audience that will have the greatest effect on its listening behavior. Then, if time and circumstances permit, acquaint yourself with other factors. Let's say that you are going to give a speech on current unemployment problems. It would be more important to learn about the socioeconomic occupational backgrounds of your audience than about its religious affiliations.

What are some of the demographic characteristics of this audience?

Keep in mind that your own attitudes and stereotypes can influence the way you relate to your listeners. You should overcome your biases so that they will not limit your ability to judge how others think and feel.

Remember, too, that people change with time, and so will your audiences. An analysis made several weeks before you speak may not alter drastically by the time you are heard, but some minor changes will naturally occur. Even if you have done a careful job of audience analysis before you walk to the podium, your listeners may change *while* you are talking. Prior analysis is only the beginning of understanding and relating to your listeners. While speaking, you must continue your examination, looking for audience reaction to the ideas you are presenting. What clues are your listeners giving you? What are their facial expressions? Are their eyes on you? Are they squirming in their seats, laughing, whispering, applauding? A successful speaker knows how to pick up on such cues, accept them, and then adapt the message accordingly.

Demographic Analysis

What are the ages of the members of the audience? What is their average salary? Is one sex more represented than the other? What kinds of occupations do the people hold? What is their level of education or religious background? These are some of the questions asked when analyzing the demographic characteristics of an audience. *Demography* is the statistical study of populations. In the demographic approach to audience analysis, specific factual information is recorded upon which probable audience reaction is based.

AGE. Consider the ages of your audience members when planning your speech. People of different ages like different clothes, listen to different music, and have many different attitudes and beliefs. It is hardly surprising, then, that young, middle-aged, and older people react differently as audience members.

Awareness concerning political affiliations is critical to speaking effectively in public.

Winston Price, a writer of popular songs for all age groups, was often called on to talk about his career and about music in general. His speeches usually resulted in a strong, positive reaction from the audience. One of the reasons for his success was his ability to alter the approach and content of his speech depending on the average age of his audience. When speaking to teenagers, he dealt primarily with "top ten" hits and popular rock groups, but these were quickly put aside when he spoke to senior citizens, to whom he talked about entertainers such as Frank Sinatra, Lawrence Welk, and Guy Lombardo. If Price spoke to an audience composed of all ages, he approached the subject in more general terms, giving examples that appealed to all members instead of a select few.

EDUCATIONAL LEVEL.   Before giving a speech, try to estimate your audience's educational level. This will help you to know what vocabulary, sentence structure, and abstract ideas will be appropriate. Also, it will let you know how many examples and definitions you will have to give in order to be understood. If you speak below your listeners' educational level, they more than likely will be not only bored but also angry when they discover they are being patronized. Likewise, if the audience is not as educated as you are, keep the vocabulary and structure of your speech at the audience's level. Too many speakers throw in technical, difficult terms to show how much they know. Your purpose as a speaker is to communicate to your audience, not to boost your ego.

Remember, there is not necessarily a correlation between the amount of education your audience members have and their degree of understanding and knowledge of a specific subject. Besides knowing your audience's educational level, you should, if possible, determine the amount of information it already has on the subject you will discuss. Before giving your speech, try to find out whether or not your listeners have done any reading on the subject, observed it, or perhaps even participated in it. You might want to talk about wind surfing because you went once or twice, but there could be members of the audience who are real pros and could speak more knowledgeably about the sport. Through analysis of your audience's knowledge, you will be able to take advantage of what your listeners already know and give them the additional information they need.

SOCIOECONOMIC STATUS.   Many of your listeners' values and attitudes are based on their economic background, so this aspect should also be taken into consideration when planning your speech. If, for example, you are asked to discuss the school budget for the coming year, a subject that influences tax level, you should be aware of the economic status of your listeners and the weight of their current tax burden.

Audience members are also influenced by their social background and experiences and by the attitudes and values they have developed. No one can totally escape his or her past. Social background, in fact, is often considered to have the strongest effect on listeners, being more important than religion, age, or sex.

OCCUPATION.   People's occupations often give clues to their educational level as well as to their information on and interest in certain subjects. Although both car mechanics and accountants may be interested in future modes of transportation, the former group would probably be more interested in a new engine part.

Different occupational groups may be concerned about different aspects of a topic. For example, postal clerks might want to know how a postal law will affect their present salaries, while publishers may be interested in how the law will influence their mailing costs. Similarly, newspaper editors may be interested in learning the facts about a new superhighway, urban planners about the ways it will change the city's environment, and construction workers about the possibility of new job openings.

SEX.   In the past, men and women were often thought to be interested in entirely different things. With the advent of the women's movement and the entrance of women into every field of endeavor, this "obvious" generalization about men and women is no longer appropriate. Some women are not only interested in airplanes, they also fly them in combat. Some men are not only appreciative of sewing, they also design clothes. Today, it is harder to differentiate audience interests on the basis of sex than it was in the past.

Nonetheless, the sensitive speaker may still be able to discern meaningful, if sometimes subtle, differences between audiences composed of men or women. For example, as a result of early socialization, males have been taught to listen more for facts, while females have been reinforced for effectively decoding relational cues. Likewise, scholars have recently suggested that women have a tendency to recall more messages than men, particularly if the messages are health-related, and emotional message appeals in particular (Lee & Davie, 1997). Women also have a tendency to integrate emotion into the rational analyses of problems, rather than separating emotional behavior from verbal analysis (Christen, 1991). The implication of these differences is that as a speaker, you may need to take these variables into account. However, you must keep in mind that generalizations are just that—and that there are countless exceptions.

GROUP MEMBERSHIP.   If you are asked to speak to a particular group or organization, such as the Dawn Sailing Club or the American Chiropractic Association, you are one step ahead in the analysis game. The groups people belong to give you many clues to their other demographic characteristics. Most clubs or associations have certain guidelines they wish all members to follow—religious groups follow certain moral codes, political associations advocate certain partisan positions, and so on.

Referring to your audience's group in your speech can sometimes create a closer speaker-listener bond. Let's say you are trying to persuade a group of women faculty members at the local community college to support a newly established women's health center with financial assistance and volunteer service. You might draw a parallel between their fierce battle against the college administration for more equitable salaries for male and female faculty members and your own group's attempt to provide good, low-cost health services despite the opposition of the community's medical hierarchy, composed mostly of men. If you are able to identify the group memberships of audience members, you may gain insight into their attitudes and determine in advance what their reactions will be to your speech.

CULTURAL BACKGROUND.   The U.S. has been called a veritable melting pot of cultures: African American, Caucasian, Native American, Hispanic, Asian, Middle Eastern—the list goes on. In labeling the United States in this way, however, we overlook the diversity that gives individuals their unique cultural and personal identities. As speakers, buying into this metaphor means missing out on vital information—information regarding attitudes, beliefs, values, habits, needs, and often definitions of appropriate communication behavior.

For example, an emphasis on family, community, and harmony with nature still permeates the lives of most traditional Native Americans in this country. Likewise, for citizens of Asian descent, family and company loyalty often supersede individual or personal rights. Thus, to approach members of a tribal council with a proposal to buy and develop sacred lands at "fair market price" would produce responses ranging from disdain to open hostility. Recommending to a group of Japanese business executives that they fire or force into early retirement their older employees would quickly destroy your credibility with the former as an international management consultant.

To gain insights into any audience that is potentially culturally diverse, learn as much as you can (in advance) about that audience's philosophies, attitudes, values, beliefs, and perceptions of appropriate communication behavior. A good place to begin is the travel, personal improvement, and business sections at your local bookstore. Another is talking with representatives of that culture prior to making your presentation. Many colleges now offer courses on multicultural diversity, especially as it relates to the business and corporate worlds.

Colin Powell's credibility contributes to his success as a public speaker.

Psychological Variables

BELIEFS AND VALUES.   According to psychologist Milton Rokeach, *beliefs* are probability statements about the existence of things, or statements about the relationships between an object and another quality or thing. For example, we may "believe in God" or believe that God is omnipotent—the former being a belief in something and the latter being a belief in a quality-object relationship. *Values,* on the other hand, are specific types of beliefs that are central to our lives and act as life guides. According to Rokeach (1973) values may take one of two forms: those that are guidelines for living and on which we base our daily behavior (*instrumental values*), and the ultimate aim or aims toward which we work (*terminal values*). An example of terminal values might be the desire to have a comfortable life. Being ambitious or cheerful is an example of an instrumental value.

Many of our beliefs and values are acquired early in childhood and, although somewhat altered by new experiences, remain the basis of many of our thoughts and actions. As a speaker, you must therefore pay close attention to these elements when analyzing your audience. As we mentioned earlier, you can appeal to an audience's values in order to persuade them to accept your point of view; but in order to achieve this end, you must be sensitive both to your own value structure and to that of the members of your audience. You must seek out the common ground that will give clues to their value structure. Let's suppose that you are going to talk to the Veterans of Foreign Wars about capital punishment, but you do not know their basic convictions. Before delivering your speech, you could read recent newspaper and magazine articles about the VFW's reaction to present-day political issues. From these you would be able to infer some of their basic beliefs and adapt the approach of your speech accordingly. Remember, however, that group associations do not always present the whole picture. The views of Democrats and Republicans, for example, often overlap on specific issues; not all Democrats feel one way and all Republicans another.

Audience Attitudes

TOWARD THE SPEAKER.   No matter how well you know your subject and how capable you are of speaking about it, you will not be effective if the audience dislikes you or strongly disagrees with your ideas. An audience's attitudes about speakers often determine their success or failure in communicating the desired message.

What criteria influence an audience's decisions about a speaker? Studies show that audiences base their attitudes on a variety of things. Some are meaningful, such as the person's experience, and others petty, such as whether or not the speaker is a member of the "in-group" and whether he or she is liked or disliked. In most cases, however, a speaker's success depends on the listeners' confidence or faith in him or her and what they feel is the speaker's worth or competence, usually referred to as speaker *credibility*, or ethos.

As difficult as it may be to "see ourselves as others see us," it is extremely important for you as a speaker to try to estimate what the audience will think of you. Whether this information is uncovered through informal conversation or through direct questioning of prospective audience members, you should seek out both the positive and the negative expectations of the audience. With this information you can make a deliberate effort to structure the message in such a way as to reinforce the positive expectations and diminish the negative ones.

TOWARD THE SUBJECT.   As stated earlier, if your audience's attitude toward the subject of your speech is favorable, your task is easier. All you have to do is give the subject a fresh approach and reinforce your ideas. But what do you do if your audience is neutral? People who have no opinions on a particular topic will probably listen to both sides of the issue and keep their minds open to all information and attempts at persuasion. At the same time, though, they may be critical of everything they hear. Neutrality toward a subject does not mean indifference to it. Neutral listeners are concerned about the subject but have not yet made any final decisions about it. As politicians have discovered, these open-minded audience members may be very important to the outcome of a persuasive speech. They can still be moved to either side of an issue. This movement is possible, however, only if the speaker presents sound evidence to support his or her ideas, relates to the audience by sharing experiences, and answers all questions.

If you feel that your audience is indifferent to your topic, make your speech as interesting as possible. You can do this by finding an appealing, exciting way to cover the topic, by using attention-getting devices, and by playing upon other interests the members of your audience may have that are related to your subject area. Members of the yacht club might not be concerned with world politics, but they could be interested in the political implications of maritime law. Literature may be exciting to elementary students when related to storytelling by writing TV scripts for their favorite show.

If you know that your audience is negatively disposed toward your subject, work to appear calm and controlled. Additionally, for audiences that are extremely hostile, try these five steps:

1. If possible, pinpoint the specific causes of your audience's hostility.

2. Determine the points on which you and the audience agree and demonstrate similarity with your listeners regarding these issues.

3. As you move to the points on which you disagree, maintain a heightened sense of neutrality and respect for the audience's position.

4. Discuss thoroughly the value (advantages and disadvantages) of your position on each point of disagreement.

5. Organize and deliver the message in such a way that each point leads to the conclusions you want the audience to draw.

Take, for example, Career Day at George Washington High, an inner-city school. Lauren, a dance instructor, had been asked to talk about her career as a professional dancer to an assembly of high school juniors. Long before she approached the podium, she knew she was going to face an uninterested, if not antagonistic, audience. But Lauren was prepared.

> You know, many football players, such as Herschel Walker, learn ballet in order to limber up and play better. Those who have tried ballet have found that it has made them more agile and has enabled them to run faster and kick farther. But football players aren't the only athletes who learn ballet; it is practiced by many gymnasts, track stars, and swimmers, as well.

By approaching her speech in this way, Lauren was able to accomplish several purposes. She lessened the opposition to her topic, gave the students someone with whom to identify, and dispelled some of the negative stereotypes connected with her subject area.

Other ways to combat audience indifference or opposition include adjusting your message, such as omitting key discrepant statements, making the message less specific, taking a less extreme position, using weaker language, and spending more time on issues and problems rather than on solutions. The most important thing to remember when confronting a negative audience, again, is to remain as calm as possible. If you hope to persuade your listeners, be careful not to show anger or impatience with their differing viewpoints. It is quite possible for you and your audience to disagree without losing respect for one another's opinions. If you present yourself and your speech in a fair and reasonable way, you may not only be able to get people to listen to your different ideas, but you may gain some converts as well.

TOWARD YOUR PURPOSE.   Every speech you make should have a definite purpose. Without the focus a well-defined purpose provides, your speech may be nothing but a collection of statements with no overall meaning. You will recall that the purpose of any speech is to inform, persuade, or entertain.

Speeches can, of course, have aspects of all three purposes, but there should be only one specific, unifying goal. If you give a speech in support of the liberalization of marijuana laws, you may inform your audience of the history of the drug's use, and perhaps relate some interesting anecdotes, but these are only means to help you accomplish your primary goal of persuasion.

The purpose of your speech will often directly depend on the audience's attitude toward the topic. Let's say that your listeners are already in favor of decriminalizing marijuana. Your purpose then is not to persuade but rather to reinforce their beliefs and inform them of the appropriate actions they can take in support of their beliefs. If your listeners are rigidly opposed to your topic, however, it might be best not to try to persuade them but simply to inform them of the facts and hope that, as a result, your audience will have obtained a more well-rounded impression of the topic. If your audience is neutral or only partially opposed, persuasion would probably be the best approach, while the interest and attention of a totally indifferent audience can often be focused on a particular issue by an entertaining delivery.

A good speaker will try to base the purpose of his or her speech on the desires and expectations of the audience. Listeners are more apt to pay attention to a speech they are prepared for and consider appropriate to their beliefs and the situation. The chances of a speech's success are greater if both the speaker and the listeners have the same purpose in mind.

Nothing angers an audience more than believing that a speaker's purpose is one thing and finding out that it is something entirely different.

> The presentation of a well-known black poet was eagerly awaited by an audience composed mostly of admirers of her work and would-be writers. Their disappointment was tinged with anger when instead of discussing her poetry, she delivered a powerful attack on Caucasian middle-class attitudes toward black Americans.
>
> Charles Marsden, a fashion designer, was asked by a women's club to speak on the history of clothing. The members felt resentful when the lecture turned out to be a sales pitch for Marsden's latest line of women's fashions.

The irritation of the audience members in both cases did the speakers much harm. Had the poet and the designer presented the expected information in a pleasing manner, they would have related well to their listeners and greatly furthered their personal causes.

If you can discover your audience's purpose and demands prior to a speech, you will know how to adapt your message to increase the likelihood of a successful outcome.

Methods of Investigating Your Audience

When preparing a presentation for one of your college classes, you already know the age, sex, relative economic status, and race of the class members. You can also make your best guesses about their opinions on issues such as censorship, job opportunities, and higher education. Difficulties occur when you are asked to speak to groups of people that you know relatively little about in terms of their demographic characteristics, values, beliefs, and attitudes.

Invitation Committee

The most obvious place to begin seeking information is from the people who invited you to speak. Immediately, questions will come to mind, such as: How many people will attend? Are there any specific time limitations or expectations? What does the audience know about the subject? Will they be required to attend? What are their ages? At first, being startled by the invitation, you may not ask all the necessary questions. If this is the case, don't hesitate to ask for additional information about your prospective audience.

Computer Technology and Mass Media Messages

Other valuable audience information comes from checking out web sites, reading community newspapers and magazines online or in hard copy, listening to local radio stations, and watching local television programs. It even may be a good idea to consult various publications for a few weeks before you speak to get an idea of important issues in the geographical area. Through the use of the Internet and various forms of mass media, you'll discover the concerns that are uppermost in the listeners' minds, such as airline strikes, terrorist activities, and military troops being activated for foreign assignments. Sometimes human interest issues surface such as celebrity or sports stars taking time out of their busy schedules to visit children in local hospitals. Even if your topic is not one of general community interest, being informed about local concerns can aid you in preparing examples and illustrations relevant to your audience.

Public Opinion Polls and Surveys

Over the years we have seen the importance of polls in predicting election results. Politicians are extremely concerned about how their platforms are accepted and how popular they are in particular areas. The information received from polls and surveys helps the candidates determine the best method of presenting their arguments and themselves. Beginning speakers can also gain insight from similar information without going to the expense of conducting actual surveys. References such as the *Gallup*

Opinion Index, Public Opinion Polls, and *Public Opinion Quarterly* provide useful data on a variety of topics for different geographical regions of the country.

Personal Interviews

If you live near your prospective audience, much can be learned about them by talking with local people. Interviews with local leaders and citizens can give you a clearer picture about who is being affected on issues such as waste water facilities, local parks and recreation departments, and health facilities. Even if you don't live nearby, after arriving in a particular area, you can talk to people with whom you come in contact (for example, restaurant personnel or gas station attendants) to find out the latest issues of concern and even language styles that might be appropriate for your particular speech.

Other Audience Considerations

Another Audience Typology

In 1935, H. L. Hollingworth developed a classification system that described audiences on the basis of their organization and orientation toward the situation in which the speech is given. This now classic approach to audiences is still highly pertinent today. As you will see, speaking before each of these audience types entails unique problems and responsibilities.

CASUAL AUDIENCES.   Frequently, in large cities, people walking down the street will stop and listen to a street orator preaching religion or some other cause, or watch an entertainer such as a magician or musician. Hollingworth calls such pedestrian audiences *casual.* These so-called audiences show very little, if any, homogeneity and, in fact, are barely audiences at all. They are just small groups of people who have gathered for a short time at the same place.

Street orators or entertainers who address casual audiences must first get the attention of the pedestrians passing by. This means that they have to spend a lot of time on their preparation and delivery. Each street orator attempts to develop his or her own unique speaking style—a specific way to hook the attention of the pedestrians. But, more important, these speakers have to *keep* the casual audience there. This means getting the listeners involved. The orator will perhaps fire questions into the crowd, and the entertainer may ask listeners to participate, emotionally or physically.

PASSIVE AUDIENCES.   The second type of audience is *passive,* or *partially oriented,* and is usually composed of captive listeners. The people who make up this kind of audience have no choice but to listen to the speaker. Students in a 400-seat lecture hall or convention goers listening to a keynote speaker are examples of passive audiences.

The size of an audience affects its behavior and reactions.

Speakers who confront passive audiences must gain the attention of the listeners and arouse their interest in the subject matter. In order to accomplish this goal, they can appeal to one or more of the interests that almost all audiences have in common. All people share basic primary interests or needs. Financial security, for instance, is one of the most basic needs of all persons. Almost everyone wants to hear about ways of earning or saving money. If you are trying to get the attention of your audience members, use some examples that are close to home and, especially, close to their wallets.

A comedian can only last till he either takes himself serious or his audience takes him serious.

WILL ROGERS

There are other common interests that, although not vital to personal welfare, appeal to audiences. Sports and hobbies are examples of such *secondary interests.* Suppose you are making a speech about an area of land you think should be converted into a state park. You might draw upon the secondary interests of your audience to advance your argument. If you have ascertained beforehand that audience members are outdoors enthusiasts, you could talk about the hiking trails, camping sites, and observation points that could be made available by such a state park. Or, if they are animal lovers, you might list the types of animals that would be protected in the park. Which secondary interests you draw on will depend on your specific audience and the results of your analysis.

Momentary interests are things that concern us for only a short time and are then replaced by other issues. A new movie or news event may be on everyone's lips for a couple of days. A speaker's reference to such a topic can be used to arouse the attention of the audience. An awareness of the momentary interests of an audience can be a great asset to the speaker.

SELECTED AUDIENCES.   Audiences who have collected for a specific purpose are referred to as *selected* audiences. These listeners normally attend a speech because they have some previous interest in the subject. Examples of such selected audiences are environmentalists who come to hear a lecture on elephant seals, New Age students attending a yoga demonstration, and members of Block and Bridle learning about a new shoeing technique.

While "interest catchers" are helpful with passive audiences, what are your responsibilities toward selected audiences that have met for a specific purpose? First, you need not try to attract attention; you already have it. Instead, you should strive to make a strong impression on your listeners so that they remember what you have said after your speech is over. A group of parents who wish to impress upon their fellow PTA members the seriousness of conditions existing in the school might invite an engineer first to inspect the buildings and then come to the next meeting to discuss the leaking roof, unsafe staircases, and broken windows.

CONCERTED AUDIENCES.   In many manufacturing companies across America, "business teams" made up of five to 15 persons meet regularly to discuss problems and issues regarding the quality of their products. These teams make up a *concerted* audience, one that has an active purpose and mutual interests, but no set separation of labor or strict organization of authority. Furthermore, the concerted audience has a high degree of orientation toward the speaker and his or her purpose. An AIDS Outreach meeting is another example of this kind of audience.

Concerted audiences are already impressed and are ready to be led to action. The speaker must therefore enforce the audience's convictions—persuading members and directing their action. Audiences may have very strong attitudes, but having such attitudes and acting on them are two different things. For example, many women who attend National Organization for Women (NOW) meetings have definite pro-women's rights views. This does not always mean that they are taking action, however. A vibrant speaker may be needed to motivate these women to take legal action in cases of sexual harassment, for example.

ORGANIZED AUDIENCES.   Finally, there is the *organized* audience, in which listeners are totally directed toward the speaker and all labor and authority lines are strictly designated. A Kansas City Chiefs coach lecturing his football team on the upcoming game against the New Orlean's Saints is speaking to an organized audience.

Organized audiences are ready for action, but they often have no direction. The speaker's responsibility in this case is to give the listeners specific instructions on the action plans. The Chiefs coach will discuss specific football moves before the big game with the Saints.

Effects of the Environment

The physical setting of your speech will greatly influence your audience's behavior. To prepare, ask yourself questions such as: Is my speech being given in a large room or in a small one? Are the chairs comfortable? How are they arranged? What kind of lighting is there, and how good are the acoustics?

Take the room itself, for instance. People will act differently if they are sitting in a large auditorium, a small classroom, or a house. Compare an audience listening to a formal lecture in a classroom with one that listens to the same speech in a coffee shop or outside under a tree.

The noises or other distractions around you must also be taken into consideration. Is the room quiet, or must you compete with the sounds of traffic outside and distractions such as loud air conditioning inside? You should learn how to adapt to such situations. You can project your voice over the noises, pause to let an intrusion pass, or incorporate the competing stimuli into the speech.

While in office, President Ronald Reagan often used noise from his helicopter to his advantage when dealing with members of the press. Rather than shout over the noise or approach the press corps close enough to hear them, he would simply cup his hand over his ear, shrug, and mouth the words, "I can't hear you." In this way, Reagan made use of the competing stimuli and avoided answering questions that he may have been unprepared to address at the time.

The atmosphere in a large auditorium with hundreds of unrelated people is, of course, very formal. Listeners usually sit in straight chairs, and all face the speaker. Compare this with a small, informal gathering in someone's home, where the listeners and the speaker have a much more intimate relationship. The listeners are more prone to ask questions and offer comments. In turn, the speaker can feel more at ease and less formal, and can more easily relate to the listeners. Additionally, he or she can use nonverbal communication more effectively to show sincerity and concern for those who are present.

The size of the audience is a physical condition that affects both your audience's behavior and your reactions to it. You will probably be more formal with large audiences than with small ones. You will also have to use more pronounced gestures and a louder voice when addressing a large audience so that members in the back rows get the full impact of the message. In a smaller group, your facial expressions and small body movements will communicate much more effectively.

The Speaker-Audience Interaction

What distinguishes an audience from a random collection of people? Three things happen when groups of people progress from a mere gathering to audience status.

POLARIZATION. The first thing that happens is *polarization,* which provides the structure for an unorganized group of people. It is at this point that audience members recognize their role as listeners and accept someone else as a speaker. Two distinct roles, then, come into existence. While the polarized audience is separate from the speaker, it is also connected to him or her by the communication that occurs. Various aspects of the public speaking situation contribute to polarization, such as seating arrangements in which the chairs face the speaker, or the stage or platform from which the speaker delivers the speech.

Polarization is both normal and necessary in public speaking situations. However, polarization can become too extreme when either speaker or audience becomes alienated from the other. Shortly after his inauguration, President George Bush accepted invitations to attend meetings at two elite, "males only" professional clubs in Washington, D.C. By doing so he drew fire from the press and damaged his credibility with feminists all across the country. Additionally, he created the potential for polarization in future meetings with this latter, highly influential audience.

SOCIAL FACILITATION. The fact that people behave differently as a function of the presence or absence of other people is called *social facilitation.* This phenomenon emerges in a number of situations. For example, when a bystander is present, weaker individuals are more likely to use violence against stronger individuals than they would without the presence of a witness (Feld & Robinson, 1998). Likewise, when we watch a situation comedy on television or by ourselves, we may not laugh aloud, even if we think the program is funny. With friends, however, we may be prompted to laugh long and loud. Social facilitation may not occur immediately. For example, a formal audience attending a theater performance may take some time to "warm up." Few people want to be the first to applaud, cheer, clap hands to the music, or stand for an ovation. Audience members look to one another for reinforcement.

Imagine that you are watching the performance of a Polish dance troupe. At the beginning of the performance, the members of the audience may be very quiet. A few people tap their feet or drum their fingers in time to the music, but most are relatively unresponsive. But as the rhythm of the music and the exuberant movements on stage affect more and more of the members of the audience, a drastic change can occur. Before you know it, you, like everyone else, may find yourself stamping your feet, clapping your hands, and cheering. Even listeners who are usually very quiet and reserved can be influenced by the excitement of an audience.

CIRCULAR RESPONSE. When the kind of communication that happens between listeners occurs between the audience and the speaker, the phenomenon is called *circular response.* The speaker says something and the audience responds with nods, applause, or frowns. From these responses the speaker knows how best to adapt what he or she says next to hold the attention of the listeners. If the response is favorable, the speaker may exert more effort, which in turn leads to more audience responses, and so on. This mutual feedback heightens the participation of both speaker and listeners and strengthens the bonds between them.

Mutual feedback heightens the participation of communicators.

Audience Analysis Checklist

Audience analysis is an art, not a science. Many variations and combinations can occur in an audience's demographic and attitudinal characteristics. Specific step-by-step rules to cover all the variables of any particular audience are difficult if not impossible to set down. However, some of the basics of audience analysis that can help you construct an effective speech are provided in Table 8.1. Also, you may ask yourself a series of questions that will help clarify your perception of your audience:

1. Before choosing my speech purpose and topic, do I know the demographic characteristics of my audience as "universal" or "particular"? What variables are most important in my conception of audience members as a "composite audience"?

2. Do I know the demographic characteristics of my audience, including age, education, occupation, personality, and so forth?

3. Have I a fairly clear notion of how much and what kind of knowledge my audience has about my topic? Will the range of knowledge among audience members be broad or narrow?

4. Have I discovered those basic religious, political, social, and moral beliefs, values, and attitudes that could affect this audience's understanding of my speech topic? Are there likely to be beliefs, values, or attitudes that may interfere with the audience's acceptance of my point of view, arguments, evidence, or examples? Have I taken these into account in planning my speech material?

5. Have I made an objective attempt to learn my audience's attitudes toward my intended purpose, my speech topic, and myself?

Audience Analysis

SUBJECT AND PURPOSE

	Your general subject area.
Purpose:	To entertain, persuade, or inform.
Specific purpose:	What you want your audience to learn; what action or response you want.
Expected purpose:	What your audience thinks the purpose is.

GENERAL CHARACTERISTICS

Personality:	Open/closed-minded, active/passive, tired/alert, calm/angry, other, mixed.
Knowledge of subject:	None—little, moderate, professional.
Knowledge of speaker:	None—little, same background, family member, friend.

DEMOGRAPHICS

Age:	Up to 12, 13–21, 22–40, 41–65, over 65, mixed.
Education:	Elementary, high school, college, graduate school, mixed.
Environment:	Rural, town, small/large city, urban, industrialized, suburbs, other, mixed.
Economic	Poor, lower-middle, upper-middle, wealthy, mixed.
Occupation:	Unemployed, student, homemaker, trade, professional, other, mixed.
Sex:	Male, female, mixed.
Group membership:	Sports clubs, lodges, occupational clubs, interest clubs, other, mixed.
Cultural background:	Homogeneous, heterogeneous.
Classification:	Casual, passive, selected, concerted, organized.

ATTITUDES, BELIEFS, VALUES

Political:	Republican/Democrat, liberal/conservative, independent, other, mixed.
Religious:	Catholic, Protestant, Jewish, other, mixed.
Attitude toward speaker:	Favorable, opposed, neutral, indifferent.
Attitude toward subject:	Favorable, opposed, neutral, indifferent.
Attitude toward purpose:	Favorable, opposed, neutral, indifferent.

ENVIRONMENTAL FACTORS

Physical setting:	Formal/informal, large/small room, indoors/outdoors, other.
Competing stimuli:	Quiet, moderate, noisy.
Size:	Small, moderate-sized, large.
Density:	Scattered, moderate, compact.
Proximity:	Audience close to speaker/far from speaker, seated in front row/back row/sides.

Source: Adapted from G. Wiseman and L. Barker, *A Workbook for Speech/Interpersonal Communication,* (San Francisco: Chandler, 1967).

6. Do I know what type of audience I will be facing? If I know, have I chosen the level and emphasis of speech materials appropriate for a casual, passive, selected, concerted, or organized audience?

7. Did I consider environmental factors that could affect the comprehension or acceptance of my ideas? Can I describe and analyze the physical setting and note its good and bad points? Are there any potential competing stimuli for which I can plan adjustments?

8. What is the occasion for which I am to speak? Is this a regular monthly meeting or an annual awards banquet? Is it a holiday or an entertainment event?

The answers to these questions will provide you with the information you need to increase the chances of a successful presentation.

Summary

Public speaking differs from other forms of communication in two essential ways: (1) Public speaking situations require two distinct roles, those of speaker and of audience, and (2) in the speaker-audience relationship, the speaker carries more responsibility for the communication interaction than does the audience.

Perhaps the most important consideration to be made before speech preparation is ethical responsibility. We talked at length about these issues in chapter 1. After dealing with ethical considerations, the speaker should select both general and specific purposes. The selection should be based on the speaker's own knowledge and interests as well as on a thorough audience analysis.

One system of audience analysis is the demographic approach. This involves the gathering of particular and factual information to predict audience reaction. A speech may be planned according to factors such as the age, educational level, and socioeconomic status of the audience. Other useful considerations are the occupations, gender, group affiliations, and cultural background of audience members. It is important to avoid stereotyping the audience, however. Demography is best used in a factual, impartial, and nonprejudiced manner.

Other variables that the effective communicator should consider are the beliefs, values, and attitudes of the audience. Familiarity with the political or religious character of the audience may provide many clues about listeners' basic beliefs and common values or convictions.

Effective communication is not likely to take place if listeners are alienated by the speaker, the subject, or the speaker's purpose. A good speaker must present the speech in a way that will emphasize the positive attitudes of the audience while minimizing its negative reactions. A message that is geared to the desires and expectations of the audience will be received more readily than one that is not.

Speaking situations vary according to another set of audience types. There are casual, passive, selected, concerted, and organized audiences, and the responsibility of the speaker is different in each case.

The person who speaks to the casual or passive audience must first attract and then hold the attention of the listeners. The select audience is a group that has met for a specific purpose, and the goal of the speaker should be to strongly impress the intended message upon them. The concerted audience is already impressed but has not yet been directed to action. In this case the speaker may try to reinforce established attitudes and motivate the listeners to take action. The final kind of audience is the organized audience. In this situation the listeners have already been persuaded of the necessity for action and are willing to carry out the specific directions of the speaker.

An intelligent public speaker must be aware of the effects of environment upon communication. Audiences react differently in large, small, formal, and informal speaking situations. Therefore, conflicting noises and distractions should be taken into account and prepared for, in order to make the smoothest possible presentation.

Those who wish to understand how a group of individuals becomes an audience and how audience reaction works should study the speaker-audience relationship. Polarization, the division of roles, establishes the speaker as separate from the listeners and establishes the connection between the two. Social facilitation involves the internal reaction of an audience to the presence of another person. Audience members reinforce the reactions of each other. Circular response involves the speaker in the sharing of excitement.

Audience analysis is an art, and like all arts must be practiced and developed by each speaker. Students of audience analysis who keep in mind the characteristics and values of the listeners, the type of audience they are addressing, and the environment in which they are making the speech are on their way to becoming effective communicators.

Exercises

GROUP EXPERIENCES
Ghostwriting

DESCRIPTION   Many audience variables need to be considered when preparing a speech or presentation for a group. Analyzing the audience is a key element in public presentations. This activity will give you the opportunity to "advise" a speaker on the elements that should be considered for a given audience and topic.

PROCEDURE   Divide into groups of four to six members. Write each of the following topics and targets on a separate piece of paper.

Topics

1. Women should pay their own way on dates.
2. The medicinal use of marijuana should be legalized.
3. Landlords should have to pay for all maintenance on apartments.
4. Mass transit (buses, subways, ferries, etc.) should be free for all users.
5. All families should be limited to two children.

Audiences

1. Corporate managers, 35 males and females, ages 45–60.
2. Women's study group, 40 females, ages 18–50.
3. Inner-city high school students, 50 males and females, ages 14–19.
4. Chamber of Commerce members, 25 males and females, ages 25–60.
5. Order of the Eastern Star, 30 females, ages 45–70.

Each group should select one topic and one target audience and should prepare a list of recommendations for things the speaker should consider. In preparing this list, the following factors should be considered:

Demographic characteristics	Cultural background
Educational level	Psychological characteristics
Socioeconomic status	Audience beliefs and values
Personality	Audience attitude toward the subject
Sex	and purpose of the speech
Group membership	

Although you have not been given all of the information just listed, you will have to make inferences about these variables. Examples of recommendations include:

1. Avoid the use of idiomatic expressions. This is a professional audience that will expect the use of professional language.
2. You will need to loosen the group up so that they will feel comfortable with one another, since they do not know one another.

Each group should identify its topic and target audience. Then, the list of recommendations should be read. Finally, the other groups should evaluate each list.

DISCUSSION   Did the group make logical inferences about the given audience? Did the recommendations reflect the appropriate concerns for the given audience? Were any important recommendations omitted? Do you think that the consideration of audience variables is important in writing an effective speech?

Audience Types

DESCRIPTION   Hollingworth developed a classification system that described audiences on the basis of their organization and orientation toward the speech situation. His audience types include casual, passive, selected, concerted, and organized audiences. This activity will give you a chance to use the Hollingworth classification system.

PROCEDURE   Each person should make up an example of two audience types. The examples should be collected and read aloud to the class. As each example is read, you should classify it as casual, passive, selected, concerted, or organized. After everyone has classified each example, the correct answers should be determined by class discussion. Check your score to see how many correct classifications you made.

DISCUSSION   Beyond the classification of audiences, of what value is the Hollingworth system? How could you use it in preparing a speech for a particular group?

Warm Up

DESCRIPTION   One of the most difficult tasks for a speaker to perform is to try to "warm up" a formal audience. Few people want to be the first to yell, clap hands to music, or even stand for an ovation. This activity will give you an opportunity to develop various warm-up techniques for different audiences.

PROCEDURE   This activity can be done either by groups or by individuals. The procedure is the same for both formats. Two descriptions of specific audiences are provided below. You are to write down all possible alternatives for warming up the given group. Your suggestions should be specific. Some examples include the following:

1. Tell a joke related specifically to the audience.
2. Bring several members of the audience in front of the group to participate in a demonstration.
3. Socialize with the group before your speech in an effort to relax them.

Setting 1
You have been asked to speak on malpractice insurance before a group of physicians. You are an attorney and have been active in lawsuits against physicians. Some members of the group resent the fact that you have been asked to speak to them. These members see you as the enemy.

Setting 2
You work for the Total Woman franchise. Your message to all women is that they should consider their husbands to be first and foremost in their lives. You have been asked to address a group of husbands who are experiencing some marital difficulties.

DISCUSSION   Have you given careful consideration to the techniques you have selected? Do any of your techniques involve nonverbal behavior, such as smiling or standing close to your audience? What are some indications that an audience is warming up to you as a speaker?

PERSONAL EXPERIENCES

1. Observe a speaker in action, but spend most of your time watching for audience response. What cues did you observe that indicated attentiveness, boredom, interest, or anger? Could you tell when (or if) the speaker won or lost the audience?

2. Have you ever considered how much information you have about people based on age alone? Consider each of the following time periods during which people were born: What do you know about people who were born during 1931–1940; 1941–1950; 1951–1960; 1961–1970; 1971–1980; 1981–1990; 1991–2000? Who were or are their heroes? What was or is the political climate they experienced?

3. Can you remember a speech that was well received by the audience? To what extent did the speaker's adapting to the audience make the speech a success?

Discussion Questions

1. How does group membership provide you with clues for presenting an effective speech?

2. What questions should you ask about an audience's cultural background before constructing a speech?

3. What environmental effects should be considered in preparing a speech for a selected audience?

4. How can you assess audience attitudes toward (a) the speaker, (b) the subject, and (c) the purpose of the speech?

5. How might an awareness of the concept of social facilitation affect your preparation of a speech for a formal audience?

References

Christen, Y. (1991). *Sex differences: Modern biology and the unisex fallacy* (68–69). New Brunswick, NJ: Transaction Publishers.

Feld, S., & Robinson, D. (1998). Secondary bystander effects on intimate violence: When norms of restraint reduce deterrence. *Journal of Social and Personal Relationships, 15*(2), 277–285.

Gross, A. (1999). A theory of the rhetorical audience: Reflections on Chaim Perelman. *Quarterly Journal of Speech, 85*(2), 203–211.

Hollingworth, H. L. (1935). *The psychology of the audience* (19–32). New York: American Book.

Lee, J., & Davie, W. R. (1997). Audience recall of AIDS PSAs among U.S. and international college students. *Journalism and Mass Communication Quarterly, 74*(1), 7–22.

Myers, F. (1999). Political argumentation and the composite audience: A case study. *Quarterly Journal of Speech, 85*(1), 55–71.

Rokeach, M. (1973). *The nature of human values*. New York: Free Press.

Communication Goals

Information Exchange, Persuasion, Entertainment

key concepts and terms

Intrinsic motivation
Extrinsic motivation
Repetition
Visual aids
Platform
Speech to convince
Speech to stimulate
Speech to move audience to
  action
Logos
Deductive reasoning
Inductive reasoning
Reasoning
Pathos
Reward appeal
Fear-arousing appeal

Efficacy message
Guilt message
Shame message
Ethos
Competence
Trustworthiness
Goodwill
Central route
Peripheral route
Experiential-schematic
  function of attitudes
Defensive function of
  attitudes
Self-expressive function
  of attitudes
One-sided message

Two-sided message
Refutational two-sided
  message
Nonrefutational two-sided
  message
Exemplar
Forewarning
Humor
Welcoming speech
Award presentation
Acceptance speech
After-dinner speech
Farewell speech
Eulogy
Impromptu speech

From:	"Annie"
To:	"Patrick" <olearypx@wfuturenet.ab.net>
Sent:	Wednesday, April 23 1:30AM
Subject:	Request for Information

Patrick,

Thank you for inviting me to speak at your next fraternity meeting about date rape. I also can't believe what happened at the Kappa house after the last keg party. Can you tell me more about what the other brothers think about the incident? How do they talk about women and sex when they're kidding around? When they're serious? I know the risks you are taking as the fraternity president just inviting me to speak on this subject at a meeting. Let me know how you would like for me to proceed.

—Annie

When we think of public speakers, we often think of politicians, CEOs, ministers, teachers, and others whose jobs require that they present messages publicly. Rarely do we think about opportunities that we may have in the future to personally affect people's lives, like Annie when she speaks at the upcoming fraternity meeting. Upon first reading Annie's e-mail, you may have thought that she was an administrator or counselor on campus. But think for a minute. Who else might she be?

Annie might be an undergraduate or graduate student who personally has experienced date rape on campus. She might be the sister, mother, or relative of a date rape victim. She might be a nurse or physician with the college or university's health center, who wants to speak because she's had to treat one too many young victims. In short, Annie could be you. And, when your time comes, you want to be ready.

In this chapter we will focus on a number of techniques for presenting a persuasive message. However, our discussion will not be limited solely to *persuasion* as a goal, but will also focus on the two other purposes of public speaking: *information exchange* and *entertainment*. As you saw in the previous chapter, you must not only know who your audience is, but you must also have a specific purpose in mind in order to be a successful speaker. Armed with this knowledge and a clear understanding of the three primary purposes of public speaking, you can begin to construct messages that win the enthusiasm, respect, and support of any audience.

Information Exchange

Ways to Increase Learning

One major goal of informative speaking is to facilitate audience learning. To do so, you must organize your speech for clarity and accuracy. However, there are several additional ways in which a speaker can increase audience learning while presenting a speech to inform. Careful attention to these areas not only improves the chances that an audience will remember what is said but also can contribute to the ease with which the speaker is able to deliver the message.

MOTIVATION.   The most significant factor in increasing learning is motivation. Before you can learn you must listen, and before you listen you must be motivated to do so. The motivation may come from within (*intrinsic motivation*) or from an outside source (*extrinsic motivation*). For example, when Min Huang attended a seminar on the Disabilities Act, he went because he wanted to be a more informed colleague. On the other hand, his lab partner Jamie went because her education professor promised to give extra credit to students who wrote reports on the seminar. Min Huang's motivation to listen and learn was intrinsic; Jamie's motivation was extrinsic. Although learning theorists disagree as to which form of motivation creates a greater increase in learning, we do know that an individual needs some type of motivation to listen to and then to learn the information being conveyed by a speaker.

If a speaker gives an audience a reason or reasons for learning the information, ideas, or skills presented, the audience gives more effort to the learning process. For example, when a representative comes to speak from the American Cancer Society and encourages the women in the audience to have a regular Pap smear and breast examination and then teaches them how to conduct breast self-examinations, she would probably tell them that doing so will increase the chances of early detection of cancer.

ORGANIZATION.   It is also the speaker's responsibility to organize his or her ideas so that the information presented to the audience is logical and easy to follow. There has been considerable research done on how the organization of a speaker's message can affect listener comprehension, speaker credibility, and listener frustration. In general, the findings of these studies support the claim that the organization of a message influences the audience in its interpretation and evaluation of a message. In studies designed to test the effects of message structure and style on listener evaluations, results indicate that messages that are more organized, logical, predictable, and factual are perceived as more comprehensible and persuasive than messages without these particular attributes (Hazleton, Cupach, & Liska, 1986). You would probably reach a similar conclusion based on personal experience. Undoubtedly, you find it much easier to understand a speaker who presents ideas clearly and logically than one who is disorganized. Most of us have trouble grasping the main idea of speakers who jump ahead of themselves or who backtrack to fill in information they left out.

EFFECTIVE DEVELOPMENT OF IDEAS.   Speakers who are presenting new information must develop their ideas effectively to sustain listener attention and motivation and thereby increase learning. There are specific techniques speakers can use to do this. One technique is to mix new and familiar ideas. Although the purpose of the speech

Effective visual aids help make ideas more clear, vivid, and concrete.

may be to present new and useful information, it is important to connect this information with something that the audience already knows. It is always easier for listeners to understand something they have experienced or can relate to. A person discussing the detrimental effects of television violence on small children would include examples of shows the audience has seen to make the information more meaningful.

Another technique a speaker can use to sustain listener attention combines the elements of conflict and suspense. If a speaker can emphasize opposition or competition through an appropriate image, the audience is more likely to note and remember that particular point. For example, an environmentalist might refer to the "race" among nations to deplete the earth's rain forests.

A strong image can serve as a focal point for a speech and give the listeners a major concept upon which they can hang other important bits of information. One key phrase can later trigger a listener's recall of important, related information. A historian describing the circumstances that led to the American Civil War could use the image of a fork in the road, one path leading to an urban, industrialized North, the other to a rural, agrarian South.

In recent years educators have talked about the need for relevance. You have no doubt sat through many speeches wondering what the information being conveyed had to do with you and your life. A speaker who can take ideas and associate them with the audience's present concerns will increase listener attention and interest. For example, a sociologist could add some interest to a discussion of primitive tribal rites by comparing them to some of the initiation rituals of various groups and societies, such as campus Greeks or urban gangs.

Another way in which a speaker can develop ideas effectively and increase learning is through the use of concrete, specific images that convey a sense of realism and vividness. A student delivering a speech on sexually transmitted diseases (STDs) could underscore their real threat to college-aged students, first, by having all members of the audience stand and, then, by seating them in groups based on actual percentages of people who will be affected by STDs in the next ten years. One of our students actually used this strategy in her classroom speech on STDs, and the effect was nothing short of amazing. Based on statistics that she confirmed with the U.S. Center for Disease Control (CDC) one day prior to her speech, she seated her classmates in the following order: "People who can have all of the sex they want in the next ten years without being affected" (a small percentage was seated, with much laughter, whooping and applause), "people who will contract STDs in the next ten years" (a larger percentage was seated, with laughter, and finger pointing especially from those already seated), "people who will know someone who has contracted the HIV virus" (the appropriate percentage was seated, and the class began to get quiet), and "people who will contract the HIV virus in the next ten years" (lots of looking around, and soft but audible, "Whoa's"). At that point, the speaker asked everyone to look around at their classmates who remained standing (again, the number reflected actual CDC percentages). Then she said, "These are the people who will not be with us at our class reunion in ten years. They will have died from AIDS if a cure isn't found in the next three years." At that point in the speech, you could have heard a pin drop in the class. Such concrete, specific images leave a vivid and lasting impression in the mind of any audience. More importantly, they remember what you had to say for years to come.

REPETITION.   In every informative speech, regardless of subject, some information is more important than the rest, and it is the speaker's responsibility to convey this to the audience. An effective speaker will increase audience learning by emphasizing the most important information through *repetition.* A speaker can mention a point, underscore its importance, mention it again in the middle of the speech, and repeat it at the conclusion. A recording engineer giving a talk to a class of would-be studio technicians might want to emphasize the need for organization during a recording session. He may mention it in the introduction as a "crucial factor." In the body of the speech, the engineer might quote the current hourly cost of studio time, pointing to the need for an organized use of every single minute. Finally, in the conclusion, organization might once again be stressed as a necessary element of good production.

VISUAL AIDS.   In addition to using verbal pictures created through imagery, the speaker may improve a presentation by using a variety of diagrams, graphs, and photographs. In turn, these learning tools may be presented by using a variety of media, including flipcharts, overhead projectors, graphics packages, handouts, charts, drawings, opaque projectors, slide projectors, and films or videotapes.

There are several advantages to using *visual aids* such as those listed above. Visual aids:

1. Reinforce the presentation.

2. Simplify complex problems.

3. Help maintain group interest and attention.

4. Clarify important concepts for note-taking purposes.

5. Aid in maximizing your credibility and professionalism.

Visual aids, then, can be of great value to you when you are presenting. You will learn more about their construction and use in Chapter 11 of your textbook.

Audience Participation

While most of our discussion of the informative speech has focused on the presentation of information by the speaker, we should mention those situations in which the audience participates in the exchange of information. One popular format in which this occurs is the *platform*.

A platform format might be used at a public hearing on drainage problems, where citizens report on property damage from recent flooding, and officials relate their efforts to deal with the situation in turn. Similarly, a member of your college placement service may give an informative presentation on how to interview effectively, after which students relate various questions they have been asked in interviews.

The classroom also offers an opportunity for the presentation and exchange of information. Examples would be a mechanical engineering class where students share their senior design projects, a technical writing class where students propose a "Rent-a-Pet" program for the local humane society, and a landscape architecture class where students offer ideas on how to rebuild parts of the inner city. In each case, while the primary speaker may be the instructor, the audience also participates in the exchange of information.

Persuasion

The degree to which an audience is actually persuaded, of course, will vary. A speaker who intends to persuade may (1) convince, (2) stimulate, or (3) move the audience to action. A person who attempts to *convince* intends to get the audience to think, believe, or feel a certain way. A person engaged in a debate, a minister preaching on the downside of materialism, and a business executive who thinks the company should merge with another firm may all use persuasive messages to convince their audience of a particular belief.

Another type of persuasion comes in the form of *stimulation*. Generally, a person who wants to stimulate an audience will attempt to reaffirm or strengthen preexisting beliefs or feelings. For example, the union leader who addresses members as they march on a picket line is trying to reinforce their belief in the importance of the strike while strengthening their feelings of solidarity.

The third level of persuasion is the speech that uses persuasion to *move members of an audience to action*. For example, if a product on the market skyrockets in cost or is believed to be hazardous to public health, different consumer groups may rally support from people around the country for an immediate boycott.

Although we make a distinction between the different degrees of persuasion, keep in mind that these purposes overlap. Obviously, before you can successfully move an audience to act, you must convince them. Because it is easier to get an audience to believe in something than to get them to act on it, the speaker who wants to activate an audience must use different techniques than the speaker who merely wants to convince.

Informative Versus Persuasive Communication

Perhaps the best way to understand persuasive communication is, first, to contrast it with informative communication. Persuasive communication differs from informative communication in three ways:

1. *Climate or environment.* When a speaker delivers an informative message, the relationship between the speaker and the audience is usually neutral. However, when a speaker delivers a persuasive message, there is an emotional atmosphere that may be hostile or inspiring, depending on the situation.

2. *Response sought.* More so than an informative speech, a persuasive speech will aim for a higher degree of audience involvement or action.

3. *Goals to be achieved.* The goal of an informative speech is to present an audience with new and useful information, from which it is hoped they will understand and learn. The goal of a persuasive speech is to change an attitude or belief, or to bring about some form of action. An informative speech that focuses on what furriers have done to date to stop the slaughter of animals on the endangered species list will be less controversial than a persuasive speech whose goal is to gain support for a boycott of the local furrier.

There are several approaches to persuasion that can help you more clearly understand the persuasive process. These include the Aristotelian approach as well as more contemporary approaches to the study of attitudes. Given the relevance of these approaches to our understanding of persuasion, we will begin by discussing each of them.

Approaches to Persuasion

The Aristotelian Approach

According to Aristotle, a speaker who wishes to create a persuasive message can choose among three persuasive modes, or appeals, in order to make his or her message effective. Aristotle labeled these appeals *logos, pathos,* and *ethos.*

Rhetoric may be defined as the faculty of observing in any given case the available means of persuasion.

ARISTOTLE

LOGOS: REASONING. *Logos* refers to a rational approach to persuasion. Based on logic and argumentation, logos is intended to appeal to an individual's sense of reason. For example, a physician trying to convince her colleagues of the value of an experimental surgical technique would do so most successfully if she uses a rational approach. Citing research studies and including statistics of successes and failures might persuade the listeners to adopt the technique. A member of a consulting firm trying to persuade a CEO to adopt an efficiency plan must present hard facts and solid figures to show how the proposed plan will either increase productivity or eliminate waste.

Logos, pathos, and ethos are reflected in the words (and actions) of effective public speakers.

Aside from facts and figures, logos includes the use of two basic types of reasoning: deductive and inductive. ***Deductive reasoning*** moves from the general to the specific. The best known form of deductive reasoning is the syllogism. The following is a classic example.

> All men are mortal.
> Socrates is a man.
> Therefore, Socrates is mortal.

A syllogism illustrates the deductive process very clearly; the final conclusion follows logically from the first generalization.

Inductive reasoning moves from the specific to the general. If your favorite disc jockey plays two enjoyable selections from a newly released compact disc, you may induce that the entire CD is good and decide to buy it.

Of course, both deductive and inductive reasoning can be false. Consider an observer at an athletic event who notices that all of the track stars are wearing a particular brand of athletic shoes. He purchases a pair for his son and is disappointed when the boy fails to finish a 5K run sponsored by the local youth organization. Just because a large number of great runners wear these shoes does not mean that everyone who wears them will be a great runner. The deductive process in this instance is fallacious and unreliable.

An example of false induction might be found in the case of a young woman who hires a small moving company to transport her furniture to her new home in another state. As she unpacks the shipping cases, she discovers that many things have been damaged, and she angrily resolves never to trust a small company again. In reality, many small companies are just as reliable as the larger ones, but she has falsely induced from her particular experience that all small company operations will be equally poor.

When you draw conclusions or make assertions, you must be able to support them by supplying the audience with the basis for your reasoning. In other words, you must convince the audience that your arguments are based on logical thinking.

Reasoning is that process of thinking by which an individual arrives at conclusions. A detective, a forensic scientist, a labor mediator, and a public speaker all use the reasoning process as a tool of their respective trades. The ability to reason or think in a logical way is one of the distinguishing characteristics of the human mind. It is through reason that humans learn about their surroundings and generalize about their environment. Without this ability we could neither adapt nor function successfully in this world.

PATHOS: FEELING.   A speaker may decide that *pathos,* an appeal to the emotions, will be more effective than logos, an appeal to reason. The effectiveness of emotional appeals depends on the audience's motivation to listen and respond, the credibility of the appeals, and the speaker's intent in creating the message. Pathos is especially effective in situations in which emotions tend to override logic. Pathos includes reward appeals, fear-arousing appeals, guilt appeals, and appeals to needs, desires, and values.

Katie Couric speaking to a Senate Special Committee on Aging about the importance of colorectal cancer screening tests.

A *reward appeal* promises the listener some personal gain or profit if he or she believes or behaves in the manner suggested by the speaker. The intended reward may be either material or psychological. For example, a high school dropout who hears a speaker at a job placement center may be persuaded to attend night school to get his diploma if he is made to feel that it will better his chances for obtaining gainful employment. When the same individual attends his first class at the adult education center, he may be even more determined to finish if the instructor speaks about the increased self-confidence and sense of achievement he may expect as a result of his efforts.

The opposite of the reward appeal is the *fear-arousing appeal.* People tend to be more vulnerable to persuasion if they perceive a threat to themselves or their loved ones. An effective speaker can capitalize on a person's fear in order to enhance a persuasive message. Advertisements for home fire alarms and various safety products are examples of this approach.

How do fear appeals work? One recent approach to their study, called the Extended Parallel Process Model (EPPM), provides an excellent overview of the process. As summarized by Kim Witte and Kelly Morrison (2000), when we experience a threat that is "serious" and "relevant," we become afraid and are motivated to take action—any action that will reduce our fear. Generally, we will respond by finding a way to *control the danger* of the threat, or to *control our fear* about the threat. If we try to control the danger itself, we find ways to eliminate or reduce the threat itself (e.g., run and hide, stay and fight, or change our attitude, behavior, or belief as recommended by the speaker). On the other hand, if we attempt to control our fear about the threat, we may deny it, repress it, avoid thinking about it, or accuse the speaker of trying to scare us and become angry.

As Witte and Morrison (2000) further noted, our attempts to control one or the other response are dependent on whether we believe we can actually perform a recommended action "easily, feasibly and effectively" (p. 3). For example, if we feel threatened by a fear appeal about STDs, we probably will follow the speaker's advice about condoms if we can "easily, feasibly, and effectively" use them to avert the danger. However, if we believe that we cannot adopt a recommendation because it's "too hard, too costly, takes too much time, or will not effectively avert the threat," we probably will attempt to control our fear instead (p. 3). Using our previous example, we might respond to a less-effective message about STDs by saying, "I can't use condoms, and even if I did, they wouldn't work anyway, so I might as well not think about STDs."

Note that a third response to a threat is possible. When we do *not* perceive a threat as "serious" and "relevant" to us, the threat will produce no response at all. In short, we simply will ignore it. These three responses are important to remember when we are making a presentation because they mean that *individual differences* in people ultimately will determine whether our message is persuasive. They are also why constructing and adapting constantly to your audience as a *composite audience* (universal or particular) are so critical. Individual differences such as demographic variables (e.g., age, gender, cultural background, socioeconomic status, education level, and occupation), psychological variables (e.g., attitudes, political and religious beliefs, and values), personality traits (e.g., anxiety, extroversion/introversion), intelligence, self-esteem, and prior experience play a key role in persuasion (Witte & Morrison, p. 5).

In addition to individual differences, speakers also must remember the importance of balancing fear appeals with other forms of evidence or arguments in our message. For example, based on a content analysis of fear appeals in 28 pamphlets advocating breast self-examination (BSE), Kline and Mattson (2000) found that threats about the severity of (and our susceptibility to) breast cancer can be effective. However, they will be effective only if they are balanced with arguments that BSE will minimize the threat of breast cancer, arguments that boost our self-confidence and help us overcome our inhibitions, or both (p. 16). In other words, we must balance fear appeals with *efficacy messages,* or messages that say my recommendation is a way to avoid a specific danger—easily, feasibly, and effectively.

Fear appeals are often used when the issue is public health. Televised public service announcements regarding AIDS, gangs, drunk driving, and drugs are other primary examples. However, fear appeals can be used in a number of other settings as well. Think for a moment about the following scenario, which resulted in harm to a university student. In a scenery workshop for the theater department of a university, the instructor presented the ground rules for participation in the class. Along with reminders to show up on time and to clean up before leaving, the students were advised to use the power saws only if supervised, to wear safety goggles and aprons when needed, to remove their jewelry, and to tie their hair back if it was long. The teacher did not really make clear the possibilities for serious harm to her audience, and the students were only too eager to start working. Some weeks later, one student lost his footing on a ladder and almost dislocated his arm when the leather bracelet he wore around his wrist caught on a protruding nail. In this case a more compelling fear appeal might have spared someone a badly wrenched shoulder and a puncture wound in the palm of his hand.

If fear tactics don't work, then often guilt or shame messages will. Probably you have experienced the negative feelings that result when someone you love calls and asks why you haven't been to visit in a while. You probably felt a rush of emotions—guilt, shame, embarrassment, remorse, regret, and humiliation simultaneously—all because of one simple question. Although it is difficult to clearly delineate between the two, Sally Planalp, Susan Hafen, and Dawn Adkins (2000) offer the following distinction between guilt and shame:

> Both shame and guilt result from failures and shortcomings, primarily moral ones, but shame is more global than guilt. With *guilt,* negative feelings are focused on the action, whereas with *shame,* the failure reflects on the entire self. One of the most concise distinctions between shame and guilt is that shame involves *being* while guilt involves *doing.* . . . When people are ashamed they feel that they are bad people; when people are guilty, they feel they have done something bad (or failed to do something good). (p. 4)

According to Planalp and her colleagues, "the United States is a 'guilt-based culture' in comparison to countries such as China and Japan, which are more 'shame-based cultures' " (p. 38). Concurring with Schneiderman in his book *Saving Face: America and the Politics of Shame* (1995, p. 5), the three authors noted, the distinction is a private (guilt) versus a public (shame) one:

> A shame culture "provides a uniform code of conduct to promote civility, propriety, dignity, integrity, and honor," whereas a guilt culture "attempts to control behavior by passing laws and punishing transgression." (Planalp, Hafen, & Adkins, p. 39)

In the public sphere, regular references to the following historical events provide examples of guilt and shame messages being used to effect persuasion. In the United States, there is guilt associated with slavery and the Civil War; the Tuskegee medical experiments on African American men; the Vietnam War; Watergate; the slaying of Martin Luther King; the Oklahoma City bombing; Monica-gate; and the list goes on. In Germany, there is shame associated with the Holocaust; in England, with the loss of Princess Diana; and, in Japan, with the inability of the royal family (at any point in history) to produce a suitable heir.

What does all of this information have to do with you as a public speaker? Clearly, the issues involve both ethics and outcomes. When should we use (or avoid using) guilt or shame messages in public presentations? Again, Planalp and her colleagues offer us a few important questions to ask before invoking guilt or shame:

1. Is the point I am trying to make important enough to warrant use of the tactic when it comes to what is valued most in my culture? ("Are sex roles important enough to shame boys for playing with dolls? girls for playing with toy trucks?")

2. Is the shame or guilt to which we plan to refer in a message "acknowledged both publicly and privately (where appropriate)"? If no, it is impossible for an audience member to reflect on causes or consequences. If yes, you still need to proceed with caution and ensure that any guilt or shame message will contribute (not hamper) psychological and spiritual growth.

3. In terms of esteem needs, are the standards we hold for the audience realistic and are sanctions for violating them appropriate? (For example, before using a shame or guilt message, teachers should ask if they are setting unrealistic standards for achievement or punishing students for mistakes that have been made due to unclear expectations. Only after being certain of answers to these questions should a teacher proceed with such a message.)

4. Does "the person (or entity) being shamed or made to feel guilty [have] any control over the grounds" for which I plan to shame them? (For instance, audience members have control over smoking or eating habits, but not over their race, gender, or status.)

5. Will my message "of shame or guilt put at risk the *connections* among people or between people and the larger society"? Always strive to maintain these connections. Without them all is at risk including the audience's sense of esteem and control. (Adapted from Planalp, Hafen, & Adkins, 2000, pp. 52–55, reprinted by permission of Sage Publications, Inc.)

In terms of the effectiveness of guilt and shame messages, O'Keefe (2000) offered additional insights. Comparing these messages based on their level of explicitness (low- versus high-), O'Keefe found that more-explicit guilt appeals indeed arouse more guilt, but are significantly less persuasive than less-explicit guilt appeals. In fact, high-explicit guilt messages actually backfire if they produce irritation, anger, annoyance, resentment, or other similar negative reactions in the listener. In a word, *caution* is the name of the game when considering the use of guilt or shame messages to persuade.

In previous examples, the needs for safety and esteem played heavily in the use of fear, guilt, and shame messages. These and other psychological *needs* can be targets for the persuasive speaker, without the use of these three appeals. The needs for survival, love and belonging, and self-fulfillment can all be used as means of persuading an individual to change attitudes, beliefs, or behavior.

An effective speaker can also use human *desires* as a means of persuasion. When an attractive actress advertises an automobile, the appeal is intended to be sexual. Similarly, promises that a particular soap or cologne will make a man virile or a woman enticing are definitely based on an emotional appeal to desire. Other common targets for the effective persuader are the desire to be powerful, the desire to be unique, and the desire to remain youthful.

Yet another type of emotional appeal aims at our sense of *values*, Homer and Kahle (1988) identified nine highly important values for most Americans. In no certain order, these include (1) self-fulfillment; (2) excitement; (3) a sense of accomplishment; (4) self-respect; (5) a sense of belonging; (6) being well-respected; (7) security; (8) fun and enjoyment; and (9) warm relationships. Speakers who understand what their audiences value can create messages that produce increased understanding or overall influence. For example, when addressing an audience regarding the importance of being tested for the AIDS virus, a speaker who appeals to the audience's need for security (value 7) and who tells how the virus devastated an important relationship in her own life (value 9) will be more persuasive than a speaker who simply argues that the audience "owes it to society" to be tested.

As stated earlier, a good persuasive speaker will take care not to alienate his or her audience with a badly organized message. One of our primary concerns as listeners is how the organization of a message will affect us on an emotional level. Studies have shown that a well-organized message prevents listeners from feeling frustrated or angry and consequently increases the chance for an appeal to more sympathetic emotions. The importance of this factor is relative to individual listeners, since some people need greater structure than others to make sense of a message.

ETHOS: SOURCE CREDIBILITY. *Ethos,* or source credibility, is the way in which a speaker is perceived by the audience. According to Aristotle, speakers will be held in high esteem if they are perceived as intelligent and moral and if they demonstrate goodwill toward the audience. Aristotle believed that these qualities alone were enough to create attitude change. Persuasion research over the last fifty years has supported Aristotle's claims. Indeed, we do analyze a speaker's ethos in terms of his or her expertness, trustworthiness, and goodwill (McCroskey & Teven, 1999). Generally, source credibility contributes much to the persuasiveness of a message, depending on the amount of direct experience or knowledge listeners have about the topic, the extent to which they are willing, interested, or able to process a given persuasive message, and their "cultural self-concepts." We will briefly address each of these three variables in the paragraphs that follow, but first let's talk about the three dimensions of ethos, or source credibility.

According to James McCroskey and Jason Teven (1999), we perceive speakers to be *competent* when they come across as intelligent, bright, well trained, informed, and experts in the subject matter being discussed. For example, a biologist who presents current information on the mapping of human genomes would be rated higher on this dimension of credibility than a high school student reading a report to a biology class. We believe speakers to be *trustworthy* when we perceive them as honest, honorable, moral, ethical, and genuine. The trustworthiness factor also operates when a source is believed to be telling the truth and not presenting falsehoods. For example, someone who makes money on the Internet by giving personal advice on investment strategies would be rated as less credible on this dimension than would a friend or relative who has succeeded in the stock market. Finally, *goodwill* is associated with the extent to which we perceive speakers to be caring, concerned, sensitive, and understanding, and to the extent to which they have our best interests at heart. For McCroskey and Teven, a speaker with goodwill is a speaker who understands our ideas, feelings, and needs; empathizes with our personal feelings; and responds to our attempts to communicate. To illustrate, Tom is chapter president of a local environmental conservation group. When he notices that an audience to which he is speaking seems uncomfortable with suggestions he is making, he takes the time to stop, acknowledge their discomfort, ask questions, and then address their concerns. The fact that he was unable to finish the speech as planned was unimportant to Tom. As a result, he earned the respect of his audience because he cared about their views.

As we said earlier, source credibility plays a significant role in persuasion especially when we know little or nothing about the subject matter, or when we are unwilling or unable to process incoming information. For example, we probably will be persuaded to think about quarks and "black holes" from a particular perspective if we hear the message from a team of physicists who view them from that perspective, and who have recently won the Nobel Prize for their work. This is especially true if we know little about physics, quarks, and black holes, but we can follow what they are saying.

Work associated with the Elaboration Likelihood Model (ELM), a "cognitive response" model to the study of persuasion, has provided us with additional insights about source credibility. According to ELM researchers, there are two primary routes to persuasion—the central and peripheral routes. Persuasion via the ***central route*** requires a listener to think actively about the issue being discussed. This necessarily involves interest, willingness, and ability to process an incoming message. For instance, Sandy is graduating at the end of next term with an advanced degree in physics. If she is listening to our Nobel Prize-winning laureates, she is probably actively processing their message about quarks. As a result of *what they say,* she may (or may not) be persuaded. In contrast, consider Max, a music theory major who is sitting in on our quark lecture for extra credit in a basic physics class. Max is hanging onto a C in the class with little more than his fingernails. He is interested in the lecture but can barely understand what the speakers are saying. According to the ELM model, Max will experience attitude change (if any) via the ***peripheral route,*** or through external cues associated with the credibility and attractiveness of the speakers, the number of arguments they make, and how well they use voice intonation and intensity to make the lecture interesting (Tasaki, Kim, & Miller, 1999, p. 197). Depending on *who* is speaking and *how* they are delivering the message, Max may (or may not) be persuaded.

Certainly these findings have emerged in studies of audiences from the United States, but what about audience members from other cultures? Do the same findings apply? Although questions about culture may seem irrelevant to our discussion at first glance, research by Katsuya Tasaki, Min-Sun Kim, and Michael Miller in 1999 showed otherwise. According to these three researchers, source credibility (particularly the *status* of a source) may be more important for listeners who have interdependent, rather than independent, self-construals. In other words, people who see themselves as highly connected with others (interdependent) are more likely to be persuaded by high status speakers than listeners who see themselves as separate from other people (independent).

To illustrate, consider Mary, who was born and brought up in Nebraska and is now a junior pursuing a degree in a North American university. As a young woman who sees herself growing in independence from her family, Mary is responsive to a social environment in which others "appraise or confirm" her as a unique individual. As a result, she is more comfortable hanging out with her friends than she is when she's visiting her family. In contrast, Choong Hyun was born and reared in South Korea. He is a friend of Mary and is studying at the same university. As a

Credibility is a function of expertise, trustworthiness, and goodwill.

young man brought up in a family that is steeped in Confucianism, he has learned the importance of honoring status differences, particularly age, sex, and family background. He values interdependence and "connectedness" with his father, mother, and older brother, and doesn't understand why Mary is so into "being her own person." Choong Hyun is responsive to a social environment that honors and reconfirms the value of interdependence with significant others (Tasaki, Kim, & Miller, 1999, pp. 200–201).

This is where culture comes into play, with independent versus interdependent self-construals. Generally, highly independent self-construals like Mary's emerge for people from *individualistic cultures* such as the United States and Great Britain. In contrast, highly interdependent self-construals like Choong Hyun's spring forth from *collectivist cultures*, such as Japan, South Korea, Taiwan, Hong Kong, and Singapore (Tasaki, Kim, & Miller, 1999, p. 200). If Mary and Choong Hyun are sitting together and listening to the same speaker, research indicates that Choong Hyun probably will have a significantly more favorable post-message attitude than Mary, even if they both perceive the lecturer to be of high status. Because Choong Hyun has been brought up to value status differences, research indicates that he will value a message from a highly esteemed source more than will Mary, who is trying to establish herself as a person with equal status.

Sometimes a speaker's ethos will be established long before a particular speaking situation. For example, a Nobel Prize-winning physicist will probably be highly regarded by an audience because of prior accomplishments. His or her message would probably be more persuasive than that of a local high school science teacher, even if they presented identical messages.

When speakers lack ethos, however, it is harder for them to persuade. Let us look at the following situation: A college president, distrusted by the student body because he or she overreacted and called in the police to deal with a nonviolent protest, convened a conference of the student government to persuade students not to discuss the protest incident with the media. The president's ethos at this time was very low, and the students were particularly resistant to this persuasive attempt.

In many situations, however, a speaker is unknown to the audience and approaches the situation without a reputation of any kind. In this case the speaker must *establish* ethos, or credibility, so that the audience will perceive him or her as demonstrating knowledge and trustworthiness.

Contemporary Approaches

Clearly, Aristotle made a significant theoretic contribution to our understanding of communication by focusing attention on strategies and attributes of the *source* that bring about persuasion. More recent advances, however, have focused on the nature of *receivers,* particularly their attitudes and the process of attitude change. Tesser and Shaffer (1990) have identified three major contemporary approaches to the study of attitude change. These include studies that address (1) the structure of attitudes, (2) attitudes as predictors of behavior, and (3) the functions that attitudes serve. We now turn to a brief overview of each approach.

THE STRUCTURE OF ATTITUDES.   Recent advances in cognitive psychology suggest that our attitudes may best be viewed as associative networks much like (cognitive) maps, with our beliefs and feelings connected both within and between our attitudes. Thus, when we hear a message, a process of "spreading activation" takes place. In other words, the activation of one attitude (such as our attitude toward racism and bigotry on campus) will "prime" or make it easier for a source to tap other elements in the map (such as our beliefs and feelings about a campus crime that was racially motivated).

How does this information on attitudes help us to be more effective public speakers? Understanding that we all have cognitive maps—some more simple and some more complex—allows us to find better ways to reach and activate the attitudes of our audience. For example, a number of variables affect our attitude structures, such as the amount of information we have on a given topic as well as how and to what extent we integrate that information. If you are speaking to an audience with expertise in your area or about some controversial issue, audience members are more likely to have knowledge both for and against your position on the subject. Thus, you will need to develop a speech that is two-sided in nature or that takes into account the sophistication of your audience's knowledge structures.

ATTITUDES AS PREDICTORS OF BEHAVIOR.   Research by Ajzen and associates (1989) has shown that the best predictor of a given behavior is our intentions, and that our intentions are a function of (1) our attitude toward the behavior, (2) whether we believe significant others in our lives would condone and encourage the behavior, (3) the extent to which we believe we can control the outcome or results of that behavior, and (4) alternative behaviors that are available to us. So powerful is this information that Ajzen and others have been able to use it to more accurately predict a variety of human behaviors, including dental hygiene, alcohol and drug use, self-examination for breast cancer, ability to quit smoking, consistency in following an exercise program, use of contraceptives, and voting behavior.

If Ajzen's theory, outlined above, has helped predict these behaviors, the theory has major implications for those of us who are interested in the nature of persuasion. For example, if you want to persuade your roommates to wash their breakfast dishes before they leave for class, Ajzen might argue that your best chance of convincing them will involve making an initial attitude assessment. This assessment should include your roommates' current attitudes toward washing dishes (positive, negative, or neutral), whether they will feel significantly rewarded by you (and each other) for washing the dishes, the extent to which they believe that washing dishes will result in desired rewards or avoided punishments, and other alternative behaviors available to them (such as not washing dishes).

Once you have made this assessment, you can begin the process of developing a message that will best fit your "profile" of their attitudes and intentions. For instance, you will need to take a more active approach if you know that they are negative toward washing dishes, feel unrewarded for doing them, believe that no significant rewards will ensue even if they change their behavior, and think that not washing dishes is the best alternative for them so far. Based on this assessment and some creative problem solving, you may be able to come up with a persuasive message. For example, you might try offering to do their dishes if they agree to make up your bed—something you loathe doing but they do well and consistently. In short, by understanding the attitudes and intentions that underlie behavior, you can better construct messages that get the results *you* intend.

THE FUNCTIONS OF ATTITUDES.   The third area of attitude research addressed by Tesser and Shaffer that has implications for public speakers is that of attitude functions. Work in this area has been conducted since the 1940s. However, a study by Kerek (1987) resulted in the classification of attitudes into three major functions: (1) experiential-schematic, (2) defensive, and (3) self-expressive.

Generally, the *experiential-schematic function of attitudes* involves the general cognitive maps that we develop about a target object, issue, person, or group (such as "needles," socialized medicine, our doctor, or medical personnel as a whole). More importantly, attitudes of this type exist as a function of our experiences with the target in question and whether those experiences have been positive, negative, or neutral. To illustrate, think for a moment about your current attitude toward lesbian or gay marriage. According to functional theorists, your attitude will be positive if (1) someone you care about has chosen this lifestyle; (2) you have had a positive personal experience with a person who has chosen this lifestyle (for instance, you have become friends); (3) you feel that it is likely that you will interact in the future with people who are gay or lesbian; and/or (4) you have had positive personal experiences with people who have gay or lesbian family members or friends. Conversely, functional theorists argue that, if you have had negative past experiences in one or more of these domains, you will probably have a negative attitude toward someone who leads a gay or lesbian lifestyle. (Kerek, 1987, p. 296). In short, if an attitude is serving an experiential-schematic function, that attitude will be based on past experiences you have had with the object, issue, person, or group in question.

The second function of attitudes is the ***defensive function***. We generally hold and express attitudes that are defensive in nature whenever we experience some form of personal anxiety or insecurity regarding the target in question. Additionally, defensive attitudes involve two major steps: the projection of unacceptable motives onto the target in question and expression of hostility as a result. (Kerek, 1987, pp. 288–289). To illustrate, consider the following scenario. You have just been given two 50-yard-line tickets to the Super Bowl and are on your way to the game. The Los Angeles Raiders are playing the Washington Redskins. You are—and have been—a Redskins fan all of your life. You have even brought along a foam tomahawk (commandeered from a friend who is an Atlanta Braves fan) to help you cheer the team. You are pumped and excited as you park the car and walk with your best friend toward the gate. However, to reach the gate, you notice that you will have to walk through a group of Native American protesters to get to your seats. How will you behave? What attitudes will drive your behavior? Functional theorists would argue that, if you prefer to avoid thinking about the protesters and their concerns because doing so makes you feel anxious, or if you experience personal feelings of discomfort as you walk through their picket line, you will probably exhibit behavior that is based on a defensive attitude. For example, you may feel uneasy and a little guilty for having screamed a "war whoop" seconds before you noticed them. Or you may even grumble to yourself as you approach the protesters that they are "trying to ruin the game." As you reach the area in which they are located, you may feel the need to avoid eye contact, to look down as you pass by, or to ignore their words and concerns. If your attitude is highly defensive, you may find yourself name calling, getting into a fight, or engaging in some other equally undesirable behavior. From a public speaker's perspective (that of the Native American protesters, in this example), such a situation is especially difficult. The "speakers" are dealing with a potentially volatile issue—in this case, especially if you (1) happen to be a Redskins fan, (2) like the mascot, and (3) love doing the tomahawk chop when your team is winning. Thus, the protesters must find ways of raising your awareness without calling out the defensive function of your attitudes—a task that is difficult at best.

The third function of attitudes is the *self-expressive function.* Self-expressive attitudes emerge every time we use our attitudes as a vehicle for expressing values that are important to us, such as having a comfortable life, a sense of accomplishment, a peaceful world, freedom, pleasure, inner harmony, or self-respect. Opinions that are based on self-expressive attitudes also involve (1) how we think people who are close to us would respond to a given target, and (2) how the target is viewed by people whose opinions we value most (Kerek, 1987, p. 296). If we have a positive self-expressive attitude toward a target (for example, someone whom we know is carrying the HIV virus), we generally will take a "live and let live" approach regarding that person. In this instance, we will value individual rights and need for personal expression—as we would with anyone who is diagnosed as HIV positive.

On the other hand, if we have a negative self-expressive attitude, we generally will resort to traditional or religious standards of what is right or wrong when perceiving the target. Think for a moment about news stories you have heard about communities banding together against a family that has a child with AIDS. In many instances, such behavior was "justifiable" to the townspeople—only as long as "everyone else" (significant others) held the same attitude. However, as soon as attitudes changed on the part of key people, or a celebrity (such as Elton John or Michael Jackson) became involved, the town generally changed its overall attitude and views.

The question becomes, how can we use this information to become more effective public speakers? Research in the area of attitude change reveals that information that is directly related to the functions that an attitude serves will be more persuasive than that which addresses concerns other than those of the three aforementioned functions (Tesser & Shaffer, 1990, pp. 502–503). For example, one study reviewed by Tesser and Shaffer revealed that messages (ads) that appeal to the "self-expressive" function of attitudes (to product image) have a positive impact on image-conscious people, for whom many attitudes serve a self-expressive function. Interestingly, the reverse would be true for people whose attitudes are driven by an experiential-schematic function. For the latter, messages that appeal to product quality over image would be more persuasive.

The ramifications of this and similar findings in attitude research are far-reaching for students of persuasion. Armed with an understanding of the structure and functions of attitudes, you are faced with a very real dilemma: determining what attitudes are driving your audience's behavior and finding ways to tap the "appropriate" attitude. That is your task and greatest challenge. However, by treating this new-found knowledge as a critical element of your audience analysis, you may begin to construct messages that are more appropriate to the audience and occasion. Given a clearer understanding of how attitudes affect behavior, we may begin a more systematic approach to understanding the structure of persuasive messages.

Persuasive Techniques

So far we have discussed key theories of persuasion. Let's now discuss specific techniques that can be used in delivering persuasive messages. Indeed, using at least one of six techniques may help you construct an effective speech. These techniques include the uses of one-sided versus two-sided arguments, evidence, forewarnings, humor, primacy and recency effects, and effective conclusions. Each of these techniques will be discussed in the following pages.

ONE-SIDED VERSUS TWO-SIDED ARGUMENTS.   When developing a speech to persuade, we must make two major decisions. First, is whether to present only one side of the issue we are supporting (a *one-sided message*) or both sides of an issue (a *two-sided message*). Second, is whether to present a refutational or nonrefutational message, if we decide to develop a two-sided message. Daniel O'Keefe (1999), a leading communication scholar, offers the following distinction. A *refutational two-sided message* is designed "to refute opposing arguments in some fashion; this might involve attacking the plausibility of opposing claims, criticizing the reasoning underlying opposing arguments, offering evidence that is shown to undermine opposing claims, and so forth" (p. 211). A *nonrefutational two-sided message* "acknowledges the opposing considerations but does not attempt to refute them directly; it might suggest that the positive supporting arguments outweigh the opposing ones, but it does not directly refute the opposing arguments" (p. 211).

Over the last forty years, researchers have offered a number of suggestions for using one-sided versus two-sided arguments. Unfortunately, without sufficient statistical data to directly support these claims, three key recommendations have emerged in the literature. The first is that we should use two-sided arguments when the audience is initially opposed to our point of view, when audience members are well educated, and when they can readily supply counterarguments. In contrast, we should use one-sided arguments when the audience is initially favorable to our position, when our listeners are "less well-educated," and when they are unlikely to think of counterarguments (O'Keefe, 1999). Researchers also have suggested that *how* we organize a two-sided message makes a difference. For instance, Jackson and Allen (1987) accurately noted three ways to organize a two-sided message: stating supporting-then-opposing arguments, offering opposing-then-supporting arguments, or alternating supporting and opposing arguments. These two researchers then suggested that the support-then-refute order might be more persuasive than the refute-then-support order for refutational two-sided messages (Cited in O'Keefe, 1999, pp. 212–213).

In order to assess the validity of these three key recommendations, O'Keefe (1999) went back and critically analyzed every article (prior to 1997) that offered suggestions about one-sided versus two-sided messages. His goal was to determine the extent to which researchers could back their recommendations with hard-core statistical data. The results of his "meta-analysis" revealed some important findings, some of which supported (and some of which refuted) past researchers' suggestions. In summary, O'Keefe learned the following:

1. Two-sided refutational messages are generally more persuasive than one-sided messages, but one-sided messages are generally more persuasive than two-sided nonrefutational messages.

2. One-sided messages are more persuasive than two-sided messages when the audience is either initially *favorable or unfavorable* to our position on an issue. When the audience is neutral, there is no significant (statistical) difference in the effectiveness of one-sided versus two-sided messages.

3. Although research is limited regarding the effects of education level, there is little basis for believing that two-sided messages are best for educated audiences, while one-sided messages are best for uneducated audiences. In fact, no significant differences seem to exist in the effectiveness of one-sided versus two-sided messages as a function of education level.

4. Likewise, no evidence is available to suggest that we use two-sided messages when an audience can produce counterarguments, and one-sided messages when they cannot. As with education level, there is little difference in the effectiveness of one-sided versus two-sided arguments as a function of the audience's access to counterarguments.

5. How we organize a two-sided message also seems to produce no significant difference in persuasive outcomes, at least when compared with the effectiveness of a one-sided message. In other words, using supporting-then-opposing arguments, opposing-then-supporting arguments, or a one-sided message can be equally effective. This finding also holds for refutational versus nonrefutational two-sided messages. However, when we interweave supporting and opposing arguments, there does seem to be an advantage in using refutational (over nonrefutational) two-sided arguments. In other words, if we offer a supporting argument followed by an opposing argument, it is a good idea to refute the opposing argument before moving on to our next supporting argument.

6. There also seems to be a significant difference in the effectiveness of refutational versus nonrefutational two-sided messages, when comparing messages that promote a consumer product or service (advertising messages) and messages that deal with social or political concerns (nonadvertising messages). When we are presenting a social or political message, we may be more persuasive if we use a refutational (rather than a nonrefutational) two-sided message. If we are promoting a product or service, neither one-sided, two-sided refutational, nor two-sided nonrefutational messages have a distinct advantage.

Given that communication researchers and teachers alike are interested in learning the best ways to persuade, O'Keefe's meta-analytic review is more than enlightening.

He refuted several long-standing beliefs about the effectiveness of one-sided versus two-sided messages. In the process, he gave us us some interesting "revised" guidelines for persuasive speaking.

USE OF EVIDENCE.   While you might expect that the use of evidence could only enhance a persuasive message, studies in this area have come up with inconsistent and contradictory findings. While some researchers have concluded that the use of evidence is advantageous, others have shown it to be of little significance. In general, the persuasive communicator must assess the subject and audience before relying on evidence to make the speech effective.

For example, a sales rep who wants to persuade a group of senior managers to implement the use of robotics in their manufacturing plant would be wise to include statistical data that supports the probability of increased efficiency. When a subject is technical, and the audience is used to data-driven decision making, using strong evidence in your message is a must.

If speakers have low credibility with their audience, then evidence (in any form) may do little to enhance their position. The audience may tune out the facts and figures, believing them to be as unreliable as the speakers themselves. On the other hand, speakers with high credibility (or power) may be able to persuade an audience without presenting sufficient evidence. (Unfortunately, audiences often accept the message of a highly credible source "at face value." As a result, they may make poor decisions based on a lack of information.)

There is some evidence to suggest that using certain forms of evidence may be effective. For example, Sundar (1998) found that online news stories that quote sources are more credible than stories that fail to cite sources. One could generalize that quoting sources in an oral presentation has the potential to increase source credibility, if not the amount of attitude change that results. Regarding journalistic writing, Brosius (1999) reported that *exemplars,* or "short quotations (verbal or visual) from concerned or interested parties that illustrate a particular problem or view, . . . influence opinions and attitudes more strongly than statistics, comprehensive overviews or official information, although the latter are doubtlessly more valid." Again, his findings would seem to be applicable in an oral presentation. Not only do personal stories add color and imagery to a presentation; they also contribute authenticity to a speaker's message.

FOREWARNING.   Does foreknowledge of a speaker's intent have any effect on the persuasion process? According to Hiromi Fukada (1986), a Japanese expert in the area of persuasion, prior knowledge of a speaker's intent when he or she plans to present a fear-arousing message reduces the effect of that message by stimulating anticipatory counterarguments. In other words, when an audience is *forewarned* of a speaker's intent to use fear-arousing appeals, audience members will generate arguments that are counter to that of the speaker during the actual presentation and will remain more resistant than audiences not forewarned throughout the message.

Of course, a speaker's intent is often well established long before he or she begins the presentation. For example, when a number of tenants refused to pay a rent increase, the landlord went before the tenants' organization. The landlord's intent was perfectly clear. The audience knew he was there to convince them that they should pay the rent increase and that the increase would mean better service. In a case like this, where the purpose is no secret, effective speakers will reveal their intent in the introduction and give a preview of what they are going to say. It thus appears that they are trying to be straight with the audience instead of trying to manipulate them.

HUMOR.   Another variable that the persuasive speaker should consider is the use of *humor*. Once again, studies have provided contradictory findings as to whether the use of humor enhances the persuasive attempt or detracts from it. However, if used properly, humor can loosen up a tense atmosphere, make people feel good, increase audience responsiveness, and reveal a more human side of you as a public speaker. Additionally, if used judiciously, humor can help emphasize certain key points and make ideas memorable. The reader is advised to remember that great care must be taken to minimize perceptions that you are speaking to entertain. Expert speakers have learned that humor is best used to keep the audience involved.

To help speakers use humor more effectively, Dorothy Leeds (1988), author of *PowerSpeak*, offers the following suggestions.

1. When you tell a story or joke, have fun with it. Your face should wear a smile and your eyes should twinkle or reflect some form of mischievousness. If you don't have fun, your audience won't have fun, and your efforts at humor will be lost.

2. Stay with the essential elements of a story or joke; avoid giving too much detail. Deliver your story briskly. Then give your audience all the time it needs to respond. Timing is everything with humor.

3. Make direct eye contact with individual members of your audience when delivering a joke. Look left to right and around the room at different people as you deliver the punch line. Practicing humor before the event will help you appear spontaneous and comfortable with your story or joke.

4. Practice telling your joke or story in different ways. After a presentation, evaluate the effectiveness of your approach and make appropriate changes the next time you give a similar presentation.

5. After delivering a humorous story or joke, move directly to the point you are making. Doing so will help the climax of your presentation to be more effective.

THE CONCLUSION.   Conclusions serve three primary functions in a public presentation. They (1) provide the audience with a sense of closure, (2) allow you to repeat your main points for emphasis, and (3) encourage your audience to think how your message applies to them As such, effective conclusions are those that directly tie back to the introduction and the purpose of the speech, thereby bringing the speech and audience full circle. Additionally, they request agreement if you desire a particular response by the audience (such as drawing a similar conclusion to yours on the issue of human rights), or they appeal for action if your presentation is persuasive in nature (such as signing up to donate blood on a regular basis).

To help you construct more effective conclusions and to end your presentation with finesse and style, consider the following suggestions:

1. Summarize the main points in your speech, just as you (may have) previewed them in the introduction. Doing so will help your audience better remember your central ideas.

2. Do not present any new information or ideas in your conclusion. Avoiding this pitfall will help your audience stay more focused on your primary points.

3. Finish with style; try concluding with a quotation, a startling statistic, humor, a rhetorical question, or a direct appeal. Challenge yourself. Stay away from the age-old phrase, "In conclusion. . . ."

4. When delivering a persuasive message, find ways to motivate your audience to action. Appealing for definite action within a specific period of time will challenge audience members, and help them to assess the full impact of your message for them as individuals.

5. When appropriate, refer back to the opening of your speech. Returning to a story, joke, statistic, or any other effective introductory device will help the audience to achieve psychological closure.

Persuasive Situations

Persuasive communication is widespread. One of the most obvious settings in which persuasion occurs is in the courtroom. Here the court must decide whether there is enough evidence to warrant a trial, or a jury must decide upon the guilt or innocence of the accused. The prosecuting attorney may use a logical form of persuasion to convince the jury of the defendant's guilt: "The culprit was also described by several witnesses as a middle-aged man wearing unusually large sunglasses and a bright green athletic jacket. The defendant was arrested several blocks from the scene of the crime wearing such a jacket. The sunglasses were found in a trash can in a nearby parking lot. From the color of his jacket and the fact that the sunglasses were found near the scene, it naturally follows that he is the man responsible for the burglary."

A defending attorney may appeal to the emotions of the jury. "The defendant was wearing a green athletic jacket, but he was on his way to his son's Little League game at the local ball park. This is the kind of family man who is more likely to wear an American flag tie pin than a pair of gaudy sunglasses." By associating the defendant with the family, the favorite American sport, and patriotism, the defense counsel attempts to persuade the jury of his client's upright citizenship and innocence.

On a less dramatic but equally effective level, persuasion is also the basis of sales and advertising. Both a student selling raffle tickets and an advertising exec making a pitch hope to gain access to your wallet. A good sales rep can be so persuasive that many states have adopted legislation that enables a person to cancel an order or void a contract within several days of the initial sale. This type of law protects the consumer who may be "talked into something" by a persuasive salesperson.

Perhaps the most effective sales pitches are the ones that appear on television, radio and the Internet, or in newspapers and magazines. So powerful are these media that manufacturers invest millions of dollars annually in advertising costs. While sponsors of such programming hope to entice the audience into buying their products—often, by introducing new multi-million-dollar ad campaigns—they also hope to expose the audience to new ideas and items. Many people go into stores and buy products that they have just heard about or seen advertised. Others are persuaded by their children to buy products whose ads have been bombarding the airwaves. Exposure and the power of suggestion account for much of the success of mass-media advertising.

Not all sales pitches come from the retail industry. In discussing persuasion, we must not overlook the charity drive. We tend to forget this form of selling, since the product we buy is either goodwill or a tax deduction. The most frequently used approach in a charity drive is the emotional appeal. While certain charity drives occur year round, they seem to be most prevalent during holiday times, particularly around Christmas. The timing is not accidental; most people are more vulnerable and charitable at this time of year.

Entertainment, Ceremonial, and Other Special-Occasion Communication

We have already taken an in-depth look at messages designed to inform and persuade. Now we're ready to focus our attention on the third category, the speech to entertain and the special-occasion speech. While these two categories are often thought to be synonymous, they aren't. Special-occasion speeches also include eulogies, farewells, and resignations, which are seldom meant to entertain. However, since many special-occasion speeches, such as introductions, acceptances, and after-dinner talks, are often intended to entertain, we will discuss them as separate but related topics.

Kinds of Special-Occasion Speeches

There are many different types of special-occasion and ceremonial speeches. Let's take a look at a few of the more familiar ones. A *welcoming speech* may be presented to an individual (or an entire group) who is preparing to join an organization or attend a particular meeting or seminar. The speaker who presents a welcoming speech should mention the group extending the welcome and should make some comment on the

Julia Roberts reacts after winning an Oscar for "best actress in a leading role."

occasion. Perhaps you remember the dean of students presenting a welcoming speech at your freshman orientation. Similarly, when you graduate, a fellow student or member of the faculty will welcome the parents and friends of the graduates. A welcoming speech should be brief and to the point. It may be humorous in nature, depending on the situation or occasion.

Two additional special-occasion speeches are the *award presentation* and *acceptance speech.* You are probably familiar with these types of speeches from having seen televised presentations of the Oscar, Tony, Emmy, and MTV music awards. It is likely that you have participated in some sort of award presentation as a presenter, recipient, or member of the audience. At some time in your life, you may have attended a high school awards assembly, a scouting club breakfast, or a church supper, where awards for superior performance were presented to deserving recipients. Whether an individual presents an award or receives one, he or she should emphasize the significance of the award. While the presentation speech focuses on the many ways in which the recipient qualifies for the award, the acceptance speech is a way of saying "thank you."

The *after-dinner speech* is often, but not always, a speech to entertain. Certainly, it is intended to make the audience feel relaxed and comfortable. The content of the speech depends on the nature of the banquet. A more formal occasion will warrant a more serious presentation. The after-dinner speech at a thousand-dollar-a-plate political banquet will probably be more serious than the one presented at an annual fraternity formal. The after-dinner speech should be relatively brief, since other announcements, introductions, and speeches are usually on the agenda.

In a *farewell speech,* the speaker expresses regrets about leaving a particular group or organization and offers thanks to those who are left behind. A person who retires or is joining another company, the valedictorian of a graduating class, the employee who has joined the ranks of management, or the man or woman going off to join the military all share a common purpose in saying goodbye and thank you to the people whom they are leaving.

One particular type of farewell is the *eulogy,* a ceremonial speech marking someone's death. A eulogy may be presented at the funeral service or at a later date as a memorial. Numerous memorial services are held on January 15 to mark the birthday of the Reverend Martin Luther King, Jr., renowned civil rights leader. The eulogy is a farewell speech that praises the virtues and accomplishments of the deceased. While a eulogy is often delivered by a member of the clergy, sometimes friends, family members, or colleagues make the presentation in addition to (or instead of) the clergy.

Although there are numerous other special-occasion speeches, the last category we will discuss is the *impromptu speech.* "Impromptu" refers to the manner of presentation. An impromptu speech is one that is made on the spot, without any formal preparation. Someone who wins an unexpected award will be expected to give an impromptu acceptance speech. Someone filling in at the last minute for a scheduled speaker may be asked to give an impromptu welcoming or after-dinner speech. The most important thing to remember when delivering an impromptu speech is to stick to the topic and try to present your message in an organized and interesting manner.

Principles of Effectiveness

In any special-occasion speech or speech to entertain, there are several principles of effectiveness that you should consider. The first of these is to use humor appropriately. Remember that not all speeches or occasions should have a humorous approach. If the occasion does call for humor, you must decide if your speech should be funny or just mildly amusing. Humor should be used as a means of accomplishing your purpose, not of offending or distracting your audience.

Another principle is to have a central theme. This is particularly important in special-occasion speeches. The speaker should know his or her purpose and relate the entire speech to that purpose.

Finally, the speaker should avoid belaboring points and should be clear, cogent, and brief. These qualities are particularly desirable in ceremonial or special-occasion speeches.

At some time in your life you will be asked to deliver a special-occasion speech or a speech to entertain. It might be at a community affair, a political banquet, or a class reunion. If you keep these principles in mind, you will increase your chances of success.

Summary

The major communication goals are information exchange, persuasion, and entertainment. In the first case, the speaker must aim for audience learning and comprehension. In the second, the speaker tries to reinforce or modify the attitudes, beliefs, or behavior of the listener. A speaker whose purpose is entertainment must strive to amuse or please the audience.

When presenting an informative speech, the speaker must keep in mind the factors that affect audience learning. The speaker must try to motivate the audience to listen and learn. The message must be organized, and ideas must be effectively developed. The speaker may emphasize important information by repetition or by the use of visual aids. Information exchange may take the form of audience participation.

Comprehending approaches to persuasion across the ages can help us better understand the persuasive process. The Aristotelian approach takes a source-oriented perspective and provides us with three modes of persuasion: logos, pathos, and ethos. Much recent work in persuasion has been based on more of a receiver orientation, emphasizing the structure of attitudes, attitudes as predictors of behavior, and the functions of attitudes. Three specific attitude functions are: the experiential-schematic, the defensive, and the self-expressive functions.

In addition to the tools this information provides in persuasive situations, speakers may increase the persuasive effects of their presentations through the use of specific speaking techniques. An appropriate use of one- and two-sided arguments, sound and sufficient evidence, or forewarning of purpose may help to change the attitude of the listener. Explicit conclusions and the proper use of humor may also be persuasive.

The final kind of public communication is the speech to entertain, whether for ceremonies or for other special occasions. The entertaining speech is intended to bring pleasure and amusement to the listener. The special-occasion speech may be a way of saying thank you, farewell, or congratulations. It may be an occasion for awarding praise or it may be a eulogy. Important elements of effectiveness in these communication situations include: appropriate use of humor; a clear, concise, and well-organized presentation; and a central idea.

Exercises

GROUP EXPERIENCES
Before and After

DESCRIPTION   Most individuals need some type of motivation to listen and learn the information that is conveyed by the speaker. Without even realizing it, most of us continually provide reasons for another person to listen to us in a dyadic conversation. If you are attracted to another person, this may provide extrinsic motivation for you to listen to what he or she has to say. On the other hand, if you have been with a person over time, attraction may no longer serve as an extrinsic motivator. In cases such as these, another form of motivation would have to be developed in order to maintain interest in the conversation. This activity will help you understand the connection between interest level and motivation.

PROCEDURE   This is a role-playing activity that is most effectively used as a demonstration technique in front of the class. There are two roles, one played by a female and the other played by a male. The team should be asked to play the following three scenes.

Before

This is your first date. You are sitting in a nightclub. You are both extremely attracted to one another and excited about being together. You hang on every word the other person says because you don't want to miss anything. Show your interest in the other person both verbally and nonverbally.

During

You have been dating for four months. You are at the nightclub again. Your relationship is gradually shifting to where you are more interested in the music than in each other. You listen to each other on an off-and-on basis.

After

You have been together for a long, long time. You are at the nightclub again. You have heard everything the other person has to say "a million times." Neither one of you listens to what the other person is saying. Carry on an entire conversation where you misinterpret or do not listen to what the other person is saying.

DISCUSSION This activity demonstrates extrinsic motivation (attraction to the other person) in the "before" scene. The "during" scene demonstrates the minimal existence of extrinsic motivation, while the "after" scene demonstrates the complete absence of extrinsic motivation for listening to the other person. Logically, it can be assumed that extrinsic motivation can be replaced with intrinsic motivation, which then would increase the probability of listening. Can you think of a time during which you listened to another person with the absence of extrinsic or intrinsic motivation? Can you provide motivation for others to listen to you on both a physical and a psychological level? In your daily conversations, do you provide motivation for the other person(s) to listen?

The 60-Second Commercial

DESCRIPTION Research suggests that many different variables should be considered when planning a speech for a particular audience. Some of the considerations include extrinsic and intrinsic motivation, organization, effective development of ideas, repetition, and visual presentation. This activity will provide you with the opportunity to use a variety of techniques in an attempt to persuade the audience to remember your product.

PROCEDURE Your task is to design a 60-second commercial on a fictitious product or service. You will be paying a high price for 60 seconds of prime time, so the commercial should be designed with extreme care. Your purpose is to motivate your audience to remember the name of your product. Be creative in the design of your commercial.

DISCUSSION The class period following the presentation of the commercials should be used to test which products were remembered. Take out paper and pencil and list all the products you remember. Next to each product you should identify why you remembered the product.

After everyone has completed these lists, check to see which products were remembered the most. Why were some products remembered, while others were not? Consider the repetition, organization, and visual presentation of the message. Do you think it is difficult to develop a "persuasive" message?

How's Your Ethos?

DESCRIPTION   Ethos, or source credibility, refers to the way in which a speaker is perceived by the audience. Some of the findings related to source credibility include:

1. Receivers tend to accept conclusions advocated by sources to possess competence, trustworthiness, and goodwill.
2. A high-credibility source can produce more attitude change than a low-credibility source, even with highly ego-involved receivers.
3. When a receiver identifies with a source, it may enhance the source's chances of producing attitude change.
4. The receiver's attraction for a source increases as perceived similarity of attitudes increases.
5. The status of a speaker can affect his or her persuasiveness.

The following activity provides you with an opportunity to see how these principles work.

PROCEDURE   Which of the above principles of source credibility does this example illustrate?

Sample Situation

In an Arizona state prison, a program was presented on adapting to society after living in prison. Two speakers addressed the group of inmates. The first speaker was Dr. Sharon Stone, a noted psychologist in the area of social adjustment. The second speaker was Ron Harnick, a former inmate who had spent five years in the state prison system. The inmates showed greater interest in listening to Ron Harnick, and, consequently, his speech had a much greater impact than Dr. Stone's.

Two principles can be identified in this example. Principle 3 suggests that when a receiver identifies with a source, it may enhance the source's chances of producing attitude change. In this case it can be observed that the inmates (receivers) identified with Harnick (source) because of the time the latter spent in prison. Principle 4 suggests that the receiver's attraction for a source increases as perceived attitude similarity between the two increases. It may be assumed that the inmates perceived Harnick to have greater attitudinal similarity with them as compared with Dr. Stone.

Now that you have a sample description, divide into dyads and write an example that will serve to illustrate each principle. You may use one example to illustrate two principles. Each dyad should read one example to the rest of the class and ask the other students to explain the applicable principle of source credibility.

DISCUSSION   After writing and listening to various examples, can you identify other principles of source credibility? What are some of the ways in which you can be perceived as more credible? Which methods are most commonly employed by politician credibility?

PERSONAL EXPERIENCES

1. Think for a moment about the last time you responded very positively or negatively to an event that occurred on your campus. That "event" might have been a protest, a heated debate, or a celebration surrounding a major victory by an athlete or team from your school. Now think of the attitudes that you had about the issues associated with that event and what attitudinal function may have been called out that contributed to your response. Was that attitude experiential-schematic, defensive, or self-expressive in nature? Did you feel your behavior being physically driven by that attitude? Have you ever found yourself embarrassed days after a behavioral response because you simply "lost control"? How does knowledge of the structure and functions of your attitudes help you diagnose your own behavior? How can you use this information to help you as you deal with other people in your everyday life? in public speaking settings?

2. Obtain a copy of a transcript of a speech, or attend a speaking situation in which the speaker is clearly attempting to persuade his or her audience. Was the speaker ethical? List your criteria for a code of ethics in public speaking.

3. A common misconception about public speaking is that the ability to make speeches is instinctive and cannot be learned. Interview one or two people in your community who are considered to be effective speakers. Find out how they began public speaking. Were they ever afraid to speak in front of groups? Did they ever deliver a "bomb"?

Discussion Questions

1. What are the criteria used to distinguish public communication from private communication?

2. What is an example of a persuasive speech to (a) convince, (b) stimulate, and (c) actuate?

3. Are the qualities of ethos, pathos, and logos inherent in every good speech? Why? Why not?

4. Describe a situation in which you used the central route to process an incoming persuasive message. What about a time that you took the peripheral route? What characteristics of the speaker, audience, and occasion played a role in how you cognitively responded?

5. Under what circumstances would a one-sided argument be more effective than a two-sided argument?

6. What forms of motivation would be most effective to use when speaking to a group of college students?

7. In what ways do persuasive messages affect your day-to-day activities?

8. What techniques can a speaker employ to increase audience participation?

9. What are some creative ways you can think of to repeat the same information in different forms?

References

Ajzen, I. (1989). Attitude structure and behavior. In A. R. Pratkanis, S. J. Breckler, & A. G. Greenwald (Eds.), *Attitude structure and function* (241–274). Hillsdale, NJ: Lawrence Erlbaum Associates.

Brosius, H-B. (1999). Research note: The influence of exemplars on recipients' judgements. *European Journal of Communication, 14*(2), 213–224.

Fukuda, H. (1986). Psychological processes mediating persuasion-inhibiting effect of forewarning in fear-arousing communication. *Psychological Reports, 58,* 87–90.

Hazleton, V., Cupach, W. R., & Liska, J. (1986). Message style: An investigation of the perceived characteristics of persuasive messages. *Journal of Social Behavior and Personality, 1*(4), 565–574.

Homer, P. M., & Kahle, L. R. (1988). A structural equation test of the value-attitude-behavior hierarchy. *Journal of Personality and Social Psychology, 54*(4), 638–646.

Jackson, S., & Allen, M. (1987). Meta-analysis of the effectiveness of one-sided and two-sided argumentation. Paper presented at the annual meeting of the International Communication Association, Montreal, Canada.

Kerek, G. M. (1987, December). Can functions be measured? A new perspective on the functional approach to attitudes. *Social Psychology Quarterly, 50*(4), 285–303.

Kline, K. N., & Mattson, M. (2000). Breast self-examination pamphlets: A content analysis grounded in fear appeal research. *Health Communication, 12*(1), 1–21.

Leeds, D. (1988). *Power Speak: The complete guide to persuasive public speaking and presenting* (117–118). New York: Prentice Hall Press.

McCroskey, J. C., & Teven, J. J. (1999). Goodwill: A reexamination of the construct and its measurement. *Communication Monographs, 66*(1), 90–103.

O'Keefe, D. J. (2000). Guilt and social influence. In M. Roloff (Ed.), *Communication Yearbook, 23*(67–101). Thousand Oaks, CA: Sage.

O'Keefe, D. J. (1999). How to handle opposing arguments in persuasive messages. A meta-analytic review of the effects of one-sided and two-sided messages. In M. Roloff (Ed.), *Communication Yearbok, 22* (209—249). Thousand Oaks, CA: Sage.

Planalp, S., Hafen, S., & Adkins, A. D. (2000). Messages of shame and guilt. In M. Roloff (Ed.), *Communication Yearbook, 23*(1–65). Thousand Oaks, CA: Sage.

Schneiderman, S. (1995). *Saving face: America and the politics of shame.* New York: Knopf.

Sundar, S. S. (1998). Effect of source attribution on perceptions of online news stories. *Journalism and Mass Communication Quarterly, 75*(1), 55–68.

Tasaki, K., Kim, M., & Miller, M. D. (1999). The effects of social status on cognitive elaboration and post-message attitude: Focusing on self-construals. *Communication Quarterly, 47*(2), 196–212.

Tesser, A., & Shaffer, D. R. (1990). Attitudes and attitude change. *Annual Review Psychology, 41,* 479–523.

Witte, K., & Morrison, K. (2000). Examining the influence of trait anxiety/repression-sensitization on individuals' reactions to fear appeals. *Western Journal of Communication, 64*(1), 1–27.

chapter ten

Developing and Organizing a Public Message

key concepts and terms

Personal interview
Survey
Introduction
Thesis statement
Body
Conclusion
Transition
Topical pattern
Chronological pattern
Spatial pattern
Increasing levels
 of difficulty pattern

Chain-of-events pattern
Inductive pattern
Deductive pattern
Cause-and-effect pattern
Problem-solution method
Progression
Metaphor
Simile
Real example
Hypothetical example
Extended example

Illustration
Story
Anecdote
Description
Comparison-contrast
Operational definition
Examples
Statistics
Testimony

From:	"PJ"
To:	"Sasha" <rasmussx@futurenet.ab.net>
Sent:	Friday, May 1 3:45PM
Subject:	Help!

Sasha. I need you. Can you still help me with my speech? I know it's only a week away, but I've done all of the research. Am just not sure how to put together a good sales pitch. As I told you yesterday, the speech has to be 5–7 minutes long. We had to come up with an invention of some sort (a real one) and now have to pitch it to a group of potential investors (the class). The audience "only has so much money," will pick the top three speakers, and will "award them with start up funds." If I'm one of them, that translates into 10 bonus points on my final point total. With a D on the mid-term exam, I really need those points. Let me know what time is good for you tomorrow or Sunday afternoon. You're a lifesaver, Sasha. I know you're engaged, but blow him off and marry me.

—PJ

American author Mark Twain once quipped, "It usually takes me more than three weeks to prepare a good impromptu speech." The question is if these words were true for Mark Twain, what do they mean for us? Most of us will never be the quintessential storytellers of our generation as Twain was for his. However, if you go back and read it again, Twain's quotation offers us a valuable lesson. Even the greatest storytellers of our times spend hours, days, even weeks preparing for public presentations.

In this chapter you will learn how to create more effective presentations by using many of the principles that successful storytellers use. However, public speakers, like storytellers, must be prepared. Speaking in public is a challenge that requires selecting a topic or approach that will enthrall, gathering information that will add not only substance but also color and form, and organizing the message with the rhythm and ebb and flow of a story. More than any other in the book, this chapter is a kind of handbook of do's and don't's. It is meant to give you practical advice. The suggestions on how to choose your topic and gather source materials will provide you with the foundation for creating more effective presentations. Likewise, we hope the information on organizing and supporting the body of your speech and on preparing an effective outline will help. (Appendix B illustrates how the process works by presenting and annotating an effective speech.) Given the importance of each of these elements to public speakers and storytellers alike, we now turn to a discussion of how to select and narrow presentation topics.

Selecting the Topic

Finding a suitable topic is sometimes half the battle. In some instances there is no choice. The topic may already have been decided for the speaker. For example, if you are a senior who is majoring in veterinarian science, you may be invited by the local Society for the Prevention of Cruelty to Animals (SPCA) to speak with their staff about the latest developments in pet psychology. Later, as a full-fledged veterinarian, you may be asked by local farmers in a nearby rural community to discuss ways to guard against cattle diseases.

You and the Topic

When you must choose your own topic, however, you should keep certain guidelines in mind. The first of these guidelines concerns you, the speaker—your knowledge, your interests, and your convictions. To help you realize the importance of these elements, consider the following illustration.

Sarah was a "thirty-something" graduate student who had returned to school later in life. Over the course of the years, she had experienced several traumatic events, a number of which had fueled her interest in the study of communication. One day, as a graduate teaching assistant for the basic communication course, she made a decision to provide her students with an example of an informative speech. The speech she gave was one she had presented to several groups in the past on the topic of AIDS, and one that was based on her own personal experience. Sarah introduced the topic of her speech by telling the following story.

> Once upon a time there were a boy and a girl who were the best of friends. They shared the same interests—skiing, cycling, the theater—and the same circle of friends. One day they looked into each other's eyes and saw that something was different. The friendship had turned to love. Soon after, they were married. Everyone came to the wedding and celebrated their union. The couple was perfect. Everyone had known that one day they would be together.
>
> For six months, their marriage was the epitome of bliss. The couple delighted in making each other happy. One morning the boy gently awakened the girl and said, "Sweetheart, I have something to tell you." The girl smiled and rolled over to face the boy she loved. His next words were, "Honey, I'm gay." The marriage was annulled immediately. It took years for the boy and girl to each put the pieces of their lives back together, but finally they did.

With a pause to cue her audience, Sarah then switched from third to first person. "One day, five years later, the phone rang. I got up and said, 'Hello.' It was Wayne. He said, 'Hello, sweetheart. I've got something to tell you.' " At that moment in her speech, Sarah's audience froze. Her next words were beyond their comprehension: "Wayne said, 'I've tested positive for the AIDS virus. I think you had better be checked.' "

As Sarah moved from her story to the body of the speech, which focused on myths and information about the HIV virus as well as how to go about being tested, she later said she could have heard a pin drop until the very end of her presentation. To her surprise, she also was approached about her speech for several weeks by students whom she didn't know. Apparently, her students had been so affected by the presentation that they had gone home and told their friends. Sarah's ultimate realization about the impact of her speech came almost three weeks later. A student who had heard about her came up and asked her where he could go to be tested. He was afraid of the results, but her story had given him the courage to face reality.

Sarah's story is true. She was one of our graduate students. Of course, her name has been changed for this book. However, if you meet her one day, in the halls of a university in which she is teaching, she will probably tell you about the time that she found a way to teach her students three critical public speaking concepts. In this instance, she discovered a way to make them see the value of considering the following three elements:

1. Know your topic.

2. Be interested in your topic.

3. Believe in your topic.

Sarah's speech provides a perfect example of how to follow these three guidelines. Sarah knew her topic well. After experiencing the trauma of a broken marriage and having to take the AIDS test, she made a point of learning more about the HIV virus. Her life depended on this knowledge, and once she learned that she had tested negative, she decided to share her experience with others. It's always easier to discuss subjects about which you are familiar than ones about which you know very little. Although a good speaker researches any topic, previous knowledge of the subject can make the selection process easier.

Obviously, Sarah's topic was also interesting to her. If your life is changed completely in one moment by as few as three words, you are going to be interested. However, you need not have experienced anything quite so dramatic as that which Sarah experienced to be truly interested in your subject. For example, if you are an art history major, you probably will feel more comfortable discussing Leonardo da Vinci than talking about the advantages of solar energy. If you are genuinely interested in the subject on which you are to speak, your enthusiasm will be communicated to your audience when you deliver your speech. Interest in your topic also increases your motivation to investigate and research it thoroughly.

Finally, like Sarah, you should consider your personal values and beliefs when selecting a topic. Make sure that your beliefs and the topic you choose are compatible. This is particularly important in persuasive speaking. For instance, you can hardly expect your audience to be convinced of the need for tougher environmental laws if you yourself are not firmly convinced. A firm belief in your topic will make the presentation more vital to you and to your audience.

Even though we have talked about three ways to approach the task of selecting a topic (i.e., it's something you know about, are interested in, or strongly believe), you may think that you still have nothing special to share with an audience. Well, that's where you're wrong. Believe it or not, some of the best and most enlightening speeches we have heard in our classes have addressed the little things in life: why we should drink water (from a student who taught aerobics); why we should attend a meeting of the city planning board to stop the building of tall hotels on a Gulf Coast beach (from a student who worked as a toll booth attendant on a bridge leading to the beach); and even how to fold a fitted sheet (by a student who simply knew how to do it exactly like the manufacturers do.) Really! All of them made A's; they made excellent presentations.

To help you get started if you don't know where to begin, consider the list of topics we've provided in Table 10.1. These are great speech topics that we (your authors and two of our closest teacher-friends) have brainstormed to prove that anything can make a great topic! Let these subjects be a starting place for your own brainstorming session. Remember that all you need is knowledge, interest, or passion about your topic—and a belief that your audience also should know or care.

Narrowing the Topic

Once you have selected a topic, you must narrow it so that it is workable. Don't be like the high school student who decided to deliver his first speech ever on "the Civil Rights Movement." How narrow should your topic be? That depends upon your purpose. The thrust of a presentation will vary according to whether it is intended to inform, persuade, or entertain. For example, in a well-coordinated effort, several elected city officials addressed their fellow citizens on the financial crisis in their city. The focus of each individual address was different. In a formal televised statement, the mayor, whose purpose was to inform the public of the crisis situation, focused on the current fiscal deficits and the long-range consequences of inaction. At a later press conference, a council member outlined the kinds of legislation necessary to relieve the crisis situation. A third member of the city council was given the job of persuading the citizens who attended a town meeting to write letters or send telegrams to state and federal government officials encouraging them to pass legislation to relieve the financial crisis. Although each speech dealt with the finances of the city, the thrust of each address was determined by the speaker's purpose.

A good speaker should consider personal purposes and goals as well. These, too, will aid you in achieving desired results and in fully informing your audience. One way that you might begin is to make a list of objectives, ideas, opinions, and conclusions that you have drawn (keeping in mind, of course, the audience and time limits involved). Next, ask yourself the following five questions:

1. *Who* in the audience am I targeting—for instance, those who are opposed to my view? those who are neutral? those who already feel as I do about the topic?

2. *What* actions, if any, do I want my audience to undertake as a result of my speech—for example, write Congress? contribute money? alter their personal

TABLE 10.1 Sample Speech Topics

INFORMATIVE	PERSUASIVE
Selecting the perfect pet	Learn CPR
Warning signs of [any] illness	Buy Japanese cars
The most maligned animals	Don't believe everything you read
The etiquette of cell phones	Stop eating fast food
Students need rest	Drink water
Four steps to break up (or make up) with your sweetheart	Volunteer
	Don't wait. Plan your funeral now
When is enough enough? Signs of binge behaviors	Celebrate mistakes
	Get a hobby
Common phrases and where they come from	Be yourself
An ideal date night	Keep a journal
The book that changed your life	Never stop being a kid
How to find your passion in life	Learn to be idle
Decorating on a shoestring budget	"Romance" is a verb
How to write your own will	Plant a tree
Travel Europe on $30/day	Buy, don't rent
You too can run a marathon	Get some sleep
What it takes to be a successful comedian	Straight A's won't make you rich
The importance of rituals	Recycle
You don't have to be a genius to change your oil	Eat low on the food chain
	Avoid city driving
The secret world of dreams	Support local mass transit
White-collar pollution	Develop a fire plan
Finding the sacred in everyday life	Read labels on food
10 fun things you can do with vanilla wafers	Conserve water
From brown thumb to green thumb: How *not* to murder your plants	Get organized
	Shop as if the earth matters
Panic attacks and other anxiety disorders	Save for the future
The keys to power bowling	Vote
Socially responsible investments	Plant an organic garden
The successful garage sale	You only fail if you don't try
What to do with old paint and other toxic materials	Cultivate your imagination
	Paper not plastic
Increasing your memory power	Live in the moment
Cruelty-free living	Importance of smoke alarms
Why boycotts work	Read the instructions first
Rain forests in the U.S.	Learn to meditate
Why vegetarian?	Buy things that will last
	Read the classics

behavior? change their attitude regarding my topic? be motivated to change? simply laugh?

3. *When* do I want the audience to take action—immediately? within the week? from this point on in their lives?

4. *Where* should the audience turn for more information if they need it? Can I provide them with enough information to bring about the desired action?

5. *How* should I structure my message in order to bring about the desired action—include stories, examples, or statistics? build a one-sided or two-sided presentation? use a cause-effect or problem-solution organizational pattern?

Determining your central thought is a final consideration when defining and narrowing your topic. One of the most glaring speaking errors of beginners and poor speakers is lack of focus. As noted earlier, good speeches are much like other works of art—stories, musical compositions, paintings, plays, or literary works. They consist of separate elements that become unified into a whole by means of a central idea or thought.

Gathering Source Materials

Once you have selected your topic and narrowed it, you can begin collecting the materials you need to build your presentation.

Use of Sources

It is usually to your advantage to select from a wide variety of sources. The type and number of sources you use will depend on the specific purpose of your speech. When presenting an informative speech on a controversial issue, you should always secure information on at least two opposing views, especially when one source of information is biased. For example, if you were presenting a speech on "ingredients in cigarette tobacco," you might discover differences in those listed by the tobacco industry and those listed by the American Medical Association. In a situation like this, you should consult several sources in order to get the true picture. Of course, when presenting a persuasive speech, you may choose to include only those sources that support your particular point of view. Even then, it is important to be aware of the opposition.

Whether you surf the Internet, conduct an interview, read a magazine article, or watch a videotape, it is essential to take notes. Your notes should include summaries of the information and direct quotations, particularly if you plan to use them in your presentation. Ethical considerations and accuracy necessitate the use of a quotation in the context in which it was found. When direct quotations are not in order, summaries of information are sufficient.

You as Source

The most basic and obvious source at your disposal is yourself. Whether you realize it or not, you represent a storehouse of knowledge, experience, and observations. The fact that you remember paying 20 cents for a slice of pizza when you were in junior high school may be trivial. If you are going to give an informative speech on inflation and the cost of living, however, this information could suddenly assume significance. In general, personal anecdotes, examples, experiences, and observations make a speech more meaningful for you as the speaker and more colorful for the audience.

Interviews

You will often find that the best source of materials for a particular subject is another person or group of people. In that case you may want to gather your material by conducting an interview.

PERSONAL INTERVIEW.   A *personal interview* is conducted on a one-to-one basis with a person who has information or knowledge about the topic of your speech. For example, if you were to present a speech on student retention in engineering programs, you might want to interview a professor, a department head, a student, and a practicing engineer. If you were presenting an informative speech on a particular diet fad, you might find it valuable to interview a doctor, a nutritionist, someone who had success with the diet, and someone who did not. Although a personal interview may provide a sizable amount of material, information or opinions obtained by this method should not be considered definitive. The impact that information from an interview will have on your audience depends on how that particular audience judges the credibility of your source.

Regardless of the subject, a good interview requires good technique. If you choose to conduct an interview, keep certain things in mind:

1. Remember your purpose and topic and avoid getting sidetracked.

2. As an interviewer, you should try to make the person you interview feel comfortable and willing to talk. Obviously, a cooperative interviewee will make your task much easier.

3. Be prepared for the interview and have definite questions in mind.

4. Since you are trying to find out specific information or opinions, phrase your questions in such a way that they will bring clear responses.

If the topic of your speech lends itself to a personal interview and an appropriate interviewee is available, you will find this method an invaluable source of material.

SURVEY.   At times you may need to conduct a survey rather than a personal interview. A *survey* is a detailed gathering of information by questionnaire, observation, interview, and so forth. A survey enables you to gain a cross-section of information and opinions. Suppose you were giving an informative speech on stress on college campuses. You might wish to conduct an e-mail survey of as large a sample of your fellow students as possible in order to obtain some firsthand information. As in the case of the personal interview, the information and opinions obtained through a survey are not meant to be definitive. Although both sources are most useful when used informally, the validity of a survey can be judged in terms of the standardization of questions and the selection of participants.

Printed Material

Printed material has long been relied on as a main source of information for speech content. Such material includes books, magazines, journals, pamphlets, newspapers, diaries, almanacs, encyclopedias, and so on. There are so many different types of printed material that it is essential to know how to locate these different sources and use them properly. Information about some subjects is found almost exclusively in printed material, although more and more is finding its way to CDs or the web. For example, historical information that cannot be gained through a personal interview may be found in books or journals, and reports about current breakthroughs in science or medicine might be located in professional journals or magazines.

Today, thanks to CDs, microfiche, and microfilm, printed material can be stored in a minimum amount of space. Libraries are the primary storage houses for printed material, but you may find it necessary or beneficial to search out other sources.

Electronic Media and the World Wide Web

Modern technology has provided us with access to vast resources and information in the form of mass media, computer databases, and web sites. Films, television, CDs, cassettes, and old phonograph recordings are all valuable sources of information that can aid you in preparing a speech. For example, the now-famous Zapruder film of the Kennedy assassination has proven to be a vital source of evidence for those who have further investigated the shooting. Many important events have been captured on videotape and film and are available as source material for you. Likewise numerous guides to help you successfully navigate the Internet have been published, such as Angus Kennedy's (1998) book entitled *The Internet: The Rough Guide*.

According to Kennedy (1998), computerized databases, World Wide Web Sites, newsgroups, and "ezines" (or electronic magazines) are probably the most easily accessible ways to gather information. For example, you can locate and order the latest books from any number of online sources like Amazon Books, Barnes and Noble, or Borders. You also can get the latest entertainment and fashion news from Celebsites, E! Online, Events Online, Fashion UK, the Internet Movie Database, MTV, and Unfurled. For information on finance there are a number of excellent sites, including Bloomberg, CNBC, Nasdaq, Wall Street Journal, and Yahoo! Finance. If you need

What type of planning is necessary when the interviewee is unknown to the interviewer?

information about government-related issues around the world, a number of sites are available, including Active Most Wanted and Criminal Investigations, the Central Intelligence Agency, Declassified Satellite Photos, FedWorld, Her Magesty's Treasury, Interpol, Police Officer's Directory, U.S. Census Bureau, U.S. Federal Government Servers, and the U.S. President (*president@whitehouse.gov*) (Kennedy, 1998).

Likewise, you can find almost every major news source in the world online, including ABC News, the Australian, BBC News, Christian Science Monitor, CNN, Drudge Report, The Economist, The Hindu, HotWired, Infobeat, New York Times, PA NewsCentre (for news from the UK), Pathfinder (which includes Time, People, Sports Illustrated, Life, Money, Fortune, Entertainment Weekly, and Vibe), Ribcast (for Russian newspapers), South Polar Times, Sydney Morning Herald, The Times (London), USA Today, and the Village Voice to name just a few! (Kennedy, 1998)

Reference works that are available include Academic Info (a research directory targeting students and teachers), the American ASL Dictionary (for sign language), Bartlett's Quotations, Britannica Online, One Look Dictionaries (allows you to search more than 300 online dictionaries at once), Rap Dictionary, Rhyming Dictionary, Roget's Thesaurus, and Strunk's *Elements of Style* (Kennedy, 1998).

A comprehensive list of electronic journals and ezines may be found on the Ezine List and Inkpot's Zine Scene. Just hop on the net, plug in one of these names (or your topic), and hit "Go!" You may (or may not!) be surprised at the world of information that is available to you.

TABLE 10.2 Guidelines for Evaluating an Electronic Source

Whenever you find an electronic source that looks good at first glance, make sure to go back and ask yourself the following questions before using the information.

1. Who is the author? Is he or she affiliated with a reputable academic institution, government entity, or professional organization?
2. Who is funding the site? What potential biases or hidden agendas may creep in as a function of being funded by a particular organization?
3. How often is the site updated? Web sites should have a date and e-mail address that you can use if you need further documentation or clarification. Some sites even furnish a toll-free telephone number for further information (e.g., the American Cancer Society and the U.S. Library of Congress). If no date, e-mail address, or phone number is provided, the content may be questionable.
4. Has the information been subjected to a credible peer review before being posted or published? Note: Some sites are bogus or rogue, and are designed for retribution or to undermine the credibility of a person, group, or company.
5. Is the source well designed? Does the content adhere to proper rules of grammar, form, and style?

Keep in mind that new resources are added every day and may not stand the test of time. Somebody must keep the information current; if not, it may not be available at a later date.

Source: Adapted From David Munger, Daniel Anderson, Bret Benjamin, Christopher Busiel, & Bill Parades-Holt, *Researching Online,* 2nd edition. (New York: Longman, 1999)

The biggest challenge to overcome if you consult *any* web source is determining whether the source of information is accurate and credible. Unfortunately, there is no easy way to discern good from bad information every time. However, to aid you in making the best decisions possible, we encourage you to consider the guidelines suggested by Munger, Anderson, Benjamin, Busiel, and Parades-Holt (1999), which we have presented in Table 10.2.

Parts of the Speech

All speeches, regardless of their purpose or length, should be composed of three basic units: the introduction, the body, and the conclusion. Each of these parts serves at least one function that is essential to the effectiveness of the speech. Although each part of the speech should flow smoothly into the next, each unit should be identifiable upon analysis of the text.

Examine the following two brief speeches, which were prepared for a training seminar for magazine salespeople. Read each presentation carefully and decide which one is more effective.

Speech 1

There are many different magazines from which a person can choose. For the sports enthusiast, there are magazines like *Sports Illustrated* and *Field and Stream*. The homemaker might want to learn new recipes or tips on decorating from the *Ladies Home Journal* or *Redbook*. Those who enjoy literary magazines may turn to the *Saturday Review* or *The New Yorker,* while others may be interested in general news magazines like *Time* or *Newsweek*. These magazines vary in price and frequency of publication and are available through our subscription service.

Speech 2

Have you ever been stuck in a doctor's office or train station without anything to keep your mind off waiting? Or maybe you were stuck inside with a cold or waiting for a delivery? Perhaps if you had an interesting magazine to read, the waiting wouldn't seem so long.

There are many different and interesting magazines from which one can choose. For the sports enthusiast, there are magazines such as *Sports Illustrated* and *Field and Stream*. The homemaker might want to learn a new recipe or tips on decorating from a magazine like the *Ladies Home Journal* or *Redbook*. Those who enjoy literary magazines may be interested in reading a copy of the *Saturday Review* or *The New Yorker,* while others might be interested in a general news magazine like *Time* or *Newsweek*. These are just a few of the many magazines that can be readily purchased by subscription.

The number of magazines published is quite large. One can safely say that there is a magazine for every area of interest, whether it be crafts, sports, science, health, automobiles, food, fashion, gardening, or anything else. And what makes it even better is that they are all available through subscription.

Although these two speeches contain basically the same information, the second speech is obviously more effective. It has a carefully developed introduction, body, and conclusion.

The Introduction

The *introduction* of a presentation or speech must first catch and then focus audience attention as well as preview the body of the message. Sometimes just getting started is one of the most crucial and difficult tasks of a presenter.

Often a speaker has to compete with a noisy or inattentive crowd. In such cases it is even more important to capture the audience's attention with an effective introduction.

Several standard devices can serve as an effective introduction. These include the use of a startling statement ("By the year 2025, the earth will run out of fresh water"), a rhetorical question ("Did you ever wonder what your life would be like had you been born in another era?"), statistics ("Two children die of malnutrition every day in Alabama"), a humorous statement ("If all the world's a stage, then a lot of us get bit parts"), or a famous quotation (from Abraham Lincoln: "You can fool all the people some of the time, and some of the people all the time, but you cannot fool all the people all of the time"). Of course, sometimes one statement produces two or more effects. For example, the statement "One out of every two marriages ends in divorce" uses statistics but may also be somewhat shocking to an audience.

THESIS STATEMENT.   The introduction of a presentation should also include a *thesis statement* that presents your specific purpose. The purpose can sometimes be worked into the opening device for getting attention. For example, a museum sponsor might begin a fund-raising speech with the following:

> You don't have to go to a peep show to see some of the most beautiful nudes imaginable. Some of the world's most famous nudes can be found right here in our museum. But, unless we can find a way to raise $95,000 for maintenance costs, these nudes are going to be left out in the cold!

The opening line of this introductory paragraph begins with an unexpected or startling statement. Chances are, at least a few ears will perk up with the words "peep show." The remainder of the paragraph suggests that the museum is in financial trouble and must raise money to continue its operations. The last sentence suggests the purpose of the speech and gives some insight into what the main text will be about.

Regardless of the technique you use in your opening, be sure that the introduction is appropriate, is in good taste, and says exactly what you want it to say. You should not use a joke or anecdote unless it is appropriate to the occasion and relevant to the subject. You should avoid telling a joke or humorous story unless you feel perfectly comfortable with it. Remember, not everyone is a comedian. You should also omit irrelevant "warm-up material" and clichéd beginnings such as, "A funny thing happened to me on the way. . . ." Your introduction should be relatively brief and direct.

The Body

The effective introduction previews the main text of the message and leads directly into the body. The *body* is generally the largest part of the speech and is intended to present the main points, elaborate on them, and clarify when necessary. It is also a function of the body to develop clear transitions between different ideas.

In an informative speech, the body contains the bulk of the information you wish to present. In a persuasive speech, the body contains the arguments and evidence that support your position, as well as a refutation of possible counterarguments. For example, if you are trying to persuade your audience to support the abolition of capital punishment, the body of the speech would probably include moral and legal arguments along with appropriate supporting material. You might also include statistics to disprove the standard counterarguments, which contend that capital punishment is a deterrent to crime, or those that attempt to justify capital punishment on the basis of "an eye for an eye."

The body of a persuasive speech should include a discussion of the nature, effects, and causes of the problem, issue, or controversy. A politician who is trying to change the juvenile justice system because it is too lenient might want to include statistics showing a high percentage of juvenile felonies, case histories of chronic juvenile offenders, and the opinions of sources who have experience in the legal system. The speaker should show why the particular problem is meaningful to the audience. The politician might try to convince the audience that it is no longer safe to go outside or that children and the elderly increasingly fall prey to juvenile criminals.

The body is the longest and most detailed part of your message, so the arrangement of its ideas is very important. There are certain patterns of organization you can follow to help you structure the body of your speech effectively. These patterns of organization include a topical pattern, a chronological pattern, a spatial pattern, and various other patterns. Simply stated, the body of a speech or presentation should be presented in a way that is logical, coherent, and easy to follow.

The Conclusion

Although the major portion of a speech is presented in the body, it is the conclusion that can leave a lasting impression. Because a speech isn't over until the speaker walks away from the podium, the *conclusion* of the speech is as important as the introduction.

In general, the conclusion of an informative speech should offer a restatement of the major ideas and a summary of the overall content. Concluding a speech on what to look for in a company to interview with, a speaker might summarize specific guidelines such as benefits, promotion practices, stock options, and office politics. Similarly, a demonstration speech on how to safely release a raptor should end with a summary of the necessary steps and equipment involved.

The conclusion of a speech gives you an opportunity to tie up loose ends and bring the speech to a unified finish. As it is impossible for the audience to listen to and remember everything that is said, the conclusion should emphasize the main points so that the audience knows what was most important.

The conclusion of a persuasive speech may be used to arouse the audience to action. Let's examine the conclusion to the speech presented by our museum sponsor:

> In conclusion, ladies and gentlemen and patrons of the arts, it is time to assure our magnificent paintings a place inside our museum. For many years you have enjoyed the beauty of these fine paintings. Now it is time to give something in return. Take out your wallet or your checkbook and give what you can to help raise the $95,000 we need to keep our museum doors open!

This concluding paragraph underscores the purpose of the speech and asks for some action on the part of the audience. A concluding call for action need not always be financial, of course. The president of a parents' group may end an address with a plea to parents to keep their children home from school as a protest against a cutback in school services. Or a union delegate might ask an audience to join a boycott of crops picked by nonunion workers. A political candidate might conclude a rally by asking for volunteers to distribute campaign literature. In each case the call for action would be strongest in the concluding paragraph.

Regardless of purpose, the concluding paragraph should round out the speech and bring it to a satisfying close. The final sentence should signal the end of the speech so that the audience will know that it is over. The speaker may want to close with an emphatic statement or use one of the devices mentioned in our discussion of the introduction. For example, if you want to leave the audience thinking, you might pose a rhetorical question. Or, depending upon the content of the speech, you might want to conclude with a famous quotation.

Sometimes you might want to coordinate the conclusion with the introduction by using the same type of device, or even the same statement. For instance, a community leader who opens with the quotation from Abraham Lincoln that we mentioned earlier may close the speech in the following way: "You cannot fool all the people all of the time; and all of us here tonight know that *now* is the time to demand an end to the irresponsible actions of the City Council." Using the same quotation or same set of statistics not only reinforces a point but also lends your speech a sense of closure and balance.

Transitions

The use of transitions is an important aspect of speech organization. A *transition* is the bridge that allows one idea to flow smoothly into the next.

The most important transitions are those between the introduction and the body and between the body and the conclusion. However, they are also necessary between the main ideas within the body. For example, in a speech presented at a block association meeting, a neighborhood detective was discussing an increase in local crimes. One major point was that in recent years there seemed to have been a tremendous increase in auto thefts and robberies. To lead into his next point, the detective added, "But, unfortunately, the problem has not remained in the streets. Latest precinct reports show that household break-ins and burglaries in the area are up 50 percent over last year." The shift from crime on the street to crime indoors was smoothly made by a simple transitional statement.

The complexity of a transitional bridge depends upon how similar the two ideas are that are being connected. Sometimes just a few words or a simple sentence will do. For example, certain phrases, such as "in addition to," "aside from," and "in conclusion," are often used as transitional bridges.

When ideas are not closely related, you may need a more substantial transition—in other words, something that draws a connection between the two ideas or parts. A woman speaking to a group of senior citizens may wish to convince them of the need for an urban renewal project and at the same time assure them of the preservation of their neighborhood. The two points may be related in this way:

> Perhaps you feel that all of these changes I have proposed will destroy the charm of our downtown area. However, along with the plans for change are many plans for the restoration of our historical sites and parks. The kind of rebuilding now proposed will be in keeping with the tastes and needs of our community.

The effective use of transitions is one way to distinguish between a good presentation and a mediocre one.

Arrangement of the Body of a Speech

Patterns for Informative Speeches

Audiences retain more information when speeches are logical and well organized. We have already mentioned several standard patterns of organization that can help you structure your speech and present your ideas with the greatest effectiveness. The pattern you choose will probably depend on your topic. Certain subjects are best suited to particular patterns of organization.

TOPICAL PATTERN.   One of the most frequently used organizational patterns is the *topical pattern,* in which information is presented according to a specific category or classification. This type of organization is particularly useful when the subject of the speech can be divided into subparts that form a whole. For example, a speaker at a children's concert might introduce the audience to various parts of the orchestra by using a topical approach. He could discuss the strings, then the brass, then the woodwinds, and finally the percussion instruments. Each of the major divisions could then be broken down according to the general characteristics of each group and the specific instruments within each category.

CHRONOLOGICAL PATTERN.   A second standard pattern of organization is the *chronological pattern,* which follows a subject in time. The chronological pattern is particularly useful when presenting biographical or historical information or when tracing the development of an idea, institution, or movement. A speech on the development of satellite communication could be presented in a chronological pattern by tracing the events from the launch of Sputnik I on October 4, 1957, to the most recent advances in satellite technology. Or a speech on American fashion in the twentieth century could be divided into decades and could mention such eras as the "flapper" style of the 1920s, the miniskirt of the 1960s, the "yuppie" look of the 1980s, and the return of the '60s look in the 1990s.

A chronological speech may span centuries or days, depending on the scope of the topic. Because it is impossible to do justice to a topic that covers an enormous period of time, even in a speech that is an hour in length, the speaker must focus on the most important information. You must also make sure that the audience is aware of the time lapse between events, especially when the events or information you are discussing have occurred at uneven intervals. For example, in presenting a biographical sketch, you might connect one event to the next with phrases such as "two years later" or "in a matter of weeks" in order to give the audience some perspective as regards the time that has passed. The use of transitional phrases is particularly important when presenting a speech according to chronology.

Remember, nobody wants to hear innumerable small details. Even in everyday conversation, an unnecessarily detailed account of an event or an experience can become very boring. Children are often guilty of this practice. For example, you may ask a child what a certain television program was about, and he will repeat an

Persuasive messages generally contain moral and legal arguments.

endless sequence of events. Obviously, each step is not an integral part of the story. However, the child has not learned how to decide what information is most important. A speaker must be able to determine the most important information, for he or she cannot include too many ideas, events, or details without causing the speech to become lengthy and tiresome.

SPATIAL PATTERN. Not every subject is suited to every pattern of organization. Topics based on the location of one part in relation to others or on a geographical progression may best be presented in a *spatial* order. A speech that traces the westward expansion of America might be divided according to the extension of different geographic boundaries. (Note that the same speech might be presented using a chronological order.) A speech based on De Soto's exploration of the New World might follow his historical routes.

A spatial organization may be appropriate for certain subjects not related to geography at all. For example, an archeologist presenting a speech on the Plains of Nazca might approach the topic from a spatial order, emphasizing the relationship between one part of the structure and another. A spatial organization enables the audience to visualize the individual parts as they relate to one another in terms of the whole.

PATTERN OF INCREASING DIFFICULTY. Because one of the primary factors in evaluating the success of an informative speech is audience understanding, the speaker must strive to present the speech as clearly and logically as possible. When a topic is relatively complex, the speaker may choose to use a pattern of organization based on *increasing levels of difficulty.* This type of structure is particularly helpful when presenting an informative talk on a subject with which the audience is unfamiliar. When a plant manager explains the changes that will take place within a factory because of the pending use of robotics, the manager may want to present the information in varying degrees of difficulty. Because the comprehension of some ideas is based on understanding other ideas, a pattern of increasing difficulty helps to ease

Using visual aids can help summarize key points at the conclusion of a message.

the progression. Audiences feel much more comfortable after they have mastered an idea or understood some particular bit of information. By carefully building one idea upon another, a speaker can present increasingly complex material to an audience whose confidence in its own interpretive and evaluative abilities also increases.

CHAIN-OF-EVENTS PATTERN. As the name implies, this pattern of organization is based on the development of a series of steps, with each step depending on the previous one. For example, a local legislator addressing members of the Young Democratic Club in her district might use the chain-of-events method to explain the sequence of events that must occur as a bill goes from the committee stage to its actual enactment as law. Similarly, a weather forecaster predicting a 50–50 chance of a hurricane striking shore might outline the series of weather events that must occur in succession in order for the storm to develop. The *chain-of-events* method is particularly useful when giving a demonstration speech that explains a certain procedure. For example, a salesperson demonstrating the use of an MP-3 recorder would show the customer how to operate it according to step-by-step directions.

Patterns for Persuasive Speeches

Various patterns of organization are particularly well suited to the persuasive speech. While these methods are not restricted to persuasive speeches, they are often used in them. Remember that the purpose of a persuasive speech is to create attitude change within the listener or to motivate the listener to action.

INDUCTIVE PATTERN. The first pattern is the *inductive pattern.* This particular pattern of organization is based on the process of inductive reasoning. In an inductive argument, you present the audience with several specific cases that serve as the basis for a generalization. The specific cases must, of course, support the generalization. Therefore, you must avoid examples that are inconsistent with or contradictory to the generalization you wish to make.

The number of specifics necessary to formulate a sound generalization will vary. Although there are mathematical calculations to determine statistical validity, you can usually rely on common sense and intuition to decide upon the minimum number of specific cases that a particular argument demands. For example, a senior citizen who condemns all teenagers as drug addicts, based on the solitary example of a neighbor's son, lacks a sufficient number of specific examples. Therefore, the generalization is invalid. When the generalization involves a large population, a greater number of specific cases is necessary.

Certain generalizations are easier to support than others. For example, U.S. health officials who sought to end the swine flu inoculation program used an inductive argument. Citing several incidents of paralysis as a side effect of the injection, officials provided enough evidence to ban the program. The argument might have followed this pattern:

Specifics: I.   Specific cases of paralysis following inoculation.

                     A. Cases of paralysis in Florida.

                     B. Cases of paralysis in Denver.

                     C. Cases of paralysis in New Jersey.

Generalization: II.   The swine flu inoculation can cause paralysis.

Conclusion: III.   Therefore, the inoculation program is potentially hazardous and should be discontinued.

Based on the occurrence of cases of paralysis following the shots, health officials decided that the inoculation could conceivably have caused paralysis and therefore concluded that the program should be discontinued. The generalization that the inoculation could cause paralysis was evolved through an inductive process based on the occurrence of scattered cases of this side effect. While some experts discounted this argument, emphasizing that the percentage of cases of paralysis was quite small relative to the number of persons receiving the shot, the program was discontinued.

DEDUCTIVE PATTERN.   The inverse of the inductive pattern is the ***deductive pattern,*** in which a speaker applies a generalization to specific cases. The generalization, if accepted by the audience, serves as the basis for an effective argument.

In a deductive pattern of organization, the speaker must draw a conclusion about a specific case based on its applicability to a previously accepted generalization. An effective argument can be organized in the form of a syllogism, the most common example of deductive reasoning. For example, a concerned member of the community may offer the following deductive argument at a public transportation hearing:

Generalization: We are all agreed that traffic lights reduce accidents.

Specifics: There seem to be a lot of accidents at the intersection of 40th and Vine.

Conclusion: Therefore, a light at the intersection of 40th and Vine would reduce the number of accidents.

If the traffic officials agree with the citizen's general statement, they might be quite willing to accept the solution. If the general statement is not accepted by an audience, however, the deductive argument will have little effect. Generalizations based on value judgments are most difficult to validate. Therefore, a speaker must have some insight into the nature of the audience. Let us examine the following deductive argument:

Generalization: All war is immoral.

   Specifics: Vietnam was a war.

Conclusion: Vietnam was immoral.

The effectiveness of this deductive argument depends on the audience's acceptance of the general statement. Undoubtedly, an audience of conscientious objectors would accept this argument. However, the same argument would probably be vehemently rejected if presented before an audience of Veterans of Foreign Wars. Therefore, in preparing a deductive argument, the speaker must be sure that the audience will agree with the general statement.

CAUSE-AND-EFFECT PATTERN.   Closely related to the inductive argument is the *cause-and-effect pattern.* In this type of presentation, the speaker establishes a relationship between two events. The speaker attempts to convince the audience that this relationship is one of cause and effect, or that a certain result is the product of a specific event. For example, at a monthly sales meeting, an assistant buyer suggests that the increase in accessory sales results from a new line of neckties. This argument could be confirmed; according to the record of sales, the new line of neckties contributed to an increase of 25 percent of the total volume of accessory sales. Therefore, the new line of neckties (cause) produced an increase in sales (effect). However, not all cause-and-effect arguments can be mathematically determined. For example, how could you substantiate a claim that natural catastrophes such as earthquakes and floods increase as a result of our tampering with the atmosphere? Although it might be argued that these disasters have been more prevalent following milestones in space exploration, it would be impossible to draw a causal relationship between the two events.

One effect is often the result of several causes. For example, when a heretofore losing team moved into a new stadium and started to win, the cheering fans were convinced that the new stadium brought the team luck. In a case like this, the exact cause of the team's success would be a combination of things, including perhaps the new stadium, an increase in attendance, errors on the part of the opposition, the return of an important player after an injury, and so forth.

PROBLEM-SOLUTION PATTERN.   Another useful pattern of organization for the persuasive speech is the *problem-solution method.* This approach is much the same as the pattern of organization used in group discussions (see Chapter 7). The problem-solving method, first described by John Dewey, includes the following basic steps:

1. What is the nature of the problem?

2. What are the causes?

3. What are the possible solutions?

4. Which is the best solution?

5. How can this solution be put into effect?

Remember our traffic light example? Let's examine this example according to the problem–solution pattern. The nature of the problem concerns the number of accidents at the intersection of 40th and Vine. Causes of the problem include the use of this route as an alternative to the parkway, with a subsequent increase in traffic, and the lack of any traffic signs or personnel. Possible solutions include a traffic light, a police officer to direct traffic, rerouting the traffic, and a four-way stop sign at the intersection. The best solution would be a traffic light, since a police officer would be too costly, a four-way stop sign might prove confusing, and rerouting the traffic would cause congestion on neighboring roads. The solution could best be put into effect by a decision by the Department of Motor Vehicles and the installation of the light by the same agency.

The problem–solution pattern is based on a logical, step-by-step analysis of a particular problem. Of course, the analysis of any problem requires considerable research and investigation.

Principles of Outlining

An outline helps you in the preparation as well as the delivery of your speech, regardless of the organization pattern you choose. The outline is a tool that allows the speaker to categorize information and separate main ideas from subordinate ones. For example, in a topical presentation the speaker would classify each aspect of the subject as a main division of the outline. Part of such an outline would look like this:

```
Parts of a Sailboat
   I.  The Rig
       A.  Standing Rigging
           1.  Shrouds
           2.  Stays
       B.  Running Rigging
           1.  Halyards
           2.  Sheets
  II.  The Hull
       A.  Hull Shape
       B.  Hull Construction
```

A chronological pattern of organization may be used in an outline that divides the topic by specific intervals such as decades, years, or weeks, depending on the scope of the topic. For example, a speech on environmental concerns in the twentieth century might be divided into discussions of endangered species at the turn of the century, in the 1940s, in the 1970s, and in the 2000s.

Although the outlines may vary in form, the basic principles remain the same. Some speakers prefer to use Roman numerals for each major part of the speech, using I for the introduction, II for the body, and III for the conclusion. Capital letters are then used for main ideas within the text of the speech. However, regardless of the form, you should remember that details presented in an outline get more specific with each subdivision. Look at the outline in Figure 10.1. Notice how the two major divisions (I and II) relate to the general topic of the outline (negative effects of air pollution). As you can see, the information gets more specific with each division, and each detail relates directly to the preceding category.

All forms of outlining share certain basic principles:

1. Keep your outline simple.

2. Account for all major parts of the speech.

3. Include at least two subpoints for each main point.

4. Use Roman numerals and indentation to structure your outline.

5. Organize main points and subpoints to underscore the relationships among them.

6. Arrange ideas in a logical progression.

To aid you in developing your outlining skills, we have provided you with three good examples of complete-sentence outlines in Appendix C.

Simplicity

An outline is used to assist, not confuse, the speaker. Therefore, as a speaker, you should keep your outline simple. Each line should represent a single thought or bit of information. Decide whether you want to use single words, phrases, or sentences, and then use them consistently throughout the outline. An outline is a valuable organizational tool if you don't let it become too cumbersome.

Accountability

When outlining your speech, make sure to include all major parts, including the following:

1. title

2. thesis statement

3. introduction

4. body

5. conclusion

6. transition statements

By accounting for all major parts of the speech in your actual outline, you will be better able to check your logic, ensure the inclusion of all major points, and better visualize your presentation as you both practice and ultimately deliver it. An example of a complete outline is provided in Figure 10.1.

Title: Air Pollution: The Silent Killer

Thesis Statement: Air pollution has an adverse effect on world health and the environment; therefore, listeners should take an active role in reducing air pollution.

Introduction

I. In the next 50 years, gas masks will not be reserved for war, but will be requisite for daily life.
  A. Current statistics regarding air pollution in major cities around the world
    1. London
    2. Paris
    3. Tokyo
    4. Moscow
    5. Montreal
  B. Current air pollution statistics in major U.S. cities
    1. New York
    2. Chicago
    3. Los Angeles
    4. Detroit

II. What are the effects of air pollution, especially on world health and on the environment?

(Transition: First, let's address the growing relationship between air pollution and world health.)

Body

I. How does air pollution affect health?
  A. Respiratory conditions associated with pollution
    1. Respiratory condition X
      a. Cases of X
      b. Deaths due to X
    2. Respiratory condition Y
      a. Cases of Y
      b. Deaths due to Y
  B. Allergies related to pollution
    1. Allergy Q
    2. Allergy Z

(Transition: Now that we've talked about the effects of air pollution on world health, let's turn to its impact on the environment.)

II. How does air pollution affect the environment?
  A. Effects on agriculture
    1. Growth of vegetation
    2. Crop yield
  B. Effects on the atmosphere
    1. Increase in carbon dioxide level
    2. Destruction of ozone layer

(Transition: As you can see, air pollution is indeed a silent killer—of men, women, children, and the environment we live in.)

Conclusion

I. Air pollution affects world health and increases destruction of the environment.
II. Join with me in attempting to reduce the problem by carpooling more often and by encouraging Congress to take measures to reduce air pollution before it's too late.

FIGURE 10.1 A Sample Outline

Inclusion of Points

When you divide a main point in a presentation, use at least two subpoints to support that point. For example, under each Roman numeral you will need to include a "point B" if you have a "point A." Likewise, under point IA, you will need to have a "subpoint 2" if you include a "subpoint 1." The only exception to this rule might be if you are providing an example or illustration for a main point. In this event, the point you are illustrating would require no subdivision.

Use of Symbols and Indentation

Using symbols and indentation in an outline allows you to organize your points, logically arrange them, and show their intrinsic relationships. For example, if used correctly, numbers, letters, and indentation show which points are of equal status and which points are logically subordinate to others. In Figure 10.1, points I and II are of greatest importance, while points A and B are subpoints of each main point or arguments that are used to develop them.

To check yourself on the appropriateness of symbols or indentation, ask yourself, "Do subdivisions A, B, and C all relate to main point I? What about A, B, and C under point II?" If the answers to these questions are "yes" and you indeed have symbolized distinctions correctly, you can avoid sloppy outlines and sloppy thinking, both of which adversely affect the effectiveness of a speech.

Underscoring Relationships

Remember that all points within a subdivision must be related. For example, consider the following partial outline on travel destinations in the eastern United States.

```
Travel Destinations in the Eastern United States
   I. Sights in Massachusetts
      A. Concord
      B. Plymouth Rock
      C. Boston Harbor
      D. Liberty Bell
```

If you know your American history, you will observe that entry D is out of place, since the Liberty Bell is in Pennsylvania. Incorrect placement of information is a relationship problem. Although the example just cited is quite obvious, the speaker may sometimes have a difficult time finding an appropriate spot for information. If the information is essential, it may be necessary to reorganize categories.

Logical Progression

It is important to arrange ideas in some sort of logical *progression*. For example, in a speech about local government, the speaker might identify the three main categories of the outline as local government in the city, in the county, and in the township. The speaker should then decide upon the order of these main categories, based on either ascending or descending order of complexity or size. The speaker should select a logical progression of ideas and remain consistent in the arrangement of major ideas and subordinate points.

Supporting Material

One of the advantages of using an outline is that it enables you to see if you have adequate supporting material. Supporting material serves a variety of functions and is essential to all speeches, whether they are to inform, persuade, or entertain.

Clarification

One of the basic functions of supporting material is to clarify an idea, opinion, or argument. Remember that in an informative speech, your goal is for the audience to understand your position. In a persuasive speech, you want the audience to understand your position. If you want to entertain or impress an audience with a story of perilous travels on the high seas, you may need to make clear the distances between ports of call or the unpredictable weather. Clarification is an important aspect of all speeches.

METAPHORS AND SIMILES. You probably remember these two figures of speech from a high school or college English class. A *metaphor* is the use or application of a name, descriptive term, or phrase to compare one person, object, or action with another, without the use of the words "like" or "as." An example would be when you describe a child using the expression, "He (or she) is a little tiger." A *simile* is a comparison of one thing with another of a different kind and necessarily includes the words "like" or "as." "She (or he) eats like a little tiger" provides a useful example. Although, at first glance, you may believe that figures of speech plan no significant role in "real-world" presentations, recent research indicates otherwise. In three experiments conducted by Richard Harris and Noah Mosier (1999), the researchers found that metaphors aid particularly well in both message recognition and recall. They also learned that concrete comparisons ("Deserts are ovens.") are remembered better than abstract ones ("Deserts are the face of mother nature.").

Given their power to aid listeners in remembering your message, both metaphors and similes can be useful to you in clarifying an idea or concept. Remember that the more colorful and engaging they are, the more your words will be remembered. This is especially true if you allow a powerful metaphor to serve as the driving force behind your message. For instance, "She is a little tiger because of (Point #1) the way she eats, (Point #2) the way she sleeps, and (Point #3), the way she plays." Or "Deserts are ovens because of (Point #1) the extremely high temperatures they can achieve, (Point #2) their arid nature, and (Point #3) their power to kill biological organisms within relatively short periods of time."

EXAMPLES.   You can clarify an idea, opinion, or concept in many ways. Another way is to use an example. The example may be real, hypothetical, or extended. Examples have been given throughout this text to help you better understand particular concepts. Some of the examples have been real, others hypothetical. A *real example* refers to an event or incident that actually happened. A *hypothetical example* is based on something that could possibly occur but that did not really happen. In the previous section on the organization of persuasive speeches, we offered two examples of inductive reasoning. The swine flu inoculation example was based on real events; the necktie example was hypothetical. Yet both examples helped to clarify a description of the inductive pattern that otherwise might have been meaningless to the reader.

An *extended example* is one that is carried out to considerable length in order to clarify or emphasize a very important idea. Often when athletes and rock stars speak to young audiences and advise them to "say *no* to drugs," they offer examples of their own personal experiences as users, and then extend the example to what might happen to audience members who do the same. Their extended examples are real. However, a speaker can extend a hypothetical example as well. For instance, a dietician might discuss the future health problems of a child born to a mother who is indifferent to the importance of prenatal diet on her unborn child.

ILLUSTRATIONS.   Another means of clarification is the use of *illustrations*. While examples are verbal illustrations, the speaker may sometimes find a visual aid very helpful in clarifying information. A surgeon delivering an informative speech on a new technique for open-heart surgery would probably find a series of diagrams useful in her presentation. If you have ever attempted to assemble an "easily assembled" piece of furniture or equipment, you may appreciate the value of a visual aid in clarifying otherwise confusing directions.

STORIES AND ANECDOTES.   Speakers sometimes use stories and anecdotes to clarify or highlight particular ideas or points of information. A *story* is an account, narrative, or tale of past events. An *anecdote* is a brief account of an entertaining or interesting moment. Stories and anecdotes are particularly useful as introductory devices when appropriate to the overall topic of the presentation. In fact, they are so powerful that cultures around the world have used them for centuries "to stimulate questions, raise issues, encourage debate, and offer listeners a view of life as it could be" (Sunwolf, 1999). For example, Native Americans use lesson stories, Sufis use wisdom tales, and Africans use dilemma tales to persuade. They accomplish this goal by encouraging self-generated thoughts, active participation, modeling, and conscious deliberation on the part of listeners (Sunwolf, 1999). What are some of your favorite personal stories? What family stories were you told as a child? The next time you give a presentation, try starting with one of your favorite tales. We bet your audience perks up the minute you begin.

Both stories and anecdotes may be real or imaginary, personal or impersonal. Although they do not offer any hard evidence, they do help clarify and emphasize your point or position. For example, a fire official delivering a speech to elementary school children on the dangers of false alarms might relate the well-known fable "The Boy Who Cried Wolf" as a way to clarify the message.

DEFINITIONS. After analyzing your topic and audience, you might decide that a definition of terms is necessary to make sure that the audience understands your points. Since language is often ambiguous, it is important that you clarify any misunderstanding relating to definitions of words.

There are several different ways to define a word, idea, or concept. Some ideas can be defined by *description*. For example, in a speech on the kibbutzim of Israel, a speaker might want to describe this type of communal living in order to clarify audience understanding of the topic.

Sometimes a word, idea, or concept can best be defined by *comparison* or *contrast*. A definition by comparison suggests the similarity of something unknown to something with which the audience is already familiar. Someone discussing musical instruments of the Middle Ages might define a lute by comparing it with a guitar. Similarly, a speaker may define a term through contrast. In the same lecture, the speaker might define a clavichord as an early ancestor of the piano, pointing out the essential differences between the two.

Sometimes a speaker has to provide the audience with an *operational definition*, one that is used only for the duration of the speech. For example, the president of a large corporation, addressing stockholders on the success of the company in the previous fiscal year, has to clarify what he or she means by "success." It is possible that the president's definition does not coincide with that of the stockholders.

Support

Using evidence in a speech supports your position while it enhances the listeners' learning process. In persuasive speeches, speakers must carefully provide material that gives substance to their messages and strengthens their positions.

The source of authority may be expert opinion, official pronouncements, religious symbols, the pomp and ceremony of institutional practice, the sayings or doings of the socially elect, or even the printed word or the tone of voice.

DANIEL KATZ AND RICHARD L. SCHANCK

EXAMPLES. When using *examples* as a form of support, you must be sure to use a sufficient number to confirm your ideas or opinions. A journalist reporting on corruption in a city agency should be able to come up with several examples of wrongdoing in order to demonstrate the problem. While one incident might make an important story, many examples would be needed to prove widespread corruption.

Successful speakers practice their speeches before appearing in public.

You also must give examples that are representative or typical of the position you support. If a psychiatrist advocates a certain kind of therapy for severe depression, he or she might support this position by citing several examples of cases in which this therapy was successful. If the cases described were not cases of severe depression, the examples would be inappropriate and unsupportive.

Examples used to support a position must also be representative of the total picture. When the owner of a nursing home sought to defend himself against media charges of poor conditions, he cited the case of one elderly gentleman who found the home so comfortable that he wrote the owner a thank-you note. Upon investigation, this example was found to be atypical and certainly not representative of what most of the patients felt. A speaker must be extremely careful when choosing examples.

STATISTICS. Another way to support your presentation is with facts and figures. *Statistics* can be very valuable if used skillfully. A business executive suggesting a merger with another company could incorporate statistics into the speech to show how the merger would be profitable for the firm. A scientist promoting a new drug would cite statistical results of different experiments.

Statistics should be used with care, however. In most situations the speaker should round off statistics to the nearest whole number. Remember, the audience is hearing the statistics for the first time, and the numbers must be easily interpreted. Statistics can be intimidating, so avoid overwhelming your audience with too many facts and figures. Fractions and decimals are often confusing and add little to listener understanding. Approximations such as "close to 30 percent" or "over a quarter of a million" give a general picture without burdening the listener with specific numbers. Nonetheless, the speaker must know when it is important to use exact figures. For example, a proponent of a particular bill narrowly defeated in Congress may quote the exact figures when discussing the issue at a press conference to show that there had been considerable support for the legislation.

If you use statistics, you must always make them meaningful for the listener. One way to do this is to present the statistics in the form of comparisons. In a speech on state aid to rehabilitation centers, a senator may tell the audience that "for every dollar spent on the rehabilitation of these citizens, they pay $17 in taxes back to society once employed." In this case, the relationship between the state expense and the state revenue is made clear by comparison.

The ethical speaker will keep in mind that statistics are often misleading and that certain statistics can be found to "prove" almost anything. The speaker and the audience should be aware that statistics do not always give an accurate representation. For example, an audience was greatly impressed when a golfer reported that he came in third in a recent tournament until they found out that there were only three participants. It is a matter of ethics to avoid such misleading information and half-truths.

Testimony

You should not overlook the value of *testimony* as supportive material. A person's testimony can often add validity to an informative or persuasive speech. Of course, the value of testimony depends on the credibility of the source. Basically, testimony can be derived either from a direct witness to an event or from an expert in a particular field. The appropriate use of testimony is determined by the nature of the subject. For example, in discussing the safety hazards in building construction, a speaker might give the testimony of several people who survived the collapse of a recently constructed hotel.

Expert testimony often proves helpful in both persuasive and informative messages. A speaker discussing the effectiveness of anti-gang advertisements might cite the testimony of actual gang members who say that threats of death are not deterrents because they live with and accept the possibility of death as reality every day of their lives. If gang members say they fear jail time more than death, they probably will (and should) be believed (Chapel, Peterson, & Joseph, 1999, p. 245).

By being careful to provide support and clarification for the ideas in your speech, you can increase the chances that your audience will understand your message and be persuaded by it. Concern for your audience as you see them and the integrity of your presentation are key issues in the preparation of a speech. When an audience feels your concern, it is likely to reward you with a positive reaction to your speech and increased credibility.

It should now be evident to you that a well-prepared speech combines many skills and carefully selected elements. Take a look at the sample speech presented in Appendix B. Analysis of any effective presentation will reveal the basics with which it was built.

Summary

Careful planning, organization, and preparation are essential when speaking in public. Athletes train for competitive events, musicians rehearse for concerts, and artists sketch before they paint. In the same way, you must prepare yourself to go before your audience. The success of your delivery will largely depend upon how well you have organized your message.

Begin by selecting a topic that interests you or one that you have some previous knowledge of or familiarity with. Make sure, if your speech is supposed to be persuasive, that your personal convictions are in agreement with your topic.

Good speeches are focused. Decide your purpose in speaking: Will you inform, persuade, or entertain your audience? Your subject should not be too general but should serve as the unifying or central idea of your speech.

As you gather information for your speech, keep your purpose in mind. An objective discussion of a controversial issue requires presentation of opposing views. If your purpose is to persuade, you may rely upon those sources that support your view. There are a wide variety of sources of information. Draw on your own experience, personal interviews, or surveys when appropriate. Take advantage of the wide range of printed materials, films, recordings, and videotapes available.

Consider the functions of the three basic parts of your speech. The introduction serves to catch and focus audience attention. Use the standard introductory devices—statistics, rhetorical questions, famous quotes—when appropriate or try telling a story. You present your main purpose and set the tone for your speech in your introduction. The body of your speech will contain the bulk of information and elaboration of your main ideas. These main ideas should be connected by smooth transitions. The conclusion should be used to leave a lasting impression on your audience and to reemphasize your main idea.

As you organize the body of the speech, decide upon a pattern of arrangement. Informative speeches may be topical, chronological, or spatial or follow the patterns of increasing complexity or chain of events. Persuasive speeches may follow inductive or deductive reasoning or develop according to patterns of cause and effect or problems and solutions.

Your outline is a map—be sure to provide yourself with a workable guide for your delivery. Remember the six main principles of every effective outline: simplicity, accountability, inclusion of all major points, proper use of symbols and indentation, underscoring relationships, and logical progression.

Supporting material is important to clarify and substantiate your ideas. Use real, hypothetical, or extended examples when appropriate. Employ illustrations, stories, or anecdotes to clarify your points. Define your terms when necessary by description or by comparison or contrast with terms familiar to the audience. You may reinforce your main ideas with the use of statistics or testimony.

The importance of good preparation cannot be overestimated. Using the methods of organization outlined in this chapter will help you in effective public speaking.

Exercises

GROUP EXPERIENCES
Come On Up and Introduce Yourself!

DESCRIPTION   As outlined in this chapter, the introduction to a speech serves several important functions. One of these functions is to catch and then focus audience attention. If you fail to capture your audience in your introductory comments, it is unlikely that you will get its attention later. This activity will provide you with the opportunity to write several different types of introductions to the same speech.

PROCEDURE   Select a topic for a speech from Table 10.1 on page 264 of the textbook. Then outline the main body of the speech. You will not have to deliver the speech itself, but you will have to deliver "introductions" to the speech. Therefore, it is important that you determine the theme and organizational structure of the speech so that you can preview the body of the speech in your introduction. Now—write three different introductions for the same speech. You may wish to review the various methods suggested in this chapter, such as the use of a startling statement, a rhetorical question, or a humorous statement. Each introduction should be no longer than 60 seconds. After hearing the introduction, your audience should (1) be motivated to listen to your speech, (2) be able to identify your central theme, and (3) have a general idea about what you will cover in the body of your speech.

Each member of the class should be asked to deliver his or her introductions to the rest of the class. The introductions should be done so that no one person will present two or three consecutive introductions. Each introduction should be evaluated by class members, based on the following three scales:

Scale 1. Did the speaker motivate you to listen to the speech? (1) not at all motivated; (2) slightly motivated; (3) motivated; (4) highly motivated.

Scale 2. With what degree of accuracy do you think you can identify the speaker's main theme? (1) not at all accurately; (2) slightly accurately; (3) accurately; (4) highly accurately.

Scale 3. With what degree of accuracy do you think you can describe what the speaker will cover in the body of the speech? (1) not at all accurately; (2) slightly accurately; (3) accurately; (4) highly accurately.

Each speaker should carefully review all the evaluations of his or her introductions. You may wish to add the total number of points possible for each scale and then the number of points actually received on each scale.

DISCUSSION   After reviewing your point totals for each introduction and each scale, can you identify problems with a particular introduction or scale? Do you need to spend more time in preparing introductions? How did your introductions compare with the others presented?

Concluding Remarks

NOTE   The procedure for this activity is the same as for the activity just described, except that *conclusions* are presented instead of *introductions*.

Patterns

DESCRIPTION   Persuasive speech patterns can easily be identified as inductive, deductive, cause-and-effect, or problem-solution. The purpose of any persuasive speech is to create attitude change in the listener; the various patterns are alternative methods for pursuing that goal. The purpose of this activity is to familiarize you with persuasive speech patterns.

PROCEDURE   Locate three speech transcripts. PBS offers an excellent collection on their web site (http://www.pbs.org/greatspeeches/). Analyze each speech to determine the speech pattern used. Keep in mind that a speech may have a combination of patterns. After identifying the patterns in each speech, write a short outline for each. For example, if you have identified a deductive pattern, you should point out the generalization, the specific statement, and the conclusion. Bring your analyses to class.

Divide into groups of four. Compare your analyses of the three speeches. If there are discrepancies among group members as to the patterns used in the speeches, determine the specific conflict. After 45 minutes each group should have reached an agreement on the patterns used in each speech and should report its results to the class.

DISCUSSION   Did you experience any difficulty in analyzing the speeches? Do you believe that organization in a speech is important for producing attitude change? Why? Why not?

PERSONAL EXPERIENCES

1. Start your own collection of jokes, stories, or other types of interesting introductions for speeches. Collect these from web sites, books, magazines, television, or public speakers. Your collection can be used for introductions to speeches, stories, or papers.

2. Collect a list of statements you read or hear in advertisements that demonstrate some form of illogical reasoning. Then consider the problems that are created when illogical reasoning is used. How often do you make invalid claims?

3. Identify all the "creative" ways in which you could collect source materials for a speech. Consider, for example, cartoons, fairy tales, and poems. Too often we look only in the standard places (reference books, interviews) for material. Consider the creative use of collections of information parallel to a multimedia presentation.

Discussion Questions

1. What are some of the principles of outlining you should use in writing a speech?

2. What are the intended purposes of the introduction, body, and conclusion of a speech?

3. Provide an example of each of the following types of supporting material: illustrations, stories, anecdotes, definitions, and examples.

4. Can a speech effectively use a combination of the spatial, chronological, and topical patterns of organization? If yes, provide an example.

5. What are the factors you should consider when preparing to speak in public? (List the factors in the order in which you believe they should be considered.)

References

Chapel, G., Peterson, K. M., & Joseph, R. (1999). Exploring anti-gang advertisements: Focus group discussion with gang members and at-risk youth. *Journal of Applied Communication Research, 27*(3), 237–257.

Harris, R. J., & Mosier, N. J. (1999). Memory for metaphors and similes in discourse. *Discourse Processes, 28*(3), 257–270.

Kennedy, A. J. (1998). *The Internet: The rough guide, 1999.* London, UK: Penguin Books.

Munger, D., Anderson, D., Benjamin, B., Busiel, C., & Parades-Holt, B. (1999). *Researching online* (2nd ed.). New York: Longman.

Sunwolf. (1999). The pedagogical and persuasive effects of Native American lesson stories, Sufi wisdom tales, and African dilemma tales. *The Howard Journal of Communications, 10*(1), 47–71.

chapter eleven

Delivering a Public Message

key concepts and terms

Public speaking anxiety
Rapport
Delivery
Gesture
Vocal delivery
Phonation
Voice

Larynx (voice box)
Resonance
Articulation
Pitch
Volume
Rate
Vocal quality

Diaphragm
Style
Accuracy
Clarity
Appropriateness
Economy
Lively quality

From:	"Jerry"
To:	"Lynda" <rasmussx@futurenet.ab.net>
Sent:	Friday, July 1 3:45PM
Subject:	Think I'm Ready!

Lyn-

Know you told me I should wear a suit when I give my SGA campaign speech, but it's just not me. So I'm wearing khaki pants and a blazer like I originally planned. That's it! End of discussion.

I did take your advice about videotaping my speech. You were right—hitting the play button was the hardest part. It wasn't pretty, but I've been able to get rid of the uhs and ums you were telling me about. Just wish you had told me I looked like a dang duck whenever I used my hands. Got that little problem under control as well. And it only took about FIFTY practice runs. Gee, I'm glad I don't have to worry about anything else right now . . . like school, or grades. Yeah, right!

Gotta run for now. Wish me luck. And thanks, Lyn! Really.

—Jerry

Throughout history, public speakers like Jerry have been keenly aware of the importance of dynamic delivery. Prophets, poets, philosophers, and storytellers have practiced through the ages to capture the minds and imagination of their audiences. As a modern student of communication, you too must develop your own unique manner of presentation. Even the most powerful speech can be ruined by a poor delivery, whereas a mediocre speech can be improved if delivered in a dynamic way.

The importance of delivery goes beyond maintaining audience interest. Delivery affects speaker credibility, message comprehension, and persuasiveness. A speaker's credibility can be established or destroyed during the presentation of a speech. The audience's perceptions are changed by nonverbal cues such as the speaker's appearance, facial expression, posture, and gestures.

However, an informed audience should always be aware of the difference between perception and reality. While an honest speaker may quite unconsciously project an image of sincerity, trustworthiness, and goodwill, a skillful speaker with the most selfish motives can sometimes create that same impression. For example, the prominent political figure who denies an accusation of wrongdoing can add to his credibility by looking directly at the audience, thereby gaining support with nonverbal communication.

Delivery also enhances message comprehension and retention. It does so primarily by eliminating many of the elements that can distract the listener from the message. For example, if Amanda presents a message without exchanging direct eye contact with her audience, she will never know whether she is getting her message across. Such feedback is vital in determining the impact of a message. Likewise, if Sam plays with his pen or the piece of chalk he is holding, he may distract the audience from his message, thus reducing the chances for message comprehension.

In addition to increasing message comprehension and speaker credibility, a strong delivery can add to the persuasive impact of a message. Perhaps one of the best examples of a speaker who uses delivery effectively is evangelist Billy Graham. Known for his sweeping gestures and his emotion-filled facial expressions, Graham maximizes his delivery for persuasive appeal.

Public Speaking Anxiety

For years we have known that people fear public speaking. In fact, for some people fear of public speaking ranks as high as fear of death, heights, and even snakes. Fortunately, its status on the top five list of fears has made public speaking anxiety a major area of study. Let us tell you what we know to date.

Long considered to be a form of social anxiety, *public speaking anxiety* is the "fear and uneasiness caused by the potentially threatening situation (real or anticipated) of speaking before a group of people" (MacIntyre and MacDonald, 1998, p. 363). Other names that it has been called are "stage fright," "audience anxiety," and (the more global term) "communication apprehension."

According to noted researchers, Ralph Behnke and Chris Sawyer, public speaking anxiety seems to stem from three key variables: inherited biological predispositions, negative conditioning that we have experienced in the past regarding speech performance, and "patterns of neurological activity associated with cognitive processing" (1999, p. 167). Based on work of Scherer (1998) in the area of emotional processing, Behnke and Sawyer described, as follows, what happens when we are asked to speak publicly:

> Specifically, emotional processes are triggered when humans perceive a novel event will occur, evaluate the pleasantness or unpleasantness of an experience, determine that the situation involves an important goal, assess the potential for coping with the situation, and appraise whether participating in the situation is compatible with the self concept (1999, p. 166).

In the language of the brain, this process occurs when three specific neurological regions of the nervous system are activated:

> "a fight/flight" system that reacts to unconditioned punishment or non-reward, a behavior inhibition system (BIS) that suppresses motor responses linked to the provocation of punishment, and a behavior activation system (BAS) that constructively engages the threat with learned adaptive strategies. Each system is regulated by a neurological circuit called the comparator, which scans the environment for any mismatch in normal conditions. Once detected, the environmental mismatch initiates a complex series of appraisals. . . . Based on this assessment of threat, the comparator selects the most effective anxiety sub-system

(fight/flight, BIS, or BAS) and continues to monitor the situation for potential shifts in threat management strategies. Adaptation to or removal of the threatening stimuli will cause the comparator to return the organism to normal functioning (p. 166).

(Whoa! Sounds like something out of *Star Trek*, doesn't it?)

With either explanation, that's where our past experiences with speech performances (of any kind) and inherited biological predispositions come into play. For example, research has shown that people with high apprehension have experienced "more intense and frequent punishment for communication" than people with low apprehension. However, the biological component seems to mediate the development of communication apprehension. As Sawyer and Behnke (1997) noted, "individuals with high communication apprehension are more susceptible and physiologically reactive to reinforcement, especially negative stimuli, while those with lower communication apprehension are less reactive to social conditioning such as punishment" (Sawyer & Behnke, 1997, p. 214).

To illustrate, consider the following examples. Judee (a 20-year-old junior) describes herself as highly apprehensive. As long as she can remember, Judee has been sensitive to what her teachers have said about her presentations and perceives that she is a "terrible public speaker." The fact that she has never received a grade higher than "B" on an oral presentation reinforces her negative self-perceptions, and makes her all the more anxious when she speaks. As a result, Judee has dropped the basic public speaking course twice, even though she needs the course to graduate. In contrast, consider Sang (an 18-year-old college freshman), who feels nervous when she speaks but describes herself as low in apprehension. Sang has ". . . always been able to hear both positive and negative comments" about her presentations, and decided at the age of 15 to use the forensics program in high school to hone her public speaking skills. Sang sees herself as a "moderately good speaker" and finds it much easier to speak in public than Judee.

Based on current research, that's what happens when we experience public speaking anxiety and three of its key contributors. But what leads us to "evaluations of pleasantness or unpleasantness" about opportunities to speak in public? Interestingly, what speakers with no public speaking training attribute to be "causes" of public speaking anxiety is actually pretty close to what we have learned through years of empirical study. For instance, Amy Bippus and John Daly (1999) asked "people without any formal background in communication or research on stage fright" to offer explanations for why people experience stage fright (p. 63). Nine major categories of answers emerged from respondents in the following order of importance:

1. *Mistakes*—People are afraid of making an error(s) during a presentation.

2. *Unfamiliar role*—Public speaking is new to many people and they aren't yet comfortable with it.

3. *Humiliation*—People are afraid of being ridiculed or rejected.

4. *Negative results*—People are afraid that adverse consequences will result from the presentation.

5. *Rigid rules*—There is a (narrow) set of expectations associated with being a good speaker, and people may be afraid they won't meet those expectations.

6. *Personality traits*—People have certain implicit traits that prevent them from being good speakers (e.g., low self-esteem, insecurity, and self-doubt).

7. *Lack of preparation*—People don't properly research and organize their presentations.

8. *Lack of audience interest*—People are afraid that the audience isn't interested in what they have to say and will be unresponsive.

9. *Physical appearance*—People are afraid that listeners are scrutinizing their personal appearance.

Again, respondents weren't too far from the mark. Indeed, research has shown that speech apprehension is actually associated with "increased self-focusing (on the part of the speaker), fear of not meeting audience expectations, believing one is dissimilar and subordinate to the audience, perceived skills deficiency, fear of evaluation, audience scrutiny, an uninterested or unresponsive audience, lack of experience in public speaking situations, poor preparation, and a contagion effect in which other speakers' anxiety increases your own anxiety" (Bippus & Daly, 1999, p. 63).

Although similarities exist between the two lists, it is also critical for you to note: *Self-reported speech anxiety is **not** significantly related to actual behaviors associated with speech anxiety (e.g., shaky voice, verbal dysfluencies, inappropriate or no facial expressions, improper use of arms and hands, and "big" body movements) nor perceptions of public speaking performance by trained observers* (Carrell & Willmington, 1998). According to Freeman, Sawyer, and Behnke (1997), other nonverbal cues that tell an audience you are anxious as a speaker are rigid or tense arms and hands; lack of movement or gesture; tense facial muscles; a monotonous voice; dead pan facial expressions; and a voice that's too soft.

What does all of this information mean for you? The ramifications are most reassuring. It means that if you're apprehensive, people don't generally notice unless (1) you actually exhibit the aforementioned anxious behaviors, or (2) you call attention to your apprehension with comments like "I apologize," "I'm just so nervous," or "Please forgive my shaking hands, I'm just new as a public speaker." It also means that, although you may be experiencing serious stage fright internally, even trained observers may not notice.

This is good news indeed. If you can master the two major tasks associated with effective message constructing (researching and organizing a presentation) and if you can deliver that message using appropriate nonverbal behaviors, your apprehension won't get in the way of your becoming a successful speaker.

Given this fairly elaborate discussion of public speaking anxiety and our presentation in Chapter 10 about how to organize a message, let's now turn to ways of reducing the number of behavioral indicators of apprehension you may be exhibiting in your delivery. If you practice these strategies, we can assure you: You will reduce the number of apprehensive behaviors you are displaying and increase the audience's perception of you as a competent public speaker.

Practice

Rehearsing a speech helps to build both speaker confidence and self-concept. If you are not prepared, you will have reason to feel tense. Consider the following example. Jennifer had just finished writing her speech for the banquet honoring her as incoming president of the Student Government Association. As she placed the finishing touches on the manuscript, her mind immediately turned to the history paper she had to finish. She knew her speech well enough—she had just written it, hadn't she? She should do fine this evening without rehearsal.

When she arrived at the banquet, she was startled by the number of people who were there. She had not anticipated an audience of 125 people, and she surely had not expected the university president to come. As the time approached for Jennifer to speak, her feelings of apprehension escalated. Her heart raced, her knees grew weak, and her hands sweated profusely. Jennifer now regretted not having rehearsed her speech.

At last, the time for her speech arrived. Jennifer stood and faced the audience. As she looked down at her manuscript, anxiety gripped her. She had not taken the time to transfer her manuscript to note cards, nor had she underlined the key points on the manuscript itself. All of a sudden, she felt herself go blank. What would she do? As she glanced at the blur of black ink on the paper, she realized her only recourse was to read her speech word for word.

Jennifer made it through the speech, as we all do, but her performance was less than stellar. She had blown an opportunity to motivate and challenge club members to greater action. Likewise, she had failed to show the university president the true level of her commitment to the club. If only she had rehearsed her speech, Jennifer could have performed more effectively and reduced her communication anxiety substantially.

Rehearsal can come in a number of forms. You can physically deliver your speech to a wall, mirror, friend, or video camera. You can run the speech through your mind the way a seasoned athlete visualizes performance before a competition, or you can deliver your presentation orally. Practicing will help you learn how both you and audiences will respond, especially if you videotape your performance or present it to a friend or group of friends. An audience of friends can also give you suggestions for improvement.

Use Physical Activity

Physical involvement in your speech helps use excess energy. If your energy has no normal outlet, it will manifest itself in trembling hands, knees, and voice. Using gestures and body movements helps use energy, emphasize points, and maintain audience attention. Like speeches, gestures and movements should be practiced and experimented with before the final presentation. If you feel that you have too much energy before speaking, try taking a few deep breaths, using isometric exercises, or using systematic relaxation.

Do Not Memorize, and Organize Well

When students try to memorize, they put themselves at a disadvantage. Speakers begin to worry about forgetting something—and usually do. If a speaker does forget, there are usually uncomfortable silences and abbreviated presentations. With proper preparation time, using a note card with a brief outline should be all that is necessary for prompting. Clear organization enables speakers to speak extemporaneously. It is much easier to remember points when they follow in a logical progression, so try to put them in sequences that build your confidence.

Get Involved with Your Topic

Confidence increases when speakers are interested in and involved with their topics. Topics should be so important and interesting to the speaker that he or she wants to get ideas across. Motivation and involvement in the topic helps focus attention on what is being said, rather than on who is saying it. As a side benefit, communication apprehension also decreases.

Develop a Proper Attitude

Proper attitudes go along with topic involvement. Speakers have a responsibility to be sincerely interested in what they have to say. Speakers must also remind themselves that their physical responses are normal reactions. The audience is an important factor to consider. Audiences usually want speakers to succeed, especially in classroom situations. The classroom audience is generally the most sympathetic audience speakers will ever encounter.

Principles

Look Natural

In order to make a successful presentation, a speaker should practice certain principles of good delivery. The first principle is to look natural. If you are stiff or artificial, you will look uncomfortable and awkward. The audience may see this as a lack of confidence, which might greatly affect their perceptions of your credibility. At the other extreme, if you seem theatrical or overly dramatic, you may be perceived as false and insincere. The good speaker strives for a natural, easygoing style of presentation.

Match Delivery and Content

The delivery should be carefully coordinated with the content of the speech. Body movement and vocal expression should add to the presentation, not detract from it. Superficial gestures and inappropriate facial expressions can distract the audience's attention. To illustrate, while practicing her welcoming speech for atheletes who were participating in the annual Race for Charity, Olivia attempted to coordinate a gesture with her opening sentence, "We welcome you with open arms." Rehearsing time and time again, Olivia tried to find the right moment to hold out her arms, palms up, facing the audience. Obviously uncomfortable with the gesture, Olivia was unsure about whether it should be used before, during, or after her spoken welcome. Although we might have laughed at Olivia's awkwardness, should we have been present in the room, we could have helped her by suggesting that she use natural gestures that would complement her verbal message—and avoid those gestures that would distract from what she was trying to say.

Although particular gestures are often associated with specific phrases, such as the one Olivia used, it is best for us to use a variety of gestures and vocal expressions. A sudden change in volume, a pause in delivery, or a firm shake of the head can all be effective in punctuating a particular idea or argument. However, the speaker's various vocal expressions and body actions should support the verbal message and not contradict it.

Make It Appropriate

Another principle of good delivery concerns the choice of an appropriate style of presentation. The delivery of a speech must be considered in relation to the audience, the situation, and the speaker. Chapter 8 presents audience analysis in terms of message selection and preparation. An awareness of audience characteristics is also important in terms of delivery. For example, the tone of voice used when speaking to an audience of children is quite different from the tone of voice used when speaking to adults. Regardless of the age of the audience, the speaker should never condescend or talk down to them. "Talking down" is more often projected by delivery than content. For instance, teachers' attitudes toward their students can sometimes be inferred from their tone of voice. Students often resent teachers who give simple instructions with overenthusiastic energy, as if to say, "Now children, today we are going to. . . ." While you may speak differently to children than to adults, you must remember that no audience, regardless of age, wants to be patronized.

A good speaker also takes into account any special challenges that members of the audience may have. For example, if some audience members experience hearing problems, the speaker should adjust his or her volume accordingly.

It is very important to make sure that the delivery is appropriate to the situation. To do this, you must first consider the occasion of the speech. For example, if you are delivering a eulogy at a funeral or memorial service, you should present your speech in a solemn manner. To do this, you should keep your volume low and the pace relatively slow. On the other hand, if you are delivering an after-dinner speech, you should seem enthusiastic and in good spirits. Lightness of tone, variation in pace, and free use of gestures, plus a happy expression on your face, are appropriate here.

You should also consider the setting for the speech. Your delivery will be influenced by whether the setting is a small conference room, an auditorium, or a large outdoor amphitheater. Your volume must vary according to the size or the acoustics of the setting.

Size, acoustics, and seating arrangement also influence the basic mood or tone of your delivery. A casual, understated, and highly informal presentation may not come across well in a very large auditorium. On the other hand, a strict sense of formality can alienate the audience in a small and intimate setting. The effective speaker will choose the degree of formality according to the setting. A quiet, casual talk would be effective in a classroom, where the audience is close enough to perceive subtle gestures and expressions, but the same kind of presentation would be inappropriate in a concert hall.

Talking and eloquence are not the same; to speak, and to speak well, are two things. A fool may talk, but a wise man speaks.

BEN JONSON

Delivery must be appropriate to the speaker's personal style or manner. The key here is to know your own personality and behave naturally—remembering that being a speaker does not mean being an actor. For example, former President Jimmy Carter was noted for his natural, easygoing style during his election campaign. He was unpretentious in his manner, and his characteristic smile helped him establish a warm relationship with his audiences. Throughout the campaign, political observers watched him gain self-confidence and increase the effectiveness of his personal, informal style.

Nonverbal messages play a significant role in public presentations.

Regardless of the situation, you will project honesty and sincerity if you are true to yourself. Aim for a delivery style that is consistent with your own personality.

Establish Rapport

If a speaker fails to develop and maintain a positive relationship with the audience throughout the presentation, the purpose of the speech will be lost. *Rapport* is almost entirely the result of delivery. For example, eye contact with the audience increases credibility and makes the audience more trusting of the speaker. A warm, conversational manner can achieve the same effect.

Rapport is also important because a good speaker-audience relationship can overshadow weak spots in the message itself. Entertainers devote much energy and overshadow weak spots in the message itself. If you don't believe us, consider the following situation. Pierre was an exchange student from Reims, a city located in the northeastern part of France. Fiercely proud of his home, where Charles VII was crowned under the watchful eye of Joan of Arc in 1429, Pierre found himself in front of his public speaking class telling them about modern-day Reims. Although he struggled with his English, Pierre's audience could tell how much he loved his subject and wanted each of them to be able to see his home as he saw it. Throughout the presentation, Pierre looked and smiled at each member of his audience with sparkling eyes, and laughed every time he got tangled up in his words. The class loved him, and they let him know by applauding loudly as his speech concluded. It didn't matter that Pierre had stumbled a couple of times in the delivery of his message. The rapport that he had developed with his audience gave Pierre the edge he needed to make his speech truly memorable.

Speak the speech, I pray you, as I pronounced it to you, trippingly on the tongue; but if you mouth it, as many of your players do, I had as lief the town-crier spoke my lines. Nor do not saw the air too much with your hand, thus; but use all gently: for in the very torrent, tempest, and—as I may say—whirlwind of passion, you must acquire and beget a temperance, that may give it smoothness.

WILLIAM SHAKESPEARE, HAMLET

Physical Delivery

The term *delivery* covers many different elements of a speaker's presentation, including physical delivery, vocal expression, and use of visual aids. The physical elements of delivery can be divided into various body movements, such as posture, gestures, facial expressions, and eye contact. Also included in the physical aspect of the presentation is the way a speaker uses accessories and audiovisual equipment, such as note cards, a lectern or computer presentation software.

Posture and Body Movements

As a speaker, you must be aware of your body as an important source of communication. In fact, the body is so expressive in communicating ideas and feelings that many of our verbal expressions are based on descriptions of body movements. For example, a person who maintains a positive attitude in times of adversity is said to keep a "stiff upper lip." Someone in great suspense or suffering extreme anxiety is said to be "sitting on the edge of his seat." These figures of speech accurately describe the body movements of people in these situations. Someone watching a movie based on a Stephen King novel may very well be sitting on the edge of his or her seat. Similarly, a candidate who does not win the election may be keeping a stiff upper lip to stop it from trembling.

Our body movements and posture are closely related to our physical and emotional states. On the physical level, posture can reveal whether a person is tired, energetic, or in pain. On an emotional level, posture can reveal whether a person is tense, relaxed, depressed, or excited. Posture also tells us something about a person's self-image. People with a healthy measure of self-confidence move about easily, stand up straight, and hold up their heads. Those individuals who are shy, ill at ease, or ashamed of themselves are more likely to slump, slouch, and keep their heads and eyes lowered.

A speaker's body movements and posture influence an audience's perceptions in many ways. Although no firm rules exist regarding the delivery of a speech, you may want to consider the following basic guidelines when presenting a speech. In order to appear poised and confident, try standing comfortably "at ease," with your weight equally distributed over both feet. Find ways to make your body relax; if you are too stiff, the audience may begin to feel uncomfortable. At the other extreme, avoid slumping, leaning on the lectern, or standing with your weight distributed on one hip or the other. If your posture is too relaxed, you may be perceived as too casual.

As a speaker, your movements, like your posture, should appear natural, not forced. Although you should stand relatively still and avoid pacing, natural movements can add to your delivery. You can use body movements to energize yourself and your audience. A speaker who does not move from one space seems dull and restrained. Appropriate body movements help to free the speaker from nervousness and spark the audience's attention. Body movements can also convey meanings. A speaker who leans forward when revealing something new suggests to the audience that they are being made privy to this information. A step toward the audience suggests that the speaker is embracing them and breaking the imaginary barrier between speaker and listeners.

Gestures

In addition to moving your whole body, you can use a variety of gestures. *Gestures* can convey many different meanings, depending upon the context and cultural background of the audience. For example, the well-known American "peace"

Gestures can convey a variety of meanings, depending on style and context.

sign—made with the first and second fingers placed in a V-shape, the third and fourth fingers curled and touching the thumb—is a vulgar gesture in some other countries. Gestures also can convey meanings in and of themselves (as emblems), while others are used as a part of the verbal message.

Traditional gestures are those movements of the hands and arms that have been associated with particular meanings. The boxer who has won a fight might clasp his hands above his head in a gesture of victory. Similarly, the modest speaker might hold up the palm of her hand toward the audience to still listeners' applause.

Other gestures are emphatic in nature and tend to punctuate the verbal message. When presenting a forceful argument, the speaker might pound a fist on the lectern to support the idea. Or a speaker may wave an index finger to focus the audience's attention on a particular thought. These gestures can serve to underscore the speaker's message, but should be used sparingly so that they don't lose their effectiveness.

Gestures can be descriptive in nature and work to enhance the verbal message. For example, try to describe a spiral staircase while keeping your hands behind your back. The feat is nearly impossible. Descriptive gestures are particularly effective when you ask the audience to visualize what you are saying. A simple gesture to illustrate size, quantity, shape, or distance can lend support to the speaker's description.

All gestures—traditional, emphatic, and descriptive—must be used purposefully if they are to add to your delivery. Here are a few guidelines to keep in mind when you use gestures:

1. Avoid gestures that make you feel uncomfortable. Awkward or self-conscious movements detract from your delivery.

2. Be careful to coordinate your gestures with what you are saying; timing is important here.

3. Avoid gestures that call attention to themselves apart from the spoken message.

4. Use gestures only when they will add to your presentation; gestures lose their effectiveness when you use them to excess. Can you imagine a speaker who pounds the lectern at each and every turn in the message? The result would probably be more humorous than forceful.

For ten additional tips for improving your physical delivery, consider Table 11.1.

Facial Expressions

A speaker's facial expressions contribute in many ways to the final outcome of a presentation. We have all sat through lectures or speeches where the speaker did little more than read a prepared message. Not only did our perceptions of the speaker's competence plummet; so did his or her "sincerity quotient" and our interest in what the speaker was saying. In short, a look of disappointment, a smile, or a frown of disapproval can be much more powerful than a spoken message.

Facial expressions are important in establishing rapport with the audience, but the skillful speaker does not want to manipulate the audience by using them. An audience can usually sense when a smile is phony in much the same way a parent can often tell when a child is lying. Once again, as with all body movements, facial expressions should be natural extensions of the verbal message. If you are genuine about the content of your speech, then your facial expressions will be consistent with your words.

Eye Contact

Good eye contact helps to establish rapport and speaker credibility. In fact, of all parts of the face, the eyes are the most important in establishing speaker-audience relationship. A speaker who looks at the audience appears more straightforward and honest than one who does not. In a study concerning speaker eye contact conducted by Atkins in 1988, speakers were judged to have "good" eye contact if they looked at the audience 90 percent to 100 percent of the time. "Minimal" eye contact was defined as looking at the audience 10 percent to 50 percent of the time. How was minimal eye contact perceived by the college students who took part in her study? Results indicated that speakers with "little" (0 percent to 10 percent) or "minimal" eye contact were judged negatively on 70 percent of the personality traits on which they evaluated speakers.

Although eye contact is important in delivery, it is impossible to look at the entire audience at one time. The effective speaker scans the audience and looks directly at individual members seated in various locations. An empty stare or unfocused, wandering eyes do not add to your delivery. To increase the effectiveness of eye contact, try to make all the members of the audience feel as if you are talking to them individually.

The Lectern and Note Cards

Most people find it more comfortable to stand behind a lectern when speaking to an audience. The key word here is stand, not *hide*. Because body movement is an

TABLE 11.1 **Ten Tips for Improving Your Delivery**

To improve the physical delivery of your message, remember these ten guidelines:

1. You don't have to *feel* natural to *appear* natural. Try to forget yourself (and your own discomfort), and focus on what you want the audience to take with them after your speech has concluded. If you touch the heart or mind of a single person in a positive way, you have made a difference.

2. When you begin a presentation, look for the friendly faces and speak to them. As you gain momentum and confidence, "go after" other members of your audience one-by-one. If you find yourself feeling apprehensive at any time, return to the "friendly faces."

3. Vary your facial expressions, body movements, pitch, volume, and rate of speech. Doing so will help you keep the audience's attention.

4. If your audience begins to look restless or bored, change something—anything. Conclude or move quickly (but smoothly) to your next point; move physically; play with your "volume" control; or do anything else you can to "awaken" them. Loss of interest isn't necessarily the kiss of death, unless you fail to counter it.

5. If you know (in advance) that you will experience a "dry mouth," take a glass of water with you to the platform. When you need to take a sip, do so without any comment. The audience will think nothing about it, unless you call attention to the matter. (The same holds true if you need to brush your hair from your eyes or unbutton your coat pocket. Casually do what you need to do. Nobody will notice unless you verbally comment or make broad or "jerky" movements.)

6. If you get lost in your presentation or forget a point, don't be afraid to backtrack or revisit. Again, avoid calling undue attention the situation. Simply say, "Let's go back for a minute to . . .," or "One key point that I should [go back and] mention is. . . ."

7. Try not to fidget. Before you speak, empty change from your pockets, dispose of that mangled paper clip, leave your pen at your desk (Clicking it will drive your audience crazy!), and sweep long hair back away from your face in a "pony tail" if you are prone to play with it.

8. Work to rid presentations of filled pauses ("ums" and "uhs"), colloquialisms ("dopey," "gypped, "belly-button"), and slang or regional words ("lame," "loser," "like, you know," "she rocks"). Most of us use them in informal situations, but they reduce credibility in public speaking settings.

9. Keep your body weight distributed equally on both feet. Avoid leaning on the lectern or a nearby table.

10. Talk *with* audience members, not *to* your audience. Even though you are speaking in a public setting, each listener will respond to you on two levels: intrapersonally and interpersonally. You are more likely to achieve a positive response if you remember that your audience is comprised of individuals.

essential aspect of delivery, you must be clearly visible to the audience. A speaker can use this spatial relationship by moving away from the lectern to develop rapport with the audience or by remaining behind it to preserve formality.

A lectern provides a space for your notes or outline. Of course, the use of written materials depends on the type of delivery. By definition, an impromptu speech would involve the use of no notes. However, an extemporaneous speech, which is carefully prepared but not memorized, might require notes or an outline, especially if the speech is long or complicated. Of course, when a speech is to be read, the complete text must be available to the speaker.

When you use note cards, be sure to prepare them carefully and to number them consecutively. If you are using computer software, an overhead projector, slides, or a flip chart, indicate their use with a color code. For example, you might try writing the letters OH #1, SL #2, or FC #3 in a different color of ink at the top left-hand corner of the card. That way, when you need to show a visual, you will know when to use it. Limit the number of note cards you use to as few as possible, and avoid rustling them (or papers) if you are wearing a microphone.

Visual Aids

As we mentioned in Chapter 10, visual aids serve a number of purposes. If used properly, they reinforce content, help explain complex problems visually, maximize group interest, aid the audience in note taking, and increase your credibility. However, the key to successfully using visual aids lies in the phrase, *"If used properly."* How many times have you watched speakers "make a powerpoint presentation" rather than use PowerPoint to reinforce their message. So easy and accessible is this popular Microsoft presentation program that the term "PowerPoint" has entered the lexicon as synonyms for "presentation software" in general (including programs like Lotus Freehand and Corel Presentations) as well as the English word "presentation" (as in, "Please fax over your powerpoint so we can make copies in advance for our people.")

In a fascinating commentary on the downside of using presentation software outside of corporate sales, Laurence Zuckerman wrote in *The New York Times* in April 1999, "Many people believe that the ubiquity of prepackaged software . . . has taken much out of the life of public speaking by homogenizing it [and actually encouraging thinking] . . . that is devoid of original ideas" (p. B9). Even the experts disagree about the value of such software, according to Zuckerman, with some saying that it reduces public speaking "to the level of an elementary school filmstrip," and others arguing that it has "elevated the general level of discourse by forcing otherwise befuddled speakers to organize their thoughts and by giving audiences a visual source of information that is a much more efficient way for humans to learn than by simply listening" (p. B9).

Even if presentation software is used well, another important question remains. As Zuckerman asked rhetorically in the title of his article, "Words go right to the brain, but can they stir the heart?" To illustrate the poignancy of this question, the journalist asked us to consider a scenario in which Martin Luther King uses PowerPoint to illustrate his inspirational "I Had a Dream Speech." Indeed, how stirring would King's speech have been then? To say the least, Zuckerman made a good argument.

So how do you go about the process of effectively using presentation software and other visual forms. To aid you in making better decisions, we have presented ten "Do's" and "Don'ts" in Table 11.2 that apply to creating and using visuals in almost any medium. As a general rule, remember, "More is less."

TABLE 11.2 Guidelines for Developing and Using Visuals

Do

1. Create visuals well in advance of presentation. (Proofread at least twice for spelling and grammatical errors.)
2. Limit yourself to six or seven lines of type per transparency or presentation software slide! (Don't even be tempted to include more.)
3. Select fonts that are easy to read. Choose fonts that are at least 20 points in height for overheads and presentation software slides; for flip charts, 2 to 3 inches, depending on the size of the room. Neatly print all flip charts.
4. Be creative with colors and designs, but don't go overboard. When creating flip charts, alternate colors for each "bulleted" point to increase readability.
5. Remember Murphy's Law! ("Whatever can go wrong will go wrong.") It seriously applies to the use of visuals. Arrive at least 45 minutes to 1 hour before your presentation to make sure visuals and equipment are properly set up. Be ready to troubleshoot.
6. Ask your host for back-up equipment, just in case. If you're using an overhead projector, ask for an extra bulb. If you're using computer-generated graphics, create duplicates of all presentation software slides as overhead transparencies, and ask for a back-up overhead projector.
7. Practice using your visuals before you speak. Once you believe you can use them well, then practice one more time.
8. Keep visuals covered before and after using them.
9. Explain the significance of each visual and tell how it relates to your presentation.
10. Give the audience enough time to view and understand your visuals.

Don't

1. Spend more time developing your visuals than you spend on creating and practicing your speech.
2. Plagiarize information when creating your visuals. Do quote sources appropriately.
3. Overuse visuals. For a 4–6 minute speech, two or three transparencies or computer presentation slides are plenty.
4. Rely on your visuals as a crutch. Visuals should support your presentation, not duplicate your message.
5. Talk to your visuals. Instead, maximize eye contact with your audience.
6. Use your finger as a pointing device. Instead, use a sharp pencil, ballpoint pen, or a pointer that *isn't* fully extended. (Also, avoid laser pointers for "everyday" presentations. They're "overkill.") Remember, do point with the hand that's closest to your visual.
7. Turn your back to the audience when using your visuals.
8. Dim the lights too low or for extensive periods of time, unless (of course) you want your audience to sleep.
9. Leave the light of an overhead or video projector burning without a slide in place. The light will blind your audience. Likewise, don't walk in front of your projector while an image is being projected.
10. Place a visual (object or handout) in the hands of the audience while you are speaking. If your visual is an object, do invite the audience to come up, view it (and handle it, if appropriate) after the presentation. If you are using handouts, do pass them out at the end of your presentation. If the audience will need to refer to a handout during your presentation, do encourage everyone to quickly familiarize themselves with it and then bring their attention back to the first page after a few seconds. *Do remain silent while they looking through the handout.* (They won't be listening.)

We encourage you to practice the tips in Table 11.2 every time you give a speech or presentation. Doing so will take you a long way toward achieving the five goals (of visuals) that we mentioned at the beginning of this discussion, and will optimize your chances of touching both the minds and "hearts" of your listeners.

Vocal Delivery

The second major element of a speaker's presentation is the voice. *Vocal delivery* involves the mechanics of vocalization, vocal characteristics (including pitch, volume, rate, and quality), and pronunciation. Inexperienced speakers often pay little attention to their vocal delivery, incorrectly believing that the voice cannot be altered in any way. Even though one's physical makeup influences vocal quality, much can be done to improve vocal delivery.

The Mechanics of Vocalization

To understand how to improve vocal delivery, it is important first to be aware of the mechanics of vocalization. Voice and speech depend on phonation. In simple terms, *phonation* is the process by which air is pushed through the vocal cords, which then vibrate to produce sound. The sounds or tones produced in this way are what we call *voice.* Because air is responsible for the vibration of the vocal cords, the breathing mechanism plays a basic part in phonation.

When you exhale, air from the lungs travels up the bronchial tubes to the larynx. (See Figure 11.1.) The *larynx,* commonly known as the *voice box,* contains two thin membranes, or vocal cords, which vibrate as the air passes through them. The sound waves that result from this vibration are the basic voice sound. Functioning like a valve, the vocal cords are controlled by muscles that regulate the amount of air passing through. In order to produce speech sounds, the cords move close enough together to partially block the escaping air and alter the tone produced.

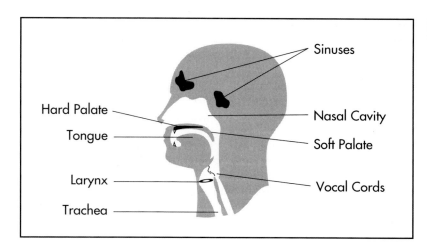

FIGURE 11.1 Elements of Vocal Delivery

The process of phonation is not complete until the sound produced in the larynx is resonated throughout the vocal chamber of the mouth, nose, and throat. *Resonance* is responsible for both the amplification and the enrichment of the voice. Without these chambers or cavities to give the sounds support and resonance, vocal quality would be quite unpleasant.

To better understand this process, place your finger on the bone of your nose and feel the vibration as you hum. The sound is resonating in the nasal cavity. When you have a cold or a stuffy nose, your voice sounds different without this additional resonance.

Articulation is the process by which voice is altered into recognizable speech sounds. These speech sounds consist of vowels and consonants, the building blocks of our speech. The consonants and vowels are formed when sounds are modified by the articulators. These include the lips, teeth, tongue, jaw, gum ridge, and palate, in addition to the nose, throat, and oral cavities. Consonants are produced as the articulators interfere with the passage of sound. Each consonant is produced by a different articulator as it interferes in some way with the flow of sound. For example, the "p" sound is made by joining the lips, which block the passage of air for a moment and are then quickly released. A "t" sound is produced when the tip of the tongue is placed along the gum ridge. The articulators in each case alter the sound produced by the vibrations of the vocal cords.

Vowels are produced by altering the size and shape of the nose, throat, and oral cavities. For example, contrast the shape of the mouth as you say "ah" and "oo." Unlike consonants, vowels do not require interference by the various articulators.

Poor articulation is usually the result of misuse of the articulators. For example, someone who has a lisp is not placing the tongue against the gum ridge to produce the "s" sound. Correction of this fault usually involves making a speaker aware of the error and having him or her practice the proper articulation of the sound.

Sometimes the problem is not one of carelessness or incorrect use. A person with a defective articulator will have problems producing proper speech sounds. For example, someone with an extreme overbite may have a lisp due to the improper meeting of the upper and lower teeth. With patience and practice, most people with such problems can improve their articulation to the point that their speech fault is negligible.

Vocal Characteristics

Now that you have a basic idea of how speech is produced, let's discuss the various characteristics of the voice. Vocal delivery involves four vocal characteristics: pitch, volume, rate, and quality.

PITCH. The *pitch* of the voice refers to how high or low the voice sounds. A person's natural pitch is determined in part by the length and width of the vocal cords. Women's vocal cords are characteristically thinner and longer than men's, so women have higher-pitched voices. Each voice can produce sounds ranging in pitch from high to low. Tensing the vocal cords produces a higher pitch, while relaxing them lowers the sound. Skillful singers and speakers are able to widen their pitch range and develop pitch control by practicing appropriate voice exercises.

When you have developed control of your pitch, you can use this skill to advantage. A variation in pitch adds color and vitality to a delivery and can also be used as a means of emphasis. The most boring speakers have little pitch variety. They speak in monotones, without emphasizing important points with their voices. As you may know, it is easy to be lulled to sleep by a monotonous voice, even when the topic of discussion is interesting.

VOLUME. The second vocal characteristic is *volume,* which means intensity or loudness. Once again, as with pitch, each of us has a volume range that allows us to project various degrees of loudness, ranging from a whisper to a scream.

A person whose voice is perfectly audible in conversation may have difficulty projecting before a large audience. Therefore, in rehearsing the delivery of a speech, you must adjust your volume to the room in which you will be speaking. Obviously, the most brilliant oration is meaningless if you cannot be heard. You should also try to overcome any distracting noise that may interfere with the transmission of the message, such as sounds from electric fans or nearby traffic.

While the most important point is simply to be heard, you can also adjust volume to add to your overall presentation. Variation in volume makes you sound more dynamic, allows you to emphasize main ideas, and helps you underscore important arguments. If you build to a crescendo as you make major points, you will add impact to your message in the same way a musician does when playing a melody.

RATE. *Rate* of speech is another important vocal characteristic. If you talk too quickly, the audience may not be able to keep pace. At the other extreme, if your speaking rate is too slow, the audience may lose interest. The main concern is audience comprehension. The nature and degree of difficulty of your message help determine a suitable rate of speech. A new or complicated message may call for a slower delivery than a subject with which the audience is familiar. An effective speaker will vary the rate of speech, pausing and slowing down to give emphasis to some material and speeding up at other points.

In addition to message comprehension, speech rate also affects an audience's perceptions of speaker competence and attractiveness. For example, a chemical engineer from New York travels to Georgia to give a lecture at a state university. Although he will arrive on campus with a certain amount of credibility because of his status, he will be evaluated less positively after the lecture if he speaks too slowly or too quickly. If his rate is too slow, he may be perceived as boring, monotonous, or patronizing. Conversely, if he speaks too quickly, he not only will be less comprehensible, but also will be perceived as less approachable and, therefore, less attractive. A situation such as this one has the potential to arise any time that a speaker travels from one region of a country to another. In our experience, the overall speech rate of audience members who are reared in the southern United States is slightly slower than those reared in more northeastern states. Similarly speech rates differ for French speakers who are reared in Paris versus Provence. (In Paris, the French language is spoken quite quickly.) Thus, if you wish to have maximum impact on an audience, you also will need to take into account both your and their normal rates of speech.

QUALITY. One of the most difficult characteristics to control is vocal quality. *Vocal quality* refers to the timbre of the voice, the characteristic that distinguishes one voice from another. In the United States, a resonant quality is desirable, so that the voice sounds deep and mellow. Voices that are too thin, strident, nasal, or breathy sound unpleasant and should be improved. Each of these qualities is the result of poor phonation. Understanding the vocal process and doing voice exercises can improve vocal quality, but it takes time to change something that feels natural to you.

Factors Influencing Your Voice

In addition to voice exercises, other factors can influence the sound of your voice. The first of these is your physical makeup. This factor involves the various parts of the vocal mechanism described under phonation—namely, the lungs, vocal cords, larynx, and resonating chambers.

Psychological factors also influence a person's voice. When you are anxious or excited, the tension may localize in the vocal cords, creating a higher pitch than normal. If you are relaxed and at ease, your voice will sound much more pleasant.

A third factor that influences voice is environment. Members of the same family often seem to have similar voices. The similarity is partially genetic and partially environmental. You pick up inflections from the people around you, including family members, peers, and members of the same ethnic group.

In addition to the influence of your immediate circle of acquaintances, your voice is also affected by regional dialects. Different regions of a country have varying speech and voice patterns that make their use of voice and language unique. In the United States, a person from the South may have a "drawl" that is quite distinct from the "twang" of a Midwesterner. Similarly, in southeast France (particularly from the people of Provence and the Cote d'Azur), you will hear "a charming droll accent" with drawn-out syllables. "You'll also hear all sorts of Italianate dialects, especially Nocois, Monegasque and Corsican" (Altman, 1989, p. 355). In short, in countries around the world, you will find regional differences. However, such regional differences usually affect pronunciation more than pitch, volume, and vocal quality.

Finally, non-native speakers of any language face a particularly daunting task when it comes to vocal delivery. For example, in a study of emotional responses that listeners in 30 countries have to their (cognitive) appraisals of a communication event, Scherer (1988) noted at least five primary ways that we respond to (or evaluate) new stimuli:

1. *Novelty*—the suddenness or unexpectedness of an event

2. *Pleasantness*—the degree to which we perceive an event to be pleasurable or enjoyable

3. *Goal significance*—the extent to which we perceive an event to obstruct or assist us in attaining a desired goal

4. *Coping potential*—the relative ease with which we can deal with an event

5. *Compatibility*—the extent to which an event is consistent with external norms (cultural norms of behavior and expectations) and internal norms (our value system or moral standards) (Scherer, 1988; as cited in Yook & Albut, 1999).

Thus, when we are listening to a non-native speaker, we may respond adversely, depending on the extent to which we are unpleasantly surprised by a "foreign" accent; the speaker's accent interferes with our ability to understand or interpret important information; we aren't used to listening to non-native speakers and are experiencing frustration; the speaker's verbal or nonverbal behavior is inconsistent with what we are "used to" hearing or seeing; and if the message is inconsistent with our values or moral standards.

As cross-cultural experts Esther Yook and Rosita Albert noted in 1999, U.S. college students' perceptions of international teaching assistants (ITAs) provide a good example. Students who enroll in college courses (particularly technical ones like engineering, computer science, mathematics, and physics) are prone to negative attributions when they walk in the first day of class and are met by an ITA. If students perceive a communication problem to exist and attribute the problem to the speaker, they will make negative dispositional attributions. If they perceive the problem to be situational rather than something the ITA can control, they will make negative situational attributions. It is important to note that, when people make negative dispositional attributions, they generally respond with anger; in the case of negative situational attributions, with sympathy. Indeed, these two outcomes emerge for students being taught by ITAs, depending on the type of attributions they make.

Fortunately, Yook and Albert also found that intercultural sensitivity training and role-playing (i.e., students playing the role of international teaching assistants) help. Individually or in combination, both instructional methods decrease the number of dispositional attributions, and increase the number of situational attributions, that we make about non-native speakers. In turn, the fewer the dispositional attributions we make, the less angry and more sympathetic we are. These findings should be good news to visitors in any country. There is hope. They also should be encouraging to you, the reader, because your chances of working with people from other cultures, and of traveling and working outside your own country, are increasing as communication becomes more global.

Improving Vocalization

The best way to improve your voice is through doing voice exercises. You must first be able to hear your own voice to decide which aspects need improvement. Try audiotaping your voice and playing it back on a tape recorder. Doing so will enable you to analyze your voice and practice a variety of exercises. You must decide, perhaps with the aid of a speech therapist or vocal coach, whether the problem concerns phonation, articulation, or pronunciation.

If the area in need of improvement is phonation, or the production of sound, then the problem may be one of force, duration, or quality. You might find that your voice often trails off at the end of a sentence, or that the volume is so low that you cannot be heard. In either case the problem is one of force.

Many people breathe incorrectly, and improper breathing can impair phonation. Some individuals lack force because they are not using their resonating chambers as efficiently as possible. Exercises to increase the use of these cavities add to a speaker's amplification.

Some people cannot speak for a long period of time without losing their voices. This can pose a serious problem for a person with many speaking engagements. Imagine the distress of politicians on the campaign trail who find their voices giving out after speaking for an extended period of time. Voice fatigue usually comes from improper use of the different parts of the vocal mechanism.

Basically, vocal sound should be supported by the partition of muscles and tendons between the chest and abdomen known as the *diaphragm.* This muscle is responsible for involuntary breathing and is one of the strongest muscles in the body. The muscles of the throat and the vocal cords are easily strained, while the diaphragm is virtually tireless. Through prescribed exercises you can learn to "support" your voice correctly and avoid hoarseness and voice loss. However, it takes time and practice to overcome bad habits that you have developed over the years. As mentioned previously, problems of articulation usually stem from careless speech habits. Unless a person must compensate for a physical defect such as a harelip, poor articulation can be improved by concentrated effort and practice. We can all be inspired by individuals who are born deaf and are never able to hear the sound of words. With a great deal of perseverance, many people who are hearing-impaired have learned to articulate well enough to be understood in conversation. Like these courageous individuals, you too can improve your articulation skills.

An understanding of how various sounds are made will help you improve articulation. Practice drills are good reinforcement for correcting problems of articulation, but you must make a conscious effort to carry over the correct production of speech sounds into everyday conversation as well as public speaking situations. Faulty articulation is particularly bad for the public speaker, since an audience is easily distracted by poor speech. Mumbling and speaking carelessly affect the audience's perception of you. A speaker whose pronunciation is clear and distinct makes a more favorable impression than does someone whose speech is sloppy.

Pronunciation

Pronunciation can be important to the improvement of both speech and voice. Standards of pronunciation are often determined by geographical area of a country or imposed by occasion or education.

For instance, in the United States Americans speak the same language, but pronunciation varies according to region. While geographic regions have changed in terms of speech patterns, one can still find a difference between Northern, Midwestern, and Southern speech. In addition to the three major regions, there are numerous subdivisions. For example, New Yorkers do not sound like Bostonians, even though they are both considered Northern.

Certain speakers do strive for what is called "standard American speech," the type of speech exemplified by national newscasters. Although still preferred in some circles, standard American pronunciation is not a prerequisite for success. Neither John F. Kennedy's New England dialect nor Jimmy Carter's Southern drawl kept either statesman from political success. The key is not regional dialect but careful articulation.

In addition to regional and national (or cultural) background, your pronunciation is influenced by the occasion and by your education. Certain situations such as job interviews or press conferences require careful pronunciation. Any person who speaks before a group should pay special attention to pronunciation. If a speaker makes an error, the audience's attention may be temporarily distracted. Poor pronunciation can create a bad impression.

Education affects pronunciation in the sense that exposure to language through reading, speaking, and listening results in increased vocabulary and knowledge of the way different words are pronounced. Education includes more than formal schooling. As you read, study, travel, and speak with educated people, your vocabulary and language skills, such as pronunciation improve.

There are several ways you, as a speaker, can improve pronunciation. If you are unsure of the way a word is pronounced, look it up in the dictionary. Be particularly careful to find out the proper pronunciation of the names of people and places mentioned in your speech. If you are quoting someone or acknowledging a particular person or organization, it is important to pronounce the name correctly.

Pronunciation, articulation, and phonation have always been concerns of the public speaker. Because we all rely on our voices for much of our communication, we should strive to improve our vocal delivery.

Style

We recognize that the Reverend Jesse Jackson has an effective style of oration, and we would all agree that His Holiness, the Dalai Lama uses a unique and powerful style of delivery. But what is style?

In simple terms, *style* is the way an individual speaker gives ideas meaning through his or her particular brand of verbal expression and delivery. Style deals with both the wording and the delivery of the message. It includes the speaker's choice of words, the use of language, sentence structure, and the characteristics of delivery. Because style is made up of so many variables, each speaker's style is somewhat different. Some speakers have pet phrases that they include in their speeches, some are very plain-spoken, and others rely heavily on the use of metaphor or flowery language.

Style also applies to syntax, or sentence structure. A speaker may invert subject and verb to achieve a stylistic effect. For example, a disgusted sportscaster might say, "Never have I witnessed such a poor display of teamwork." Run-on or choppy sentences can also be used to achieve a stylistic effect. Although a good speaker should adhere to the rules of grammar, "poetic license" of sorts can be used to achieve a desired effect.

Our primary concern here is with the element of style that applies to a speaker's physical and vocal delivery. Of course, while every speaker develops a personal style, you should be able to adapt your style to fit the audience, occasion, topic, and purpose of your speech. Basically, your style may be formal or informal, with varying degrees in between.

Logically, a formal style is best suited for formal occasions. For example, we expect both a world leader's state of the nation address and a college graduation address to be formal. A casual treatment of either of these speeches would demean their importance. The characteristics of a formal style include a serious and impersonal tone, correct use of grammar, sophisticated stylistic devices, and avoidance of slang. Physical and vocal aspects of a formal delivery style reflect dignity and seriousness.

A serious tone is projected by the manner in which you present yourself and your message. Although you need not be solemn, you should be dignified. There is no room for flippancy in a formal presentation. To emphasize the importance of the message, you should keep an impersonal tone by avoiding the use of personal pronouns.

More often than not, the speaking engagements in which we find ourselves tend to be more casual than formal and require a less formidable style. An informal style is characterized by a light and personal tone, use of fairly simple sentence structure and vocabulary, and a bending of grammatical rules, if necessary. An informal style allows the speaker to add warmth to the presentation with informal language and humor.

Very few speaking situations are either strictly formal or strictly informal. As most fall between the two extremes, you will have to adapt your style accordingly. For example, although we might think of an after-dinner speech as being informal, the appropriate presentation would depend on the nature of the occasion as well as the audience. You should evaluate each speaking situation individually to determine the right delivery.

Characteristics of Style

Although each speaker is different, there are certain desirable characteristics that help make any speaker's style effective. The first of these is *accuracy*, which requires a precise use of words. You may know what you want to say but have trouble getting the idea across to the audience. If an audience walks away not knowing what was said or misinterpreting the message, then you have failed in your basic purpose. As a speaker, you must choose the words that most accurately convey your message. Avoid words that are too abstract or general, as well as words that are open to many different interpretations. Words such as *good, bad,* and *nice* are really ambiguous and add little to a presentation.

Closely related to accuracy is *clarity.* The main consideration here is audience comprehension. A complicated description of a medical procedure that is perfectly clear to a surgeon may be totally confusing to an audience of lay people. Therefore, you must adapt your language and style to fit the needs of the audience.

Appropriateness is another characteristic of style. As mentioned previously, a speaker's style should fit the occasion, the audience, and the type and purpose of the speech. Each presentation should reflect consideration of all of these factors.

Another characteristic of effective style is *economy,* or the greatest efficiency of language. If you use the right words in the most efficient way, your message will be more meaningful. There is no need to use many words when a few will do. If you are concise, you generally will achieve accuracy and clarity as well. However, conciseness should not undermine comprehension, which sometimes makes it necessary to repeat ideas.

The final characteristic is a *lively quality* in the selection of words. Although economy is a virtue in terms of style, sometimes a speaker will use a phrase or expression that leaves a lasting impression on the audience. A poetic statement, a memorable expression, an unusual figure of speech, or a melodic phrase will jump out at the audience and capture its attention. The speaker must not overuse this quality, however, or the impact will be weakened.

Style, like good public speaking skills in general, can be learned, but not without the interest and effort it takes to achieve any valuable goal. An impressive style can only be achieved with careful preparation and practice.

Summary

The importance of delivery in public speaking cannot be overestimated. A speaker's delivery is the vehicle for the communication of the message. Good delivery is essential in capturing and maintaining audience attention and also affects speaker credibility, audience comprehension, and persuasive impact.

Public speaking anxiety can affect a speaker's delivery, and stems from inherited biological predispositions, negative reinforcement for past speech performances, and patterns of neurological activity. Public speaking anxiety can be treated. To reduce its impact on speech performances, the speaker can (1) practice, (2) use physical activity, (3) avoid memorization and organize well, (4) get involved with the topic, and (5) develop a proper attitude.

Principles of good delivery include a natural appearance, consistency of expression and content, rapport with the listeners, and a presentation that is appropriate to the audience, the situation, and the speaker. The physical aspects of delivery include body movements, posture, gestures, facial expressions, eye contact, and the use of the lectern and note cards. An awareness and natural use of these elements can greatly enhance the verbal message.

The effective public speaker understands the vocal aspects of public speaking. Good phonation, resonance, and articulation are essential to message audibility and comprehension. An awareness of pitch, volume, rate, and voice quality will enable the speaker to capture and hold the listener's ear. Vocal delivery is influenced by physical, psychological, cultural and environmental factors. Serious students of public speaking can improve their powers of vocalization by practicing appropriate vocal exercises.

Pronunciation is another element of vocal delivery not to be overlooked. Good pronunciation is essential to message comprehension and speaker credibility.

The style of delivery may be as important as the content of the message. The speaker may choose between varying degrees of formality. Most speakers eventually develop a unique personal style. Choice of words, use of language, and syntax are all effective stylistic elements. The speaker should aim for a style that is accurate, clear, appropriate to the occasion and setting, economical, conscious, and not overly dramatic.

Exercises

GROUP EXPERIENCES
Coaching on the Sidelines

DESCRIPTION Politicians have long been aware of the importance of public speaking. Today ghostwriters, communication consultants, and many other specialists work together to help "present" the politician to the public. This activity will give you the opportunity to act as coach or consultant to a politician.

PROCEDURE Divide into dyads. You and your partner have been hired to help Laura Martinez present herself to the public for the upcoming campaign. Laura is totally inexperienced in public speaking. She does not know what to do with her hands, how fast to talk, what to say, or how to say it. Needless to say, you have a big job ahead of you. Write a plan for getting Laura ready for the public. You might want to incorporate some practice speaking sessions, including the use of videotape and so forth, to prepare Laura. Share your plan with the other groups and compare the strategy plans.

DISCUSSION Did you forget any important steps in your plan? Can you improve a person's speaking ability? Can you create "charisma" in a person? How can delivery affect the credibility of a person?

Timing

DESCRIPTION A good delivery is absolutely essential for a successful presentation, as are voice, gestures, and body stance. They all play an important role in a public speaking situation. A good delivery should be carefully coordinated with the content of the speech. If the gestures and facial expressions do not come at the right time, they will distract from the speech itself. This activity gives you an opportunity to see the effects on an audience of the timing of facial expressions and gestures.

PROCEDURE If you have a theatrical flair or a dramatic side to your personality, then this is the activity for you. Write a three-minute speech designed to sell a product of your choice. Practice the delivery of the speech several times until you have completely *uncoordinated* your gestures and facial expressions with your words. This will be difficult, because when your voice is excited, your face will have to look bored. If you state that there are three good reasons to buy your product, you may want to use a hand gesture *after* you finish saying this. In whatever way possible, by making the timing wrong, your "presentation" should look like a comedy routine. Try it out by presenting it before a class or a group of people.

DISCUSSION What were the reactions to your poorly timed talk? Did the audience remember what you had to say or the way you said it? Did you feel self-conscious or overdramatic? Whatever effect you created, chances are good that the lack of timing did hurt the impact of your speech. Next time you give a speech, be natural, and you will see that the facial expressions, gestures, and content of the speech will complement one another.

Voice Lessons

DESCRIPTION A speaker's vocal delivery involves four things: pitch, volume, rate, and quality. By studying and practicing each quality, you can improve your speaking voice. The following voice drill is designed to help you identify specific characteristics of your voice.

PROCEDURE Divide into dyads. With the help of your partner, practice the following line: "A person whose voice is perfectly audible in conversation may have difficulty projecting before a large audience." Say the line six times for each characteristic, focusing first on pitch, then volume, then rate, then quality. For instance, with rate, the first time you should say the line very slowly, and gradually get faster, so that by the sixth time you are saying it very fast. Your partner should select which repetition (first to sixth) is the best rate for an audience, and then do the same for the other characteristics.

Pitch: Go from a very high pitch to a very low pitch.

Volume: Go from a very soft voice to a very loud voice.

Rate: Go from speaking very slowly to speaking very quickly.

Quality: Go from a very nasal quality to a deep and resonant quality.

DISCUSSION Are you surprised by any of the selections made by your partner? Feedback is important, particularly about the voice, for we cannot hear ourselves the way others hear us. A common problem in speaking is rate. Speakers tend to think they are speaking at a slower rate than they actually are. Try to remember and practice what your partner selected as the best rate, volume, pitch, and vocal quality for you.

PERSONAL EXPERIENCES

1. Listen to a live speaker or a televised speech. Listen carefully to the vocal characteristics of the speaker (pitch, volume, rate, and quality). Is the speaker using his or her voice for maximum effectiveness? What things, if any, would you change about the speaker's voice?

2. Observe the kind of gestures you use when talking to another person. Do you use a lot of gestures? Do you make gestures in close to your body, or are they expansive? Do you feel self-conscious when you use your hands? You use gestures as a natural part of your everyday conversations; there is no reason why your gestures cannot be just as natural in a speech. Watch them. Feel comfortable with the way your hands move. If you feel comfortable, so will others.

3. Imagine that you are going to give a speech before an audience of a hundred people. In addition, you will be talking about something that excites you. Since looking forward to giving a speech is very important, what could you do to "psych" yourself up?

Discussion Questions

1. How can communication apprehension be used to *enhance* your delivery of a message?
2. What are the basic factors to consider in the presentation of a speech? Is any one factor more important than the others?
3. What physical aspects of a presentation are important for a speaker to consider?
4. What things make you "unique" as a speaker? (Consider style, vocal quality, delivery, and so on.)
5. What methods can you use to improve your delivery?
6. What plan would you make for yourself in order to improve your public speaking skills?

References

Altman, J. (1989). *Berlitz: Blueprint France*. Lausanne, Switzerland: Berlitz Guides.

Atkins, C. P. (1988). Perceptions of speakers with minimal eye contact: Implications for stutterers. *Journal of Fluency Disorders, 13,* 429–436.

Behnke, R. R., & Sawyer, C. R. (1999, April). Milestones of anticipatory public speaking anxiety. *Communication Education, 48,* 165–172.

Bippus, A. M., & Daly, J. A. (1999, January). What do people think causes stage fright? Naïve attributions about the reasons for public speaking anxiety. *Communication Education, 48,* 63–72.

Carrell, L. J., & Willmington, S. C. (1998). The relationship between self-report measures of communication apprehension and trained observers' ratings of communication competence. *Communication Reports, 11*(1), 87–95.

Freeman, T., Sawyer, C. R., & Behnke, R. R. (1997). Behavioral inhibition and the attribution of public speaking anxiety. *Communication Education, 46*(3), 175–187.

MacIntyre, P. D., & MacDonald, J. R. (1998, October). Public speaking anxiety: Perceived competence and audience congeniality. *Communication Education, 47,* 359–365.

Sawyer, C. R., & Behnke, R. R. (1997). Communication apprehension and implicit memories of public speaking state anxiety. *Communication Quarterly, 45*(3), 211–222.

Scherer, K. (Ed.). (1988). *Facets of emotion: Recent research.* Hillsdale, NJ: Lawrence Erlbaum Associates.

Yook, E. L., & Albert, R. D. (1999, January). Perceptions of international teaching assistants: The interrelatedness of intercultural training, cognition, and emotion. *Communication Education, 48,* 1–17.

Zuckerman, L. (1999, April 17). Words go right to the brain, but can they stir the heart? *The New York Times (Arts and Ideas Section),* B9, B11.

chapter twelve

Mass Communication in the Twenty-First Century

key concepts and terms

Print media	Mass communication	Advertising
Electronic media	Niche markets	Public relations

From:	"Shura"
To:	"Tay" laurets@futurenet.ab.net
Sent:	Saturday, August 12ᵗʰ 10:20AM
Subject:	Glad we're friends!

Hi, Tay.

Today, I was watching CNN and saw a horrifying story. You may have heard about it.

A girl was kidnapped from State College last Friday night. Apparently, these two guys grabbed her at a fraternity party and nobody noticed she was missing until the next day around 1:00. Her best friend had phoned her over and over again on Saturday, and when she didn't answer, he called the police.

The police looked for her for 2 1/2 days and found her lying in a ditch beside the Interstate. The two morons had raped her and left her for dead. But she wasn't, thank goodness. The police credited the media with getting the word out about her kidnapping. They said some farmer had read about it in the newspaper and had seen a picture of her on the local news. (His daughter went to State College, and he was really upset that it could have been her.) So he got in his truck and drove around the area for two days checking all the back roads around State. On his way home, he was driving along the Interstate and saw something red out of the corner of his eye. So he pulled off the road, got out, and sure enough it was the girl's red jacket. It was lying about 20 feet from her body. Thankfully, he had a cell phone and was able to call the State Police. The CNN story said she was able to identify the two guys, and the police arrested them this morning at some truck stop just this side of the state line.

Tay, it was like a flash back. Remember last year when you couldn't find me the day after the Kappa party? That could have been me! What a nightmare! And what a great friend you are! What would we do without TV and cell phones? OR E-MAIL?

Guess I have to run. I'm running late for practice. Just wanted to thank you again for being such a great friend. You're the best, Tay!—Shura

Skeptics today say there are no happy endings. But there are. Had the same events transpired even 25 years ago, the girl in the CNN story above might never have been found alive. But, with information provided via the media and "the hero's" access to communication technologies, indeed a happy ending occurred.

The uses of mass media and communication technologies like those described above are the primary subjects of this chapter. Specifically, we will focus on the characteristics, functions, and effects of print and electronic media in an attempt to broaden your understanding of their purpose and viability as communication tools.

Mass Communication: An Overview

Although all forms of mass communication affect our lives, the most widely used and influential forms may be divided into two major categories: print and electronic. *Print media* include newspapers, books, and magazines. *Electronic media* include radio, television, sound recordings, motion pictures, and the Internet (Hiebert, 1999, p. 5). Perhaps, the importance of these media can best be expressed in numbers. At the end of the twentieth century, there were approximately 10,100 daily and weekly newspapers published in the United States alone, not including shoppers' guides, entertainment listings, and tabloids. Approximately 40,000 book titles and 11,000 daily, weekly, or monthly consumer magazines were published annually (p. 5).

The role of the newspaper keeps changing. At first it was entirely informative in nature; then, before the days of electronic media, it developed an important entertainment function, which disappeared after the advent of radio and TV. Yet today, because of keen competition among papers and other forms of media, newspapers once again include many features in addition to the daily news. This broad coverage of information is evidenced by the success of *USA Today. The New York Times, The Washington Post,* and the *Los Angeles Times* all offer sections devoted to the home, entertainment, and lifestyles.

Although many Americans are children of the computer generation or television age, statistics about radio broadcasting help us realize the continued importance of radio as both a news and entertainment medium. According to Hiebert (1999, p. 5), at the end of the 1990s, there were close to 10,000 radio stations in the United States alone. Such a demand for the use of the airwaves made it necessary long ago to regulate the air frequencies and to use AM and FM bands in the interests of fairness and efficiency.

At the end of the twentieth century, there were approximately 1,550 commercial television stations and 350 educational channels. More than 100 cable and premium channels of programming extended the numbers even higher. About 250 recording labels were responsible for the vast majority of all cassette, CD, video, and disk sound recordings. Interestingly enough, only seven major motion picture studio companies produced greater than half of the new feature films made in America (Hiebert, 1999, p. 5).

However, the most staggering numbers associated with mass media are reserved for personal computers and the Internet. According to Brian Winston (1998), author of *Media and Technology Society: A History from the Telegraph to the Internet,* 35 million American households owned personal computers by 1995. By 1997, approximately 3 million people were believed to be using Internet technology (p. 335).

Characteristics of Mass Communication

Peter Orlik (1997), author of *The Electronic Media,* defined **mass communication** as "the process of rapidly conveying *identical* information, assertions, and attitudes to a potentially *large, dispersed,* and *diversified* audience via mechanisms capable of achieving that task" (p. 11). The four characteristics of mass media that he identified are italicized in his definition.

By *identical* information, Orlik obviously meant the *same* information, like that which is conveyed in *The Wall Street Journal* no matter what part of the world in which one is reading it on a given day. The same definition holds true for visual and audio images of the Olympics or Oscar Awards when they are formally broadcast around the world. Whether one is viewing them in Sydney, London, New York, or Los Angeles, the only difference lies in the time zones in which they are viewed.

For Orlik, the term *large* was defined by "the quantum leap" that results when you compare live versus televised versions of a State of the Union Address or a Broadway show like *Miss Saigon* or *Cats.* Rather than offering us a single number that constitutes the term "large," Orlik simply compared the leap in numbers from 2,000 to 2 million people when one compares the venues of live versus broadcast theater.

The *dispersed* characteristic is associated with *where* the audience is located: in a single or multiple locations. To illustrate, revisit Orlik's distinction between live versus broadcast theater. With a live production, the audience travels to a single location to see the musical or play; with a broadcast production, the event travels via cable or satellite to the audience, whose members are geographically dispersed, or located around the world. Finally, to be considered mass communication, the message must reach an audience that is *diversified.* In other words, the audience must represent "a broad spectrum of society" (Orlik, 1997, p. 13).

One important postscript that Orlik (1997) added was that the Internet is changing the way that we define and characterize mass media. As originally conceived, mass communication was considered to be a one-way process. Media outlets were the message *producers,* and audiences were the message *consumers.* This particular distinction is rapidly changing. To illustrate, consider the differences that Orlik noted between online and conventional mass media audiences: "(1) [an online audience] is highly segmented across tens of thousands of sites with some message transactions, at a given time, being as intimate as a telephone conversation; (2) also like a traditional phone chat, these transactions can be *two-way*" (p. 21).

Telephone call-in shows like *Larry King Live* and online surveys by CNN and MTV serve as excellent examples. The *one-way* mass media messages of the past are fast becoming *two-way* interchanges.

Mass Communication Media

Now, more than at any time in history, we are a media society. No day goes by without our feeling the effects of mass communication. "That's not true," you may say.

These children are viewing an underwater video of dolphins and a trawler net, something they would not be able to see first hand.

"I don't watch TV every day!" Maybe not, but did you listen to your radio or CD player on your way to school today? wear a Walkman the last time you worked out? read a book or magazine article in the last few days? surf the net for a paper you are writing? We employ mass communication daily by using it to inform us of world events, to help escape into another realm, or to plan our weekends based on weather reports.

We have already examined the characteristics of mass communication. We will now look at five of the most important forms of mass communication: radio, television, sound recordings, motion pictures, and the Internet.

Radio

Ever sit at a traffic light and watch the person next to you sing along with the radio, commercials and all? Driving to class or work, or driving out of town, many of us turn the radio dial, looking for a favorite station. It is usually fairly easy to find a station to meet our needs, since approximately 5,000 AM stations and 5,000 FM stations play all types of music. Although it has not always been so convenient, radio has been popular for over 70 years. During the 1930s and 1940s, radio was the television of today, with situation comedies, musicals, political addresses, and game shows. The late 1940s were a time of great change because of the development of television. Sponsors were quickly changing over to the visual medium. To save radio, a deejay format was introduced in 1951. With the deejay format, stations began to design programs for specific audiences; today we have everything from all-music to all-talk radio.

The success of radio often has been attributed to its mobility. We can carry portable radios in our pockets and bring them anywhere, from beaches to offices. Radio is still the most reliable form of communication during emergencies because it can use batteries instead of electricity and is easily portable. Further, radio is beneficial to advertising. Many small organizations that cannot afford the expense of TV commercials can still get inexpensive publicity through radio advertisements.

Television

Your parents were members of the television generation. You probably are, too. We find it easier to identify with television personalities like Jennifer Aniston, Courtney Cox, Will Smith, and Regis Philbin than with members of the president's cabinet or former school teachers. In 1941, fewer than 10,000 homes in the United States had televisions; today, 98 percent of all homes in America have at least one television.

Like radio, sound recordings, and motion pictures had being doing for years, television in the late 1970s and early 1980s began to target *niche markets,* or specialized groups of audience members. This change from targeting every television viewer to more narrowly defined audiences emerged as a function of the widespread availability of cable programming, direct-broadcast satellite (DBS) transmission, and home-shopping networks. Indeed, television in the early twenty-first century targets every group imaginable: Baby Boomers (Home and Garden Television and Style); Generation X (MTV and VH-1); young adult audiences (Fox, the WB Television Network, and United Paramount); children (Disney Channel, Family Channel); women (Lifetime); men and sports buffs (ESPN , ESPN2); black Americans (Black Entertainment Network); and people whose preferences run the gamut from movies (TNT, American Movie Classics) and religion (Faith & Values) to soft pornography (some pay-per-view outlets). Indeed, the variety and flexibility of television, cable and satellite programming make it America's most popular form of entertainment.

Television is the first truly democratic culture—the first culture available to everybody and entirely governed by what people want. The most terrifying thing is what they want.

CLIVE BARNES, AMERICAN CRITIC

Sound Recordings

Is there a special song that reminds you of the first time you fell in love? Do you play a certain CD when you're lonely and want to think? Can some music make you tap your foot or rock out? Music is everywhere in our society, from Muzak in doctors' offices, to country music or grunge rock in local nightclubs. Just as we remember songs from different periods in our lives, we also remember different decades by the music that was popular at the time. The Big Band and swing era of the 1940s gave birth to the first recording hero, Frank Sinatra. The Comets arrived in 1955 with "Rock Around the Clock," and Elvis helped usher in rock 'n' roll in the late 1950s. The early 1960s were best known for the Beatles and later for songs of social discontent and alienation. The 1970s were a decade of no real trend, with gentler rock, hard rock, disco, punk rock, new wave music, and the rise of country and western music. During the 1980s, the trend was toward music that raises our social consciousness—for example, about famine (Michael Jackson and Quincy Jones, "We Are the World"), child abuse (Suzanne Vega, "Luca"), the plight of AIDS victims (Dionne Warwick, Elton John, and others, "Friends"), moral responsibility (U2, "The Joshua Tree"), and lifestyles (Tracy Chapman, "Fast Car"). The Band-Aid, Live-Aid, and Farm-Aid concerts represented a few of the efforts of musicians in that decade to step out and help their fellow humans.

In the 1990s, R.E.M., Kenny G., Ice T, and Clint Black dealt with emotions that varied from love to angst. "Crossover" artists (ones that appeal to more than one listener segment) were at an all-time high. Rappers like Eminem were heard from coast to coast. Dr. Dre challenged social barriers, while Madonna pushed the sexual envelope.

The recording industry produces music for all ages and tastes. When you visit a music store, the walls are filled on three sides to the ceiling with categories from A to Z. One visit can convince even the staunchest critic that the music industry is alive and well. Not everyone who tries to make it big succeeds. But, in a garage band somewhere, the next Sting, Whitney Houston, Barbara Streisand, or Stephen Sondheim is warming up to claim a place in the music world.

Motion Pictures

From its beginning as a method of recording history, film has developed into a major form of recreation and entertainment. Films and movies have been around longer than any other electronic medium, and they stay alive because they are the most creative and artistic of all media. The motion picture experience shows us the universal emotions of love, hate, jealousy, fear, and delight. Each era has its own unique theme of the time. Trends have included the 1920s era of Charlie Chaplin silent movies; 1930s musicals with Fred Astaire and Ginger Rogers; patriotic pictures featuring Humphrey Bogart in the 1940s; 3-D and youth-oriented themes of the 1950s; experience/involvement movies like *Psycho, The Sound of Music,* and the Beatles' movies of the 1960s; and disaster pictures such as *The Poseidon Adventure, Jaws,* and *The Towering Inferno* of the 1970s. The 1970s also gave us social commentaries such as *One Flew Over the Cuckoo's Nest, All the President's Men,* and *Coming Home;* the late 1970s and early 1980s often gave us movies focused on music, such as *Saturday Night Fever, The Buddy Holly Story, The Rose,* and *A Star Is Born.* In the 1980s, motion pictures also revealed our enchantment with and curiosity about space exploration and travel, particularly films such as *Star Wars, E. T., Close Encounters of the Third Kind, Cocoon* (parts I and II), and *My Stepmother Is an Alien.* The 1990s brought greater technical wizardry and special effects such as those in *Terminator II, Independence Day,* and *Beauty and the Beast.* What's next? Although no one knows what next year will bring, we do know that there will be something for everyone, because motion pictures readily adapt to the events and needs of the times.

The Internet

In his book *Media Technology and Society: A History from the Telegraph to the Internet,* Brian Winston (1998) provided some interesting insights into the development of the present-day Internet. For example, he noted that, while computers, machine "languages," and telecommunications networks had been in existence for years, the 1945 publication of an article by Vannevar Bush in *Atlantic Monthly* was the first to articulate the idea of "data arranged as webs rather than the branchings of a tree which computing power would. . . [at the time], most easily allow" (p. 323). As Bush noted,

> When data of any sort are placed in storage, they are filed alphabetically or numerically, and information is found (when it is) by tracing it down from subclass to subclass. It can only be in one place. . . . The human mind does not work that way. It operates by association. With one item in its grasp, it snaps instantly to the next that is suggested by the association of thoughts, in accordance with some intricate *web* of trails carried by the cells of the brain (Bush, 1945, p. 105, emphasis added; as cited in Winston, 1998, p. 323).

From the time Bush's article appeared, it was almost 20 years until headway was made in actually constructing the Internet.

In the 1960s, two prominent researchers who worked with the "military establishment" emerged as leaders in the field. They were Paul Baran, an American researcher who worked for Rand, and Donald Watt Davies, a British computer pioneer who worked at the National Physical Laboratory (NPL). Although working separately, both were directly (or indirectly) working toward the creation of a "nuclear-bomb-proof communications system," through which computers could be backed up in case of nuclear attack (Winston, 1998, p. 325). Overall, the development of the prototype was associated with work at the NPL and the Advanced Research Projects Agency (ARPA). The latter agency was created by the U.S. Department of Defense in response to Russia's launch of Sputnik. Not surprisingly, their prototype was named ARPANET.

Although ARPANET was primarily a military-based project at first, a number of universities began to work on its development, particularly the University of California at Los Angeles (UCLA). Although early demonstrations focused on remote chess games, quizzes, and interactive programs, a short time later two major network functions emerged: international communication and electronic mail (Winston, p. 329). According to Winston, two of the first e-mails were sent to and from a meeting held at the University of Sussex in 1973. Vint Cerf, a former UCLA professor who had worked on ARPANET, sent an e-mail to the conference saying his arrival would be delayed due to the birth of his child. Another man, who had left the conference early, sent an e-mail back to a friend requesting that he try to locate a razor, which the former had left at the conference (p. 330).

By 1973, the first international e-mails became possible and, in 1975, mail lists emerged. Primarily available to a handful of the "university elite" and, of course, the military, ARPANET had a bumpy ride through the Vietnam War era. The ride got especially rough when radical students on campuses around the United States learned that it was being used in the war effort. However, with the help of the National Science Foundation and $5 million in start-up funds, ARPANET was joined by the development of CSNET, the Computer Science Research Network, in 1979. Shortly thereafter, the National Science Foundation agreed to allow "commercial exploitation," and online services began to emerge. Many of you may be familiar with the first of these services: Compuserve. By 1994, Compuserve claimed 3.2 million users in 120 countries. That same year, its competitors, America Online and Prodigy, claimed 3.5 and 1.4 million users respectively (Winston, pp. 331–333). (Interestingly, according to Winston, the words *cyberspace* and *cyberpunk* were coined in 1989 by author William Gibson in his novel, *Neuromancer.*)

Now that we have provided you with a glance at the five most important *forms* of mass communication, we turn to a discussion of its primary *functions:* to inform, entertain and, persuade.

It was not so long ago that people thought that semiconductors were part-time orchestra leaders and microchips were very, very small snack foods.
                                        GERALDINE FERRARO (1935–) AMERICAN POLITICIAN

Functions of Mass Communication

To Inform

The dissemination of information belongs primarily to the news media, both electronic and print. Yet the news media have come a long way from just "telling it like it is." In the 1990s local news shows throughout the country expanded their formats to include human-interest stories as well as news features. Co-anchors came to be known as "news teams." Friendly newscasters "shared" the news with their audience rather than stating just the facts (Whetmore, 1991). Viewers were encouraged to participate in news gathering by using their home video cameras. The Rodney King incident in Los Angeles, in which police officers were filmed beating a suspected traffic violator, was one incident in which a home videotape became a part of the national news. A home video camera also captured footage of the crash of the Concorde in 2000, which made international news. Indeed, ordinary people have become a part of the news team. Even the actual coverage of the news has changed dramatically over the years. Instead of merely reporting events, reporters and broadcast journalists have become news analysts and prognosticators who discuss the implications of important news stories.

PUBLIC BROADCASTING SERVICE. One cannot talk about the media as a source of information without mentioning educational television or the Public Broadcasting Service, a nonprofit organization that attempts to emphasize the educational and enlightening aspects of television. Unlike commercial networks, which sell air time to sponsors, educational stations buy programs from the PBS network with money obtained from donations, federal funds, and commercial grants. You might notice that at the beginning or end of a program on PBS, the source of funding for the program is announced: "This program was made possible by a grant from. . . ." This type of sponsorship, which eliminates the need for advertisers, represents one of the most striking differences between commercial and public broadcasting.

Unlike commercial networks, PBS has attempted to realize the educational values of television. Many of its programs are instructional in nature, the most widely known being *Sesame Street,* a program for preschool children. PBS also provides a forum for many experimental and innovative programs that would be too risky for commercial sponsors.

The new source of power is not money in the hands of a few but information in the hands of many.

JOHN NAISBITT, MEGATRENDS

To Entertain

The most common function of mass communication is entertainment. Although radio, TV, and motion pictures function as information sources, entertainment provides the primary source of their revenues.

Entertainment covers many different things. For example, entertainment sections in newspapers include comics, horoscopes, and advice columns, as well as crossword puzzles and other word games. In television, entertainment includes music videos, game shows, situation comedies, soap operas, movies, dramas, and sporting events. Radio entertainment today consists primarily of music, although talk shows make a major contribution. When we talk about motion pictures, we are talking mainly about an entertainment medium, with the possible exception of documentaries. Finally the Internet and personal computers provide us with hours of entertainment via web sites, chat rooms, and electronic games. What do all these forms have in common? By nature, an entertainment medium is one that provides the consumer with some sort of escape or diversion from the realities and anxieties of daily living.

To Persuade

Another function of the mass media is persuasion. Advertising for products, political candidates, service organizations, charities, businesses, and so forth all use persuasion. Both electronic and print media have great persuasive potential, but, depending on the nature of the message, a full-page ad in a major newspaper can sometimes have greater impact than a minute of air time. There are media specialists who analyze where and how messages should be placed to have the greatest influence. For example, research concerning persuasive appeals in political campaigns has suggested that campaign strategies using "attack" commercials against other candidates are rated less favorably when followed by the opponent's "issue" commercials. This knowledge can aid political campaign managers in planning and programming mass media campaigns more effectively. (Roddy & Garramore, 1988).

Advertising

Each day our dreams, fears, desires, and concerns are analyzed by advertisers anxious to sell products. *Advertising's* chief purpose is to persuade people to buy, and to continue to buy, certain products. Radio . . . TV and online advertisements are geared to the particular audiences that will tune in or log on. During a weekday afternoon, soap operas that attract millions of viewers are interrupted with commercials featuring laundry, cleansing, beauty, and feminine hygiene products. Football games are sprinkled with commercials for beer, sturdy trucks, and men's underwear. Saturday morning TV is filled with advertisements for sugar-coated cereals and the latest action figures and toys of the future. Through various means of measuring audiences, companies have learned about the types of people comprising their target audiences and what products they would be most interested in buying.

Many of you can easily recall certain advertising slogans or commercials. These advertising messages must do more than keep attention to be successful. No matter how interesting an advertisement may be, if it fails to influence consumer buying habits, it fails. Advertising has been widely accepted in the print and broadcast media, but many people still view television & online advertising as an invasion of privacy. They resent their lack of control over the type and length of commercials. For this reason, many TV viewers are turning to cable television or remote-control devices to turn off advertising. Commercials now invade local movie theaters and rental videotapes before you can see the feature presentation. Consumers can have a voice in methods of advertising. Because of consumer complaints about exaggerated claims, broadcast regulations now govern the content of advertisements.

One medium can be more successful than another for certain products. Radio is most effective in announcing items where the visual appeal is not as important as the information. Television and the Internet are highly successful where both visual and verbal content is important. Seeing how a drop of super-strength glue suspends a 500-pound weight is more effective than just hearing about it. So is viewing a product and reading its specifications, as is possible on many web sites.

Advertisers and politicians depend heavily on mass media. How else would sponsors promote new products, or candidates introduce themselves to the general public? Very often, however, consumers are unaware of the widespread influence of the mass media. A consumer may buy a product without realizing that the seed for that purchase was planted by a TV commercial, newspaper ad, or web site.

Public Relations

While a fine line is drawn between advertising and public relations, advertising is generally concerned with selling a product, and public relations with selling an image. *Public relations* is a more subtle form of advertising, which is designed to influence attitudes and beliefs. McDonald's is interested in selling its food products, but it also tries to gain recognition by giving contributions to charity and hiring people with disabilities.

Corporations are not the only organizations interested in public relations. Nonprofit groups, governmental agencies, churches, and universities are all involved with publicity campaigns. These organizations use public relations agents and agencies to get specific information to the public via the news media. One of the goals of public relations is to utilize space free of charge. Television news coverage of a political candidate participating in a national walk-a-thon is probably more influential in projecting a favorable image than a 30-second, $150,000, prime-time TV spot would be. So, too, is setting up a web site that people can visit, and which can be updated over and over again.

Although many people resent the persuasive impact of advertising and public relations, we must also realize that this influence can sometimes be constructive. Self-help groups such as Alcoholics Anonymous and different social service agencies use the media to help make people aware of the groups' existence as well as to persuade those in need to seek out their help.

Effects of Mass Media

Widening Gaps

To date, three of the most profound effects of mass media and communication technologies have been the widening gender, socioeconomic, and racial gaps between people, both in the United States and around the globe. These gaps have been reflected in stereotypes that have emerged, and the growing divide between the "haves" and "have nots."

THE GENDER GAP. Until the late 1980s and 1990s, the mass media generally reflected society's attitudes toward gender roles. Women were portrayed as passive, men as aggressive and powerful. Women were portrayed as sex symbols with little brainpower (e.g., Marilyn Monroe), men as sexy and amazingly smart (e.g., Sean Connery, Roger Moore, and Pierce Brosnin in their portrayals of James Bond). Around that time, however, a shift began toward presenting men and women in more realistic roles. In television, shows like *Murphy Brown, Roseanne,* and *Grace Under Fire* depicted women as family breadwinners, and as capable of competing professionally with men. By the late 1990s, both women and men could be found anchoring night-time news programs, acting as commentators at professional sporting events (including American football), and serving as on-air war correspondents during the Gulf War crisis with Iraq.

During that same time period, movies like *Working Girl, Baby Boom,* and *Men Don't Leave* began to change depictions of women in the workforce. In music, a number of artists waged battles against gender stereotyping, including Boy George and Madonna. Additionally, magazines designed exclusively for working women began to emerge in the marketplace, including *LEARS, New Woman, Working Woman,* and *Redbook.*

At the beginning of the twenty-first century, however, considerable gender stereotyping (and division) remains, especially in the world of computing, which is heavily dominated by men. According to David Bolt and Ray Crawford (2000), women today still run the risk of being shut out of the digital world by not wanting to be perceived as "too smart"; by preferential treatment of boys in the classroom, particularly in math, science, and, consequently, computer technologies; and "a dearth of computer games that appeal directly to the interests or needs of girls" (pp. 75–93). Although, at the time of this writing, considerable efforts were being made to provide men and women with equal access to information (and the Internet), greater efforts are still needed to make communication technology more "gender neutral."

SOCIOECONOMIC AND RACIAL GAPS. In 1999, the U.S. Department of Commerce released its third annual survey regarding the use of computer technologies in the United States. Results of their study revealed that computer ownership among European-American households was 46.6 percent in 1999, compared with 25.5 percent for minority groups like Latinos. Additionally, when computer ownership was compared based on amount of annual income, 80 percent of households earning incomes of $100,000 reported having computers at home, while only about 20 percent of those earning less than $30,000 reported having home computers. Similarly, Internet usage during the mid-1990s increased disproportionately, with European Americans up by 38 percent and African Americans up by only 12 percent (cited in Bolt & Crawford, 2000, pp. 98–99).

Certainly the ability to afford computer technology is a major contributor to the growing digital divide around the world today. Interestingly, Trish Millines Dziko, founder of the Technology Access Foundation, offered another important observation regarding this phenomenon in an interview that she granted to Bolt and Crawford:

> When you talk to kids, [the use of computer technology] is something that the white kids do. . . .You know, you say, "Who is a scientist? What does a scientist look like? What does a computer repair person look like?" You know, they'll almost always draw a white

person and it's always a man. It's the same stuff they see in advertisements. It's the same things they see on TV. In their community, maybe. They need to have a little variety in role models who are willing to spend time with them, not just stand in front of them and say, "Well, I build computers." (pp. 100–101).

If her statement is valid for kids around the globe, Dziko offered a compelling statement about the ways in which the mass media continue to reflect, if not, shape racial and ethnic stereotypes. Let's consider the evidence.

At the time of this writing, you need to look no further than the number of television programs featuring actors of color to see evidence of such inequalities. Very few programs depict the lives of people other than European Americans. When you then consider the types of programming most likely to present people of color, you find a disproportionate number of situation comedies at the top of the list. It was precisely this observation ("Comedy, not Drama!") that helped to spark the development of Spike Lee's controversial movie *Bamboozled* in 2000.

To summarize, one of the most profound effects of mass media on people in almost every culture is the gap that exists between the "haves" and "have nots." Another is the number of gender and racial stereotypes that continue to be reflected and promulgated by twenty-first century mass media. We now turn to another equally important effect of mass media: the extent to which they shape cultural events.

Computers and the Internet are now a part of many people's everyday lives.

Shaping of Cultural Events

Mass media and communication technologies are so important in our lives that they often have an effect on the shaping of the events they cover. Sometimes events are planned with an eye toward media coverage. The Super Bowl is a perfect example of a spectacular event that grew out of the media. On a smaller scale, basketball and football games that are broadcast live allow time out for a word from the sponsor.

There are numerous examples that show how media and technology can shape events. A politician may delay a press conference until a broken TV camera is repaired, or a track star may be asked to repeat a final lap so that his or her action can be recorded on film. At one time, a group of people even speculated that the first landing on the moon was "faked" and that subsequent visits were nothing more than media manipulation.

The media sometimes overstep their bounds in shaping events. For example, in 1998, Cable News Network (CNN) and *Time* magazine broke a story claiming the U. S. military used nerve gas to kill enemy troops, women, children, and American defectors in Laos during the Vietnam conflict. The operation, code named Operation Tailwind, was reported to have taken place in 1970. Less than a month later, CNN retracted the story, citing "serious faults in the use of sources who provided them with the original reports" (http://www.cnn.com/US/9807/02/tailwind.johnson/). Key CNN personnel associated with the story were promptly fired. However, to date, questions continue to linger about the credibility of the story, the people involved, the U. S. military, as well as CNN and *Time* magazine.

Children and TV

There has been considerable investigation of the effects of TV on children. Not all findings are consistent. Some theories suggest that television provides vicarious reinforcement; that is, imaginary participation in an activity that is rewarding for the characters on the screen will reinforce this same type of behavior in a real-life situation. This does not imply a negative or positive value. Yet, when the activity is violent, or when youngsters cannot separate themselves from fantasy, this effect can be harmful. To support this claim, Sparks investigated developmental differences in children's reports of fear that is induced by mass-media programming. Results of his study revealed that younger children (ages five through seven) tend to report fright from programs that depict "impossible content" (that is, present grotesque, ugly figures or portray physical transformations of the main character), whereas older children (ages eight through eleven) report fright from programs that portray "possible events" or contain violent content (Sparks, 1986).

Another criticism of television is that it stifles a child's creativity. To test this claim, a research team from the University of Southern California exposed 250 intellectually gifted elementary school students to three weeks of intensive television viewing. Based on pre-test and post-test evaluations, the study found that the children showed a "marked drop in all forms of creative abilities except verbal skills" (What TV Does to

Kids, 1977). This study provided empirical data on an effect that many elementary school teachers have been observing for some time. A study by Rosenkoetter, Huston, and Wright (1990) indicated a relationship between heavy television viewing and less advanced moral reasoning judgment in kindergarten students. How much effect early television viewing has on humans is not yet known. Further studies that follow the development of children over time will tell us more about the ways in which viewing habits change our ability to view or participate in society.

Because children watch television for a number of reasons, ranging from boredom to loneliness, they unknowingly become involved in a process of "observational learning"; that is, they learn certain things simply by watching the behavior of TV characters. The amount of observational learning that takes place depends upon several factors, which include the following (Pearl, 1984):

1. The age of the child (two-year-olds are more prone than teens to imitate behavior, given that they are unable to see a relationship between behavior and motives.)

2. A belief that behaving in the way presented on television will be rewarded.

3. The degree to which a child identifies with a television character.

4. The degree to which a child rehearses a given behavior by daydreaming about it or using it in make-believe play.

Children learn many things through observation, including skills, values, norms, roles, and sex stereotypes. What children learn can be either positive or negative, depending on behaviors they observe.

Another important effect of TV is that it often replaces parental influence and supplies role models for children and adolescents who have inadequate ones at home. The TV set can become a substitute parent, a baby-sitter, and a replacement for family interaction. This effect is not usually in the individual's best interest.

TV VIOLENCE. We cannot discuss TV and children without emphasizing the effects of TV violence. Once again, not all findings agree. However, an extensive body of literature demonstrates that exposure to television violence indeed contributes to increased levels of aggression among the young. In one such study, the researcher was interested in the effects of realistic TV violence versus fictional violence on aggression in children. To test the effects of violence, he presented to preadolescents a six-minute newscast that featured a fight scene as one story, and to a different group of children the identical fight scene as a part of a movie preview promotion. Both the fantasy and reality fight segments produced higher scores on a hypothetical situational aggression test than were obtained in the control group, which completed the test without having viewed either film segment. Alarmingly, Atkin (1983) also found that scores were higher on the aggression measure completed by children who viewed the news version than by children who viewed the fantasy segment of the fight scene.

It is interesting to note how TV violence, in addition to producing aggressive behavior, affects our reactions to violence in real life. It is sometimes said that exposure to very violent scenes makes viewers more sensitive to the painful consequences of violent actions. Yet, there seems to be more support for the notion that TV violence "desensitizes" its audience to violence in real-life situations. According to this view, the audience becomes apathetic toward or accepting of violent acts in society (Rule & Ferguson, 1986). However, recent research supports the theory that television viewing does not make us more violent. Researchers from this camp argue that each individual is born with a certain level of aggressiveness and that, as with alcoholism, only those susceptible to the effects of violence will show more aggressive behaviors (Lynn, Hampson, & Agahi, 1989).

For example, one study examined how death was portrayed on television and the influence of these portrayals on a child's perceptions and ability to discuss death. The findings indicated that adolescents enjoyed watching violent deaths, but showed ambivalence about younger children viewing the same scenes. Many of the children were uncomfortable speaking to their parents about death, and often overestimated the amount of dying on television news and entertainment programs (Wass, Raup, & Sisler, 1989).

The movie industry has also been faced with pressure concerning violence in films. The rating system imposed by the movie industry in the late 1960s was an attempt to deal with this matter, although both sex and violence determine the rating. While the rating system does not alter the content of a film, it does serve to keep children from seeing certain films and warns other viewers of what to expect. This same function is served by the disclaimers that precede certain TV programs.

TELEVISION COMMERCIALS. The effect of television advertising on children is another area of concern. Especially on Saturday mornings, children are bombarded by enticing cereal, candy, toy, and game commercials. In a 36-minute time period, at least six minutes are devoted to advertising. Like the advertising designed for adults, children's advertising encourages youngsters to persuade their parents to buy and use certain products. The commercials often offer rewards and prizes, such as iron-on decals and toys inside the box.

Parents display mixed emotions about children's television advertising. Faced with endless demands for certain products and specific brand names, they often feel at the mercy of televised commercials that have influenced their children. However, a study by Galst (1980) suggests that parents may have the resources to fight back—and to influence their children's preferences for snacks. In Galst's study, three- to six-year-old children were exposed over a four-week period to cartoons, with interjected commercials for food products with added sugar or commercials for food products with no added sugar. Additionally, pro-nutritional public service announcements (PSAs) were included in the segments, with or without additional adult comments to the children about the product portrayed. Following each televised segment, the children were allowed to select a snack from a snack table which included all advertised products to which the children had been exposed, as well as similar product types (such as additional candies and fruits). The form of intervention that was found to be most effective in reducing the selection of snacks with added sugar was exposure to commercials for food products without added sugar and pro-nutritional PSAs with accompanying positive evaluative comments by an adult. Indeed, it seems that parents *can* fight back—but parental monitoring of television viewing is the key.

I am entirely persuaded that the American public is more reasonable, restrained and mature than most of the broadcast industry's planners believe. Their fear of controversy is not warranted by the evidence.

EDWARD R. MURROW

Political Campaigns

Some people believe that mass communication is the key to political victory. In fact, certain political observers have suggested that presidential candidates have lost debates and elections because they weren't as "telegenic" as their opponents.

Television, if used effectively, can aid a political campaign. However, candidates must be selective in choosing their strategies and media. In order to use the television medium most effectively, candidates apparently have to purchase television spots to introduce themselves and their ideas. Although televised news coverage is free and spot commercials are expensive, the commercials have a much greater

Today, mass media are increasingly global rather than local.

impact. Whether or not this exposure reinforces or changes viewers' voting habits is still unknown. In terms of exposure and information, however, the advertising spots have a much greater effect than television news coverage.

Of all forms of media, television is the most expensive and therefore must be used most efficiently. Advertising agencies may plan a media campaign for a political candidate in much the same way that they promote a new product. In fact, books such as *The Selling of the President,* by Joe McGinniss, have explored this similarity.

The Future of Mass Communication

Unlike other forms of communication, the development of mass communication has depended on advances in technology. The first major contribution to this development was the invention of the printing press, which led to the print media. For hundreds of years, print was the only form of mass communication. Radio, television, and film did not become realities until the twentieth century. Because the electronic media have such a powerful impact on our daily lives, it is almost impossible to imagine what our lives would be like without them.

Yet many advances in mass communication have occurred in just the last few decades. Words such as *DAT* (digital audio tape/technology), *CD* (compact disc), and MP3 music files are now part of almost everyone's vocabulary, although they were developed fairly recently. The development of mass communication has certainly not stopped; we can expect that as our technology becomes even more sophisticated, there will continue to be additions to the realm of mass communication.

In the realm of communication technologies, the future offers us endless opportunities for growth and development as human communicators. Dr. James Canton, president of the Institute for Global Futures, an internationally recognized think tank that focuses on the impacts of technology, offered his readers hundreds of predictions about twenty-first century technologies. Our top ten favorites were:

1. Computers will become powerful extensions of human beings designed to augment intelligence, learning, communications, and productivity (p. 17).

2. The Net will become the first global knowledge network connecting billions of people with an unlimited number of channels (p. 47).

3. The convergence of the Net, digital TV, and wireless phones will support interactive multimedia features that will transform business and society (p. 47).

4. Artificial Life (A-Life)—computer-generated entities—will mimic human appearance, language, reasoning, and personality (p. 71).

5. Companies will learn to manage customers' relationships by virtually serving their needs "24X7"—24 hours a day, 7 days a week (p. 109).

6. Educational content will be delivered by new computer, interactive TV, satellite, and Internet technologies (p. 139).

7. The convergence of biotech and computers will accelerate the genetic redesign of all living things (p. 155).

8. Medicalbots, nonhuman intelligence agents, will dispense medical care to patients and doctors worldwide to save money and share expertise (p. 183).

9. Nano-enhanced humans will have physical, intellectual, and sensing powers superior to other human beings (p. 205).

10. Advanced virtual reality bundled with digital agents and holographic entertainment worlds will transform our experience of entertainment (p. 223).

If Canton's (1999) book, entitled *Technofutures,* is successful in predicting even half of the changes on the horizon, the "textbooks" your children read on the subject of communication will differ vastly from than this one, both in form and in content.

As you can see, the shapes of mass communication and communication technologies are rapidly changing. Indeed, the possibilities are limitless, as the power of imagination today becomes the reality of tomorrow.

Summary

The most widely used and influential forms of mass media can be divided into two categories: print and electronic media. Print media include newspapers, books, and magazines. Electronic media include television, sound recordings, motion pictures, and the Internet.

Mass communication is defined as the process of rapidly conveying identical information, assertions, and attitudes to a potentially large, dispersed, and diversified audience via mechanisms capable of achieving that task. Thus, the four characteristics of mass communication include the transmission of (1) *identical information* to a (2) *large,* (3) *dispersed,* and (4) *diversified audience.* However, the Internet is changing the way mass communication is defined by moving toward the exchange of two-way messages.

Mass communication serves a number of functions. It can be used to inform, to persuade, and to entertain. The informative function of mass communication is primarily concerned with the news media. Newspapers and radio are still important forms of news media, and under some circumstances they are even more effective than TV in fulfilling this function.

The entertainment function of mass communication is quite diversified. Both comics in newspapers and a quiz show on TV entertain an audience. TV and film are primarily entertainment media.

The persuasive influence of the media is recognized in advertising for political candidates, service organizations, charities, and manufacturers. The relative persuasiveness of one medium over another depends upon the nature of the message as well as the individual medium.

While there has been considerable research on the effects of the mass media, many of the findings are inconclusive. Educators, psychologists, and sociologists are among those interested in the effects of mass media. Some of the areas they have explored include the effects of the media in terms of the widening gender, socioeconomic and racial gaps between people, the shaping of cultural events, children and TV, and political campaigns.

We can only guess where the advances of the future will lead us in terms of mass communication and communication technologies. However, where we go is limited only by the boundaries of imagination.

Exercises

GROUP EXPERIENCES

Delayed Feedback

DESCRIPTION Mass communication, by definition, suggests a widespread audience separated from a source by a considerable distance. As a result, a receiver's feedback or response to a message is usually limited and delayed. There are varying degrees of delayed feedback, ranging anywhere from a few minutes to several weeks or months. For example, a television commercial urging a customer to purchase a particular brand of detergent may have a delayed response of several weeks until the consumer runs out of his or her current brand of detergent. This activity will give you the opportunity to identify various degrees of delayed feedback.

PROCEDURE Television and radio both operate on the premise that a receiver's feedback or response to a message is both limited and delayed. For this activity you are to identify two examples from radio or television of (1) immediate, (2) delayed, and (3) long-term feedback. For the purpose of this activity, we will define immediate feedback as a response that occurs within a 30-minute period; delayed feedback includes responses within up to two weeks; long-term feedback involves responses that require more than two weeks.

DISCUSSION What are the effects of the varying degrees of delayed feedback on the receiver? Have you ever considered writing to a television show for a specific purpose and later decided that it would take too long to get an answer? Do you think that the nature of television and radio feedback reduces the number of written responses from viewers? How do television and radio stations attempt to accurately assess the feedback of receivers? Are you aware of the various degrees of delayed feedback with which you respond to mass media?

The Big Debate

DESCRIPTION One of the most compelling questions with regard to television is the effect of television on children and adolescents. Although there has been considerable research on the effects of television, findings are inconsistent. Some of the criticisms of television are that it stifles creativity, promotes violence, and has a negative effect on social morality. This activity will give you a chance to view both sides of the controversy.

PROCEDURE All class members should research the effects of television on children and adolescents. Half the class should be instructed to find evidence to support the continuation of television programs, while the remaining half should find evidence of the negative effects of television. After the research has been collected, four class members should be selected to participate in a debate. One team (two members) will represent the position that television produces negative effects on children and adolescents (the negative position). The second team, also consisting of two members, will represent a major network (the affirmative position). The following format should be used for the debate:

Affirmative speaker 1: 5 minutes

Negative speaker 1: 5 minutes

Affirmative speaker 2: 5 minutes

Negative speaker 2: 5 minutes

Negative speaker 1: 2 minutes

Affirmative speaker 1: 2 minutes

Negative speaker 2: 2 minutes

Affirmative speaker 2: 2 minutes

Following the debate, the class members should reevaluate their positions on the topic.

DISCUSSION What is your opinion on the effects of television on children and adolescents? Can you support your position with research findings? Can you identify any of the effects television has had on you? Can the effects of television be controlled or directed? How?

PERSONAL EXPERIENCES

1. For a period of one week, watch a late-night movie every night. Try to watch a combination of romantic, humorous, violent, and horror shows. Keep a TV dream diary in which you record in detail all the dreams that you have. It would be best to record your dreams first thing in the morning, before you do anything else. What relationship, if any, do your dreams have to the television shows that you viewed?

2. How are you influenced during presidential campaigns? List the various ways in which you receive information about the candidates. How many of those sources involve some form of mass communication, such as televised debates, radio, newspapers, or the Internet? How has mass media changed national elections?

3. How does television reinforce or alter stereotypes? Select six different television shows and identify whether or not they reinforce gender and racial stereotypes. Identify the methods by which programs characterize people according to gender or racial stereotypes. Are there programs that attempt to change or even revise these stereotypes? If so, which ones?

Discussion Questions

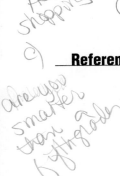

1. How do mass media differ from other communication systems (intrapersonal, interpersonal, and group communication)?
2. What are the positive and negative effects of television on its viewers?
3. What do you envision for the future of mass media? Describe the advances in technology that you feel will take place in the next 30 years.
4. Identify the television shows that are used primarily to (a) inform, (b) persuade, and (c) entertain. Are the most successful shows a combination of all three purposes?
5. How often do you use the Internet? For what major reasons do you surf the Net for information or entertainment?

References

Atkin, C. (1983). Effects of realistic TV violence vs. fictional violence on aggression. *Journalism Quarterly, 60*(4), 615–621.

Bolt, D., & Crawford, R. (2000). *Digital divide: Computers and our children's future.* New York: TV Books LLC.

Canton, J. (1999). *Technofutures: How leading-edge technology will transform business in the 21st century.* Carlsbad, CA: Hay House, Inc.

Galst, J. P. (1980). Television food commercials and pro-nutritional public service announcements as determinants of young children's snack choices. *Child Development, 51,* 935–938.

Hiebert, R. E. (Editor). (1999). *Impact of mass media: Current issues* (4th ed.). New York: Longman.

Lynn, R., Hampson, S., & Agahi, E. (1989). Television violence and aggression: A genotype-environment, correlation and interaction theory. *Social Behavior and Personality, 17*(2), 143–164.

Orlik, P. B. (1997). *The electronic media: An introduction to the profession* (2nd ed.). Ames, IA: Iowa State University Press.

Pearl, D. (1984). Violence and aggression. *Society, 21,* 17–22.

Roddy, B. L., & Garramore, G. M. (1988). Appeals and strategies of negative political advertising. *Journal of Broadcasting & Electronic Media, 32*(4), 415–427.

Rosenkoetter, L. I., Huston, A. C., & Wright, J. C. (1990). Television and the moral judgment of the young child. *Journal of Applied Development Psychology, 11,* 123–137.

Rule, B. G., & Ferguson, T. J. (1986). The effects of media violence on attitudes, emotions, and cognitions. *Journal of Social Issues, 42*(3), 29–50.

Sparks, G. G. (1986). Developmental differences in children's reports of fear induced by the mass media. *Child Study Journal, 16*(1), 55.

Wass, H., Raup, J. L., & Sisler, H. H. (1989). Adolescents and death on television: A follow-up study. *Death Studies, 13,* 161–173.

What TV does to Kids. (21 February 1977). *Newsweek,* 63–70.

Whetmore, E. J. (1991). *Mediamerica* (4th ed.). Belmont, CA: Wadsworth.

Winston, B. (1998). *Media technology and society: A history from the telegraph to the Internet.* New York: Routledge.

Preparing for a Job Search

Anyone who has looked for a job knows that the interview is the most important step in the job-hunting process. If you do not perform well in a job interview, chances are you won't get the position, no matter how well qualified you are. Likewise, if you as the job interviewer do not know the correct skills, you may discourage qualified applicants or simply choose the wrong person for the job. Yet few executives and supervisors make an effort to learn specialized interviewing skills; they underestimate the importance of these interactions. Instead, they handle interviews with little advance planning, relying only on experience and improvisation. An understanding of the interviewer responsibilities should give you insights into how to prepare for your first interview.

Responsibilities of the Interviewer

Even though you may never be a personnel recruiter, there will be times when you will be responsible for conducting interviews. There are formal rules for interview situations. James Black (1970), for example, offers a classic checklist of principles on sound interviewing practices that is clearly relevant today. Black first suggests that as an interviewer, you prepare yourself for the task of gathering a lot of information in a limited period of time. Because the interview is so short, you must decide in advance how much time you wish to devote to each area of discussion. Preparation also includes studying the data already received about the interviewee so that no time is wasted in asking unnecessary questions.

Second, you must define your objectives and follow an organized plan to achieve them. A directionless interview is inefficient and will probably annoy the interviewee, giving him or her a poor impression of the company. Thus, the reason for the interview and the information to be obtained from it must be clear in the minds of both you and the person being interviewed.

Third, the environment of the interview must be considered. Positive communication often depends on comfortable surroundings. The room should be well lit and quiet. To ensure good eye contact and attentiveness, the two participants should always sit facing each other. The accommodations should be relaxed, pleasant, and above all, private. Taking telephone calls in the middle of an interview is rude and wastes valuable time.

Fourth, as the interview opens, it is up to you as the interviewer to break the ice—to make the other person feel at ease. Perhaps a question about an outside interest or about the person's family can serve this function. When interviewing, you should use words and phrases that the interviewee can understand. Trying to impress someone with your high-powered vocabulary will only block communication. Since you would like a productive interview, you must be able to develop a friendly relationship quickly, and, even more important, you must create a feeling of trust and confidence. The only way to do this is to be genuinely open and receptive rather than distant, authoritative, or condescending. These positive attitudes show the interviewee that you are sincerely interested in what he or she has to say.

Fifth, as the interviewer, you should decide the nature of the questions that will give you the necessary information. These questions should evoke more than a simple "yes" or "no," which would force you to do all of the talking. Also, the conversation must be free and open, and not become a cat-and-mouse game in which you try to trap the person with trick questions. In this situation you will lose the trust of the person you are interviewing, who will then reveal as little information as possible.

Sixth, you must listen attentively and intelligently. If your eyes wander or if you are constantly glancing at papers on the desk when you interview, the people you interview will feel uneasy. They will either speed up their answers or break off before they finish all that they have to say. On the other hand, if you show interest and attention, they will speak openly and freely and may even give more information than expected. Empathy is also important when listening. You should try to put yourself in the place of the person being interviewed and understand the real meaning behind the spoken words.

Seventh, interviewees should not be rushed into careless answers at the end because you must hurry them out. The interview should end gracefully and naturally. The interviewee will know it is coming to an end by the type of questions being asked and by the way you use your voice.

Eighth, at the end of the interview, interviewees must be told what to expect in the future: when they will find out whether they got the job, or what action will be taken to handle the matters that were discussed.

Finally, when the interviewee leaves, the interviewer's work must be completed. While the interview is fresh in your mind, you should make notes and evaluate the information you received. This evaluation should be as objective as possible. As the interviewer, you must put aside your own prejudices and must not distort the facts. Therefore, you must possess sound judgment, emotional stability, and the ability to make objective decisions.

Responsibilities of the Interviewee

Now that you are familiar with some of the tasks facing the interviewer, it's time to look at your responsibilities as an interviewee. You may think that all you'll need to do is to answer a few questions, but these questions will probably be the most difficult you've ever encountered, especially if you haven't prepared for the interview in advance. Job hunting is hard work, and sometimes even your preparation might seem difficult. The next few sections provide guidelines and principles to follow while preparing for your first interview.

SELF-EVALUATION.   Do you know who you are? We all think we know ourselves pretty well, but during the next few minutes you may begin discovering parts of yourself that you never knew existed. The first step in preparing for your job search is to conduct a personal inventory. Most interviewees think they know the type of job they're looking for, where they'd like to work, the type of people they would enjoy working with, and so on, but campus recruiters find that students often fail to evaluate their personal and professional goals. Figures A.1 and A.2 give guidelines for you to follow when conducting personal and job inventories.

Before you find a satisfactory position, you will need to evaluate your qualifications, preferences, knowledge, training, and experience. Don't just look at your strengths; also look at areas where you need improvement. A favorite question that recruiters ask applicants is, "Now that we have talked about some of your strong points, tell me some areas you feel weak in, and tell me what you are doing to overcome these weaknesses." That's a tough question, and unless you've prepared before the interview, you may have difficulty answering it effectively.

Jason, an English major, wants to work in a consulting firm developing communication training programs for business and industry. After Jason makes a list of his skills and training, he realizes that he's never taken business or organizational communication courses. Jason can overcome this potential job-hunting weakness by taking appropriate courses or by getting a part-time job in business and industry.

The evaluation form in Figure A.3 is excerpted from a book by William N. Yeomans (1977). It is designed to help you evaluate your job marketability. By now you should have thought about who you are, what you have done, and what talents, skills, and interests you possess. With all this firmly in mind, complete this questionnaire. The scoring has not been scientifically tested, but it does view applicants in the same way organizations evaluate potential employees.

Listed are 50 characteristics that many employers consider positive and important. They are qualities that anyone could have, but not everyone does have. Rate yourself from "1" to "5" on each factor. Note that this list is not comprehensive; include other traits under number 51.

	(Poor) 1	2	(Average) 3	4	(Excellent) 5
1. Honest	( )	( )	( )	( )	( )
2. Dependable	( )	( )	( )	( )	( )
3. Motivated	( )	( )	( )	( )	( )
4. Assertive	( )	( )	( )	( )	( )
5. Outgoing	( )	( )	( )	( )	( )
6. Persistent	( )	( )	( )	( )	( )
7. Conscientious	( )	( )	( )	( )	( )
8. Ambitious	( )	( )	( )	( )	( )
9. Punctual	( )	( )	( )	( )	( )
10. Creative	( )	( )	( )	( )	( )
11. Intelligent	( )	( )	( )	( )	( )
12. Mature	( )	( )	( )	( )	( )
13. Emotionally stable	( )	( )	( )	( )	( )
14. Enthusiastic	( )	( )	( )	( )	( )
15. Flexible	( )	( )	( )	( )	( )
16. Realistic	( )	( )	( )	( )	( )
17. Responsible	( )	( )	( )	( )	( )
18. Serious	( )	( )	( )	( )	( )
19. Pleasant	( )	( )	( )	( )	( )
20. Sincere	( )	( )	( )	( )	( )
21. Analytical	( )	( )	( )	( )	( )
22. Organized	( )	( )	( )	( )	( )
23. Appearance	( )	( )	( )	( )	( )
24. Able to get along with coworkers	( )	( )	( )	( )	( )
25. Able to get along with supervisors	( )	( )	( )	( )	( )
26. Oral communication skills	( )	( )	( )	( )	( )
27. Written communication skills	( )	( )	( )	( )	( )
28. References	( )	( )	( )	( )	( )
29. School attendance	( )	( )	( )	( )	( )
30. Job attendance	( )	( )	( )	( )	( )
31. Willing to work long hours	( )	( )	( )	( )	( )
32. Willing to work evenings and weekends	( )	( )	( )	( )	( )
33. Willing to relocate	( )	( )	( )	( )	( )
34. Willing to travel	( )	( )	( )	( )	( )
35. Willing to commute a long distance	( )	( )	( )	( )	( )
36. Willing to start at the bottom and advance according to own merit	( )	( )	( )	( )	( )
37. Able to accept criticism	( )	( )	( )	( )	( )
38. Able to motivate others	( )	( )	( )	( )	( )
39. Able to follow through on something until it is done	( )	( )	( )	( )	( )

FIGURE A.1   Analyzing Your Personality Strengths

	(Poor) 1	2	(Average) 3	4	(Excellent) 5
40. Able to make good use of time	( )	( )	( )	( )	( )
41. Goal or achievement-oriented	( )	( )	( )	( )	( )
42. Show initiative	( )	( )	( )	( )	( )
43. Healthy	( )	( )	( )	( )	( )
44. Able to follow directions	( )	( )	( )	( )	( )
45. Detail-oriented	( )	( )	( )	( )	( )
46. Able to learn quickly	( )	( )	( )	( )	( )
47. Desire to work hard	( )	( )	( )	( )	( )
48. Moral standards	( )	( )	( )	( )	( )
49. Poised	( )	( )	( )	( )	( )
50. Growth potential	( )	( )	( )	( )	( )
51. Others	( )	( )	( )	( )	( )

FIGURE A.1 **Analyzing Your Personality Strengths (continued)**

Listed are factors that many people value in jobs and organizations. Rank the factors from "1" to "3" in terms of their importance to you. Put an asterisk beside the five most important factors.

1—Not Important   2—Average Importance   3—Very important

	1	2	3
1. Challenge	( )	( )	( )
2. Responsibility	( )	( )	( )
3. Stability of company	( )	( )	( )
4. Security of job within company	( )	( )	( )
5. Size of company	( )	( )	( )
6. Training program	( )	( )	( )
7. Initial job duties	( )	( )	( )
8. Advancement opportunities	( )	( )	( )
9. Amount of contact with coworkers	( )	( )	( )
10. Amount of contact with the public	( )	( )	( )
11. Starting salary	( )	( )	( )
12. Financial rewards "down the road"	( )	( )	( )
13. Degree of independence	( )	( )	( )
14. Opportunity to show initiative	( )	( )	( )
15. Degree of employee involvement in decision making	( )	( )	( )
16. Opportunity to be creative	( )	( )	( )
17. Type of industry	( )	( )	( )
18. Company's reputation in the industry	( )	( )	( )
19. Prestige of job within the company	( )	( )	( )
20. Degree of results seen from job	( )	( )	( )
21. Variety of duties	( )	( )	( )
22. What the boss is like	( )	( )	( )
23. What the coworkers are like	( )	( )	( )

FIGURE A.2 **Analyzing Factors of Importance to You in Jobs and Companies**

Source: From *Interviewing . . . A Job in itself.* Copyright Lois Einhorn and The Career Center, Bloomington Ind., 1977, 3–6.

Scholastic Standing	Score
Phi Beta Kappa; top 10% of class	6
Top 25% of class	4
Top 50% of class	2
Lower 50% of class	0
Academic Rating of Your College	
Very high; Ivy League caliber	6
Good, well-respected academically	4
Not known for academic excellence	1
Barely accredited or not accredited	0
Work Experience	
Full-time work in your major field	6
Summer or part-time work in your major	4
Work in unrelated field or community service experience	2
No work experience	0
College Expenses Earned Yourself	
75–100%	6
50–75%	4
25–50%	1
Under 25%	0
Campus Activities	
Major elected offices; many activities	4
Minor elected offices; some activities	2
No elected offices but some activities	1
No elected offices and no activities	0
Personality	
Popularity-plus. Well-liked; meet people easily	4
Pretty well-liked; meet people easily most of the time	3
Some friends; not too great at meeting people	1
Zero personality	0
Height (If Weight Is Proportionate)	
5'10" to 6'4" for men	3
5' to 6' for women	3
4'1" or under, 6' or over, or overweight, for women	0
Under 5'10", over 6'4", or overweight, for men	0
Bearing (Voice, Posture, Eye Contact)	
Commanding, immediately impressive	3
Mostly impressive	2
Not too impressive	0
A laugh	0
Total Score	_____

Results

31–38   Outstanding! You should be able to pick and choose a suitable position. However, people rarely score this high, so evaluate yourself again to be sure.

19–30   Excellent prospect. You should have several job possibilities without much trouble.

7–18   Average candidate. Job opportunities will depend on the economy and labor market. Need to try to develop some different areas to increase your chances.

0–6   Not so good. You will probably have difficulty in getting a desirable job. Need to think of ways to improve your score, or you may have evaluated yourself too severely.

FIGURE A.3   Job Marketability Evaluation Form

You may already know the type of positions for which you'd like to apply, but you may now know what's available to someone with your major, background, and skills. You may have chosen a major because the prospects for earnings looked good, the courses were easy, your parents suggested it, or it was something you'd always wanted to do. After getting your degree, and maybe after getting a job, you realize that you won't be challenged or happy working in this area for an extended period of time. Some people, for example, major in elementary education, get a job, and realize that children drive them crazy. Others get preprofessional degrees and then are not accepted into medical school, law school, or graduate school. What then? An inventory of your job preferences can help you look for positions to meet your needs. For additional help, go to your campus career planning office or to professional personnel agencies, study self-help manuals, or take a course on career planning. Laird Durham's book *100 Careers: How to Pick the One That's Best for You* is very useful. We hope that the exercises and examples in this section have given you greater insight into what your strengths, weaknesses, training, preferences, and other qualifications are so that you'll know what you have to offer during a job search.

WRITTEN PREPARATION.   You have now evaluated your assets and liabilities and know what you can expect from an organization. With your job objectives clearly in mind, you need to find a way to get an interview. The most widely used method of introducing yourself to an organization is through a letter of introduction and a *résumé*. Although cover letters and résumés are the most commonly used method of getting an interview, many have the opposite or no effect. Abbott P. Smith (1977), a professional recruiting and placement specialist, offers 12 basic guidelines to help you ensure that your next résumé is not your obituary.

1. Do some soul searching before you begin (conduct a personal and job inventory).

2. Write your objective (what do you want to do?).

3. Sell yourself (tell what you have done and what you can do).

4. Be brief and nonrepetitive (aim for a one-page résumé).

5. Write it yourself (steer away from professional résumé-writing services).

6. List the jobs you have held (include job titles and dates).

7. Forget the references (applicants list references who will give positive comments).

8. List personal information first (name, address, phone number, e-mail address, etc.).

9. Don't elaborate on personal information (keep it brief).

10. Make it neat (this may be the time to invest in a professional typist or printing job).

11. Write a neat, short, personal cover letter (give reason for writing and what you know about the organization).

12. Put yourself into your résumé (find a way to stand out from the other candidates).

Résumé formats and what is included in résumés differ considerably. Figure A.4 provides an example of a résumé. You may be able to apply for several types of positions. If you do, you may need to write different résumés directing the content of each to a particular position. Applicants looking for a position in education usually use an academic vita, which has a different format. A valuable source book to help with your preparation is *What Color Is Your Parachute?* by Richard Bolles, which is updated annually. Just as the résumé is important, so too is your cover letter.

Field and Holley (1976) found that personnel managers consider five items important in a cover letter:

1. The position the applicant is seeking.

2. The applicant's job objective.

3. The applicant's career objectives.

4. The applicant's reason for seeking employment.

5. The indication that the applicant knows something about the organization.

Because you are trying to get an interview with a particular person, it is also advisable to request an interview in the cover letter and to refer to your enclosed résumé.

FINDING JOB POSSIBILITIES. The interview is the most important step in the hiring process. Some of you may have a job waiting for you, but most of you must find a way to get an employment interview. Four major methods of securing a job interview include (1) answering ads in newspapers or listed on Internet sites, (2) taking advantage of college placement centers, (3) visiting employment agencies, and (4) making cold calls.

Newspaper ads are the least popular form of organizational recruiting because they often expose employers to unknown problems, cost a lot of money, and release competitive information to other companies. Some companies use blind newspaper ads with only box numbers to give themselves greater flexibility. Because of the anonymous nature of a blind ad, the employer is not forced to answer inquiries, leak information to competitors, or conform to governmental equal employment opportunity guidelines. Although newspaper ads have advantages, they get fewer responses than Internet ads.

When reading ads, you must learn to understand advertising tactics. Recruiters advertise for the maximum qualifications they can get, with inflated requirements that are not absolute. Of course, some positions will require special expertise. A nurse shouldn't apply for a physician's position, and a brick mason shouldn't apply for an electrician's position. When answering an ad, you either will be offered the job, rejected, or offered a position not listed in the advertisement.

The simplest way to get an interview is through your campus placement center. All you have to do is sign up; yet even with this easy procedure, many students fail

TABLE A.1 Some Do's and Don't's in Successful Interviewing

DO	DON'T
Act natural	Criticize yourself
Be prompt, neat, courteous	Be late
Prepare self and job analysis inventories	Present an extreme appearance
	Become impatient
Ask relevant questions	Become emotional
Allow the employer to express himself or herself	Oversell your case
	Draw out the interview
Make yourself understood	Make elaborate promises
Listen to the other person	Come unprepared
Present informative credentials	Try to be funny
Think of your potential service to the employer	Linger over what the company will do for you (such as benefits, salary, promotion)
Act positively	Unduly emphasize starting salary

Source: Reprinted from *Planning Your Future* by permission of the College Placement Council, the copyright holder. In R. A. Vogel and W. D. Brooks, *Business Communication* (Menlo Park, Calif.: Cummings, 1977), 42–43.

to take advantage of placement center opportunities. Some think that their grade point average is too low, that only small companies recruit on college campuses, that companies look only for business majors, or that a lot of extracurricular activities are required. Students need to reevaluate the placement center interviewing option because it offers opportunities to students with a variety of backgrounds, experiences, and education.

It may help to familiarize yourself with how the placement center works. Placement offices usually have orientation meetings at the beginning of each quarter or semester, giving essential procedural information. The placement center provides forms and starts personal files for interested students (including alumni). Files include standard data sheets, résumés, letters of recommendation, and interviewing histories. Some centers also provide interview workshops, career counseling, career libraries, and employer information. Centers use open sign-up systems (first come, first served), staff sign-up systems (counselors place students), or card systems (batches of high- and low-priority cards are given for company preferences). No matter which system is used on your campus, you should go through your placement center to get valuable interviewing experience.

You may now be wondering what happens after you've signed up for an interview. Company recruiters are given placement center data sheets and a list of interviewee names with time slots. Your interview begins before you meet the recruiter,

---

Julie D. Jordon

6500 Jefferson St.	Kansas City, Missouri 64113	(816) 361-8162

EDUCATION: University of Missouri, Bachelor of Journalism. Minor-English

EXPERIENCE:

Lifestyles Editor
Opelika-Auburn News (Opelika, Alabama) November 1999 to March 2001. Responsible for daily Lifestyles page(s) including two weekly 10-page sections. Duties included writing, editing, design, pagination, and composing.

Entertainment Editor
Opelika-Auburn News (Opelika, Alabama) August 1999 to March 2001. Responsible for writing, editing, design, pagination, and composing of weekly entertainment magazine; duties included writing weekly opinion column and two weekly Lifestyles feature.

Assistant Editor
Weekend magazine (Columbia, Missouri) January 1999 to May 1999. Responsible for writing, editing and composing of weekly magazine.

Executive Assistant
Weekend magazine (Columbia, Missouri) August 1998 to May 1999.

Copy Editor
Communications, Eighth Edition (Prentice Hall Press) Summer 1998 Worked in association with author D. Larry Barker.

Staff Reporter
Missourian (Columbia, Missouri) January 1998 to May 1998. Covered neighborhood beat on city desk for daily newspaper.

Administrative Assistant
Business Journalism (University of Missouri) August 1997 to May 1998. In association with the Society of American Business Editors and Writers with James Gentry and the Missouri Interscholastic Press Association with Dr. Robert Knight.

Technical Assistant
KBIA Newsroom (Columbia, Missouri) August 1996 to May 1997.

HONORS AND ACTIVITIES:
William Randolph Hearst Foundation Journalism Awards Program
Fourth Place in 1998 National Feature Writing Competition
Pi Beta Phi Fraternity.
Elizabeth Jennison Scholarship
Sabra K. Beri Scofield Scholarship
Olga Bak Scholarship

Reference Available Upon Request

FIGURE A.4   A Sample Résumé

as he or she examines your placement file. Next, the recruiter enters the lobby or waiting area and calls your name. Introductions are made, handshakes are exchanged, and then you are led into a small room or partitioned area. The interview area usually consists of two chairs, with one placed behind a desk for the interviewer. Most campus interviews last from 15 to 20 minutes. At the end of the interview, recruiters usually tell you when you should be hearing from the company.

Finally, after you leave, the recruiter quickly jots down impressions before moving on to the next interviewee. This can be a grueling process for both the recruiter and you; but again, you should get as much interviewing experience as possible.

A third method of getting an interview is through an employment agency. Employment agencies vary in size, style, cost, and purpose. Some agencies may have only one or two people placing applicants, while others have divisions for sales, management, engineering, professional, or technical positions. Agencies may treat you very professionally, with preinterview testing and counseling, or they may send you to an interview without preparation. Employment agencies stay in business through the fees they collect from either the employer or the interviewee or both. You may pay 10 percent to 20 percent of your first year's salary, or the company may pay all fees. As often as possible it is best to interview with fee-paid organizations. Some professional search agencies charge 20 percent and higher but guarantee job satisfaction, testing and training, and résumé-writing services. The purposes of employment agencies also differ. Agencies fill temporary vacancies, place technical or specialty personnel, find executives, or say they can place anyone.

Advantages of using employment agencies include their efficiency, saving time by having others do the searching for you, and confidentiality. One of the best methods of selecting an employment agency is to look at the classified section of your Sunday newspaper to see which agencies do the most advertising. Then scout several agencies and select two or three that seem most suited to your needs. Tell the agencies that you have registered with other agencies to let them know they have competition. As an interviewee, you must be prepared for critical analysis from agency counselors. They want to increase your job marketability and will sometimes get tough to help you perform more effectively during appointment interviews.

The final way to get an interview is by making cold calls. You can either send a résumé, or phone, or go in person. As mentioned earlier, it is best to go in person, yet this is probably the most difficult and ego-deflating situation of all. Having a job places you in a better bargaining position, but whether you have a job or not, you have to be persistent and make use of special cold-call tactics.

The best time to show up is about 10 A.M. or 3 P.M., because these are the least hectic times in organizations. When making plans, also try to go on Tuesday, Wednesday, or Thursday rather than Monday or Friday. The beginning of the week is busy and at the end of the week you'll find that the important people may be away. It is best to apply before November 15 and after January 1 because of holidays and fiscal years. If you want to make one friend before seeing a personnel director, it should be the company receptionist. Receptionists have the power to help or hurt your chances of getting an interview. However, even though you want to make friends with receptionists, don't give them your résumé. After you turn over your résumé, you lose bargaining power and may never get a chance to talk to the people who make hiring decisions. You'll learn tricks of the trade with experience. Just remember not to give up until you get the interviews you want.

RESEARCHING THE COMPANY.   It is essential that you find out about the company before the actual interview. Just as you feel good when someone you meet knows something about you, recruiters are also flattered when you know something about what is important to them—their company. Know everything possible. The knowledge will increase your confidence and ease during the interview. However, remember too that timing is important. Don't interject some obscure company fact at inappropriate times.

The best place to begin is at your placement office. It usually has company literature, annual reports, brochures, and fliers. If not, check their website, or write or phone the organization and ask someone there to send you the information. Next, try to talk with people who work in the organization. They'll give you greater insights than any written material could provide. Finally, local libraries usually have information in business periodicals, newspapers, stock market reports, and so on. The questions you will want to answer depend on the type of organization you are investigating. In applying for a teaching position, you'd want to know the number of schools in the district; for a manufacturing firm, you'd be interested in plant locations and competition; and for a bank, you'd probably like to know if it was nationally or state chartered and how many branches it had. Remember, the answers to the questions are intended to help you. Now that you have examined the responsibilities of interviewers and interviewees, you should be ready to think about your first interview. Your confidence should be high because you have evaluated yourself, completed a formal résumé, found the job openings, researched the company, and gotten an interview.

The Interview

When you are being interviewed, your chief responsibility is to yourself. During an employment interview, you owe it to yourself to obtain as much information as you can, so that should you be offered the job, you can make an intelligent decision. Make sure you understand the requirements of the job (just what it is that you will be expected to do). If you don't understand something, ask questions until you do. State your qualifications in a positive way, and don't be afraid to mention potential weaknesses in your background (but try to balance them with strengths). The most important thing to do during any kind of interview is to communicate—listen, speak, question, respond, and understand.

The employment interview incorporates everything we've discussed about communication, and more. After your first interview you will be aware of additional areas that you'll need to prepare for the next time. One area that needs no further preparation is that of honesty. There is a misconception that you should say anything to get the job. However, this doesn't pay off. One young man decided to alter his grade point average on his résumé. Instead of putting down his cumulative average, he listed the average in his major course work, which was considerably higher.

He interviewed with his placement center and was offered a job in a major duplicating corporation. After he accepted the position and had started training, the company sent for his college transcripts. The personnel director noticed the discrepancy between the grade point averages and called him in to ask him about it. After he told the director what he had done, he was fired for dishonesty.

Lying may not get you fired, but it could cause even more serious problems. New interviewees often fall into the trap of trying to please the interviewer with all their answers. If they are asked if they'd mind traveling, some say "no" even if they do; or they may say they enjoy working with people, when in actuality they would rather work by themselves or with machines. You may get a job, but your dishonesty will only hurt you. Too many people are miserable in positions they should never have accepted or applied for. When you see that you would be dissatisfied in a position you're applying for, acknowledge it to the recruiter. There may be another position that you'd be better suited for, or the recruiter can keep you in mind if something does become available.

We have already mentioned a few questions that are used during employment interviews. The following list of frequently asked questions should help prepare you further for your first interview. Questions are designed to serve as indicators of your personal background; human relations skills; work background; accident, safety, and health histories; education and training; and personal objectives.

1. What do you see yourself doing in five, 10, 15 years?

2. How have childhood experiences influenced you?

3. How would your closest friend describe you?

4. Why did you decide to go to your college or university?

5. If you could change anything about your education, what would it be?

6. Do you work well under pressure? (give some examples)

7. Would you rather be a leader or a follower?

8. What motivates you to give the most effort?

9. Are your grades a good indicator of your academic achievement? (explain)

10. Do you have plans for continued study? (explain)

11. How do you evaluate success?

12. Who is the person you admire most? (why?)

13. If you could have an ideal job, what would it be like?

14. Why should I hire you over other candidates?

15. Do you work better alone or with supervision? (explain)

16. Why are you interested in working for our company?

17. What have you learned from your mistakes?

18. What are you looking for in a job?

19. Are you a leader? (explain)

20. What qualities should an effective manager have?

21. How do you accept criticism? (explain)

22. Tell me about yourself.

23. What work experience helps qualify you for this position?

24. How do you spend your free time?

25. What qualities do you think I should be looking for in this position?

The ability to answer these and other questions should give you a good edge over unprepared candidates. Questions you will be asked are important, but you should also be giving some consideration to questions you should ask the interviewer. Toward the end of an employment interview, the interviewer usually asks if you have any questions. A few sample questions follow.

1. What type of training program do you have, and how long will it last?

2. What is the advancement potential in your organization?

3. Does your company help pay for employees to continue their education?

4. Will I have to relocate?

5. How are your employees evaluated?

6. What opportunities do you see for a person with my background?

7. What have been your most rewarding experiences with the company?

8. What is the employee turnover rate?

9. Does the company pay for moving expenses?

10. What weaknesses do you see that I should try to improve?

Job interviews do not consist solely of questions and answers. Several factors work together to make your interview a success or failure. The list of do's and don't's in Table A.1 should serve as a useful reminder before your interview. Making sure that you do all the do's will not necessarily land you a job, but doing one don't could cause you not to be hired.

In this section we have covered the three Ps of interviewing: preparation, presentation, and post-analysis. The preparation phase involves four steps: (1) self-inventory, (2) occupation inquiry, (3) preparation of letter of introduction and résumé, and (4) putting it all together. The interview presentation itself has four stages: introduction, background, matching, and closing. The post-analysis calls for follow-up and reevaluation of your performance. The important thing to remember about this process is that no two interview situations will be exactly the same. The most you can do is understand the overall process; prepare for that process; and go in with a positive and professional attitude, thinking, "I have something to offer you."

After the Interview

Before breathing a sigh of relief, remember that your job search is not over yet. It is not complete until you've secured the position that you've applied for. After each interview, applicants can follow three simple steps to increase their chances of getting hired.

Immediately after leaving the interview, write down your recruiter's name, title, and address. Forgetting your interviewer's name could be detrimental to you later, when a secretary calls to set up a second interview and asks if you were interviewed by Mr. Barton, Ms. Kendall, or Mr. Barfield. The recruiter is now a personal contact with the organization, and all additional correspondence should be directed to him or her. You may be asked to send in letters of recommendation, transcripts, or job applications at later times, so be prepared.

After making sure that you remember your interviewer's name, find time to evaluate your interview participation by reconstructing the interview situation. Do you think that the outcome will be positive or negative? What impressions did you make? Why? After self-analysis you may remember biting your fingernails, interrupting the recruiter, looking at your watch, answering the wrong question, or using profanity. There is a tendency for us to focus on our mistakes rather than to look at the total process. Try to force yourself to remember areas of outstanding performance as well as areas that need improvement, so that your next interview will be more successful.

One last way to leave a favorable impression with a recruiter is to write a letter of appreciation. These letters usually thank the recruiter for his or her time and for the opportunity to meet, and express interest in the organization. You want the recruiter to remember you; even if a company doesn't have a position at the present time, he or she will be more likely to think of you in the future if you keep in touch. By following these three post-interview guidelines, you should increase your chances of success.

References

Black, J. (1970). *How to get results from interviewing* (1). New York: McGraw-Hill.

Field, H. S., & Holley, W. H. (1976, March). Résumé preparation: An empirical study of personnel managers' perceptions. *The Vocational Guidance Quarterly,* 229–237.

Smith, A. P. (1977, May). How to make sure your next résumé isn't an obituary. *Training,* 63–66.

Sample Speech*

Introduction

getting
attention

I am here today in three capacities. The first is as a native Californian—this has been my home for most of my life, and I only regret that my job requires me to be away from the Golden State most of the time. I have been here, though, for most of the last month, enjoying the sun and the ocean, my friends and my family—including the newest addition, my four-year-old grandson.

establishing
ethos

I mention him—his name is Patrick Elton Dunne—because being here in California and seeing him has reminded me again of what a wonderful place this is to raise children, and also because my second capacity today is that of a parent—a person who has children, and now a grandchild as well, and who thinks often of the many large and small influences that shape our children into adults.

stated
purpose

My third capacity today is that of a broadcaster, which I have been most of my adult life—a person who has some responsibility for one of those influences, the television set in the living room. It is only in the last few years that most of us, parents and broadcasters alike, have realized just how sizable a role television plays in the lives of our children. The realization has been a sobering one. We have spent a great deal of effort trying to discover just what it is that our children get from their television watching—and when we haven't liked the answers, trying to improve the situation. We have asked what the proper role of television ought to be in the growth of our children and where the responsibility for it lies. In the next few minutes, I would like to offer a few of my own conclusions on this subject.

*Elton H. Rule (President, American Broadcasting Companies, Inc.), "Children's Television Viewing: The Parent's Role," in *Vital Speeches*, 43, 1 (15 October 1976), 24–26. Speech was delivered before the Rotary Club of Los Angeles, Los Angeles, California, 3 September 1976.

Body

ethos
ethics

Let me begin by admitting one of my own personal prejudices. We have all heard a great deal about what's wrong with the younger generation: that they are alienated, apathetic, illiterate, promiscuous—and so forth. No doubt there are a good many children who do have those and other problems. But my own feeling is that, by and large, today's youngsters are turning out very well. At six and at 16, they are often surprisingly mature and interesting people—people who know more about their world, and themselves, than I would have expected.

assertion

suppport

If there's any truth to this impression, I also believe that the presence of television may have been one positive contributor. Television is, after all, a window on the world wider than any previous generation has ever known—one that offers an incredible exposure to people, places, and events that were once only topics in textbooks. And television is an effective communicator—from one recent study in Michigan State University, we know that there is a distinct correlation between how much television young children watch and how much they know about current events and discuss these events with their parents. More than that, television can aid personal, emotional development; in entertainment as well as informational programs, children can gain insights into how other people live, how they relate to each other, and especially how they deal with problems common to us all.

problem
counter-
support vague
testimony goal

That's not to say television cannot cause problems for children. It can. This has been brought home to us very forcefully by parents of all descriptions since television began to assume a greater role in their home lives. Beginning about five years ago, our industry—and ABC in particular—embarked on an intense and still-continuing search for ways to improve its programs as they relate to younger viewers.

examples

This effort has involved not only those in the industry, but a broad spectrum of educators and child psychiatrists, not to mention a great many parents and children. It has brought to the screen programs altogether new to the medium—from Saturday morning news programs for children to original weekday afternoon dramatic specials both for and about children. It has brought a new policy, called "family viewing," to evening television; it provides for early-evening programs which are suitable for viewing by the entire family. And it has completely changed the face of the weekend programs made specifically for children.

problem
assertion
goal

One major area of concern has been the portrayal of violence (or the threat of violence) in these programs. Early on, we at ABC pledged ourselves to eliminate gratuitous acts of violence from our programs, and as a result of similar actions throughout the industry, the overall amount of violence has been declining on television. To eliminate all acts of violence would be to deny reality, however, so we needed also to learn to ensure that what violence remained had constructive value. We knew relatively little about how to do this at the beginning, so we spent $1 million on two five-year research projects by three distinguished experts in the area.

That phase of their work is now completed, and from their findings we have been able to develop some workable guidelines for the producers of our programs and for our own editors. Let me cite some examples: The presentation of violence should exclude details which could be imitated by a viewer; it should be used clearly as a dramatic example of what should not be done; and the negative consequences of such violence should be demonstrated. There is much more to be done in this area, and our research is continuing, but I think we are definitely moving in the right direction.

In addition to the question of violence, we were concerned about the ideas young viewers were getting from the programs they watched. Recently, one of our consultants, Dr. William Hooks of the Bank Street College of Education, made a list of some of the qualities we would like to shine through our programs. It is keyed to the word "respect," and I would like to repeat it here:

respect for the individual;
respect for differences;
respect for religious beliefs and ethnic qualities;
respect for all animal life and for the environment;
respect for private and public property;
respect for moral values;
respect for the feelings and sensitivities of others;
and, not least, respect for oneself.

We hope all the programs our young viewers see can live up to this principle of respect. We take very seriously our responsibility for our younger viewers.

But let me emphasize that ours is only a part of the overall responsibility for the effect that television has our children. We in the television industry can control our programs and what happens to them right up to the point where they enter the home. But in the living room or the family room, control can be exercised only by parents. The most constructive use of television for children can come about only through the sharing of responsibility by broadcaster and parent.

Recently, the Roper Organization asked a national sample of parents with children under the age of 16 what sorts of rules they had for their children. As you'd expect, a sizable majority had strict rules about what their children ate, what time they went to bed on weeknights, when they did their homework (if they had homework), and knowing where they went when they left the house.

But the Roper people also asked parents what sorts of rules they had about television viewing. And they found that only about two-fifths had rules about what programs their children were allowed to watch. Less than a third of those with children under the age of 12 have rules about letting children watch television after 9 P.M. And those who do have such rules based them on the lateness

Margin annotations:

examples

problem

testimony

repetition
device

assertion

solution

support

statistics

assertion

of the hour, not on the kinds of programs which are on at that hour. We know, too, from other research, that most parents are not present when their children do the greatest part of their viewing.

What this appears to mean is that parents who take active charge of most of the elements of their children's upbringing allow a kind of anarchy to prevail where television viewing is concerned. To me, this is a cause for real concern. Children are unique creatures, with their own personal areas of knowledge and ignorance, their own needs and fears and insecurities. No television program, no matter how sensitively it is designed, can be guaranteed to affect all children in the same way.

support & clarification anecdote

A given television program may inform a child—or it may confuse him. It may delight a child—or it may disturb him. The difference is the degree of his parent's involvement. Eda LeShan, a noted expert in the field of child psychology, tells the story of a mother whose marriage was collapsing. She thought she and her husband had shielded their problems from their 11-year-old son, until the day she and her son watched an ABC Afterschool Special dealing with divorce.

The mother reported that "as the program went on, Andy kept inching closer and closer to me. I put my arm around him and suddenly realized his whole body was trembling. It was a terrible shock. I realized that he had known all along what was going on, was terrified, and that my husband and I should have discussed it with him a long time before. That program kicked off the most honest and important conversation I'd ever had with my child." We can all wonder what effect the program would have had on the child if his mother hadn't been there.

note transition support

That's an extreme example, but a revealing one. Let me offer a different one, from a study conducted at the University of Texas not long ago. An episode of a television program was shown in which playing hooky was involved. With one group of preschoolers, a teacher commented during the show that "that boy is in trouble. He did not go to school when he was supposed to. He was playing hooky, and that is bad." The other group didn't get that comment. Before and after the show, both groups were asked whether they thought playing hooky was all right. For the boys, the percentage of those who thought playing hooky was a bad idea increased 75 percent among those who heard the teacher's comment; it decreased among those who didn't. For the girls, the number improved 120 percent among those who heard the comment, and 80 percent among those who didn't.

statistics

assertion

Based on observations of this sort, the Texas study concluded that "parents are the single most important contributor to a child's development. Furthermore, while most parents believe they are in hopeless conflict with the ever-present television, the project's results indicate parents can directly and easily moderate the influence of television. The results indicate that parents should not

assertion

let the television become a surrogate parent. Instead, parents should watch television with their child and talk about the programs."

Problem

testimony

Eda LeShan put the same thought very succinctly: "No [television] program can seriously damage a child in any way if a concerned and loving adult shares the experience and uses it as an opportunity to talk about feelings."

Solution

So much for the problem. How is it to be solved? To begin with, I do not believe that parents are thoughtless, selfish creatures who have abandoned their children to the television set—any more than I believe that television is a vicious electronic monster programmed to corrupt the youth of America. I do think, though, that there are a good many parents who are still learning how to cope with the presence of the television set in their home, who—not knowing quite what to do about it—do nothing at all about it.

ethos

For that reason, we have tried to draw together from our outside consultants—people like Dr. Melvin Heller, an eminent child psychiatrist at Temple University, and the people at the Bank Street College of Education—a few suggestions for parents to help them deal with their children and their television set. They may sound a little obvious, but they can make a difference.

solutions
assertions
clarification

First suggestion: Know what your children watch. See the programs for yourself, and read about them as well. Not every program is suitable for every child of every age, especially late at night when we offer programs designed for more mature audiences. All the television networks provide advisory notices when the subject matter of a program may be unsuitable for younger viewers, but the final decision must rest with the parents, who know their children best. It is imperative that parents make those decisions actively, not by default. And it's useful, too, if children know the standards by which their parents select programs for viewing.

clarification

Second suggestion: Watch television with your children. No, this does not mean watch every program with your children; there's absolutely no harm in their watching television while you snatch an extra hour's sleep on Saturday morning. But do try to watch some of the things your children watch, in the morning and the afternoon as well as the evening. That is the only way to know how they react, as well as what they are reacting to.

clarification

Third suggestion: Comment on the things you see with your children. When you read stories to your children at bedtime, you probably comment on the things you are reading. Even the smallest remarks, such as "gee, that was scary, wasn't it?" can make a difference in the effect an episode has on your children.

clarification

Fourth suggestion: Use your family television viewing as a basis for conversations. Many families find serious discussion difficult during their children's growing-up years; communication about personal feelings and experiences is

clarification

sometimes almost nonexistent. But those feelings can often be unlocked and those experiences shared, if parents will use similar situations seen on television to initiate dialogue with their children. And there are also a number of educators who have devised games and other techniques by which parents can use television to further their children's education.

ethos

And, finally, a fifth suggestion which does not come from our consultants, but from me: Let us know what you think of the programs you watch with your children. It is an unfortunate truth that exceptional programs, for children as well as for adults, cost more than routine programs. We do not begrudge the cost of exceptional programs for children, any more than we begrudge the cost of covering a presidential election or the Olympic Games, but we need to know when our efforts succeed.

Conclusion

repetition of
main points

problem

Whether a child watches five hours of television a week, or 25, his viewing is an important part of his life. Knowing that imposes an awesome responsibility on all of us in the television industry, and we have committed ourselves in the strongest possible terms to live up to that responsibility. But the quality of our efforts can only be as good as the use to which they are put in the home. For parents who pay little or no attention to their children's television viewing, television is no more than an electronic baby-sitter, an informative and entertaining gadget whose value will vary from child to child in unpredictable—and sometimes undesirable—fashion. This we must try to avoid.

solution

On the other hand, for parents who grasp firmly their share of the responsibility, who actively involve themselves in their children's viewing experience, television can be—and will be—a significant and constructive contributor to the growth of the generation of young people that will take over where we, their parents, leave off. That is the goal all of us should work toward. At ABC, we are doing everything we can to reach that goal, and we hope all of you will share this responsibility with us.

Sample
Student Outlines*

Outline 1 Title: The Role of Comic Books in American Society

I. Introduction
    A. "Outside, the London nightlife is just beginning. Trafalgar Square is crammed with curious tourists, St. Martin's Lane bustling with anxious theatregoers. Inside, a lone woman makes a fateful decision. "Is this what I've become? A thief? A scavenger? Heaven help me, I'm reduced to stealing food to live. Is this my curse for becoming the Spider-woman?"
    B. Comic books are a part of every kid's and many adults' lives.
    C. Comic books are a part of the media in the United States.
        1. As a medium, comic books reflect some of society's attitudes and values.
        2. Three comic books, *Red Sonja, Ms. Marvel,* and *Spiderwoman,* reflect our notions about women.

II. Body
    A. Three comics are published by Marvel comics, but each has its own history.
        1. *Red Sonja* first appeared in 1975.
            a. The origin of Red Sonja is unclear.
            b. Red Sonja lives in the "Hyporian Age" in the distant past.

---

*These outlines were prepared by Debbie Smith of Southwest Texas State University and are reproduced with her permission.

       2. *Ms. Marvel* was presented in January 1977.

         a. Ms. Marvel has amnesia and does not know her origins.

         b. Ms. Marvel is a superhero in the tradition of Superman.

       3. *Spiderwoman* is the newest of the female superheroes, with her first issue appearing in April 1978.

         a. Jessica Drew (Spiderwoman) is half-spider, half-woman from another world.

         b. Spiderwoman is attempting to learn to live on earth.

  B. Violence is an aspect of all three comics, but each deals with violence in a different way.

       1. *Red Sonja* is a graphically violent comic book.

         a. The only weapons Red Sonja uses are her blade and sword.

         b. Red Sonja kills for self-preservation and pay.

       2. Ms. Marvel fights violence in true superhero tradition.

         a. The violence in the comic is beyond the comprehension of mortal man.

         b. *Ms. Marvel* involves fantasy violence where no one is killed or seriously injured since they are super villains.

       3. Spiderwoman uses violence only for justifiable reasons.

         a. Spiderwoman fights for the good of society.

         b. In the first issue, she does not use her full power even against a criminal.

  C. Each of the three comics makes a statement about women.

       1. Red Sonja is considered the "she-devil with a sword."

         a. The comic does not deal with women's rights specifically since it is set in the distant past.

         b. Red Sonja fights her battles alone.

       2. It is obvious from the title *Ms. Marvel* that this comic has been influenced by the women's movement.

         a. Ms. Marvel's slogan is, "This female fights back."

         b. Carol Danvers (Ms. Marvel's alter identity) is the editor of a feminist magazine.

       3. Spiderwoman is learning how to deal with her identity while living on earth.

         a. The comic says, "To know her is to fear her."

         b. Spiderwoman is searching for her own identity.

III. Conclusion

  A. The comics present strong, independent women.

  B. Solo female superheroes, while not very real, do suggest a growing awareness of women.

  C. But perhaps the comics say it best: "Like the Valkyrie guards of Valhalla, she sweeps across the face of the earth, arms as widespread as an eagle's wings, eyes burning, jaw set, every sinew throbbing with battle anticipation . . . her name is her own, but for want of something better we may call her Marvel, Ms. Marvel, and because of her the world may never be the same."

Outline 2   Title: Crime and the Elderly
  I. Introduction
    A. A New York couple—Hans Kabel, 78, and his wife Emma, 76—were assaulted twice in less than two months.
    B. The older people in our cities are viewed as victims or potential victims of criminals.
      1. Most are poor and unable to move.
      2. The elderly are living in fear in the cities.
  II. Body
    A. Fear of a criminal attack is now the major concern of the elderly.
      1. New York City officials believe that there are 30 victims for every crime reported.
      2. Chicago demonstrates the plight of the elderly.
        a. On the South Side, the elderly are faced with gangs of potential assailants on the first of the month, when Social Security checks arrive.
        b. On the West Side, no one goes out after dark.
      3. Statistically, the elderly are not victimized more than any other age group, but the impact is more severe.
        a. Physical injury is greater for the elderly in an assault.
        b. Emotionally, elderly persons' lives are governed by fear of an attack.
    B. The assailants of the elderly are primarily young juvenile criminals.
      1. The crimes are called "crib jobs" because it is like taking candy from a baby.
        a. The youngsters usually operate in teams.
        b. The elderly are young criminals' ideal victims.
      2. The rights of juveniles are so well protected that it is almost impossible for there to be repercussions.
        a. About 75 percent of the juveniles apprehended have been arrested before.
        b. Prosecutors are prevented from revealing a juvenile's arrest record.
      3. Judges do not know if they are dealing with a first offender or a longtime criminal.
      4. A juvenile who had beaten and robbed an 82-year-old woman was released on a $500 bond even though he had 67 previous arrests, one for murder.
      5. Violent crime against the elderly is increasing.
        a. In Seattle, violent street crime has increased 18 percent.

        b. In New York, two 16-year-olds raped a 75-year-old woman.

        c. In Detroit, an 80-year-old woman was killed because she clung to her purse.

    C. Cities have started several programs to help solve the problem.

       1. Seattle engages policemen to serve as decoys.

       2. Chicago, Los Angeles, and New York have received federal funds to start self-help and victim assistance programs.

       3. San Francisco provides an escort service for the elderly.

       4. In Charleston, West Virginia, elderly residents call in to the police department each day.

       5. In some cities, high school students serve as escorts for the elderly.

    D. The best solution is to have more police patrolling the streets.

       1. New York City has done this in a few areas, and it has been very successful.

       2. It is the solution most often recommended by the elderly.

  III. Conclusion

    A. Crimes against the elderly are significant and increasing.

    B. Solutions exist that can help solve the problem.

    C. Unfortunately there are also counterproductive solutions. The Kabels, the elderly couple mentioned at the beginning of the speech, used a counterproductive solution—dual suicide—saying they did not want to live in fear anymore.

Outline 3   Title: Implications of Group Ownership in the Newspaper Industry

  I. Introduction

    A. In 1960, chains and conglomerates controlled 30 percent of the nation's newspapers and 46 percent of the readership.

    B. In 1977, chains and conglomerates controlled 59 percent of the newspapers and 71 percent of the readership.

    C. There has been a growing concern about the increasing group ownership of American newspapers.

  II. Body

    A. Increasing chain ownership is not viewed as threatening by some people.

       1. Chain ownership saves newspapers.

         a. Small newspapers that are going under are bought by large chains.

         b. The chains have more money to invest in the newspapers to keep them in business.

       2. The chains are improving the quality of the newspapers they buy.

         a. The chains hire more staff for the newspapers.

         b. The chains add additional news services.

       3. Some of the leading newspapers in the country, such as the *Washington Post* and *Los Angeles Times,* are owned by conglomerates.

B. Chain ownership is perceived as destructive to the press in the United States.
  1. Chains are concerned with profits.
     a. Profits take precedence over quality.
     b. Concern with profits conflicts with serving the public interest.
  2. Competition is necessary for a good press.
     a. Without competition an inferior product can be produced without challenge.
     b. With chain ownership there is no competition.
  3. Chains do not improve the quality of the newspapers.
     a. Papers tend to stay mediocre if bought by a chain.
     b. Outstanding newspapers have never been created by chains.
C. Chain ownership threatens the free press.
  1. Chain ownership violates the intent of a strong, free press.
  2. Newspapers play a special role as sources of opinion and information that should not be controlled by a limited number of owners.

III. Conclusion
  A. Chain ownership has reached epidemic proportions.
  B. The trend is continuing at a fast rate.
  C. Something should be done to prevent domination of such an important source of public information as newspapers.

Selected Bibliography

AJZEN, I. (1989). Attitude structure and behavior. In A. R. Pratkanis, S. J. Breckler, & A. G. Greenwald, (Eds.), *Attitude structure and function.* Hillsdale, NJ: Lawrence Erlbaum Associates, 241–274.

ATKIN, C. (1983). Effects of realistic TV violence vs. fictional violence on aggression. *Journalism Quarterly, 60*(4), 615–621.

ATKINS, C. P. (1988). Perceptions of speakers with minimal eye contact: Implications for stutterers. *Journal of Fluency Disorders, 13,* 429–436.

BARKER, L. L., JOHNSON, P. M., & WATSON, K. W. (1991). The role of listening in managing interpersonal and group conflict. In D. Borisoff & M. Purdy (Eds.). *Listening in everyday life.* New York: University Press of America, 139–162.

BLACK, J. (1970). *How to get results from interviewing.* New York: McGraw-Hill.

BOHANNON, J. N. III, MACWHINNEY, B., & SNOW, C. (1990). No negative evidence revisited: Beyond learnability or who has to prove what to whom. *Developmental Psychology, 26*(2), 221–226.

BRODER, S. N. (1987). Helping students with self-disclosure. *School Counselor, 34*(3), 182–187.

CALTABIANO, M. L., & SMITHSON, M. (1983). Variables affecting the perception of self-disclosure appropriateness. *Journal of Social Psychology, 120,* 119–128.

CANARY, D. J., CUNNINGHAM, E. M., & CODY, M. J. (1988). Goal types, gender, and locus of control in managing interpersonal conflict. *Communication Research, 15*(4), 426–446.

CHANEY, R. H., GIVENS, C. A., AOKI, M. F., & GOMBINER, M. L. (1989). Pupillary responses in recognizing awareness in persons with profound mental retardation. *Perceptual and Motor Skills, 69,* 523–528.

CHRISTEN, Y. (1991). *Sex differences: Modern biology and the unisex fallacy.* New Brunswick, NJ: Transaction Publishers.

DANCE, F. E. X., & LARSON, C. (1976). *The functions of human communication.* New York: Holt, Rinehart & Winston.

DEWINE, S., AND CASBOLT, D. (1983). Networking: External communication systems for female organizational members. *The Journal of Business Communication, 20*(2), 57–67.

EKMAN, P., & FRIESEN, W. V. (1969). The repertoire of non-verbal behavior: Categories, origins, usage, and coding. *Semiotica, 1*(1), 49–98.

FIELD, H. S., & HOLLEY, W. H. (1976). Résumé preparation: An empirical study of personnel managers' perceptions. *The Vocational Guidance Quarterly* (March), 234.

FUKADA, H. (1986). Psychological processes mediating persuasion-inhibiting effect of forewarning in fear-arousing communication. *Psychological Reports, 58,* 87–90.

GALST, J. P. (1980). Television food commercials and pro-nutritional public service announcements as determinants of young children's snack choices. *Child Development, 51,* 935–938.

GAMBLE, T. K., & GAMBLE, M. (1982). *Contacts: Communicating interpersonally.* New York: Random House.

HAN, PYUNG. (1983). The informal organization you've got to live with. *Supervisory Management, 28,* 25–28.

HAZLETON, V., CUPACH, W. R., & LISKA, J. (1986). Message style: An investigation of the perceived characteristics of persuasive messages. *Journal of Social Behavior and Personality, 1*(4), 565–574.

HESS, H. (1965). Attitude and pupil size. *Scientific American, 212*(4), 54.

HOLLIMAN, W. B., & ANDERSON, H. N. (1986). Proximity and student density as ecological variables in a college classroom. *Teaching of Psychology, 13*(4), 200–203.

HOLLINGWORTH, H. L. (1935). *The psychology of the audience.* New York: American Book.

HORNSTEIN, G. A., & TRUESDELL, S. E. (1988). Development of intimate conversation in close relationships. *Journal of Social and Clinical Psychology, 7*(1), 49–64.

JANIS, I. L. (1982). *Victims of groupthink: A psychological study of foreign policy decisions and fiascos* (2d ed.). Boston: Houghton Mifflin.

KEREK, G. M. (1987). Can functions be measured? A new perspective on the functional approach to attitudes. *Social Psychology Quarterly, 50*(4), 285–303.

KLEINKE, C. L. (1986). Gaze and eye contact: A research review. *Psychological Bulletin, 100*(1), 78–100.

KNAPP, M. L. (1984). *Interpersonal communication and human relationships.* Boston: Allyn & Bacon.

LAZOWSKI, L. E., & ANDERSEN, S. M. (1990). Self-disclosure and social perception: The impact of private, negative, and extreme communications. *Journal of Social Behavior and Personality, 5*(2), 131–154.

LEEDS, D. (1988). *PowerSpeak: The complete guide to persuasive public speaking and presenting.* New York: Prentice Hall Press.

LUFT, J. (1984). *Of human interaction.* Palo Alto, CA: National Press Books.

LYNN, R., HAMPSON, S., & AGAHI, E. (1989). Television violence and aggression: A genotype-environment, correlation and interaction theory. *Social Behavior and Personality, 17*(2), 143–164.

MAASS, A., SALVI, D., ARCURI, L., & SEMIN, G. (1989). Language use in intergroup contexts: The linguistic intergroup bias. *Journal of Personality and Social Psychology, 57*(6), 981–993.

MASLOW, A. H., & MINTZ, N. L. (1956). Effects of esthetic surroundings. I. Initial effects of three esthetic conditions upon perceiving "energy" and "well-being" in faces. *Journal of Psychology, 41,* 247–254.

MILLARD, R. J., & STIMPSON, D. V. (1980). Enjoyment and productivity as a function of classroom seating location. *Perceptual Motor Skills, 50,* 439–444.

MULAC, A., WIEMANN, J. M., WIDENMANN, S. J., & GIBSON, T. W. (1988). Male/female language differences and effects in same-sex and mixed-sex dyads: The gender-linked language effect. *Communication Monographs, 55*(4), 315–335.

NASH, L. L. (1990). Ethics without the sermon. In W. M. Hoffman and J. M. Moore, *Business ethics: Readings and cases in corporate morality* (2d ed.). New York: McGraw-Hill.

NEIMEYER, R. A., & MITCHELL, K. A. (1988). Similarity and attraction: A longitudinal study. *Journal of Social and Personal Relationships, 5,* 131–148.

NORRIS, P. (1986). Biofeedback, voluntary control, and human potential. *Biofeedback and Self-Regulation, 11*(1), 1–19.

PEARCE, W. B., & CONKLIN, F. (1971). Nonverbal vocalic communication and perceptions of a speaker. *Speech Monographs, 38,* 235–241.

PEARCE, W. B., & CRONEN, V. (1980). *Communication, action, and meaning.* New York: Praeger.

PEARL, D. (1984). Violence and aggression. *Society, 21,* 17–22.

PRIZANT, B. M., & WETHERBY, A. M. (1990). Toward an integrated view of early language and communication development and socio-emotional development. *Topics in Language Disorders, 10*(4), 1–16.

RODDY, B. L., & GARRAMONE, G. M. (1988). Appeals and strategies of negative political advertising. *Journal of Broadcasting & Electronic Media, 32*(4), 415–427.

ROSENKOETTER, L. I., HUSTON, A. C., & WRIGHT, J. C. (1990). Television and the moral judgment of the young child. *Journal of Applied Developmental Psychology, 11,* 123–137.

RULE, B. G., & FERGUSON, T. J. (1986). The effects of media violence on attitudes, emotions, and cognitions. *Journal of Social Issues, 42*(3), 29–50.

SALTER, C. A., & SALTER, C. D. (1982). Automobile color as a predictor of driving behavior. *Perceptual and Motor Skills, 55,* 383–386.

SELLERS, D. E., & STACKS, D. W. (1990). Toward a hemispheric processing approach to communication competence. *Journal of Social Behavior and Personality, 5*(2), 45–59.

SMITH, A. P. (1977). How to make sure your next résumé isn't an obituary. *Training* (May), 63–66.

SPARKS, G. G. (1986). Developmental differences in children's reports of fear induced by the mass media. *Child Study Journal, 16*(1), 55.

STANAT, K. W., & REARDON, P. (1977). *Job hunting secrets and tactics.* Milwaukee: Westwind Press.

STEIL, L. K., BARKER, L. L., & WATSON, K. W. (1983). *Effective listening: Key to your success.* Reading, MA: Addison-Wesley.

STEWART, C. J., & CASH, W. B. (1983). *Interviewing: Principles and practices* (3d ed.). Dubuque, IA: Wm. C. Brown.

TESSER, A., & SHAFFER, D. R. (1990). Attitudes and attitude change. *Annual Review of Psychology, 41,* 479–523.

WASS, H., RAUP, J. L., & SISLER, H. H. (1989). Adolescents and death on television: A follow-up study. *Death Studies, 13,* 161–173.

WATSON, K. W., & BARKER, L. L. (1991). *Presentation skills manual: A guide to effective oral presentations.* New Orleans, LA: Spectra, Inc.

WATSON, K. W., & BARKER, L. L. (1992). *Personal listening preference profile.* New Orleans, LA: Spectra, Inc.

WHAT TV DOES TO KIDS. (21 February 1977). *Newsweek,* 63–70.

WHETMORE, E. J. (1991). *Mediamerica* (4th ed.). Belmont, CA.: Wadsworth

Glossary

Abstract Representing feelings or thoughts that cannot be sensed directly.

Accenting Use of gestures such as nods, blinks, squints, and shrugs to help emphasize or punctuate spoken words.

Acceptance Speech A speech designed for the acceptance of an honor or award.

Accuracy Precise use of words.

Action-Oriented Listener Listener who is task-oriented and prefers information to be presented in a logical, organized way.

Active Listening A series of interrelated processes including attending, perceiving, interpreting, assessing, and responding.

Advertising Method of persuasion concerned with influencing people to buy, or to continue to buy, a product.

Affect Display Body change that conveys internal emotional states.

Affective Dimension The dimension of listening associated with emotional or feeling states.

After-Dinner Speech In general, a form of entertainment speech intended to make the audience feel relaxed and comfortable.

All-Channel Network Communication network in which all positions send and receive messages to and from all other positions.

Alternating Monologue Unproductive communication in which each person knows the other is speaking but does not listen openly to what is being said.

Ambiguity Language difficulty caused when one symbol (word) has several different meanings.

Ambiguous Feedback Response that gives no indication that the message has been received positively or negatively.

Anecdote A brief account of an entertaining or interesting moment.

Antientropic The possibility for a system to move away from randomness or disorganization as a function of communication.

Appraisal Interview Designed to get and evaluate information about a worker's past performance and future potential.

Appropriateness Use of language style that is adapted to the occasion, audience, and type and purpose of the speech.

Articulation Process by which the voice is altered into recognizable speech sounds.

Assessing Making judgments about a message and its importance to us.

Assimilation The process of incorporating some aspect of the environment into the whole set of mental functionings in order to make sense of what goes on around us.

Attending The initial step of the listening process. Involves focusing attention on a message.

Attitude Learned tendency to react positively or negatively to an object or situation.

Attraction Positive attitude, movement toward, or liking between two people.

Audience Analysis The act of acquainting yourself with the audience before giving a speech.

Autocratic Leader A leader who is extremely goal-oriented, has firm opinions on how to accomplish these goals, and is highly direct in his or her leadership approach.

Avoiding Relationship disintegration stage in which one or both parties act as though the other person does not exist.

Award Presentation A speech designed for the presentation of an honor or award.

Barrier Factor that causes incorrect meanings, or no meanings, to be communicated.

Behavioral/Interactive Dimension The dimension of listening associated with our awareness of the relational elements of communication.

Behavioral/Nonverbal Dimension The dimension of listening associated with the nonverbal behavior we exhibit.

Behavioral/Verbal Dimension The dimension of listening associated with the actual verbal behavior we exhibit.

Belief Probability statements about the existence of things or statements about the relationships between an object and another quality or thing.

Biofeedback A form of external self-feedback used to control physiological processing.

Biological Perspectives View human communication as derived from genetic, biological, physiological, and neurophysiological processes.

Body Manipulator Movement originally associated with body functioning, but that has come to be used unconsciously and independently of bodily needs.

Body of a Speech Portion of the speech that elaborates and clarifies the main points for an audience.

Bonding Final stage of relationship development; usually signifies commitment through a formal contract.

Bureaucracy An organization that relies heavily on rules, regulations, and policies to establish authority, rather than on a single charismatic leader.

Business Meeting Small group within an organization that meets to disseminate information or develop solutions to current organizational problems.

Bypassing A situation in which people are actually talking past each other.

Casual Audience Small, heterogeneous group of people who gather at the same place for a short period of time.

Cause-and-Effect Pattern In a speech, a persuasive structure of organization that establishes a relationship between two events.

Central Route According to the Elaboration Likelihood Model, one of two means of persuasion. Persuasion that results when a listener thinks actively about an issue being discussed.

Chain Network Similar to the circle communication network, except that the members at each end of the chain send messages to and receive messages from only one position.

Chain-of-Events Pattern Informative organizational structure based on the development of a series of steps, with each step dependent upon the previous one.

Change Agent One who is responsible for making policy and creating change.

Channel The conduit through which a message is sent.

Chat Room A technology-based group of people who regularly take part in real-time conversations online.

Chronological Pattern Informative pattern of organization that follows a subject through time.

Circle Network Communication network in which messages are sent to the left and right of a position, but not to other members in the group.

Circular/Interaction-Based Models Models of communication that generally include all of the elements of linear models plus the concept of feedback.

Circular Response Mutual feedback between speaker and audience that increases participation and strengthens the bonds between them.

Circumscribing Controlled disintegration stage with less total communication and expression of commitment.

Clarity The art of saying exactly what is meant, thus increasing audience comprehension.

Cognitive Dimension The dimension of listening associated with formal (and active) information processing.

Cognitive Processing Storage, retrieval, sorting, and assimilation of information.

Cohesion The degree to which group members identify themselves as a group or team, rather than merely a collection of individuals.

Comparison-Contrast Defining a word, idea, or concept by pointing out similarities and/or differences between it and something with which the audience is already familiar.

Competence One of three dimensions of source credibility, which speakers are perceived to possess when they come across as intelligent, bright, well trained, informed, and experts in the subject matter under discussion.

Complementary Relationship A relationship in which one person is more dominant and the other person is less so.

Complementing Messages Nonverbal messages that complete or accent explanations and/or descriptions.

Composite Audience An audience that is heterogeneous in terms of demographics, attitudes, beliefs, values, and attitudes toward the speaker, subject, and purpose of a presentation.

Concerted Audience Collected group of individuals with an active purpose and mutual interest without separation of labor or strict organization of authority.

Conclusion of Speech Final portion of speech, which summarizes and reinforces the speaker's point of view.

Concrete Symbolizing objects or events that can be pointed to, touched, vicariously experienced, or directly experienced.

Conflict Management Means by which two or more people settle disputes or conflicts.

Conformity Occurs when all group members agree to abide by the outcome of a group decision.

Connotation Meanings beyond the objective reference of a word (abstract meaning).

Constitutive Rule A rule that defines what a given act (or behavior) should "count as" and allows us to decide what each others' behavior "means."

Constructive Conflict Type of conflict that leads to innovation.

Content-Oriented Listener Listener who focuses easily on the content of a message and tends to critically evaluate all incoming information.

Context Circumstances that surround and give meaning to words and statements.

Control The dimension of interpersonal relationships that focuses on the distribution of power.

Coordinated Management of Meaning Theory of communication that focuses on how humans coordinate and manage meanings in everyday life.

Covert Stimuli External changes or actions received at the subconscious level.

Cultural Diversity The sum total of the different ways of life, behaviors, and beliefs reflected by the individuals who constitute a particular group or team.

Cultural/Social Perspectives View human communication as a process that is learned via cultural and social influences.

Dampening Strategy used by listeners to calm a speaker when he or she is experiencing a negative emotional state.

Deception Cues Cues that suggest possible falsehood but do not tell what information is being withheld or falsified.

Decoding The process of interpreting or translating incoming stimuli (e.g., words) into thoughts, ideas, and concepts.

Deductive Pattern Persuasive structure that applies a previously accepted generalization to a specific case.

Deductive Reasoning Moves from the general to the specific.

Defense Mechanism Method of resolving anxiety produced by intrapersonal conflict.

Defensive Attitudinal Function Function of attitudes expressed whenever we experience some form of personal anxiety or insecurity regarding the target in question.

Delivery Physical and vocal elements of a speaker's presentation.

Delivery Function Function of nonverbal communication associated with how humans use nonverbal cues for self-expression and the exchange of information about the outside world.

Demassification Using channels of communication to reach highly specialized interest groups.

Democratic Leader A leader who guides rather than directs a group.

Demography Statistical study of populations (age, sex, educational levels, etc.).

Denotation Objective reference of a word (its factual, concrete meaning).

Description Method of defining a word, idea, or concept.

Destructive Conflict Type of conflict that leads to disharmony that often damages relationships.

Differentiating Relationship state characterized by increased interpersonal distance.

Diffusion of Information Manner in which the public learns about new events, products, and changes in policy, ideas, philosophies, and so forth.

Digging Strategy to help listeners discover underlying issues and concerns by reflecting on the emotions and thoughts of speakers.

Directive Interview Structured and planned interaction situation that is generally conducted by using a step-by-step outline or format of questions.

Discourse Ethic The art of questioning oneself and others before constructing a persuasive message.

Discussion Group Group of three or more persons characterized by cooperation among members, face-to-face interaction, shared perceptions, and verbal and nonverbal communication.

Dogmatism Personality trait characterized by a closed mind and a reluctance to accept new ideas and opinions.

Downward Communication Information messages directed to subordinates within an organization.

Dyad Two people in close physical contact.

Early Childhood Period of language learning that takes place from approximately 24 to 48 months.

Economy Use of the right words in the most efficient manner.

Efficacy Message A persuasive message often associated with fear appeals, which focuses on the benefits of adopting the speaker's position rather than on the consequences of not adopting the position.

Ego Needs The human need to think well of ourselves.

Emblem Commonly recognized sign (usually a gesture) that communicates a message usually unrelated to an ongoing conversation.

Emotion Function Function of nonverbal communication associated with the stimulus-response process that motivates an organism to engage in behavior that is essential for the survival of its species.

Emotional Processing Nonlogical response of an organism to a stimulus.

Employment Interview Situation in which employers and applicants attempt to get pertinent information before making hiring decisions.

Encoding The process of translating ideas, concepts, and intentions into verbal and nonverbal messages.

Entropy The tendency of a system to become random or disorganized.

Episodes Interpretable and meaningful patterns of behavior that emerge through communication.

Equal Time Rule Stations must give all political candidates the same amount of time under the same terms.

Equifinality The idea that there are many ways for a system to reach its goals.

Ethic of Care The extent to which we respond with compassion and love to the needs of another person while we are communicating with him or her.

Ethic of Resistance While communicating, the extent to which we maintain a space for ourselves and others to position themselves as freely choosing agents even in the face of oppressive practices and discourses that threaten to marginalize or constrain them.

Ethical Communicator As a communicator, the extent to which you create messages that are "right, proper, just, honorable, decent, upright, principled, fair, honest, good, and virtuous."

Ethos Perception of the speaker by the audience (source credibility).

Eulogy Farewell speech that marks someone's death.

Evaluation Group Uses information from the fact-finding group to determine the scope of a problem and the priorities in finding a solution.

Exemplar Short quotations (verbal or visual) from a credible source that are presented in a message to illustrate a particular problem or view point.

Exit Interview Situation designed to find out how an employee feels about the company, work environment, and job conditions after he or she has decided to leave the position.

Experiential-Schematic Attitudinal Function Function of attitudes that involves the general cognitive maps that we develop about a target object, issue, person, or group.

Experimenting The "do you know" period of interaction development.

Extended Example Illustration or story carried out to considerable length in order to clarify or emphasize a very important idea.

External Self-Feedback Part of a person's own message that is heard by the person.

External Stimuli Stimuli that originate in the environment outside of the human body.

Extrinsic Motivation Motivation that arises from an outside source (such as extra credit points).

Face-to-Face Group A group whose members meet in the same locale, and are able to see and hear one another during the process of interacting.

Fact-Finding Group Type of problem-solving group that gathers as much information as possible about a particular issue or problem.

Fairness Doctrine All stations must provide time to discuss controversial issues and must encourage opposing viewpoints.

Farewell Speech Expresses regret about leaving and thanks those left behind.

Fear-Arousing Appeal Threat or scare tactic designed to persuade.

Feedback A listener's response to a speaker's message.

Field of Experience The sum total of a person's cultural and life experiences, beliefs, values, attitudes, language, and so on.

Focus Group A group comprised of members of a certain target audience that uses a particular product or service.

Focusing Taking responsibility for the success of communication by preparing oneself to listen.

Forewarning Information about the speaker's intent given prior to the speech.

Formal Communication Structured communication situation in which more attention is paid to both verbal and nonverbal messages.

Formal Communication Structure Rules, regulations, and procedures within an organization.

Formal Presentation The most structured form of organizational communication, in which responsibility is placed on one person to create interest and motivation to listen.

Formal Structure The formal (often written) lines of communication that constitute a group or organization.

Forum Type of public discussion in which the audience actively participates in the discussion.

Functional Role Role that aids the group in accomplishing its objectives by keeping the discussion on course.

Functional Theory of Interpersonal Communication Theory that delineates three primary purposes of communication: linking, mentation, and regulation.

Gatekeeper Individual or organization that controls or influences a mass communication message.

Gender Diversity Differences in people as a function of masculine and feminine socially learned behavior.

Gender Role Behavior that is ascribed, defined, and encouraged by each society's culture to be appropriate for either males or females.

Gestalt Viewing an object or event as "a whole" rather than looking at its individual components.

Gesture Movement of the body that communicates messages to others.

Global Team Generic term that encompasses two types of teams: intercultural and virtual global teams.

Global Village Theory that the world is "smaller" than before due to advances in mass communication.

Goodwill One of three dimensions of source credibility, associated with the extent to which we perceive speakers to be caring, concerned, sensitive, and understanding, and to have our best interests at heart.

Group Any number of people who share a common goal, interact with one another to accomplish their goal, and see themselves as part of a group.

Guilt Message A persuasive message (implied or tacit) based on the premise that the audience has done something bad (or failed to do something good), and that atonement will result if the speaker's position or argument is adopted.

Hawthorne Effect The fact that work productivity increases in an organization when human factors are considered.

Holism The idea that systems exist as whole entities rather than as isolated parts.

Homophily Degree to which two interacting individuals are similar in characteristics such as beliefs, values, education, social level, and so on.

Human Communication A biologically and culturally based, complex, continuing, and interactive process in which two or more people use verbal and nonverbal symbols to shape, reinforce, or change one another's behaviors, either immediately or over time, for the purpose of satisfying their respective needs and, in turn, ensuring the survival of both the species and the individuals.

Human Messages Messages that focus on the relational element of the organization and that are associated with and directed by the attitudes, values, preferences, likes, and dislikes of organizational members.

Humor A variable a persuasive speaker should consider.

Hypothetical Example An event or incident that could possibly occur but that did not really happen.

Identification An attempt to find security by forming a psychological bond with other persons or groups.

Identification Function Function of nonverbal communication associated with our ability to distinguish humans from animals, males from females, and individual differences among people.

Illustration Use of verbal examples or visual aids to help clarify information.

Illustrator Body expression that accents or adds emphasis to a word or phrase, shows the direction of thought, points to an object or place, depicts spatial relationships, rhythms, or bodily actions, or demonstrates shape.

Imitative (Learned) Behavior The belief that interaction with other human beings is necessary for language development.

Impromptu Speech Presentation made on the spot without any preparation.

Increasing Levels of Difficulty Pattern Informative organizational structure used to present complex topics clearly and logically.

Inductive Pattern Persuasive structure that presents several specific cases that serve as a basis for a generalization.

Inductive Reasoning Moves from the specific to the general.

Infancy Period of language learning that occurs from birth through approximately 12 months.

Informal Communication Relaxed communication situations in which speakers are free to be themselves.

Informal Communication Structure Interpersonal relations that develop among employees in addition to the formal communication structure.

Informal Network Messages sent haphazardly within an organization (grapevine, rumor, etc.).

Informal Structure The informal (often unwritten) lines of communication that constitute a group or organization (e.g., "rumor mill" or "grapevine").

Ingroup People with whom we are taught to associate.

Initiating Relationship development stage in which conscious and unconscious judgments are made about others.

Innateness Theory Belief that evolution is responsible for the ability to produce and use language.

Innovative Messages Messages that help an organization adapt to the changing environment; associated with projects, new products or services, planning sessions, focus groups, and brainstorming sessions.

Instrumental Values Guidelines for living and on which we base our daily behavior.

Insulation Isolation of contradictory feelings and/or information.

Integrating Relationship stage when two persons agree to meet each other's expectations.

Intensifying Relationship stage when steps are taken to strengthen the bond between two persons by asking for and reciprocating favors.

Intensity Determines which stimuli individuals will attend to when bombarded by many different ones.

Intentional Communication Occurs when messages are sent with specific goals in mind.

Interaction The sharing and communication of ideas and emotions with oneself or others.

Interaction with Empathy Communication that involves deep understanding between the participants, feeling their pain and sharing their joy.

Interaction with Feedback Communication situation in which there is give-and-take by both participants.

Intercultural team Group of people from different cultures that meet face-to-face to work on a project.

Interdependence According to systems theorists, the argument that all parts of a system affect every other part of that system.

Interference Any factor that negatively affects communication.

Intergroup Conflict Conflict between groups.

Internal Self-Feedback Messages picked up through bone conduction, nerve endings, or muscular movement.

Internal Stimuli Stimuli that originate from within a human's body.

Interpersonal Communication Informal, spontaneous, loosely organized exchange of messages between two or more people to achieve some goal.

Interpreting Process of understanding the meaning of a message.

Interrupting Response Response that breaks into the words and thoughts of another person.

Interview Dyadic communication situation designed to get information for employers and applicants by asking and answering questions.

Intimacy The degree to which two people can uniquely meet one another's needs.

Intimate Distance Spatial zone of interaction stretching from actual contact (touching) to 18 inches.

Intragroup Conflict Conflict within a group.

Intrapersonal Communication The sending and receiving of messages within an individual.

Intrinsic Motivation Motivation that arises from an internal source (such as desire to learn).

Introduction of a Speech First portion of a speech, which captures the audience's attention and prepares them for the rest of the speech.

Irrelevant Response Response that does not apply to the topic being discussed.

Kinesics Study of body movement.

Labeling Identifying an object, act, or person by name so that it may be referred to in communication.

Laissez-Faire Leader A leader who avoids directing a group at all, but rather sees him- or herself as a potential source of information and feedback only.

Language Communication of thoughts and emotions by means of a structured system of symbols (words).

Language Acquisition Device Innate device in humans that helps them sort out language and understand grammatical rules.

Larynx (Voice Box) Transforms vibrations of air to produce basic voice sounds.

Lateral (Horizontal) Communication Information messages between peers at the same hierarchical level.

Leader Person who leads (and is followed) by others.

Leadership Any kind of behavior that helps a group to achieve its goals.

Leadership Style The means by which a person motivates others to accomplish goals.

Leakage Nonverbal behavior that implies that information is being given inadvertently.

Linear Models Models of communication that focus attention on the sender's use of messages to influence other people.

Linguistic Stereotyping Assuming automatic relationships between linguistic styles and personal traits.

Linking Function The function of communication that allows a person to interact with his or her environment.

Listener The person receiving the message.

Listener Feedback Involves verbal and nonverbal responses to a message.

Listener Preferences Preferences developed for types of information and sources and that emerge as a function of socialization and reinforcement patterns.

Listening A process that involves hearing, attention, understanding, and remembering.

Lively Quality Selection of words that leave a lasting impression.

Locus of Control Degree to which we perceive reinforcement either as contingent upon our own efforts or actions (internal locus of control) or as a result of forces beyond our control and due to chance, fate, or some other external force (external locus of control).

Logos Rational approach to persuasion based on logic and reasoning.

Long-Term Memory Permanent storage of information for future reference.

Maintenance Role Functional role that is concerned with the feelings and emotional behavior of the group.

Management Team A collection of managers who meet on a regular basis to make decisions and determine the future direction of a unit or organization.

Manipulation Method of dominating and controlling others, frequently through skillful use of verbal and nonverbal communications.

Mass Communication Process by which messages are transmitted rapidly and inexpensively through some mechanical device to a large, diverse audience.

Maturity Differential stages of personal growth and behavior patterns.

Media Richness Extent to which a message can overcome various constraints of time, location, permanence, distribution, and distance; transmit the social, symbolic, and nonverbal cues of human communication; and convey shared understanding.

Memory Storage of information that a person chooses to remember.

Mentation Function The function of communication that allows humans to conceptualize, remember, plan, and evaluate.

Message The behavior that an individual produces in order to communicate.

Metaphor The use or application of a name, descriptive term, or phrase to compare one person, object, or action with another, without use of the words "like" or "as."

Negative Feedback Response that indicates that a receiver has misunderstood a message.

Network Interconnected channels or lines of communication used in organizations to pass information from one person to another.

Networking The process of developing and using contacts for information, advice, and moral support.

Noise Interference between a speaker's intended message and a listener's reception of that message.

Non-Allness Korzybski's law that states that a word cannot symbolize all of a thing.

Nondirective Interview Planned interaction situation in which freedom is given to participants in terms of how they ask questions and give responses.

Non-Identity Korzybski's law that states that a word is not the thing it represents.

Nonrefutational Two-Sided Message A persuasive message that presents both sides of an issue without addressing why opposing arguments are in error.

Nonverbal Communication Communication via behaviors such as facial expressions, tone of voice, gestures, body movement, clothing, and so on.

One-Down Message A message that relinquishes control in a relationship.

One-Sided Message The structure of a persuasive message that presents only the side of an issue that a speaker advocates.

One-Sided Presentation Persuasive speech approach in which the speaker presents only the side of the issue he or she supports.

One-Up Message A message that exerts control in a relationship.

Open (Public) Discussion Group meeting conducted before an audience who listens and/or participates.

Operational Definition Defining or delineating a term by establishing the means by which it can/will be measured.

Opinion Positive or negative reaction to or statement of an attitude.

Opinion Leader Receiver of information from a change agent, who then disseminates it to the general public.

Oral Communication Messages that are transmitted aloud from one person to another.

Organization Collected group of individuals constructed and reconstructed to work for goals that could not be met by individuals acting alone.

Organizational Communication Focuses on ways to analyze and improve leadership ability, develop greater responsiveness to clients, create more efficient work environments, build effective self-management teams, and optimize the flow of information within organizations and with their publics.

Organized Audience Group of listeners who are directed totally toward the speaker with strict labor and authority lines.

Outgroup People with whom we are taught to avoid association.

Overt Stimuli Internal or external changes or actions received at the conscious level.

Panel Type of open discussion in which a group of well-informed people exchange ideas before an audience.

Paralanguage Variations in the voice that give clues about emotional states, sex, age, status, and so on.

Participative Management Rensis Likert's employee-centered approach to management in organizations that encourages the creation of interlocking participative groups (or teams), each of which has multiple group memberships. Via such groups, employees throughout the organization may aid in decision making.

Particular Audience An audience that constitutes one segment or another of humanity, which has a known group identity.

Passive (Partially Oriented) Audience Captive listeners who have no choice but to listen to the speaker.

Pathos Approach to persuasion that appeals to the emotions.

People-Oriented Listener Listener who is primarily concerned with how his or her listening preferences influence relationships with other people.

Perceiving Use of one or more of the basic senses to receive verbal and nonverbal messages.

Peripheral Route According to the Elaboration Likelihood Model, one of two means of persuasion. Persuasion that results as a function of processing external cues, such as speaker attractiveness, number of messages presented, or vocalics.

Personal Distance Spatial zone of interactions from 1½ to 4 feet, used for casual interactions.

Personal Interview Interaction conducted on a one-to-one basis with a person who has information or knowledge about the topic of your speech.

Phatic Communication A formal term that is synonymous with "small talk."

Phonation Process by which air is pushed through the vocal cords, which then vibrate to produce sound.

Physical Needs The human need for the basic elements of life including food, water, sex, and shelter.

Physiological Processing Subconscious and conscious physiological responses to internal stimuli.

Pitch Highness or lowness of vocal tones.

Platform Situation in which the audience participates in the exchange of information.

Polarization Point at which the audience members recognize their role as listeners and accept someone else as a speaker.

Policymaking Group Makes changes or takes actions after the evaluation group offers its recommendations.

Positive Feedback Response that indicates that the receiver has understood a message.

Prejudice Preformed judgments about a person, group, or thing.

Primary Group (Psyche Group) Collected group of individuals who function as a support system for its members.

Principles of Scientific Management Guidelines that emerged in the 1800s for organizations to follow, based on the work of such pioneers as Taylor, Fayol, and Weber.

Private (Closed) Discussion Group meeting held without an audience to listen or participate.

Problem-Solving Group A group of people who work together to solve a problem by collecting information, reviewing that information, and making a decision based on their findings.

Problem-Solving Pattern/Problem–Solution Method Persuasive structure of organization based on a logical, step-by-step analysis of a particular problem.

Professional Worker characterized by commitment to his or her job.

Progression Arrangement of ideas in a logical order in a speech outline.

Projection Attributing personal traits, motives, or behaviors to others.

Proxemics Study of how people react to the space around them, how they use it, and how their use of space communicates information.

Public Communication Usually a one-way process in which one person addresses a group in a lecture or public speech.

Public Distance Spatial zone of interaction from 12 to over 25 feet, used in formal addresses or lectures.

Public Relations Method of persuasion concerned with promoting an image.

Public Speaking Communication situation in which one speaker directs a message to an audience.

Public Speaking Anxiety Fear and uneasiness caused by the potentially threatening situation (real or anticipated) of speaking before a group of people.

Quality Circle A group of persons from three to ten in number who meet periodically to suggest ways of improving work life, increasing employee commitment, implementing suggested changes, and building attitudes geared toward problem prevention.

Rapport Development and maintenance of a positive relationship with an audience throughout a speech.

Rate Speed at which words are spoken.

Rationalization Attempt to justify personal failures or inadequacies.

Reaction Formation A defense mechanism by which an individual denies personally or socially unacceptable drives by reacting in the opposite direction.

Real Example An event or incident that actually happened.

Reasoning Process of thinking by which an individual arrives at conclusions.

Recall Reconstruction of information that has been stored.

Receiver The person or person for whom the source intends a message.

Reception Process by which the body receives stimuli.

Recognition Awareness of familiar information based on previous experience.

Redirecting Strategy used by listeners to help a speaker get back on track from an inappropriate or lengthy digression.

Referent Actual object as it exists in reality.

Reflecting Strategy by which listeners test their understanding of or clarify messages.

Refutational Two-Sided Message A persuasive message that presents both sides of an issue and points out why (possible) opposing arguments are in error.

Regulation and Policy Messages Messages that take the form of policy statements, organizational procedures, agendas, schedules, orders, and control measures that ensure that the organization will function properly; associated with formal and informal rules of the organization.

Regulative Rules According to rules theorists, rules that tell us with whom it is appropriate to communicate about certain topics, when we may do so, and how we should act during an interaction.

Regulators Body movements or expressions that control verbal communication.

Regulating Function The function of communication that allows us to regulate our own and others' behaviors.

Relational Communication Theory Theory that addresses interpersonal communication by examining the dimensions of relationships.

Relationship Function Function of nonverbal communication associated with intimacy and control, two variables that affect the creation and maintenance of relationships.

Repeating Nonverbal behavior that conveys the same message as the verbal message.

Repetition Means by which audience learning may be increased via the presentation of material in a recurring fashion.

Repression Keeping thoughts and feelings beneath the conscious level.

Resonance Variations in voice from a thin and quiet voice to a loud and booming voice. Also, movement of air through the mouth, nose, and throat, which gives amplification and richness to the voice.

Responding The completion of the communication process by the receiver through verbal and/or nonverbal feedback.

Retrieval Bringing back into conscious awareness information that previously has been stored in the brain.

Reward Appeal Persuasion that promises listeners personal gain or profit if they believe or behave in a desired manner.

Second Law of Thermodynamics Principle from physics specifying that all systems have a tendency to develop entropy or disorganization.

Selected Audience Group of people collected together for a specific purpose.

Selective Perception Screening out a large number of stimuli to permit an individual to attend to just a few.

Self-Awareness The extent to which you are cognizant of (and open to) incoming information about yourself and the world around you.

Self-Disclosure Process of revealing significant aspects of the self to others.

Self-Esteem Enduring evaluation of the self.

Self-Expressive Behaviors Behaviors that emerge when we use our attitudes as a vehicle for expressing values that are important to us.

Self-Feedback Perception of a person's own nervous system via muscular movements as the person hears himself or herself speak.

Self-Reflexiveness Korzybski's law that states that a word can refer both to something in the real world and to itself.

Self-Serving Role Counterproductive role that has a negative effect on a group's emotional climate as well as on its ability to reach its goal.

Semantics Study of relationships between word symbols and their meanings.

Sense Subjective feelings about a symbol (word).

Sensory Storage Ability to hold some information for a fraction of a second after the stimulus disappears.

Shame Message A persuasive message (implied or tacit) that is based on the premise that the audience has done something unworthy of them as human beings, and that atonement will result if the speaker's position or argument is adopted.

Short-Term Memory Process by which data are analyzed, identified, and simplified to be conveniently stored and handled.

Simile A comparison of one thing with another of a different kind and necessarily includes the words "like" or "as."

Small Group A system of three to fifteen individuals who think of themselves as a group, are interdependent, and communicate by managing messages for the purpose of creating meaning.

Small Group Communication Process involving three or more persons with a common goal and potential for interaction between members.

Social Distance Spatial zone of interaction from 4 to 12 feet, used by people meeting for the first time or by people conducting business.

Social Facilitation Influence of one audience member on another.

Social-Oriented Listener Listener who easily listens to sources of information that are charismatic and entertaining.

Social Needs The human need for connections to other human beings.

Sorting Selection of the most relevant information from the brain's storehouse of knowledge.

Source The person (or entity) who originates a message.

Spatial Pattern Informative organizational structure based on the relation of one part to others or to geographical progressions.

Speech to Convince Speech intended to get an audience to think, believe, or feel a certain way.

Speech to Entertain Informal speech designed to bring the audience pleasure.

Speech to Inform Speech designed to increase audience learning and comprehension.

Speech to Move an Audience to Action Persuasive speech that seeks some form of action on the part of the audience.

Speech to Persuade A deliberate attempt by one person to modify the attitudes, beliefs, or behavior of another person or group of people through communication.

Speech to Stimulate Speech intended to reaffirm or strengthen preexisting beliefs or feelings.

Speech to Welcome Presentation to a group, or to an individual, about to join an organization or attend a meeting.

Stagnating Relationship disintegration stage in which all efforts to communicate are abandoned.

Statistic A numerical fact or datum.

Stimuli Elements that cause a reaction in one or more of a person's senses.

Stimulus-Response Interaction Communication situation in which the speaker proceeds in a set manner, independent of responses made by the listener.

Story An account, narrative or tale of past events.

Study Group A gathering of people who get together to learn new information or skills.

Style Individual selection, organization, and use of language.

Substituting Using nonverbal messages to take the place of words.

Support Group A group of people that focuses on learning to cope with situations to meet the needs of its members.

Survey Detailed gathering of information by questionnaire, observation, interview, and so on.

Symbol Word or nonverbal sign used to represent objects, ideas, and feelings to others.

Symbolic Process Use of words as symbols to represent objects or concepts.

Symbolization Visual form of coordination, subordination, and progression of a speech outline.

Symmetrical Relationship A relationship in which partners often mirror each others' behavior.

Symposium Form of public discussion in which a group of experts presents its views, one speaker at a time.

System An entity comprised of components that interact with, or mutually influence, one another in ways that enable the entity to achieve a goal or goals.

Systems Perspectives View human communication as a total process in which biological, cultural, and social variables play a vital role.

Tangential Response Response that sidetracks a conversation.

Task Messages Messages that focus on the products, services, and activities of an organization.

Task-Oriented Role Functional role that is directly related to a group's goal.

Task Team A group that is formed for a specific period of time to work on a particular problem or issue.

Team A group of people working together in a collaborative effort to achieve a common goal.

Technology-Based Group A group of people that must depend on technology in order to communicate.

Teleconferencing Three or more people talking via telephone at a pre-specified time and date.

Tempo Rate of speech in a given amount of time.

Terminal Values Ultimate aim(s) toward which we work.

Terminating Final relationship disintegration stage, which may be either rapid or delayed.

Territoriality Possessive desire or ownership reaction to the space and objects around us.

Testimony Information derived from a direct witness to an event or from an expert in a particular field.

Thesis Statement Sentence that presents the specific purpose of a speech.

Threshold of Consciousness Boundary between conscious and unconscious awareness of stimuli.

Time and Motion Studies Associated with the Classical/Scientific Management approach to organizational management; studies designed to reveal the one best way for workers to design and implement tasks.

Toddlerhood Period of language learning that takes place between approximately 12 and 24 months of age.

Tolerance of Ambiguity Ability to accept poorly defined and unclear situations.

Topical Pattern Informative organizational structure in which information is presented according to specific category or classification.

Tracking Encouraging others to continue talking until their message is complete.

Trait Quality that distinguishes one person from another.

Transactional Leader A leader who controls the team through negotiation, or exchanging rewards for accomplishments.

Transactional Models Depict the simultaneous interaction of complex, multilayered elements of the communication process.

Transformational Leader A leader who empowers and develops personal leadership in individual team members.

Transition Statement that smoothly connects one idea to the next.

Transmission Process by which messages are sent from a source to a receiver.

Trust The responsible acceptance of the control dimension in a relationship; includes both trusting and trustworthy behaviors.

Trusting An admission of dependency on the part of persons involved.

Trustworthiness One of three dimensions of source credibility that speakers are perceived to possess when they come across as honest, honorable, moral, ethical, and genuine.

Turn-Denying Cues Cues that we use when we are listening, the speaker wants us to take a turn, and we do not wish to speak at that time.

Turn-Maintaining Cues Cues that are used when we are speaking and do not wish to yield the floor to the listener.

Turn-Requesting Cues Cues that are used when we want to take a conversational turn.

Turn-Yielding Cues Cues that tell the listener that we no longer wish to speak for the moment and want him or her to take a conversational turn.

Two-Sided Message The structure of a persuasive message that presents both sides of an issue: that which the speaker does (and does not) advocate.

Two-Sided Presentation Persuasive speech approach in which the speaker presents both sides of an issue.

Unintentional Communication Messages (usually nonverbal) that are sent without communicators being aware of them.

Universal Audience An audience to whom you speak as "rational human beings."

Upward Communication Information messages directed to superiors or those of higher status within an organization.

Vagueness Caused by the relative meaning of words that need more precision in usage.

Values Specific types of beliefs that form the core of our belief system.

Verbal Communication Communication via the words that we use.

Virtual Global Team Group of people whose individual participants remain in their separate locations around the world to conduct meetings via different forms of technology.

Visual Aid Anything (other than the speaker) that is used to get a message across to an audience.

Vocal Delivery Mechanics of vocalization, vocal characteristics, and pronunciation.

Vocal Quality Timbre of voice that distinguishes one voice from another.

Voice Sounds or tones produced through phonation.

Volume Intensity or loudness of speech sounds.

Wheel Network Two-way communication network with all communication directed to and from a centralized position.

Word Structured system of symbols that when joined with other words creates language.

Work Team A collection of individuals who form natural work groups within an organization.

Written Communication Primarily verbal messages conveyed in writing.

Y Network Communication network in which the central position does not communicate with one of the members.

Index